# *Official Macromedia*
# *Director® Studio*

# Official Macromedia Director® Studio

*Tony Bové*
*Cheryl Rhodes*

WITH MARC CANTER AND STUART SHARPE

**RANDOM HOUSE**
**ELECTRONIC PUBLISHING**

New York

*Official Macromedia Director® Studio*

# Contents

# *Foreword*

As I look back over the past decade, Macromedia Director (and its predecessors VideoWorks and MacroMind Director) have been used for almost every type of multimedia project you can imagine: trade show displays, interactive sales presentations, guided tours for the Macintosh and a host of other applications. Developers around the country—and around the world—have picked up Director and combined it with some of the other tools available on the Macintosh to create a whole new communication medium. Nothing in words can express my excitement and amazement over the wide range of presentations and products that our users have created with Director. But the number one reason why I think Director has had such an influence in today's multimedia market is its remarkable ease of use compared to other multimedia animation systems.

Professional users who have been exposed to traditional cel animation stands, or computer controlled slide shows, love Director's real-time interactive responsiveness, and especially appreciate the immediate feedback aspects of its notational editing system. The time line featured in Director's user interface is a direct representation of time; and after all, time is what animation, sound, and video are all about.

Time, as represented by the score in Director, is the single aspect that differentiates multimedia from flat media, such as paper. Time is the insight that once you understand, you'll never forget. Time is the element of Director's user interface that I think most people latch onto almost instantly; "Oh, I get it, this comes before that, but after this. And that's what's going on at the same time."

It's the combination of Director's time-line score and its WYSIWYG (what-you-see-is-what-you-get) layout capabilities that creates an intuitive system for multimedia composition. When we first created VideoWorks, we felt that users would want to see their entire time-line sequence represented, while at the same time see the particular instance of time that they were "at."

By combining the direct manipulation of objects (whether they are text, graphics, or drawings) in space (on the screen), with a direct representation of time (in a spreadsheet-like score), we felt that we could leverage off some of the best aspects of the Macintosh user interface. The score enabled users to drag and select ranges of time, just like they selected ranges of cells in a spreadsheet, and the stage enabled users to lay out and place objects on the screen, just like MacDraw (or the later PageMaker).

It all seemed to make perfect sense to us back in 1984, but then again everything was simpler then. We only had 128k of memory to work with, so in those days all we needed were 64 cast members. Twenty-four channels also seemed quite adequate in those days. But now, and certainly for the future, we realize that there should be no boundaries to what someone could do with Director.

You should only be limited by your imagination when you're using Director. Now that Director can record onto videotape one frame at a time, there is literally no difference between what your computer and a few peripherals can do compared to a professional, multi-million dollar animation studio. Creating 24-bit animations with Director is equivalent to using a Quantel Harry and Paintbox, together with a few special effects devices.

But of course that's not enough. We designed Director to go beyond what traditional animation systems can offer. Director enables you to create interactive documents—applications that let you browse through information, randomly jump around a presentation—for a gamut of uses from presenting study materials for review to a young learner, to training an experienced professional. Director enables you to create interactive marketing brochures for distribution by mail, or for setup as a kiosk in a shopping mall. Most importantly, Director gives an artist the interactive programming capabilities of HyperCard (or other authoring systems), by simply using "go to" commands.

Solving the artists' needs has always been MacroMind's (and now Macromedia's) focus. Not surprisingly, MacroMind was made up almost entirely of artists, musicians, and actors when it was founded; people who were patiently doing their day jobs, but really waiting for their moment in the sun, their day on the stage of life, their 15 minutes of stardom. We've always used our products ourselves, of course for marketing and sales presentations but also as training disks for our products and as a means of simulating our next generation products. And of course we've tried to create great art with Director, synchronizing our animations, artwork, and interactive environments with state-of-the-art, MIDI-composed rock music and new age ballads.

I'll always remember an image I had when we first started MacroMind. I felt that even if the company didn't take off, that we'd at least have some monster tools that I could go off onto a mountain top and use. At the time, we (the three founders of MacroMind) were working for Bally/Midway, the giant video game company.

We were using fairly advanced tools for the day (our own version of FORTH, with special editors for alien attack formations, mother ships, or sound effects), but these editors still lacked some of the obvious enhancements that we really needed. So when the Macintosh came out, it seemed like the right thing to do to create a series of SoundVision tools that could be used for video game development work (and start a company at the same time).

These original tools became VideoWorks and MusicWorks and the rest is history, but the moral of the story is that we were originally inspired by the high-end, expensive tools that were used in professional video and audio recording studios. We felt that desktop computers would eventually be able to do everything these expensive machines could do, but that the software for these machines was impossible to use, often requiring a C programmer (or Pascal programmers in those days) to accomplish anything.

Our goal was to create tools that were as powerful as those professional tools, but as easy to use as video games. Of course it has been a long road, but I think we're finally getting real close to reaching that ideal. Technology will continue to become cheaper over time, and it's Macromedia's role to bring high-end workstation-based tools down onto the desktop and to make those tools accessible and easy to use. Someday we will have the same software tools to run on hardware that costs $250, $2,500, $25,000 and $250,000. The key will be to be able to move our documents around between each of these systems and to have the software work identically regardless of the environment.

Over the years there have been many attempts to write a book about VideoWorks or Director. I even tried to do one myself in 1986, only to find out that we were a little too early for the industry. Tony and Cheryl have stuck with it, climbing over all the obstacles, and have created a book I can be proud of. Of course I think our manuals are pretty good, and hopefully none of you will forego reading our manuals thoroughly, but this book-disc will give you a complete multimedia solution that will help you make decisions about all the accompanying pieces of hardware that Director controls so very well.

In closing, I want to tell you of another story that really changed my life, and set VideoWorks and Director onto the course that they remain on today. We were selling VideoWorks for $100 at the time (1985) and positioning it as a tool for education and fun (we dubbed it "creativity tools"). At one MacWorld Expo, an engineer walked up to me and showed me the animation he had just created for work. On the screen I saw synthetic fiber molecules flying through the air and forming into some sort of Helix-shaped cluster. Suddenly I realized (a) how Nylon was developed, (b) that there were many other ways to use animation, and (c) that we had to position VideoWorks (and now Director) as a visualization tool for communications, learning, and technical professionals who needed to implement their ideas without spending a fortune.

That underlying image has driven MacroMind (now called Macromedia) since 1985, and very much inspired the publication of this book. Visualization is really why computers were invented in the first place. Computers help humans solve problems and communicate ideas, without having to fly to the moon or journey to the bottom of the oceans. I hope you will find hours of enjoyment and fulfillment not only with Macromedia Director, but also with this book. Good luck.

Marc Canter, Founder
Macromedia
San Francisco, CA
July 25, 1990

## *Fast foreword...*

I write this 1994 addition to the foreword of Tony and Cheryl's Director book-disc as I embark on a new career in the field of interactive content. It's an appropriate theme for this piece, for it is interactive content that will fulfill the "promise" of multimedia.

Little did I realize years ago (when I toiled to send numbers out of digital-to-analog converters, interface knobs to laser beams, or move pixels around the screen) that I was really participating in the birth of a new era of communications, entertainment, publishing, education, and just about everything else.

All we thought we were doing was using "video game" techniques in the business world. It's appropriate that most of the money flowing into multimedia today is really in search of the next, killer shoot-em up video game, a field that I abandoned over 12 years ago.

I'm set on a mission to show what's possible besides simple video games. There's got to be something else that we spend our time on, and our intellect.

I think interactive music videos are the way to salvation and nirvana. Others have created such precedent-setting products as *Sim City, Freak Show* and *Total Distortion*. But all it seems that Hollywood and publishers want is games, games, games. In fact, the game world seems obsessed with violent, male-oriented themes, which is bad news for all of the meaningful, well-intentioned content developers out there today. So, how can we halt this trend and make interactive content into a new medium of creative expression?

We could look to the music industry. That's *another* $5 billion that actually has very little to do with shooting, killing, flying or driving. Sure, rap and heavy metal music cover a few violent topics, but Atlantic, Virgin, or Geffen seem to know what girls and women want a lot better than Electronic Arts or Accolade. Don't developers understand that if content doesn't rock, it's never gonna roll!

Or perhaps we could learn a little from the world that we all admire so well—the sports industry. Or TV, where heroes come and go based upon their latest antics, winner take all. In the cutthroat game industry, you've got to commit yourself to one platform or the other and line up like lemmings to buy the next sequel of cartoon trash spurting death and destruction.

Either way, nothing's gonna change this world unless we play by their rules and create some kick-ass content that nobody will argue about. If you make the content good enough, they will come. They may be terrified, but they will come!

M.C.
July 4, 1994

# *Preface*

**We live in media, as fish live in water.**

Ted Nelson

The emergence of desktop computer tools for creating and editing media (text, graphics, sound, animation, video, film, etc.) has changed the artistic and cultural landscape. These tools empower a new generation of multimedia artists—not just to secure rewarding careers in multimedia development, but to attain new heights of creative expression and communication without high-end production costs. These desktop tools are just as good, if not better, than high-end equipment because they cost less and require less training. Now, nearly every aspiring media producer can obtain the production quality typical of a well-financed project without the financing.

Macromedia Director is the most popular tool for creating interactive presentations, CD-ROM titles, software demonstrations, and information or demonstration kiosks, especially if animation is required. It works well with other tools, particularly QuickTime on the Macintosh and Video for Windows on Windows PCs. A version of Macromedia Director 4.0 is available for both the Macintosh and Windows platforms.

Macromedia Director evolved from a humble beginning in 1985 as a program for creating on-screen animation (called VideoWorks, then renamed to MacroMind Director, and finally to Macromedia Director). It now combines sophisticated animation tools with facilities for integrating text, sound, images, animated sequences, and full-motion video into a multimedia presentation or information product. It also includes features for navigating through information in an interactive, nonlinear fashion, as well as a fully featured programming language used for "authoring" or "scripting" interactive information products and presentations.

We first heard the term "multimedia" used to describe an artistic performance involving the use of multiple media—music, film, projected images, dance, mime, and even printed material. As video became a medium for art, the term was extended to include the use of video (which includes sound) and animation.

As computers filtered down to the art world as production equipment, they also came to be recognized as creative tools. Computer-generated graphics became a new medium for art, as well as for business presentations. The personal computer, arriving in the 1980s as an inexpensive information tool, caused dramatic changes in the workplace, and evolved to be capable of playing animation and sound as well as displaying high-resolution graphics. The term "multimedia" was reborn as a description of computer-generated animation, sound, and even video.

If you have the opportunity to communicate an idea effectively, you can change the world, or at least your part of it. The purpose of this book and CD-ROM is to explain and show by example how you, as a Macromedia Director user, can create materials for multimedia projects, and how you can use a personal computer as an interactive medium for communicating ideas.

*Medium* can mean many things, but for this book/disc, *medium* (plural: *media*) carries two meanings: It is a means of mass communication, such as newspapers, television, and radio, and it is a type of artistic technique or means of expression determined by the materials used or the creative methods involved. *Multimedia* describes the use of several techniques or means of expression for communication. The word also is used to describe a project or application that uses text, graphics, sound, animation, and video to describe information.

## Why Macromedia Director?

It took the introduction of Macromedia Director software on the Apple Macintosh to bring this new medium out of its infancy and into mainstream business, art, and entertainment.

Macromedia Director provides a measure of control over the creative process never before possible and offers a new form of expression for the computer screen: the simulation, the demo, the slide show with a soundtrack, and the animated storyboard.

Director uses the stage production metaphor that includes a *Stage* for displaying presentations, a *Cast* for holding cast members that serve as sprites (actors) on the Stage, and a *Score* with instructions on how cast members are arranged on the Stage. All of this is explained in detail in this book. The Score can also accommodate instructions, called *scripts,* for controlling animation and interactivity. Scripts are written in a language called Lingo.

Director divides the Score into frames to measure time in a relative fashion suitable for animation and still-image display. Director is not designed to be a video editor that measures real time with timecode, but the program does allow users to import movies that were edited with such video editors, and composite those movies with animation scenes.

Macromedia Director version 4, a major upgrade that includes a Microsoft Windows version, is also a major step forward for the venerable authoring tool that helped launch the multimedia industry. It not only slices and dices animation with interactivity, it also lets you create productions without as many limitations and constraints as the previous version. Other authoring tools have approached Director's level of functionality but never surpassed it; Director 4 is now way ahead of the competition.

Developers who have in the past used Director for animation and proprietary C code for interactivity and performance may take a second look at using Director for the whole project. Director's now-compiled scripts help developers achieve that C-level performance, and the capability to protect files and remove the source code make Director more useful for authoring entertainment products.

# Features of This Book and CD-ROM

This book introduces the concepts of animation and interactivity, and explains how you can use Macromedia Director for a variety of multimedia projects. It includes many tips and techniques for producing outstanding special effects.

This book also demonstrates how anyone can put together presentations and information products using Macromedia Director. We provide helpful examples of real applications and suggestions about how to implement multimedia projects. The CD-ROM interacts with the book and provides everything you need to become a Director user.

## Features of the CD-ROM

The CD-ROM accompanying this book provides you with 650 megabytes of tools, media, and reference material you can use in your own presentations—all packaged in a multimedia interface that itself was created with Director 4.0. Here's what's on the disc:

- Hundreds of megabytes of clip media—images, textures, sounds, video, animations—that you can use in your presentations. These are found in the Freebies section.

- A number of useful utilities, including a collection of Director XObject scripts that you can use to customize your presentations, QuickTime for Macintosh and Windows, Equilibrium's Debabelizer Lite graphics file format converter, and more. These are also found in the Freebies section.

- The full retail versions of Director 4.0 for Mac and Windows, SoundEdit 16 for Mac, Sonic Foundry and SoundForge for Windows, Adobe Photoshop for Mac and Windows, Adobe Premiere for Mac and Windows, and Turtle Tools for Windows. You can test drive all of these applications up to three times, and can then *purchase any of them directly from the CD-ROM* by calling an 800 number (details on the CD)! These are found in the Software Store section of the disc.

- Animated tutorials and movies that supplement the book by showing you step by step how to get great results from Director's powerful features. Movies that directly relate to passages in the book can be found in the Tutorial folder/directory.

- A full hypertext version of this book with animated figures.

- For Macintosh users, a demo of gray matter design's hot new MediaBook CD-ROM, containing usable XObjects and product demonstrations.

## Overview of the Book

The book begins with an introduction to multimedia and to the equipment required for different types of applications. It first describes tasks such as using scanned images and predrawn graphics and making "live" computer presentations with "clip" art and animation that you can use right out of the box, requiring little or no specialized skills.

It then describes how to make your own animated sequences, which requires some design skill but not specialized knowledge. It also describes a variety of painting and drawing techniques that require some artistic sensibilities but little artistic talent or drawing skill.

The book then moves on to the most popular animation techniques and introduces you to interactive features. The scripting of interactive presentations is explained in more detail for those who want to produce interactive training, education, simulation, or engineering projects.

Finally, the book presents power user's tips and tricks for getting the most of of Director. Here's a more detailed rundown:

Chapter 1, "Multimedia and Director," defines the elements of multimedia and describes the appropriate equipment and Macintosh configurations for developing a variety of different applications. It explains the use of disk storage devices, displays, scanners, digitizers, sound recorders, video equipment, system software, and Macromedia software.

Chapter 2, "Your First Movies," introduces the Auto Animate function, and then gently introduces most of the features of Director while examining a sample movie. The chapter provides five tutorial lessons with information ranging from examining and editing a movie to using sounds, creating an interactive movie, and printing movie information.

Chapter 3, "Elementary Animation," explains how to perform all of the regular animation techniques. It shows how to perform in-between operations and edit animation information in the score. It also explains how to do essential things such as locking the animation speed.

Chapter 4, "Painting Techniques," introduces graphics features and explains the differences among painting and drawing tools that enable you to create black and white, gray, and color graphics and images. This chapter also explains the use of sophisticated painting and transformation tools, color palettes, and special ink effects and patterns. Tips and techniques are provided that are used by many different multimedia artists who are able to harness the power of Director's extensive graphics features.

Chapter 5, "Animation Techniques," explains by example how you can do special effects to enhance your presentations and information products. It presents a compendium of tips and techniques, using successful projects as examples. You will learn all about film loops, techniques for adding sophisticated titles and fancy text effects, methods for animating with color effects, compositing tricks, and cast management including sharing cast members among several movie files.

Chapter 6, "Elementary Scripting," introduces you to the art and techniques of interactive media. It is the first stop for anyone who wants to learn Lingo, the interactive scripting language used with Director. It shows you how to find the scripts, create buttons and hot spots for executing scripts, and trace script execution. You'll learn about events (such as mouse clicks) and how Director handles them. You will also learn about puppets and moveable sprites. This chapter concludes with a description of how to make projector files for distributing Director creations.

Chapter 7, "Using Sound," explains how to use analog and digital sound in presentations. The chapter explains in detail how sound is sampled into digital form, edited with a sound editing program, and then imported into Director. The chapter also covers the use of CD Audio Tracks, and synchronizing sound to animation.

Chapter 8, "Using Video," explains how video works, and how you can use video equipment to enhance presentations, such as capturing still images, and displaying live or prerecorded video in a window. It also covers digital video in detail, including importing and exporting digital video movie files. This chapter also describes how to record Director movies onto videotape.

Chapter 9, "Tips and Advanced Techniques," is a collection of the most-requested tips and tricks, culled from our experiences and those of many others who communicate on various Macromedia-sponsored bulletin boards and newsgroups on the information highway. We currently edit tips and techniques in a monthly journal, *Macromedia User Journal* (published by HyperMedia Communications), where some of these tips originally appeared. The tips include establishing timers for controlling playback, exporting PICS files, and blurring edges of line art and text. Important techniques include synchronizing sound and animation, creating various button styles, playing movies inside other movies, and using Lingo extensions such as XObjects. Also included are tips on cross-platform Macintosh-Windows development.

## *Producing This Book and CD-ROM*

As you begin assembling equipment suitable for desktop multimedia applications, consider what was used to produce this book: the Macintosh Quadra 950, PowerBook 180, and Quadra 700 were all used at one time or another, along with a Compaq 486 PC.

Macromedia Director 4.0 was used by Aaron Marcus & Associates to create the CD-ROM user interface. We also used Macromedia Director 4.0 to create the electronic book on the CD-ROM (with programming by Steve DeBevec), and to create all animations. Adobe Photoshop and Macromedia Director were used to retouch artwork and to keep track of graphics elements. Capture (Mainstay Software) was used to capture screen images. Syquest cartridges were used to receive Director files from artists and to create backups. Modems and the AppleLink and CompuServe information services, as well as the Internet, were also used to transfer text, images, and animation files.

The clip media contained in the Freebies section of the CD-ROM were licensed and assembled by Random House, while the major applications offer for purchase in the Software Store section were licensed by InfoNow Corporation. InfoNow also provided the unique test drive and purchase engine, as well as the final disc programming, content assembly and mastering, and sales services for applications purchased from the disc.

The best part of this experiment is that it worked! We were a bit apprehensive, since this CD-ROM would be one of the first to work in both Macintosh computers and PCs. We thank everyone involved for bearing with the incredibly tight schedule.

# 1

# *Multimedia and Director*

**Freedom of press is guaranteed only to those who own one.**

A. J. Liebling

Liebling's quote was used in the 1980s to introduce the revolutionary topic of *desktop publishing*, mainly because the emerging technology of the time made it possible for writers like ourselves to control nearly all aspects of publishing except the actual printing. The point of desktop publishing was to control the means of production, thereby reducing the cost and time it took to create publications. Unfortunately, desktop publishers still had to deal with a paper-based result. We could not fit an offset press, or any other volume printing machine, on a desktop (nor could we afford such equipment). So, we were still locked into a process that required a third-party printer or publisher to take our electronic pages and reproduce them on paper.

A decade later, we now have tools and a technology called multimedia that enable us to publish information without paper. We can put information, such as this book, in electronic form and display it on computer screens. Anyone with a computer screen can receive and display the information without the need for a printing press.

However, if electronic pages were the only benefit, this book would be interesting only to paper publishers. In fact, this technology has percolated through the entire arts and entertainment media, resulting in the placement of multimedia tools and opportunities in the hands of artists and musicians. Marc Canter's MediaBand, a group of artists and musicians that puts on interactive multimedia experiences rather than simple rock concerts, is an example of the potential for enriching communication through the use of multiple media (animation, sound, and video) and interactive navigation (Figure 1.1).

**Figure 1.1**
**The *House Jam*
excerpt from
Marc Canter's Me-
diaBand CD-ROM
(HOUSEJAM in
the TUTORIAL
folder/directory).
Click various ob-
jects, and click
the eye in the
globe to exit. (Mu-
sic performed by
the MediaBand,
with animation
by Stuart Sharpe
and other artists.)**

The development of multimedia is actually far more revolutionary than desktop publishing ever was. Multimedia technology gives artists the tools necessary to create a product without requiring expensive studio equipment. Indeed, the publishing function for a multimedia project, whether for *CD-ROM (compact disk–read-only memory)*, hard disk storage, or transmission over networks, is mostly a front office function, not a manufacturing one.

The term *multimedia* dates back to the pioneering cubist painters, who first created what are now called collages. Subsequent artists extended these works into a new realm, creating *assemblages* (the French word for multimedia). In the 1960s, artists combined images from television, photography, and movies to create mixed media projects. The psychedelic light shows of that period, created for trips, festivals, and be-ins, were actually called multimedia shows.

If anyone can claim the first use of the term with regard to computers, it would be Marc Canter, the founder of Macromedia. He first coined it in 1983, when his company was called MacroMind. Marc's company created the first major author-ing tool, known then as VideoWorks and now as Macromedia Director. It is still the most popular interactive animation tool for creating multimedia projects.

One indication of how multimedia technology has changed communication and expression is that teams usually work on multimedia projects. They include writers, editors, artists, musicians, actors, video editors, animators, and programmers. You would never think of hiring all of these people simply to write a book or magazine article. However, you need nearly all of these disciplines to create a multimedia project that involves the use of text, graphics, sound, animation, video, and interactive menus and branches.

It is not in the scope of this book to explain every aspect of multimedia. It will, however, lead you by the hand through the process of using Macromedia Director and other tools to create nearly every type of multimedia presentation, or project, including CD-ROM titles, and especially *interactive* CD-ROM titles. One of the hallmarks of this technology is that it allows you to create a presentation that lets the user navigate through the information in any sequence, without having to go through the entire presentation in a linear fashion, as you would with a videotape.

This ability to interact with the information more than enhances the informational content of the presentation; it makes that content accessible with no artificial barriers.

The goal of many presentations is to persuade others to accept and build upon an idea. The goal of learning is to increase the ability to comprehend ideas. The goal of art is not as easy to define, but entertainment should be pleasing, attention grabbing, and, well, entertaining.

Multimedia is a tool for attaining these goals. It provides an environment for navigating through complex information. A multimedia presentation can condense a complex subject to make it more palatable. Animation by itself can convey much more information than static art; when combined with sound, it can provide the illusion of life; when combined with video, it helps you see beyond reality. One look at the intense interest on the audiences' faces when they are viewing a multimedia presentation will convince you that multimedia brings the message home. It makes the message easy to comprehend, and firmly stamps it into your viewers' memories.

## Multimedia Applications for Director

Multimedia technology is making an impact in entertainment, professional training, education, sales, and marketing communications. We expect it to eventually change the nature of television, information retrieval, and business management. Right now, the potential users of this technology are as vast as the entire mainstream entertainment and business markets, encompassing everyone who must communicate and present ideas.

You can create Macromedia Director presentations for a large variety of applications (Figure 1.2). The pieces can be put together by a group of content experts and graphic artists, or by animation and design firms that specialize in

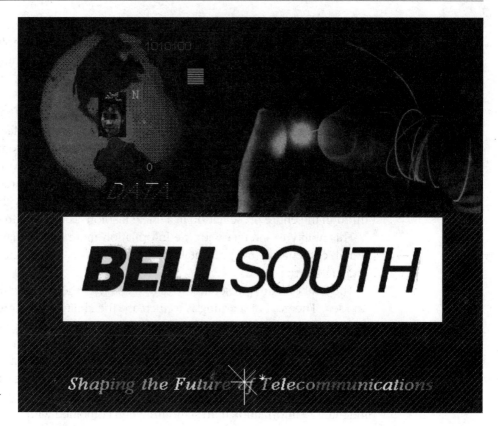

**Figure 1.2. Stuart Sharpe created the BellSouth presentation (the movie *Bell Tour*, filename: BELLTOUR.DIR, in the Tutorial folder/directory on the accompanying CD-ROM) using an early interactive version of Macromedia Director called Video Works Interactive. The presentation offers speech in different languages.**

creating modular animated presentations. These larger components can then be incorporated into presentations by anyone with minimal experience, and played either on the computer (either Macintosh, or PC running Microsoft Windows, using Macromedia software) or recorded onto videotape.

There is no such thing as a typical multimedia presentation. However, there are several mainstream applications for multimedia tools. They are:

- Business presentations (such as animated bullet-list items for marketing and sales).

- Visualizations (such as simulations and prototypes, used to communicate an abstract idea).

- Learning experiences (such as topical CD-ROMs and interactive demonstrations).

- Job reference tools (such as employee directories and product information databases).

- Kiosks (such as information kiosks in malls and airports, or shopping kiosks in stores and malls).

- CD-ROM titles (such as entertainment titles *Spaceship Warlock* from Reactor, *David Bowie's Jump They Say* from ION, *From Alice to Ocean* by Rick Smolen, and educational titles *Oceans Below* from Amazing Media).

- Interactive television, such as demonstrations by Apple, Microsoft, and others who are implementing video-on-demand, home shopping, and other interactive services to deliver to homes and businesses.

See the CD-ROM bundled with this book for demonstrations of presentations created with Director.

The most dedicated users of Director are multimedia CD-ROM artists. Some make all of their revenues from projects in which Director is the main tool. In fact, Director is by far the most popular *authoring tool* for computer-based CD-ROM titles. (*Authoring* is the process of creating an interactive multimedia presentation—it combines the disciplines of a writer, editor, graphic artist, photographer, animator, movie director, music producer, and programmer.) Classic examples of CD-ROM titles authored in Director include: *Spaceship Warlock* from Reactor, *From Alice to Ocean* by Rick Smolen, *Oceans Below* from Amazing Media, *The Journeyman Project* from Presto Studios, *Iron Helix* from Drew Pictures, and *Freak Show* from The Voyager Company.

In the production of CD-ROM titles, it is possible to work on the project and test it on various computers, then transfer the files to a master CD-ROM disc in only a few minutes with a desktop CD-ROM recorder. A large volume of CD-ROM discs can then be manufactured for less than $1 per unit from the master. Director makes it easy to create such titles on both Macintosh and Windows-based computers.

Executives and corporate communicators are also major users of Director, employing it to jazz up in-house presentations, public informational kiosks, and on-the-job learning and reference tools. Graphics programs have for years now been used in a variety of business and professional applications, as well as in slide presentations. However, once you've seen one slide presentation, you've seen them all. With Director you can go another step further in this evolutionary process: make the slides move, and give them a voice and sound.

Public relations and advertising agencies, consultants, market researchers, designers, and training companies use Director, as do educators, and even the military. Advertising agencies use it to prototype commercials, saving time and money on revisions and refinements. A client's first reaction to a visual element, gesture, or selection of spoken words can make or break a presentation, and can be critical for gaining approval for a project.

The film industry is another large market for multimedia tools. For example, for the film *Star Trek V*, special effects artist Lynda Weinman put together animated sequences that served as part of the storyboard for describing scenes

**Figure 1.3
Where no Mac
has gone before:
scenes from ani-
matics created by
Lynda Weinman
presenting ideas
and concepts for
the movie** *Star
Trek V.*

in the film (Figure 1.3). She used VideoWorks II (the predecessor of Macromedia Director) on a Macintosh with a color monitor to present the animatics to the director of the film and to the special effects crew. The animatics were used only for prototyping the actual scenes, although the director expressed a wish for the future capabilities of actually producing scenes entirely on the desktop.

## *Introducing Animation, Sound, and Video*

Although text is considered the traditional form of communication, graphic images have been around much longer, and human expression even longer.

Artists have tried to introduce motion to art since the beginning of recorded history. When Cro-Magnon man drew animals on the walls of caves, there was a suggestion of movement that brought out a feeling for the life force represented by the inanimate drawings.

The inventions of the motion picture camera and roll film made animation possible. The early animators created drawings that, when projected sequentially onto a screen at a constant speed, provided the illusion of animation—a persistence of vision.

As a form of communication, animation offers more choices in the style and detail of the content. Animators can choose to draw the subject in fine, intricate detail, or draw the subject in caricature, employing satire and ridicule. Emotions can be expressed as well, or kept hidden. Vladimir Tytla, an early animator for Walt Disney, once summarized animation to a group of aspiring artists, "Animation is not just timing, or just a well-drawn character, it is the sum of all the factors named.... What you as animators are interested in is conveying a certain feeling." One of the greatest opportunities with animation is the ability to convey human feelings with graphics, images, body language, and symbolic gestures.

Now, animation—and even real-time video—can be created, processed, and combined in presentations by nearly anybody through desktop tools such as Macromedia Director.

Director provides a painting, drawing, and animation studio in one package, making it easy to flip through drawings and animated sequences. The typical color display of a Windows PC or Macintosh provides 256 (out of a possible palette of 16.7 million) colors at any time. Macromedia Director can swiftly change the palette of 256 colors so that a Director movie can display every possible color. The range and depth of available colors, plus the painting and animation capabilities made possible through Director, combine to form a satisfying color experience.

Sound can also play an important role in a learning environment. It can highlight a presentation, draw attention, provide a realistic simulation, and present content. Every Macintosh, and every Windows-based Multimedia PC (MPC), offers the built-in capability to play sound, with a jack for connecting the computer to stereo speakers and amplifiers. Therefore, using Director, you can design multimedia presentations to include sound with the knowledge that every Macintosh and MPC owner will be able to hear it.

Add real-time video to animation and sound, and you can present complex information simply and quickly. If you have the proper ancillary hardware and software to prepare digital video for use in a Director presentation, you'll be able to add immeasurable impact and excitement to your message (see the hardware section later in this chapter).

Animation can be more effective in some cases than video because you have complete control. You can avoid the awkwardness of videotaping, since you can control the lighting, the perspective, and how much detail should be revealed. Some graphic design skills are essential, as with publishing and presentations, but talent can be acquired by using artists to create original graphic material. Animation is ultimately far less expensive than hiring a professional video crew and paying for studio editing. Of course, bad animation can make a business presentation seem like a frivolous diversion. Bad video, on the other hand, can be far more costly. It makes sense to try your ideas with animation first.

Video, when produced properly, can be extremely entertaining and direct, capturing attention and providing much more information in a sequence of images better than any other medium. Video information enhanced with computer graphics and text in Director can be saved on videotape for use with a VCR, or played back on the computer screen. You can also use a digitizer to capture live video still images and full-motion video clips in digital form, then use the images or clips in Director movie documents.

The applications of desktop video include all forms of training and entertainment. CD-ROM titles can include digital video as part of the content. Professional video production studios are using Macromedia Director for animatics. Advertising firms are using Director to do rough edits of commercials to obtain approvals and make final adjustments. TV stations are using Director to produce transitions between programs and animated graphic overlays.

However, animation, sound, and video are only part of the Director story. With Director you can use the computer's most distinguishing capabilities to create *interactive* media projects.

## Introducing Interactive Media

The next step beyond the presentation of information is the ability to interact with it. The user can stop and rerun a video or animated sequence, jump to some detailed information reference, see a simulation of something, or jump to a completely different area of the presentation. The computer changes from a sequential player of information to a tool for exploring all of the information through many different paths.

**Lingo**

Director offers a *scripting language* called Lingo for building interactive presentations and CD-ROM titles. *Scripting* is the writing of scripts that perform functions that allow users of presentations to interact with the presentation and explore topics. Scripting languages such as Lingo are designed for use by nonprogrammers and are not as complex to use as some programming languages. On the other hand, you can create very complex scripts with Lingo, because it offers the power to control animation and all forms of interactivity.

To create an interactive presentation controlled by scripts, you first define the animated sequences to occur over frames, using graphic and text objects, then you attach scripts to frames and objects to give the user of the presentation control over navigating through the material.

For example, Lingo offers the Go to instruction you can use in a presentation at a certain point to allow the users to jump to another frame or to another movie document, as they wish. A user can navigate through an interactive presentation, such as a movie that shows how to operate a machine on a factory floor, jumping from one screen to the next, in sequential, or any, order. He or she could also simply follow references to other parts of the presentation.

This linking is accomplished by defining a *hot spot* on the screen. When the user clicks on it with the mouse, the hot spot executes a script containing a Go to instruction that moves Director's playback head to another frame of animation or to another movie. In the example of a movie that shows how to operate a machine on a factory floor, the movie may have hot spots defined on certain dials, levers, or controls on the machine. The user can click these areas of the machine and see more information about them. There are numerous examples on the CD-ROM supplied with this book.

Lingo's interactive features offer considerable other advantages, such as the ability to create objects (called *sprites*) that can be edited, resized, and animated at the click of a mouse, and then moved around the screen while animated. Director also supplies a set of *extensions* to Lingo for controlling various devices such as laser videodisc players, so that users can play different video sequences at the click of the mouse. For more details, see the discussions of Lingo later in this chapter and in Chapter 6, "Elementary Scripting."

## Interactivity at Work

The applications of interactive media tools are wide-ranging. Learning experiences, such as topical videos, animated brochures, information kiosks, and product demonstrations, can be designed in Director to allow users to browse information in different ways. Users can interrupt a particular topic presentation to jump into another topic or subtopic. Reference tools, such as employee directories, product information databases, research databases, and catalogs, can make workers more productive by increasing the speed of access to information as well as the comprehension of that information. Visualizations, such as simulations and prototypes, can be created to communicate an abstract idea or process. Self-paced training presentations allow trainees to explore areas of interest and try simulated exercises while expert systems can demonstrate processes, explain concepts, respond to user queries, and take into account user responses.

Especially in art and entertainment, where the highest quality methods are the norm, the interactive media tools in Director open up new possibilities for an art form that changes with audience interaction. For entertainment, there is a constant need for new games with interesting visual and audio elements. Imagine a form of interactive TV news in which you can pause the newscaster and delve deeply into a related subject. You can summon newspaper stories, research figures, an animated timeline of events, and other video clips, with voice narration and sound. You decide where and how deeply you want to go, and when you want to return to the main subject.

Interactive media is immensely more powerful than print because it can provide an associative learning experience and present large, complex ideas and models. Director makes it possible for this experience to reach the public, through business as well as learning and entertainment applications.

## Macromedia Director 4: A Quick Tour

By now you are probably anxious to explore some of Director's specific features as they relate to multimedia. Here's a quick summary. All features are explained in more detail in Chapter 2, "Your First Movies."

Macromedia Director is a full-featured painting, animation, and multimedia layout program. It can present on-screen shows of images, with sound and animated sequences (called movies), and even allow the transfer of presentations to videotape. To summarize, Director allows you to:

- Create "digital movies" and artwork from scratch for presentations.
- Modifiy existing movies and artwork.
- Create interactive presentations for computer playback.
- Record presentations to videotape.
- Control a variety of multimedia devices such as laserdiscs.

To create and edit presentations, the program allows you to combine:

- Formatted text
- Graphics
- Video still images
- Digital video movie files
- Video from analog sources
- Transition effects
- Automatically animated text and graphics
- Prerecorded sound and music

**Director Files**

Director files are called *movies*. You can also create self-running Director files called *projectors*, which allow your audience to view presentations without the presence of the Director program.

You do not need to convert your movie to run on one platform or the other—the movies created with either the Mac or Windows version of Director 4 are completely compatible and should be able to run on either platform without modification, if you have followed the design guidelines.

## The Interface

Director 4 for the Macintosh offers an improved user interface, and other enhancements from previous versions of Director. Director 4 for Windows is a new program that offers complete compatibility with Director 4 for the Macintosh.

Earlier versions of Director for the Macintosh (such as version 3.1.3) comprised two modules: the Overview and the Studio. Version 4 of Director eliminates the Overview, combining all of the program's features into what was formerly called the Studio.

Director offers:

- A Stage, where Director movies are played, with a Control Panel (which can be displayed or hidden) for controlling playback.
- A Cast window for keeping track of multimedia elements and scripts that will be used in a presentation.
- A Paint window for creating bitmap artwork or importing and editing existing artwork.
- A Score window for creating movies and film loops, which repeat animated sequences in a movie.
- A Text window for typing text elements and styling the text with fonts, borders, and shadows.
- A Tools window for creating shapes and text directly on the stage.
- A Color Palettes window for switching color palettes.
- A Digital Video window for adding digital video movies to the Cast.
- A Script window for adding and editing Lingo scripts.
- A Message window for testing Lingo scripts.
- A Tweak window for moving selected elements precisely.
- A Markers window for adding comments associated with markers you can set in the Score.

## The Stage and Control Panel

The Stage area is where Director animations are played. You can change the size of the Stage to match your playback environment. For example, you might choose a small Stage size to play digital video movies, or you might choose a Stage size that equals an entire 14-inch (or 13-inch) display with 640 by 480 pixels.

Director offers a Control Panel with icons representing standard VCR controls (play, rewind, pause, etc.). The Control Panel lets you dynamically change the tempo and other playback aspects of the Stage, such as looping animation, turning sound on and off, locking the movie's playback speed, and changing the color of the background. Both the Stage and the Control Panel are described in detail in Chapter 2.

## The Cast Window

The cast members in the Cast window make up the elements of your movie: text, graphics, images, sounds, and digital video clips.

To help you identify a cast member, the program displays a thumbnail of each one in the Cast window. An icon in the lower right-hand corner of the thumbnail identifies the cast member's type. These cast-type icons include: Text, Button, Shape, Script, PICT, Linked PICT, Digital video, Palette, Embedded bitmap, Linked bitmap, Embedded sound, Linked sound, Film loop or embedded movie, and Linked movie.

Additionally, a Script indicator appears in the lower left hand corner of the thumbnail if a particular cast member has a Script. The names of cast members which are part of a shared cast movie appear next to the cast number in italics. (This is provided you haven't turned off the Indicate Cast Members with Scripts check-box in the Cast Window Options dialog box, which is normally turned on.) The Cast window is described in more detail in Chapter 2.

When you double-click a bitmap cast member in the Cast window, Director displays the Paint window. If you double-click a text cast member, the program displays the Text window; a digital video cast member, the Digital Video window; and so on.

## The Paint Window

Director's painting tools in the Paint window (Figure 1.4) let you scale, rotate, flip, invert, and otherwise distort graphic objects.

With Director's paint brush, you can paint with the currently selected color, ink effect, or fill pattern, and you can define several brush shapes to be available while painting. Director includes a lasso and a rectangular selection tool that can shrink, or tighten, the selection around an irregularly shaped object. Director also offers an airbrush tool that can be modified by choosing different ink effects from a pop-up menu. The Paint window is described in detail in Chapter 4.

## The Score Window

The Score window (Figure 1.5) describes the animation over time, using frames as units of time, and channels as layers of objects on the Stage. In the Score window, channels appear as horizontal rows, and frames are vertical columns.

By employing multiple channels as layers, Director lets you animate with some of the techniques of traditional *cel* animation, in which the layers are pieces of celluloid. Cel animation allows you to move elements around the Stage while leaving the background unchanged.

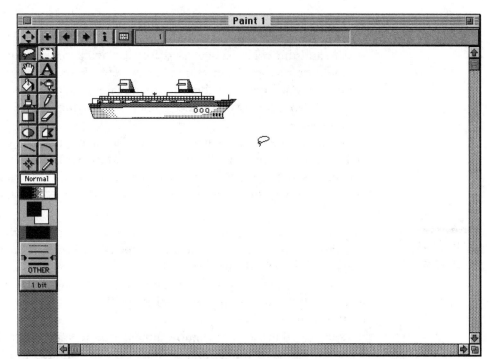

**Figure 1.4
Artwork can be
created in or im-
ported into Direc-
tor's Paint
window, which
offers a complete
set of color and
grayscale paint-
ing tools (air-
brush, custom
brushes, shape
drawing, etc.).**

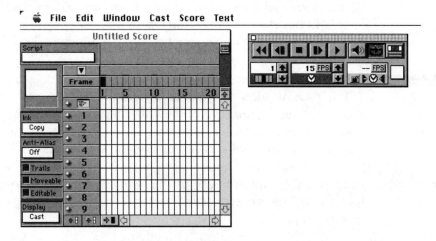

**Figure 1.5
The Score win-
dow for playing
director and
"shooting" ani-
mated sequences
with sound and
viewing frames
of animation**

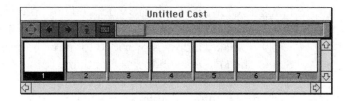

The Score window includes special channels such as the Tempo channel, which controls the movie's speed, and the Palette channel, which controls color cycling effects and the color palette used for displaying color images. The Transition channel controls special transition effects between frames, and the Script channel contains frame scripts in the Lingo language that can do a variety of things. Director also offers two sound channels for playing two different sounds or a stereo sound.

The Score menu offers many options for manipulating cast members in the score, including the Auto Animate command for automatically creating animated text effects such as bullet and bar charts, zooming text, banners, and credits. Score window features are described in more detail in Chapter 2.

## The Text Window

The Text window is available for adding text to a presentation. When you type text into the Text window, a text cast member is created. You can use different fonts and styles for a text cast member.

You can edit any text on the Stage in the Text window by double-clicking the text. Also, you can use the text tool in the Tools window to create text directly on the Stage.

Text created in the Text window animates more slowly than text created in the Paint window as a bitmap image, but you can continue to edit the text in the Text window, which is an advantage if you will be modifying the presentation later. You can always convert the text to a bitmap image as the last step before finishing a movie. Text cast members are described in detail in Chapter 3.

## Other Editing Windows

Director includes other windows for creating and editing cast members.

The Tools window is available for creating shapes and text directly on the Stage, including interactive buttons that highlight when the user clicks them. These shapes animate more slowly than bitmap images, but they take up less memory. The Tools window is described in Chapter 4.

The Color Palettes window lets you switch the sets of colors to be used for displaying the Stage. You can use this window to edit your own custom palettes (color sets). This is described in Chapter 4, which includes a technique of creating a common palette for a group of images.

The Digital Video window is for adding and editing digital video movies. The Macintosh and Windows digital video standards are used. Even if you are not familiar with other digital video editing programs, Director's Digital Video window is simple to understand and is described in detail in Chapter 8.

The Tweak window is provided for moving selected elements precisely on the Stage. The Markers window is for adding comments associated with markers you can set in the Score window, and for jumping to marked areas of the Score. These and other features of animation editing are described in Chapters 3 and 5.

## Interactive Features and Lingo Support

In addition to animation features, Director provides a complete scripting language called Lingo. Lingo is used to create interactive presentations and simulations. Director also offers a set of external *driver* routines called XObjects to drive (control) various devices such as laser videodisc players and professional video recording decks from Director's Lingo scripts.

Lingo has been in development for many years. The VideoWorks Interactive Toolkit, a predecessor to Director, included a preliminary version of Lingo that was used to create a variety of famous interactive presentations, including Apple's Macintosh SE Tour and Reactor's *Spaceship Warlock*.

To use the interactive features of Director 4, you should first become familiar with the techniques for creating animated sequences and editing in the Score window. The score lets you control events over time, such as executing a script at a particular frame.

Scripts are available in the script entry area of the score, and by clicking the script icon for script cast members and other cast members containing cast scripts. A Script window appears whenever you click a script icon to create or edit Lingo scripts. The Message window is available for testing Lingo scripts. All of this scripting stuff is described in a gentle way in Chapter 6.

## Macromedia Utilities

With Director, Macromedia supplies sample movies, as well as the Guided Tour (an interactive presentation developed with Director) and tutorials developed with Director. Director also offers extensive on-line help available as a Help button in most dialog boxes. *Lingo Expo* shows examples of commonly used Lingo commands. An Extras folder supplied with the Macintosh version of Director 4 includes XFCNs and XObjects for controlling devices such as Sony Videodisc players and VTRs, and Pioneer Videodisc players.

Also supplied in the Extras folder/directory is the ClipMedia Sampler folder/directory, containing sample animations, music, sounds, videos, graphics, and color palettes from the Macromedia ClipMedia series, Business and Technology Volume 1. The Macromedia ClipMedia series (available separately) of Clip Animation, Clip Sounds, Clip Charts, and Clip Movies provide a library of items to help you start your projects. The series is available on Mac and Windows-compatible floppy disks.

Some of the examples in this book draw their original artwork, sounds, and animations from the clip libraries you can use without copyright restriction. Other examples in this book use animations created by Stuart Sharpe, an expert Director user and top animator, who has used Director from day one, and animations created by other top Director users. These animations are on the CD-ROM contained in this book, in the Tutorial folder/directory. You can open these movies with Director and examine how the experts create Director movies, to learn new tricks and techniques from them.

Macromedia provides two FKey utilities in the Extras folder for the Macintosh for automatically capturing the screen image. They are:

- ScreenClip, Command-Shift-6, places the image in the Clipboard.
- Scrapbook, Command-Shift-8, places the image in a Scrapbook.

The Scrapbook file is a standard Macintosh graphics file that you can import directly into Director's Cast or Paint window.

To import the images in a Scrapbook file into a Director movie, use the Import command, and Director will place each image into the cast as a separate cast member in the Cast window.

Previous versions of Director included the Macromedia Accelerator utility. Accelerator was used with earlier versions of Director to make movies run faster by preloading the composite screens from accelerator files. The accelerator files were large and required a lot of RAM to run.

If you have accelerator files that you need to use, you must use Macromedia Player 3.1 for the Macintosh to play them. Files you created with Macromedia Accelerator can't be converted to Director 4 movie files.

Director 4 runs movies more quickly than earlier versions of Director, and the Accelerator is no longer necessary. Director 4 movies can be accelerated in Director by selecting the Export command from the File menu, then exporting the movie file as a digital video movie file (such as a QuickTime movie). Then import the digital video movie into Director and play it back as a digital video cast member. QuickTime cast members can be played at faster or slower rates using options you set in the Digital Video Cast Member Info dialog box. (Select the digital video cast member and press the Info button in the Cast Window or the Digital Video window to display the Digital Video Cast Member Info dialog box.)

# Version 4 Features

Those of you who already use Director will find version 4 to be a tool that delivers a faster, more compact presentation, with extra features that make it easier to create complex presentations. Director 4 frees the multimedia artist from such artificial constraints as file size and score channel limitations. It also addresses many other limitations and includes several new features.

For those of you who already know how to use Director, the following summary of new features will make sense. For those of you who don't, you can safely skip this section and read on.

Director hackers! Size will no longer be a constraint. There are twice as many score channels. The upgrade also addresses many other limitations and includes several new features.

## New Features

One important new feature is an increase from 24 to 48 channels in the Score, which doubles the capacity for simultaneous sprites on the stage. With twice as many sprites available, users will be able to design more complex interactive animations.

Another important feature, needed especially by designers of CD-ROM titles and complex productions, is the increased numbers of cast members per movie, from 512 to 32,000. The previous file size limitation of 16 megabytes has been removed; files now can be any size.

An improvement that benefits all users is the capability to add color in the Score to easily identify sprites for editing. Colors can now be used to organize the Score information so that it is much easier to follow the logic of interactive controls and debug interactive movies.

Other enhancements include: an improved Cast window that scrolls, permitting quick view of cast members, and a cast member drag-and-drop into the Score window, into a selected channel/frame cell range.

With Director 4's purge priorities in the Cast, you can have explicit control over removing cast members from memory, in order to free up memory space for other cast members. You can also set a cast member to never be purged from memory, so that it remains available.

Director 4 also offers a Save and Compact command to save a file in the most compact and optimized way for playing back, which provides better performance from CD-ROM.

An exceptional new feature, called *movie in a window*, allows multiple Director movies to play at the same time, with each movie retaining full interactive features. It is possible to use this feature to control various movies at once and pass messages from one movie to another.

Macromedia also improved the way Director saves files, compressing them further and providing for faster loading from CD-ROM. While some of these file-saving improvements appeared in version 3.1.3, Director 4 uses a revised file layout that reduces disk access time and is binary-compatible between the Macintosh and Windows versions. This means that a Director file created in either the Macintosh or Windows versions of Director can play on both Macintosh and Windows platforms without modification. Another improvment is the capability to create a projector file directly from Director, without having to use a separate utility (Macromedia Player in previous versions).

A neat new feature is the placement of the playback head at the top, rather than the bottom, of the Score window. This makes it easier to locate. Another is that cursors can now be cast members, rather than resources. This makes it easier to port the movie to Windows (where such resources aren't attached to files, as in the Macintosh), making it easier to change those cursor images to conform to Windows standards.

## Differences from Earlier Versions

Several authoring techniques and methods available in previous versions of Director have been dropped because they were not appropriate for cross-platform authoring, or no longer make any sense in the new version of Director.

For example, Director 4 no longer supports unlinked QuickTime cast members, to maintain compatibility with the Windows version, which works with either QuickTime or with other digital video formats (such as Microsoft's Video for Windows).

In addition, direct MIDI support has been dropped in favor of standard platform-specific methods, such as the *Media Control Interface (MCI)* in Windows, and QuickTime 2.0 in the Macintosh System. Developers can still use third-party XCMDs, XFCNs, or XObjects to integrate MIDI control with Director animation.

The Overview module has been eliminated, but the Auto Animate feature from the Overview remains (there is now no need of a separate Studio module). Also, Director 4 no longer supports Accelerated movies, due to compatibility with the Windows version. However, there are now other techniques for achieving the same result, such as using digital video formats that are compatible.

Some of the old keyboard shortcuts are different. You can no longer play a movie with Command-A (use Command-P), nor can you stop it with Command-W (use Command-period). The new keyboard shortcuts are more in line with the conventions for Macintosh and Windows applications.

You can update an entire folder of Director 3 files to Director 4's format. In the process, Director automatically changes the old macro-style script definitions into real handlers, making the modular programming techniques more consistent. Director also takes the frame scripts, sprite scripts, and movie scripts, and turns them into cast members that can be edited, moved around, copied, and pasted into other movies. The result: It is now much easier to find and edit scripts, and you can even share scripts more easily than before.

Macromedia also added the option to Allow Outdated Lingo in the Movie Info dialog. This makes it possible to use scripts and conventions already embedded in Director 3 files. Director 4 also supports playing Director 3 files. However, there are considerable performance benefits if you upgrade them from Director 3 to the Director 4 format, including compatibility with the Windows version of Director 4.

**Lingo
Scripting
Improvements**

An improvement that every professional user will applaud is the increase in performance of Lingo. You can now compile Lingo scripts for faster execution and improved memory management. New Lingo instructions provide explicit control over removing cast members from memory, in order to free up memory space for other cast members. There are new commands that simplify the creation of reusable code for separate movie files. Professionals will also like the new capability to hide Lingo scripts from view with new security features.

Over 160 new commands, functions, keywords, and properties were added. Scripts are now stored as cast members. Also, Director lets you create an enormous number of *handlers* (routines defined by a separate name), and allows you to share them among movie files by putting them in a file called SHARED.DIR and storing that file in the same directory or folder as the movie files.

A Find Handler menu command lets you quickly find handlers in a movie. More controls over cast properties were introduced. You can use Lingo scripts to duplicate cast members, copy cast members to the clipboard, import cast members, and change the script of a cast member.

Message-passing to the script handlers has been improved to allow explicit control. A new Pass statement lets you pass an event to the next level of script execution. New event and messaging keywords were added, including keyUp, enterFrame, and exitFrame for more precise control. You can also get more information about the operating environment with functions such as movie FileSize, searchPath, and getNthFileNameinFolder.

An exceptional feature that requires a bit of forethought to use is the object-parent mechanism for creating child objects that inherit the methods and handlers of their parents. This mechanism can be used instead of the more complex factory and method definition of previous versions of Director.

Director 4 also provides the ability to create and manage lists, with new Lingo instructions for sorting, searching, adding, and deleting list items. Previously, factories were used to create simple lists, but the new list feature is better because it offers automatic garbage collection for better use of memory. You can also create lists of lists for three-dimensional arrays.

Director 4 for the Macintosh is compatible with most existing XObjects, XCMDs and XFCNs that can extend Director's functionality. However, the Windows version of Director 4 may require Dynamic Link Libraries (DLLs) as replacements for these extensions in the Windows environment.

**Upgrading
Movies to
Director 4**

It is a simple process to upgrade older movies to the Director 4 movie file format, which is compatible with the Windows version of Director. Simply open the movie in Director 4 on the Macintosh, and save it.

If you want to convert more than one movie, use the Update Movies command in the File menu, which converts one, or a folder of movies, to Director 4's file format. The original movies are preserved, and the new Director 4 versions are saved in a new folder you specify in the Update Movies dialog box.

To create a projector from a movie file that was created with an earlier version of Director, you must first open the movie with Director 4 and save it as a Director 4 movie.

Any unlinked QuickTime movie cast members in the older movie are converted to linked cast members in the Director 4 movie. A QuickTime movie file is created for each unlinked QuickTime movie cast member and stored in the same folder with the converted Director movie.

Note that Sound File sounds are not converted. Overview and Projector movie documents created in Director 3.1, and movies created with Macromedia Accelerator can't be converted to Director 4 movies.

## Installing and Using Director

For many of you, the first experience you have with Director is the out-of-box experience. If you bought Director from Macromedia, before this book and CD-ROM came out, you received a slew of floppy disks to use to install Director onto your hard drive. However, if not, you can make a phone call to purchase and unlock the version on the CD-ROM supplied with this book and install Director from it onto your hard drive. (You can also test drive it three times before purchase!). See the CD-ROM for details.

**Macintosh Version**

Director is as easy to install as any other Macintosh application. Insert Disk #1, and its contents appear on your desktop. Double-click the Install Macromedia Director icon. Since Director comes in a compressed form, it must be decompressed with the Install program. This program asks if you want the standard installation or a custom job; you should click the button for a standard installation, unless you already know what you want to install. The program then asks for the folder in which to store the Director program. Choose an appropriate folder to hold the program and its files. You need about 32.4 megabytes of disk space for a standard installation. When it finishes installing Director, the program returns you to the Finder. You can then start Director by double-clicking the Director icon, or by double-clicking any sample Director movie document.

A hard disk is necessary, because you need quite a lot of disk space to store Director and movie files. You should already know how to use the Macintosh Finder to drag files and folders from one disk to another, and how to create a folder. The Finder information is in any tutorial book on using the Macintosh System, and in the Macintosh System manuals. In fact, every Macintosh comes with an animated tour, created in a precursor to Director called VideoWorks Interactive, that explains how to manipulate files and folders using the Finder.

**Windows Version**

Director is as easy to install as most Windows applications. Insert Disk #1, and run the setup.exe program from the File Manager. This program asks if you want the standard installation or a custom job; you should click the button for a standard installation, unless you already know what you want to install. The program then asks for the directory in which to store the Director program. Choose an appropriate directory to hold the program and its files. A hard disk is necessary, because you need quite a lot of disk space to store Director and movie files.

When it finishes installing Director, the program displays the "read me" file that supplies the latest information on this release of Director. This is an ordinary Windows text window. You should already know how to use Windows and the File Manager to drag files and directories from one disk to another, and how to create a directory. The Windows information is in any tutorial book on using Windows, and in the Microsoft Windows manuals.

You can then start Director by double-clicking the Director icon in the window of the Program Manager (or similar Windows shell), or by double-clicking any sample Director movie files (which have the ".dir" file name extension).

**Starting Director**

When you first start Director, it asks for your name and the name of your organization, so it can personalize your copy of Director. The program also asks you for a serial number, which should be listed on the packaging.

Director uses no copyright protection scheme, so you can freely copy the program from one disk to another to make a backup copy. However, if you are working on a computer connected to a network, each user on the network must have their own copy of Director. This is because the program will only run one copy per serial number at one time.

## *Configuring an Authoring System*

Now that you have the big picture of Director and what it can do, it's time to consider what equipment you will need for authoring and playing back multimedia presentations.

The type of equipment you need depends a great deal on the application. If you are designing a kiosk, you may need special equipment such as a touchscreen and a laserdisc player. For CD-ROM titles, you will need an authoring system that can allow you to edit more than twice (or even three times) the capacity of a CD-ROM disc, which holds 650 megabytes. You will need as much

RAM as you can get, so that you can run a fully installed system with many applications.

If you are designing animation that will run on a slower machine, use the slower machine to test the playback speed. When you have the desired speed on the target machine, you can use Director to lock the timing (in the Control Panel) so that the animation always plays at that speed. This means the movie will never play faster than this speed, although it may play slower due to other factors. You can, however, design your movies to run quite acceptably on a less powerful computer, no matter which system you use to create them.

**Computer**

Any Macintosh with a 68030, 68040, or PowerPC processor and at least 4 megabytes of RAM can run the Macintosh version of Director 4. More RAM is, of course, recommended (at least 8 megabytes).

Any PC with an Intel 486/33 or Pentium processor and at least 8 megabytes of RAM, running Microsoft Windows 3.1, can run the Windows version of Director 4. More RAM is, of course, recommended (at least 16 megabytes).

A greater processor is always recommended; the faster, the better. We use Director with Quadra 950 and 700 models (68040 processors), a PowerMac 8100 (PowerPC processor), and a PowerBook 180 (68030 processor). We also use a Compaq 486/33 PC with the Windows version of Director.

Don't even think of trying to run Director on slower PCs, such as 286-based or 386-based PCs. The experience will no doubt be frustrating.

With a 4-megabyte Macintosh and a less powerful processor, such as a 68020, you can barely run Director with System 7 or higher. Note that you can't use QuickTime movies on a Macintosh based on the 68000 processor (older Mac Plus, Classic, SE, and PowerBook 100 models).

Note that projector files on both platforms can run movies in minimally configured computers, such as 386-based PCs and 68020-based Macs. On the Mac, projector files can run with MultiFinder and System 6, but System 7 is recommended. However, such minimal configurations can't support the use of Director for authoring.

The use of color requires a color display and possibly a display adapter, depending on which Macintosh or PC you have. Most Macs (including the PowerBook 180) can drive a 12-inch, 13-inch, or 14-inch Apple Color Display. Some will drive larger displays. With a color display adapter of some kind, which occupies a slot in the computer, you can support larger displays and additional monitors. PC color laptops are sometimes adequate for authoring, but color PCs, with Super-VGA video displays, are recommended.

Some computers are better than others for creating color animations, especially if you are using scanned color images, because processing speed and disk capacity are limiting factors. The best advice for multimedia production is to get the fastest possible machine as long as it is reliable. Computers that are only a few months old may have compatibility problems with third-party equipment (such as display cards) and software; after the machines are tested and reviewed favorably in magazines, this problem will have been resolved.

## Sound Support

Sound can be recorded and played back with any Macintosh. Some models have built-in stereo speakers, and all other models have built-in monaural speakers. All models offer stereo output jacks for connecting to stereo equipment. In addition, many newer Macintosh models (such as Quadras and PowerBooks) have built-in sound digitizers for recording sound (although these digitizers do not record at the highest possible quality).

Any Macintosh can be outfitted with an external sound digitizer if needed, such as Macromedia's MacRecorder, to record monaural sound, and you can use two MacRecorders to record stereo sound. The MacRecorder connects to one of the two serial ports (modem and printer) on the back of any Macintosh; you can connect two MacRecorders by using both ports. Higher-quality digitizers, such as the DigiDesign Audiomedia II card, usually occupy a slot, or are included in a video card such as RasterOps' MediaTime.

Multimedia PCs running Windows 3.1 can support sound cards such as the Creative Labs SoundBlaster Pro, Media Vision's AudioSpectrum models, and so on. Some multimedia PCs have sound cards already integrated with the machine. If the sound card works with Windows 3.1, it should work with Director (any exceptions are listed in the "read me" file accompanying Director).

Sound occupies a lot of disk space and RAM, as do color images. The more RAM you can afford, the bigger presentations you can build. However, you must keep in mind the final presentation device and its RAM capacity when designing a multimedia presentation. If the presentation will appear on a low-RAM machine, you will have to refrain from using color graphics and a lot of sound in one movie. If it will be on an 8-megabyte machine with a color display, or on videotape, you are not as limited. We describe in more detail how to manage the use of sound in movie documents in Chapter 7.

## Displays

An important decision to make is which kind of display to use. The choices are limited for older Macintosh models that have no slots, and for laptops. However, the choices are virtually unlimited for modular Macs and most 486-based and Pentium-based PCs.

PCs typically include a VGA-compatible monitor. Director works in the 640 by 480 pixel resolution mode with either 16, 256, or more colors. There are a zillion display monitors that fit this configuration, and VGA or super-VGA adapters are available on the open market. However, Director does not work with all of the adapters available for PCs, especially ones that do not work with Windows 3.1.

For the Macintosh, Apple offers a complete line of display monitors that set the standard for third-party offerings for the Macintosh. Built-in color capabilities vary from one model to the next, but standards are adhered to so that a presentation created for one type of display will still play on another. With the capability to display 8-bit color, or gray, the number of colors that can be displayed at one time is 256 out of a possible 16.7 million. The same display, when set to gray in the Monitors control panel on the Macintosh, can display 256 levels of gray (including black).

Some Macintosh models have enough video RAM to expand your color range to include all 16.7 million colors simultaneously (24 bit), or thousands of colors (16 bit). Some PC models and adapters offer similar capabilities. Both the Macintosh System 7 and Windows 3.1 offer support for different color resolutions. Thus, with some adapters, you can display photorealistic images with Director. However, animation of 24-bit images is slow on some computers unless it is accelerated with an adapter (or built-in accelerator chip), or run on faster processors.

For displaying 24-bit images, we recommend using an accelerated display adapter, or a very fast processor (Pentium or PowerPC). For real-time animation on computers with slower processors, use the 8-bit display mode (256 colors). To record photorealistic images, frame-by-frame, onto videotape, use 24-bit mode. All modular Macs and most multimedia PCs support the use of third-party video frame grabbers and video digitizing cards, as well as video-out cards (described later).

The Macintosh has the inherent capability of supporting several display monitors at the same time, spreading the desktop over all the displays rather than duplicating the same information. You can place separate windows on the separate monitors to compare them and drag items, such as icons and windows, from one monitor's display to another. You can even spread windows to appear on more than one monitor. Director supports the use of multiple monitors so you can put the presentation on one monitor, yet keep the controls, Score window, Cast window, and Notes window on another monitor facing the speaker. You also can design animation that can move from one monitor to the other, and design a presentation that uses more than one monitor for the stage area.

There are many third-party monitors that are useful for desktop presentations. A monitor frequently seen at trade shows in exhibit booths is the Mitsubishi XC3710. This 37-inch monitor (with a 35-inch diagonal viewing area) can display 800 by 560 pixels and vibrant color images, due to the 30-MHz bandwidth of the supplied video amplifier. The monitor is housed in a casing with two stereo speakers. A unit without speakers is available for wall or ceiling mounts. The monitor can automatically adjust to the scan rate of a Macintosh video card, and is compatible with all Macintosh models and PCs.

**System and Software**

The Macintosh operating system and file system software modules are called the System and the Finder (or MultiFinder in System 6). The Finder provides a mechanism for organizing files in folders and for launching programs. With System 7, you can open several applications at the same time and switch from one to another quickly. Note, however, that if you are going to be using several applications at once, including Director, you may run out of RAM. This is particularly true if you use sound and complex graphics in your movies.

Windows 3.1 is the most widely used system for DOS-based PCs. There are so many books about using Windows that we won't bore you with our version of these well-known instructions. As a Windows user, you already know that you always need more RAM. No amount seems to be enough. Start with at least 8 or 16 megabytes.

On both platforms, the operating system controls any peripheral devices connected to your computer. It controls the use of programs, desk accessories, which are stored in the System file, and fonts (also stored in the System file).

The system software will most likely be updated by the time you read this (Apple updates System 7, Microsoft updates Windows). Ask your computer dealer for the latest version, which is System Version 7.1 for the Macintosh, and Windows 3.1 for the PC, as this book is written.

Macintosh and Windows applications tend to look very similar to others like them on the same platform, because they generally use the same menu conventions. Both the Macintosh system and Windows provide for the display of pull-down menus with commands and options. The systems also provide the display of dialog boxes with settings and the OK and Cancel buttons.

Nearly all Macintosh and Windows programs use these conventions, so that you are not completely lost when you start up a new program for the first time.

When working with different applications, some operations you will use often are the Cut, Copy, and Paste commands (found in the Edit menu of most applications, including Director). You can use these commands to transfer text and graphics within an application and from one application to another. For example, you can use this feature to transfer a graphic image (or a piece of a graphic image) from a program such as Swivel 3D to Director (on the Macintosh). Also, you can use the Macintosh's Scrapbook desk accessory (or a substitute such as Solutions Inc.'s SmartScrap), or a similar Windows utility, to receive copied or cut elements from different applications. Then, cut or copy the elements one by one from the scrapbook file into another file.

Part of nearly every Macintosh or Windows application is the ability to undo an action that you've just performed. You will find the Undo command under the Edit menu. It only undoes the results of the most recent operation. You must use it immediately, before doing anything else, if you are not sure about something that you did. If, after using Undo, you decide that the original operation was correct, you can re-do the operation.

Most applications also offer a Revert command in the File menu that reverts back to the last saved version of your file. This command lets you return to a previous version, throwing away the current version of the file. You would only do this if you really did not want to save the current version. In addition, every dialog box has a Cancel button and/or a Close box (Close Window in Windows), so you can always back out of a dialog box. These features make the computer experience as pleasant and nonthreatening as possible.

# Disk Storage and Backup

First, the good news: Artwork for multimedia applications, and scanned images, do not take up as much space as they would for publishing applications because you do not need as much resolution. For example, you can scan a grayscale, or color, image at 75 dots-per-inch resolution, and 256 levels of gray or colors, if you intend to display it on a 256-color monitor or record it in NTSC video format. For publishing applications, where the image will be printed on paper, you need at least 300 dots-per-inch resolution. Such images require up to four times more disk space per image.

Now the bad news: Just one second of sound can occupy from 5 to 22 kilobytes of disk space, and you need at least 1 megabyte to hold about 45 seconds of medium-quality music. In addition, photorealistic color and video images that carry 24 bits of color information (potentially displaying 16.7 million different colors) are usually three times larger than 8-bit color images (which display 256 different colors). The processor can't move this much information fast enough to provide smooth animation. Fortunately, Director can change which 256 colors to use in each image, and you can get by using 8-bit images for animation. Director can also display and animate 24-bit images, but performance depends on the speed of the processor.

As you add new types of information to your communications toolkit, such as sound and color images, you may be increasing your storage requirements exponentially. One reason is that both computer display and video media encourage the use of images and color, as well as sound.

Projects exist as files that are grouped together (in folders on the Macintosh, or in directories on Windows-based PCs). The smallest storage unit that you can use is the floppy disk. However, these only hold up to 1.4 megabytes of data. Their small capacity makes floppies inconvenient for storing or transferring project files and presentations including sound, even if you use compression techniques. It is possible to compress files to about half their size with compression utilities, but the compressed files must decompress onto a hard disk before you can use them.

You can divide your storage media needs into these useful categories: on-line, archive, project backup, and dynamic backup.

*On-line* means that a file is available to the computer without anyone having to load a cartridge or insert a disk. Typically the on-line storage requirements are one or more hard disks, ranging from 40 megabytes (for running presentations) to well over 200 megabytes (for designing them).

The *archive* medium can be anything as long as it is somehow damage-proof and suitable for long-term storage. In many cases this means keeping a duplicate copy of everything in the archive, and storing the archive in another location. The most convenient archive medium is one that is also transportable, at least in individual units. Floppy disks are popular and economical but, as noted, have very limited capacity and are not convenient for sound files and large images, even with compression utilities (although you can compress to save space).

Convenience is important for *project backup*. You want to keep all the files for a given project together, on one disk if possible, so you can load it when necessary, or transfer an entire project to someone else. We have used Syquest removable hard disk cartridges (see below), which hold either 44 or 88 megabytes each (44 is standard, yielding about 42 megabytes), and a Mirror Syquest-compatible removable cartridge drive.

A *dynamic backup* is a copy of all the information that is available on-line at any given time, as well as the state of the system and applications (a system-wide and project-in-progress backup). This type of backup is insurance against having to reconstruct the on-line information if your on-line equipment fails catastrophically. The idea is to store everything that is currently on-line onto a slower, relatively nonvolatile medium that can hold the entire on-line capacity. Tape cartridges are popular for this function, as are removable hard disk cartridges and extra hard disks (which is what we use). You may be able to handle dynamic system-wide backups with one or more hard disks with the same capacity (or more) as the on-line disks (this is what we do).

Most users will want to have one and possibly more magnetic hard disk drives for on-line storage. These components have been in use for many years and have proven themselves worthwhile for all interactive applications. However, they are not ideal for backup and archive, nor for distribution of information to other users, because they are bulky and fragile.

High-capacity hard disks are cost-competitive with all other technologies and are usually the fastest storage medium. The problem with hard disks is that the data is never permanent. Disks can fail, and static electricity and other ambient factors can cause reliability problems. The only better way to have a large-capacity storage device available for on-line interactive access is to "press" a CD-ROM (described later).

Removable hard disks provide speed close to the performance of fixed hard disks plus the convenience of removing the information and using a removed disk as a backup. There are two forms of removable hard disks: removable disk cartridges and removable disk drives.

## Syquest Cartridges

The Syquest-designed cartridges contain disks that are removable from the drive mechanism. The ubiquitous 44-megabyte cartridges are usually interchangeable among different Syquest-based systems. They are reliable as long as you handle them carefully, but may have a shorter use cycle and may need to be reformatted periodically, due to the strain of inserting and removing the disk cartridges. We have found that some units have problems with power supplies and other components. However, the units are usually warranted, and such failures usually happen early in the product's life cycle.

## Removable Drives

Removable disk drives are similar to Syquest cartridges except that you remove the entire drive assembly and disk from the chassis. However, there is no standard chassis among manufacturers, so the removable drives are not interchangeable. Removable disk drives are much faster than removable cartridges. In fact, some removable hard disks are faster than fixed hard disks with the same capacity. Such drives are usually more expensive than fixed hard drives. You can't expect to exchange information with other users unless they have the same drive.

## Tape Backup

Tape backup is still the recognized standard device for backing up large-capacity hard disks. The portability of tape cartridges is a major advantage, since certain tapes are interchangeable with different drives. However, tape is a sequential-access medium (you can't go quickly to a section and read a single file), and tape backup devices are slow and often as expensive as hard disks. A form of digital tape used in music recording, called *Digital Audio Tape (DAT)*, is faster and higher in capacity.

## WORM Discs

WORM (write-once, read many times) removable optical discs write new data after the old—the old data can't be erased. WORM discs are useful for audit trails and archives, but not for system-wide backup, or storage of data that must be overwritten on a regular basis. Currently available WORM discs can hold from 200 to 400 megabytes each, but are much slower than hard disks. As with removable hard drives, WORM discs from one drive are not usable in another, due to the wide variety of proprietary formats.

**Magneto-Optical Discs**

Erasable magneto-optical discs are attractive for backup if you can afford them. Enclosed in cartridges that are about the same size as WORM discs, erasable magneto-optical discs are reasonably priced and can be used interchangeably in drives from different manufacturers. The higher-capacity M-O discs can hold more than 2 gigabytes of data.

**CD-ROM**

You can distribute or publish multimedia presentations on CD-ROM (compact disc–read-only memory), which offers a storage capacity of 650 megabytes. This format is also suitable for archiving data. CD-ROM discs are the exact same size as standard audio compact discs. Although CD-ROMs must be recorded at a mastering facility or by means of a desktop CD recorder, they are excellent for high-volume duplication and not prohibitively expensive for test "pressings." The cost per disc drops quickly as you increase the volume. Desktop CD recorders are coming on the market at under $8,000.

The CD-ROM is ideal for publishing because it is a read-only medium and is virtually damage-proof. Its read-only nature makes it attractive for distribution of copyrighted material, such as large databases, software, image libraries (clip art), animation libraries (clip animation), and sound files. It is also useful for large visual and audio presentations and for music. One example is the CD-ROM supplied with this book, which contains hundreds of megabytes of Director movies. However, interactive presentations that must save new information have to be designed to store that information on the user's hard disk, since file-saving operations to CD-ROM either cause error messages or are simply ignored.

Digitized stereo music, scanned images, and video images take up precious disk space. They must be in digital form for editing, modifying, and retouching. However, you can store the original source material (music, images, video) in its original analog medium. To change information in any way you should first convert it into digital form. With any other method you run the risk of degrading the quality of the original material. Digital copies of digital files are exact copies, so you can expect to retain the highest level of quality once the information is in digital form.

## Tools for Still and Moving Images

The steepest part of a multimedia project's development path is at the beginning, when you need to start with images. It is not easy to visualize what you want and to create the graphics and images from scratch. Fortunately there are other ways to acquire graphics and images than to painstakingly draw them. In fact, there are hundreds of megabytes of graphics, sound, and video clips available on the CD-ROM packaged with this book. Nevertheless, a scanner is indispensable as a multimedia developer's tool.

## Scanners

A desktop scanner captures an image from a slide, a piece of paper, or whatever is placed on its copierlike platen, and converts the image into digital information. Once the image is in digital form, you can retouch, alter, and copy it as digital information without any loss in quality.

With a simple black-and-white scanner you can scan hand-drawn illustrations for automatic or manual tracing with a drawing program. You then use the result of the tracing in a Director movie. Sometimes the actual scanned illustration is good enough to use in Director. Once the image is in Director, you can use the paint window's distortion tools to change it.

With grayscale or color scanners you can scan photographs and capture up to 256 levels of grayscale information or up to 16.7 million colors. You can adjust, or change, the colors or gray levels in Director's paint window. A specific color can be substituted for another. For example, you can scan photos and retouch them, or simply change their contrast and brightness values, before using them in a movie.

One not-so-obvious use of a desktop scanner is to scan patterns on fabrics for use as backgrounds and textures for graphics. Color scanners can be useful for capturing textures and designs from fabrics. Clothing designers now use them to prepare pattern examples for printing on color printers, and to prepare animations to show how they will look in certain lighting conditions. Grayscale scanners are useful because you can scan images and graphics in black and white, and then colorize them in Director or in other graphics programs.

Scanners vary greatly in size and price. At the high end are drum scanners for prepress printing applications, where prices range as high as $65,000. In the middle range (about $2,000–$5,000) are desktop scanners that can sense black and white only (1-bit) up to 16.7 million colors (24-bit color), with 300 dots-per-inch resolution. Low-end or hand-held scanners, available for a few hundred dollars, can do perfectly suitable scans for some types of screen applications. You don't need higher resolutions if you are displaying the results on a screen. High-resolution scanners are often used for the print medium. The type of scanner you should use depends on the size and type of source material you wish to scan.

For portability and convenience, you can carry a hand scanner into libraries to scan passages of text, into laboratories to scan the results of experiments, or onto the factory floor to scan parts lists and specifications. However, hand-held scanners require a steady hand when scanning, and you must pull straight as you drag the scanner over the paper or flat object. If you move too quickly, you may cause streaks in the image and shortened sections of line art. Move too slowly, and it may not align properly.

Desktop scanners are more expensive and highly sensitive; some can sense up to 24 bits of color information (16.7 million different colors) at higher than 300 dots-per-inch resolution. If you are preparing a multimedia presentation for a standard Macintosh or PC color monitor or for NTSC video, 8 bits of color information (256 colors or grayscale levels) is usually enough. Seventy-five dots-per-inch resolution is all that is necessary (for highest image quality you would choose 24-bit color). You don't need resolution higher than 75 dots per inch for on-screen display of a presentation and for saving onto videotape. If you perform a variety of tasks with the same images, you may want to store them at a higher resolution, such as 300 dots per inch, and make a copy of the image at a lower resolution for use in Director.

**Analog Video Tools**

Video is an effective medium for entertainment, art, training, and education. You can design interactive video projects that let users explore the video presentation from many different entry points without having to sit and watch the entire video presentation in sequence.

With Director you can prepare a videotape of an animated presentation, or overlay animated graphics on top of a video presentation and save the result on videotape. In addition, you may want to record live video and synchronize it with animation, or prepare it for an interactive presentation or information tool.

It is possible to work directly with the standard video signal used in television and video recorders. You can either display video on a separate monitor (from a source device controlled by Director), or display video in a window on the display. The Macintosh AV models, such as the Quadra 840AV, offer a video-in connection to display analog video in a window on the screen, and a video-out connection to record the entire screen onto videotape.

Devices that convert signals from video source devices (such as camcorders, VCRs, and laser videodiscs) are called *video digitizers*. Some digitizers can perform this digital conversion at the speed of NTSC video (30 frames per second). (NTSC, the acronym for National Television System Committee, describes a type of video signal defined in 1953 that encodes and transmits color television in the U.S.) They can use a variety of video equipment. Others (known as *frame grabbers*) can digitize only still frames of video.

A still video image is similar in format to a scanned grayscale or color image. You can edit and retouch it just like a scanned photo, although the former is usually lower in resolution than the latter. Director provides a color palette for 256-color (8-bit) displays that includes the standard NTSC colors that work well with still video images. Director lets you save custom palettes that can include any colors and shades of gray. You can even combine a grayscale image with a color image in the same 256-color display by using a combination of gray shades and colors in a single palette. (See Chapter 4, "Painting Techniques," for information on color palettes and creating a common palette.)

There are several hardware products available for Macintosh and PCs that can display full-motion analog video in a window on the display without your having to create a digital movie file from the analog video. The applications for analog video on the screen can be as simple as watching TV while working. However, it can be as complex as integrating video with a multimedia presentation, or overlaying text and graphics on a video image, and recording the result onto videotape.

One way to add prerecorded analog video to a multimedia presentation is to use a separate video monitor for the video portion of the presentation; then control the video source device (usually a laser videodisc player) from Director. Director offers external commands in its Lingo scripting language, called XObjects in the Macintosh version and the Media Control Interface in the Windows version, to control laser videodisc players, such as the Pioneer 4200 and the Sony industrial players. With these extensions to Lingo, a multimedia presentation involving animation synchronizes with a videodisc player.

## Digital Video Tools

Another way to add video to a multimedia presentation is to convert the analog video into digital video (in a process called *digitizing*), and compress the digital video to fit on disk and play back from CD-ROM.

The Macintosh offers a digital video architecture called QuickTime that also runs on Windows; Microsoft offers another digital video architecture called Video for Windows. There are numerous programs for capturing, digitizing, and compressing video into digital form, and numerous hardware digitizer cards for PCs and Macintosh computers. Digital video is described in more detail in Chapter 8, "Using Video."

Director offers a method to convert a Director presentation into a digital video movie, such as a QuickTime movie on the Macintosh. Also, you can convert to either a QuickTime for Windows movie file, or a Microsoft Video for Windows (.AVI) file. These digital video movies can then be imported into Director movies. The digital video features of Director are described in Chapter 8, "Using Video."

## Video Recording

It is also possible to record animation directly onto videotape in real time. Director provides Tempo and Actual displays in the Control Panel to show the speed of your movie in frames per second. You can speed up, or set a Lock button to control the Actual timing of movies, so they can be recorded to videotape. However, some projects require frame-by-frame recording to videotape. Macromedia provides XObjects for the Macintosh version of Director to record images, frame by frame, to professional videotape recorders (such as those using Video8, ¾-inch, and 1-inch formats) driven by intelligent controllers.

Recording frame by frame to videotape is the preferred method for showing animations of 24-bit photo-realistic images, which are slow when run in real time on most computers. However, when recording animation frame by frame, you may lose some of the transition effects between frames. Special transitions are provided for recording frame by frame, and accelerated movies using other special transitions can be recorded to videotape in real time. Design tips and techniques to record movies to videotape appear in Chapter 8.

# Sound Tools

Every Macintosh model offers a built-in capability to play sound and a mini-phone jack for connecting the computer to stereo speakers and amplifiers. Therefore, you can design multimedia presentations to include sound with the knowledge that every Macintosh owner can hear it. Users running Windows MPC PCs can also play back sound. In either case, the sound can be in stereo and played on the monaural speaker or on stereo equipment.

To use sounds with Director, you can either digitize the sound and play it through the computer speaker, or mini-phone jack, or control a CD-ROM player to play sounds stored on the audio tracks of compact discs. The CD-ROM player also has a mini-phone jack. You can also trigger musical instruments and synthesizers with the use of a *MIDI (Musical Instrument Digital Interface)* sequencer. All of these methods are described in detail in Chapter 7, "Using Sound."

For most applications that do not require high-fidelity music, digitizing the sounds and storing them on disk is the best choice. Any Macintosh can play the sound without the need for additional equipment. Multimedia PCs also come with sound playback support or can be configured to have an inexpensive sound card. The other methods require additional equipment, for example, a CD-ROM player with speakers, or MIDI equipment.

You use a *sound digitizer* to record sound and convert it to a digital format for storing on disk as digital sound. Macromedia's MacRecorder for the Macintosh is a widely used sound digitizer. The MacRecorder is a device for recording, and it includes SoundEdit 16, a program for editing, mixing, and storing sounds in disk files for use with Director. Each MacRecorder can record audio by means of a built-in microphone, external microphone, or line-in source. With two Mac-Recorders you can record in stereo. You can also use the SoundEdit software as a multichannel mixer.

For the PC, cards such as the Creative Labs SoundBlaster Pro and the Media Vision AudioSpectrum 16 can digitize sound and create digital sound files. They are provided with software for capturing and editing sound in digital form.

To store sound in digital form, a sound digitizer takes *samples* of the waveform—it measures the exact location of the waveform—at evenly spaced intervals of time. The sound digitizer records these samples at a rate of, for example, 22 kHz (you can usually pick a higher or lower rate), which is suitable for voice narration. Some digitizers can be set to sample as high as 44.1 kHz in stereo (CD quality).

You can set the sound digitizer to record at a lower sampling rate (*downsampling*) to conserve disk space. This, however, will result in lower quality sound. The basic tradeoff is that you lose more high frequencies, but you can make a longer recording using the same amount of memory and disk space. Sound sampling is described in detail in Chapter 7.

The Macintosh and PC internal speakers are not good enough to convey the quality of medium- or high-fidelity sound. High-fidelity sound delivery can be achieved with speaker systems that can be attached directly to the Macintosh's built-in stereo mini-plug port or the PC's sound card mini-plug. You also can connect the computer's sound card or built-in sound port to a conventional stereo amplifier or receiver.

## *Playback Considerations*

You know you have a machine capable of playing the best interactive CD-ROM titles if you can play the "TECHNORM.DIR" movie supplied in the TUTORIAL folder/directory, which is part of Marc Canter's MediaBand CD-ROM (Figure 1.6). This movie requires at least 5 megabytes of RAM on a Macintosh, or 8 megabytes of RAM and a sound card on a PC, and a 640-by-480 pixel color display.

The Macintosh product line is sufficiently consistent so that you can create a projection file and run it on almost any Macintosh. For example, all Macintosh models with built-in CD-ROM drives come with at least 5 megabytes of RAM. The PC universe, however, is a lot less predictable.

The differences among computers basically are:

- **Memory**. The amount of RAM determines the size of the Director movie file you can play. A minimum of 5 megabytes is required to run a QuickTime movie, and Macintoshes with built-in CD-ROM drives are configured with 5 as the base amount. We recommend at least 8 megabytes for either Macintoshes or PCs, and more if you can afford it, because you can run more than one program at a time if you have enough RAM.

- **Digital video**. The 68000-based Macintoshes (e.g., Macintosh Classic, PowerBook 100) can't run QuickTime, so you can't include a QuickTime movie with your Director movie if you are playing it back on a 68000-based

**Figure 1.6**
**The "TECH-**
**NORM.DIR"**
**movie, an ex-**
**cerpt from Marc**
**Canter's Media**
**Band, pushes the**
**playback ma-**
**chine to the limit**
**of what you can**
**expect from a CD-**
**ROM title.**

Macintosh. Similarly, QuickTime for Windows and Video for Windows won't run properly on 286-based PCs or slow 386 machines.

- **Display size**. Displays range from 9 inches up to 20 inches and possibly more. Macintoshes with NuBus or direct slots can also support multiple displays, and some PowerBooks (such as the PowerBook 180) can output to a 13-inch (also known as 14-inch) or smaller external display. PCs have displays of all kinds. Depending on the project, you might design your presentation for a standard 9-inch display (512 by 384 pixels) as a common denominator, as described in Chapter 2, because every Macintosh and PC can probably display it. If NTSC video is the final delivery medium, use a standard 13-inch setting (640 by 480 pixels) and obey the rules about recording to videotape (see Chapter 8).

- **Color**. Some Macs and PCs have color displays, others don't. Since no two monitors are alike in every way, there is no guarantee that every color will reproduce exactly the same way. NTSC video also poses several challenges to designing in color, as described in Chapter 8. As for PowerBooks, the Macintosh System with QuickTime automatically dithers color images to display them. The results may not look as good as you might want, which is why some designers use grayscale images. Director offers a grayscale palette for such images.

Projector start   PROJECT

**Figure 1.7**
**Projector icons are displayed for stand-alone Macintosh Director movies that run without Director present. On the left is a Projector icon created by Macromedia Player for Macintosh from a Director 3.1 movie. On the right is a Projector icon created by Director 4 for Macintosh using the Create Projector command in the File menu.**

## Projectors for Distribution

With Director 4, you can convert movie files into projector files, which can play back without Director. You can freely distribute the projector files. Projector files are ideal for distribution because they can run without the Director program. You can run Projector applications by double-clicking them (Figure 1.7). You can distribute projectors and play them on computers without any other software.

The playback environment is the same as described above for running Director, except that projector files can also run in more limited environments and slower machines. The best way to find out if a projector file works on a particular machine is to try it.

Projector applications can be distributed either with related movies embedded within them, or with the related movies as separate projector files in the same folder. Any linked movie files (movies called from within the projector movie file) should be included in the folder to ensure that the projector can find them.

Another advantage of creating a projector file to distribute to users is that users cannot edit the movie file or open it with Director. The projector version of the movie is compacted and protected from being opened, and the file size may also be reduced. The projector file is a play-only version of your movie(s). These movies will play in the order you list them in the Create Projector dialog box, when the projector is created. For this reason, you should make, and save, a copy of the movie file(s) for yourself. You should do this before you create the projector, in case you need to make any changes to the movie(s) later.

Director 4 provides the Create Projector command in the File menu to create projectors. Earlier versions of Director were supplied with a separate utility, Macromedia Player, for building projector files, but this is not necessary with Director 4. In fact, the old Player utility does not work with Director 4 files.

While Director movie files can be played on either Macintosh or Windows platforms, projectors created with the Macintosh version of Director 4 will play only on a Macintosh. Projectors created with the Windows version of Director 4 will play only on a Windows PC. You can create a projector with a movie that calls external movie files, so you need only create one projector for Macintosh

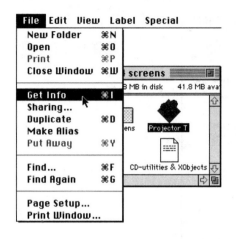

**Figure 1.8
Using the GetInfo
command in the
Finder's File
menu to look at
the memory par-
tition size.**

computers and one for Windows to distribute a presentation that uses the same
movies to play on both platforms.

When you distribute projector files that will play back on a Macintosh with
System 7's Finder (or System 6's MultiFinder), you need to check the memory
size allocated to the projector application file. Use the Get Info command in the
Finder's File menu (see Figure 1.8).

Director can play back some movies in as little as 2 megabytes, but the more
random access memory (RAM) allocated to the application, the better the
performance. To specify the amount of RAM to allocate to the partition of a
Macintosh projector, use the Get Info command as shown above. Type a number
(representing kilobytes) into the field titled Current Size (Figure 1.9). You will
have to experiment to determine the optimal size for your projector files.

**Cross-
Platform
Authoring**

Although the Macintosh is the most popular computer for multimedia development, the PC running Microsoft Windows is perhaps the most ubiquitous
computer of all time.

The highest quality software for multimedia development first appeared on the
Macintosh because its environment is enriched for graphics and sound applications. The common feature of multimedia programs is that they represent
information with graphical icons, and the editing of information is represented
with appropriate graphics on screen. The Macintosh excels at presenting screen
graphics, and its system is intuitive and easily understood by graphically oriented
people. In addition, every single Macintosh has built-in sound playback capability. So there is no question about it: Although other computers can be used for

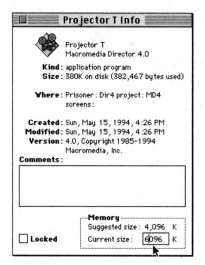

**Figure 1.9
Changing the
memory parti-
tion size in the
Get Info dialog
box.**

multimedia applications, the Macintosh offers the best graphics computing
platform for integrating the activities of artists, writers, musicians, directors, and
producers.

Many of the high-quality software tools for multimedia development have
migrated over to the Windows platform, including Director. Windows offers a
similar graphical environment for presenting multimedia information, and the
proliferation of low-cost audio cards for PCs ensures that sound capability is easily
obtainable for less than $500.

All PCs with 386, 486, or Pentium central processors, and at least 5 megabytes
of RAM, an 8-bit audio card, and a single-speed or double-speed CD-ROM drive
can play Director movies started by a projector file. There are many PCs in the
market that fit that description. (Note, however, that for authoring, you need at
least 8 megabytes of RAM to run the Windows version of Director.)

The aspirations of multimedia developers, who want to create a single
presentation or title, which can run on all possible machines, are well served by
version 4 of Macromedia's Director. It is capable of playing multimedia on both
types of systems and from the same file. You can create the Director file in a
Macintosh or Windows version of Director 4, and play it on either system.

However, you need to make certain design decisions when you create your
movie to guarantee getting the results you expect. For example, your choice of
color palettes (and the color resolution setting of cast members) will affect the
look of the movie. If you create your movie using the Macintosh version of
Director 4, use a palette designed for the PC, such as the VGA or System-Windows
palette. This will result in a movie that always uses the exact same colors, with
either platform.

Other design decisions to make concern:

- Font choices. Macintosh and Windows machines use different fonts that may cause text to appear at different sizes.
- Palette effects (such as fades and color cycling).
- Use of sound.
- QuickTime movies.
- Ink effects (some ink effects are slower on Windows PCs—some are so slow that they are not recommended for cross-platform movies).
- Lingo commands.
- File and folder naming conventions.

Indeed, the names you give files and folders must be no longer than 8 characters, if you are to be compatible with Windows 3.1. See Chapter 9 for more details on cross-platform design.

In this book, we explain what you need to know at each step to make the right design decisions for cross-platform playback.

If you expect to use Director 4 for cross-platform development, be aware that Director Player for Windows 3.1 will not play Director 4 files. You must use the Windows version of Director 4 to play Director 4 movies and to create a projector file that plays Director 4 movies on the Windows platform.

## *Chapter Summary*

In this chapter, you were introduced to animation, sound, and video, which make up multimedia presentations. You also learned about the applications of interactive media and Director's interactive control features, including its scripting language, called Lingo.

This chapter described how to configure your Macintosh or Windows system with hard disks and other storage devices, displays, utility software, scanners, video digitizers, sound recorders, and projection equipment.

You also learned about the new features of version 4 of Director, and the differences between version 4 and previous versions. The enhancements to the program and to the Lingo scripting language were summarized, and you learned about cross-platform authoring.

You can start using Macromedia Director right away, as described in the next chapter, without any graphics skill. The example movie in the next chapter can be created by anyone. You will want to become graphics literate when you create visual presentations and animation, but Director is useful no matter what level of graphics skill you have acquired.

# 2

# *Your First Movies*

**Animation can explain whatever the mind of man can conceive.**

Walt Disney

In this age of information overload, animation can condense a complex subject to make it more palatable to novice viewers—allowing them to get over the early problems of comprehension. By adding sound, you can illuminate the material in a new dimension. The presentation becomes more effective the more you can customize it for a particular audience, keeping that audience awake and interested in what you have to say.

The animation does not have to have realism, nor the quality and style of a Disney cartoon. With simple flourishes, moving titles, and transitions, you can create a dazzling performance.

To get used to this new medium, you should start your Director experience by opening a simple Director movie and seeing how it works. In this chapter, you'll do just that, learning how to modify and to customize a movie for your needs. With this information, you'll be able to modify many of the clip animation files on the accompanying CD-ROM. By the end of this chapter you will know how to put together your own movies.

## *Your First Look*

Animation, video, and film have one thing in common: Still images, called *frames*, play in sequence so quickly that the human eye is fooled into seeing movement. The slight differences between each frame are indistinguishable individually and are perceived as continuous motion. This phenomenon is called *persistence of vision*. It is the principle behind animation techniques.

41

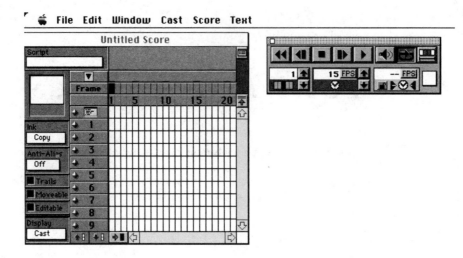

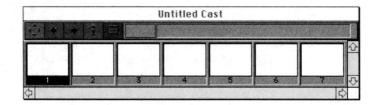

**Figure 2.1
Director displays
the Cast and
Score windows
and the Control
Panel.**

Director displays the passage of time, or frames, with a spreadsheet-like interface called the *score*. When you first start Director, the program opens the Score window, the Cast window, and the Control Panel (Figure 2.1).

All visible animation in Director occurs in an area of the screen called the *stage*. The stage can fill the entire screen, or it can be smaller than the screen size. The stage area is behind everything else and is always present, although other windows may partially or fully obscure it. The Window menu provides options for displaying the Score window, the Cast and Control Panel windows, and other windows. You can also close any windows by clicking the window's close box in the upper left corner. As a shortcut, on the Windows version of Director you can close an open window with Control-W, or close all open windows with Control-Alt-W (or hold down the Alt key and choose Close Window from the File menu). On the Macintosh version of Director, you can close all open windows by holding down the Option key while clicking the close box of the active window.

The Score window describes the animation over time, using numbered frames as units of time, and numbered channels as layers of objects on the stage. In the

Score window, channels are shown as horizontal rows, and frames are vertical columns. The frame numbers appear along the top of the chart in multiples of 5 (that is, 1, 5, 10, 15, 20, and so on).

The other visible window is the Cast window, which holds the elements used in the movie. These elements can be images, text, graphics, sounds, and digital video clips. Each individual element in the Cast window is a *cast member*. This is Director's metaphor: In an opera, cast members appear on the stage in scenes connected to musical numbers. In Director, the stage is an area on the screen, and the scene is a sequence of frames. The score is the Score window that provides the detailed information on the position, appearance, and duration of cast members and sounds for each frame.

If all this sounds confusing at first, don't worry—just try these simple lessons to get acquainted with Director.

## Lesson 1: Using Auto Animate

You say you are not an artist or cartoonist. You have no painting or drawing skill, and you've never before created anything as dramatic-looking as animation. Nevertheless, Director puts the power of animation tools in your hands.

One fundamental difference with using Director over any other method of animating is that Director can do it for you: It has extensive *automatic* animation capabilities.

By pointing and clicking at menu choices, you can instantly build a presentation with shimmering titles, darting bullets in a bullet list, scrolling movie-style credits, and so on. You can enhance even the simplest, sincerest, and most business-like presentations with Director's auto animate feature.

You can combine a familiar visual cue, such as a corporate logo or a background image, with animation. However, for the purpose of introducing Director's features with the simplest example, we'll create a bullet chart.

**Animating Bullet Charts**

To build a simple presentation, start by double-clicking the Director program, or if you are already in Director, select New from the File menu (Figure 2.2). (Note: If you don't already own Director, you can follow along using the Test Drive available on the accompanying CD-ROM.) To give the presentation a name, select the Save command from the File menu. Type a name for the movie, such as EXAMPLE1. It is helpful, when using movies with both Macintosh and Windows systems, to keep your file names to a maximum of eight or fewer text characters to conform with PC file-naming conventions.

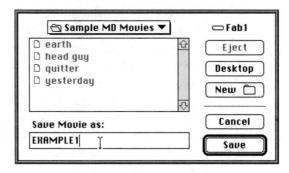

**Figure 2.2**
**Using the Save**
**command in the**
**File menu to save**
**the file by name.**

Next, click inside the cell in channel 1, frame 1 in the Score window (Figure 2.3).

Choose the Auto Animate command in the Score menu, which displays a submenu of Auto Animate choices (Figure 2.4).

Choose the Bullet Chart option, and Director displays the dialog box for defining the bullet list text and animation features (Figure 2.5).

You can type the words to be animated, in place of the dummy words (Figure 2.6), and set the text style and font (or use the default settings).

The dialog box offers a number of choices for animating a bullet list. You can set the speed of the animation as well as the motion of the bullet list items, such as from the right side of the screen. For example, the text can start scrolling from

**Figure 2.3**
**Clicking inside**
**cell 1, in channel**
**1 of the Score, to**
**start an automat-**
**ic animation se-**
**quence.**

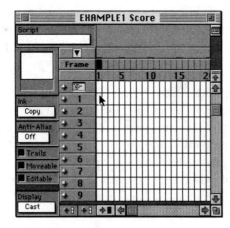

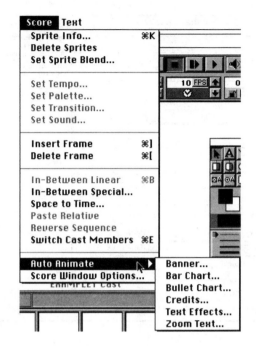

**Figure 2.4
Choosing the
Auto Animate
command in the
Score menu.**

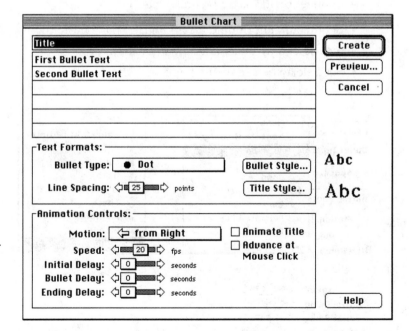

**Figure 2.5
The Bullet Chart
dialog box with
options for creat-
ing an animated
bullet list of text.
You can change
the dummy text
to your own.**

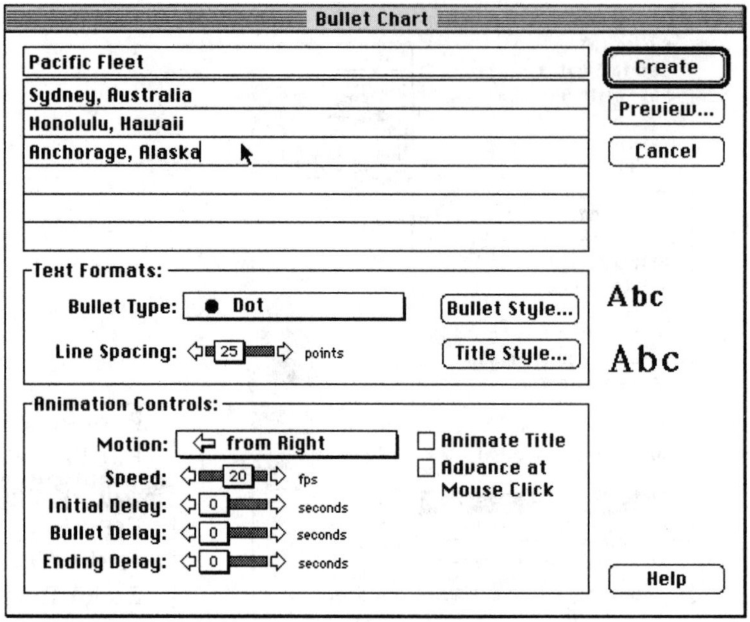

**Figure 2.6
Changing the
text in the Bullet
Chart dialog box,
but keeping the
default font and
size.**

the right, from the left, from below, and so on, or simply appear in a reverse of
a dissolve. You also can set the type of bullet, such as a flying arrow (Figure 2.7).
The Bullet Chart dialog box also lets you:

- Set the amount of time for an initial delay before the list appears.
- Set the ending delay after the animation.
- Set a delay before the text appears, after the bullet appears (Figure 2.8).

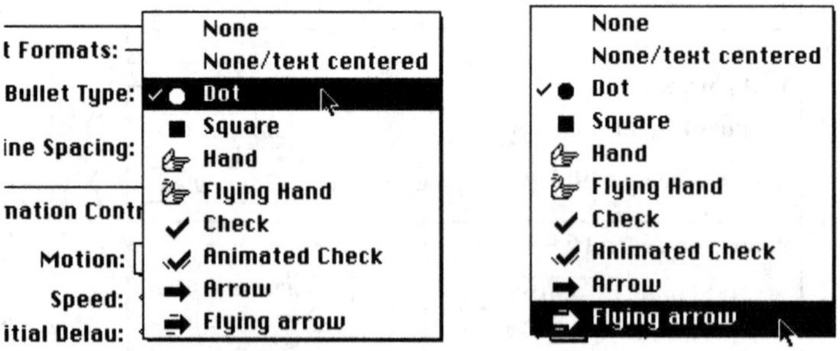

**Figure 2.7
Changing the bul-
let type to a fly-
ing arrow.**

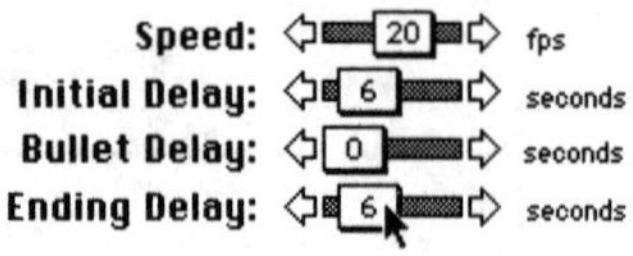

**Figure 2.8
Setting delays
and the overall
speed of the bul-
let list items.**

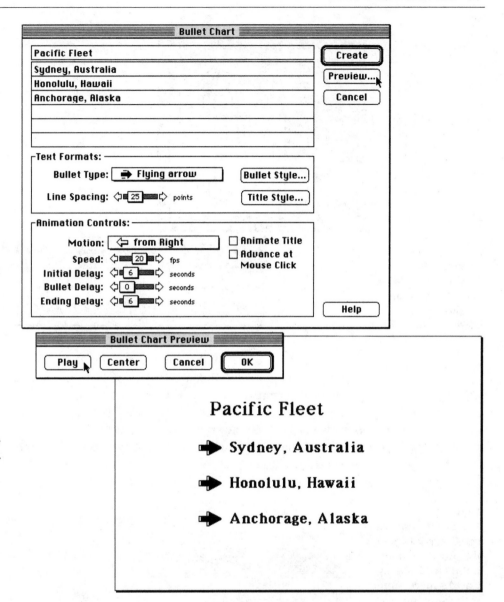

**Figure 2.9**
**Click the Preview button in the Bullet Chart dialog box to see a preview of the animation and its position on the stage. Click the Play button to see the preview repeatedly.**

A speed setting controls how fast the overall animation plays. You also can override the bullet delay setting with the Advance at Mouse Click option, so that list items move into place only after you click the mouse. Click the Preview button to see the animation (Figure 2.9).

When you click in the Preview window, the animation moves to a new starting point based on where you clicked, so you can place the animation exactly where you want it on the screen. Click the Center button to move the animation starting

**Figure 2.10**
**The result of the Auto Animate operation is a completed animation.**

point back to the center of the stage. Click the OK button after previewing, and the Create button for the Bullet Chart dialog box, and your automatic animation is complete (Figure 2.10).

To play the animation, look for the play button on the Control Panel, which looks like a VCR remote control (Figure 2.11).

You may have to "rewind" the animation to the first frame with the rewind button (Figure 2.12).

**Figure 2.11**
**The play button on the Control Panel is the one the cursor points to. The gray-tinted square button is the stop button.**

**Figure 2.12**
**The rewind button in the Control Panel returns the playback head to the first frame to start play.**

**Figure 2.13**
The Bar Chart op-
tion in the Auto
Animate sub-
menu of the
Score menu.

If the windows are blocking the animation, hold down the Shift key when you click the play button. To stop the animation when the Control Panel is not visible, press Command-period on the Macintosh. The Command key is the key with an Apple symbol, or a clover-leaf symbol, found between the Option key and the space bar. On Windows systems, Control-period (the Control key is labeled Ctrl on some keyboards) stops the animation.

There you have it: your first movie. Use the Save command in the File menu to save it.

Remember that bullet charts are most effective when you have three or four points to make. For visual clarity, you want to keep the text simple and save the details for other methods of communicating.

## Animating Bar Charts

Bar charts are common in presentations, and Director provides a way to automatically animate them.

First, select New from the File menu to start a new movie. As before, click inside the Score window in frame 1, channel 1. Select the Bar Chart command from the Auto Animate submenu in the Score menu (Figure 2.13).

The Bar Chart dialog box of options appears with default options for a solid bar style and no delays (Figure 2.14).

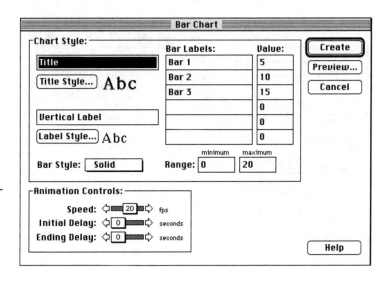

**Figure 2.14**
The Bar Chart dia-
log box with
dummy text and
values, set to a
solid bar style
and no delays.

**Figure 2.15
Filling in the text
in the Bar Chart
dialog box.**

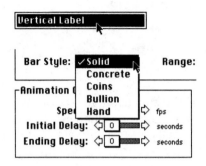

**Figure 2.16
Choices for the
bar style in the
Bar Chart.**

In this dialog box, you can change the text style of the title and labels (including font, size, and style), type labels and values for each bar, and the minimum and maximum numbers representing the bar chart's range. The minimum value is where the axes meet, and the maximum value defines the height of the vertical axis; you can enter any positive values between zero and 32,000. Bar labels appear underneath each bar, and the Vertical Label (Figure 2.15) appears to the left of the chart.

By clicking on the Bar Style pop-up list, you get a list of choices for the bar style (Figure 2.16). You can also set the speed of the animated bar chart, and the initial and ending delays. The delay sliders show numbers that are relative to the speed of your computer, not absolute units of time. Change the Bar Chart dialog box as you want (Figure 2.17).

You can then click the Preview button to see the animation. When you click in the Preview window, the starting point for the animation changes to the point

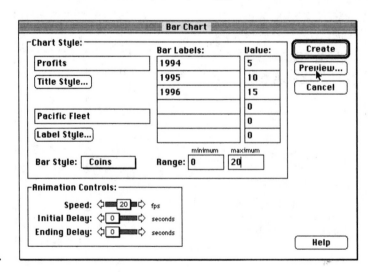

**Figure 2.17
Click Preview to
see a preview of
the bar chart
with these values.**

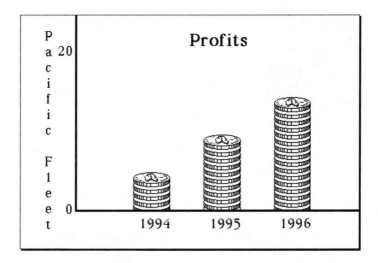

**Figure 2.18**
**Previewing the**
**automatic bar**
**chart.**

where you clicked, so you can place the animation exactly where you want it on the screen. You can also click the Center button to place the animation in the center of the window (Figure 2.18).

When you click OK, you return to the Bar Chart dialog box, where you can make even more changes if you want, and then click Create to finish the animation.

As you can see by the Score window, this automatic animation occupies far more cells in the score (Figure 2.19).

Use the Save command in the File menu to save the movie. Bar charts are useful for comparing values of the same kind, such as growth percentages, revenues, profits, and so on. Director lets you animate up to six bars, which is a practical limit for visual reasons. You can create more complex charts by using animation techniques described in the next chapter.

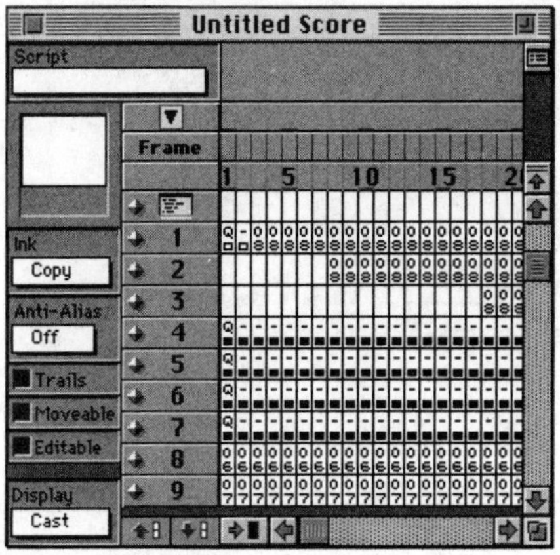

**Figure 2.19**
**The result of the**
**automatic bar**
**chart animation**
**in the Score win-**
**dow.**

**Figure 2.20**
**Selecting the**
**Credits text ef-**
**fect from the**
**Auto Animate**
**submenu.**

## Using Title and Text Effects

Animated titles add visual interest to any type of movie. Director offers a variety of animated title effects including:

- Zoom, to zoom text from tiny to regular (or from regular to tiny) size in the center of the screen.
- Banner, to run text across the screen as in a banner.
- Credits, to scroll text up from the bottom as in movie credits.
- Letter slide, for text made up of letters sliding into place, one at a time.
- Typewriter, for text that appears as if typed, one letter at a time.
- Sparkle, for text sparkling in the center of the screen.

For this part of the lesson, select New from the File menu to start another new movie. As before, click inside the Score window in frame 1, channel 1. Select the Credits option from the Auto Animate submenu in the Score menu (Figure 2.20).

A dialog box appears for setting up text to scroll up from the bottom of the display to the top, like movie credits (Figure 2.21).

**Figure 2.21**
**The Credits dia-**
**log box for set-**
**ting up film-style**
**scrolling credits.**

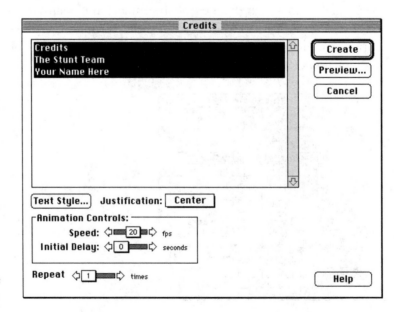

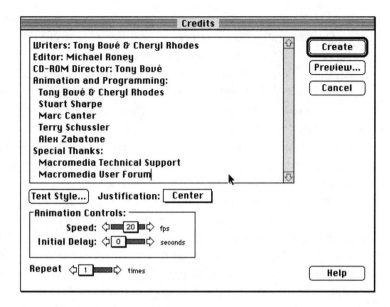

**Figure 2.22**
**Replacing the**
**dummy text in**
**the Credits dialog**
**box with new**
**text, keeping the**
**default type size**
**and font.**

You can type as many lines of text as you need, up to 32,000 characters, ending each line with the Return key or letting lines wrap around to the next line (Figure 2.22).

You can set the text style, font, and justification (center, left, or right). The speed slider controls how fast the text scrolls up the screen, and the initial delay slider sets the delay before starting the animation. Be careful to set a speed that enables ordinary users to read text as it scrolls by.

Click the Preview button to see a preview of the animation, and to set its position in the window (Figure 2.23).

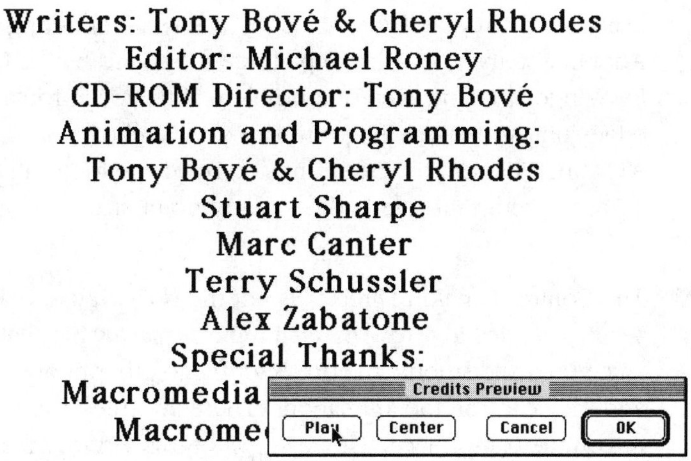

**Figure 2.23**
**Previewing the**
**credits text ef-**
**fect, using the**
**Play button to re-**
**peat the anima-**
**tion, and the**
**Center button to**
**center it on the**
**stage.**

Writers: Tony Bové & Cheryl Rhodes
Editor: Michael Roney
CD-ROM Director: Tony Bové
Animation and Programming:
Tony Bové & Cheryl Rhodes
Stuart Sharpe
Marc Canter
Terry Schussler
Alex Zabatone
Special Thanks:
Macromedia
Macrome

Credits Preview
Play   Center   Cancel   OK

Click OK to go back to the Credits dialog box, where you can change the speed, set an initial delay, or set the number of times to repeat the animation or to repeat it continuously. Click the Create button to finish the animation.

Another title effect that is popular is the moving horizontal banner. It is simple to set up: Select the Banner option, as you did for the Credits effect, after starting a new movie. The Banner dialog box offers a text entry field for typing the banner text, and the now-familiar speed and delay controls.

Since it is more difficult to read text that is moving in a horizontal direction, you might want to slow down the speed of the animation. Use the Preview function to check the speed, and you can click the play button to see the Preview over and over before clicking the OK button to return to the Banner dialog box. You can then adjust the speed and add an initial delay, if you like, or even specify how many times to repeat the animation.

The Zoom Text effect, named after the camera technique of changing from a long shot to a close-up (zooming in), lets you set the text to zoom into the center of the stage window, and either stay there or zoom back out again. You create this animation in exactly the same way as the other effects, except that you choose the Zoom Text option from the Auto Animate submenu.

The Text Effects option provides several other effects, including the Letter slide, in which individual letters slide across the display to form the words. A title effect that grabs attention is the Sparkle effect, which we often use to make an idea appear precious or exciting. A sparkle appears on the characters from left to right. To set up the Sparkle effect, simply choose it from the submenu, type the text, and use the Preview function to see how it looks. The Sparkle effect works best with large point sizes.

You get better results with any text effect if you choose a screen font and point size that is already installed in your system, or a PostScript Type 1 font if you are using ATM (Adobe Type Manager, a screen-rendering outline font utility from Adobe Systems), or a TrueType font (supported by the Macintosh's System 7 and by Windows). However, one problem with screen fonts is that they show jagged edges unless the specific point size you've chosen is already present. If you use ATM and PostScript Type 1 fonts, or TrueType fonts, all of your fonts will display correctly without jagged edges at any point size.

## Creating a Projector

The Control Panel in Director is not the only way to play a movie. You can play several movies in a row by creating a *projector* file that contains the movies. In fact, you can distribute the projector file to other people who don't have Director, and they can run the animation. (There are rules about the use of projector files in commercial projects. However, as of this writing, the distribution of projector

**Figure 2.24**
**Using the Create Projector command to create a projector file to distribute movies to others. The projector files can run by themselves, without the need for Director.**

files is virtually free as Macromedia does not charge a royalty, and only requires that you include the Director logo on commercial products.)

To combine the last three movies you created into one presentation, use the Create Projector command in the File menu (Figure 2.24).

This command brings up a dialog box (Figure 2.25), in which you can select each movie file to be played back and add each to the sequence inside the projector.

As you click each movie and click the Add button, the movies line up on the right side in the order you specified for playback. Click the Options button (Figure 2.26), and in the Projector Options dialog box, turn on the Play Every Movie option so that the entire list of movies will be played in sequence.

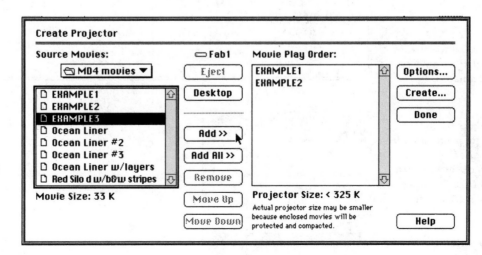

**Figure 2.25**
**The Create Projector dialog box lets you add movie files to a projector and play them in a specified order.**

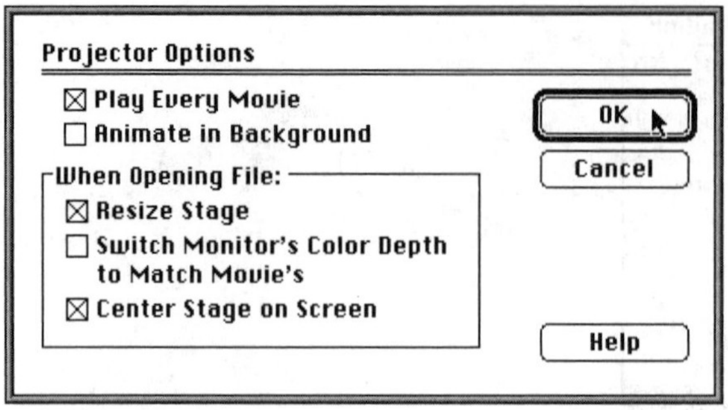

**Figure 2.26**
**Click the Options button in the Create Projector dialog box to set the projector options. Turn on the Play Every Movie option.**

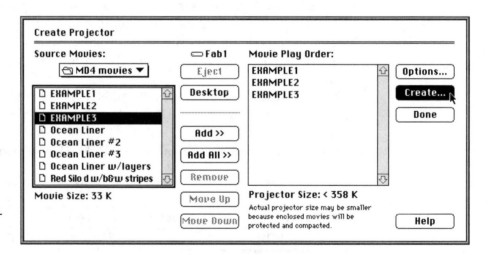

Now you can click the Create button to create the projector file (Figure 2.27), give it a name, and store it on disk.

Click the Done button in the Create Projector dialog box to return to Director. You now have a projector file you can distribute to others on floppy disk, or over a network, or via modem, or even CD-ROM. The recipient can play the projector file by double-clicking it (Figure 2.28).

**Figure 2.27**
**Create the projector file and give it a name.**

**Figure 2.28**
**The projector file has an icon that is different from a Director movie icon. You can double-click a projector file to play it.**

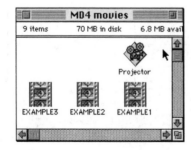

The other movie files (EXAMPLE1, 2, and 3) are not needed—they are included inside the projector file. The Director program also is unnecessary to run the projector. However, if you want to open or change the movie files, you must keep them as well as the projector, because you can't open a projector with Director. Projector files are simply for playing, and can't be edited or changed.

## Lesson 2: Examining a Movie

To understand how to construct a simple movie, let's examine one of the example movies supplied in the Tutorials folder/directory on the accompanying CD-ROM, called *Ocean Liner* (filename: OCEANLIN.DIR). Use the Open command in the File menu to open the file (Figure 2.29).

When the movie first opens the stage is set to a 9-inch screen size. If it is viewed on a larger screen there will be a border around it. If the Control Panel and other windows are obscuring the stage, you can remove them automatically by selecting the Stage option in the Windows menu (Figure 2.30).

In the Stage view on a 13-inch or larger display, movies designed for smaller displays appear in the center of the display, and the menu bar stays visible. The Stage view causes the menu bar at the top of the display to disappear, but you can still select any menu by clicking in the position where it would normally appear.

**Figure 2.29
Opening the
*Ocean Liner*
movie (filename:
OCEANLIN.DIR),
which is on the
CD-ROM that
comes with this
book.**

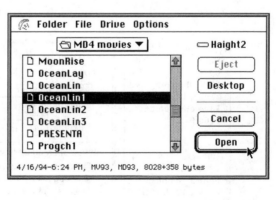

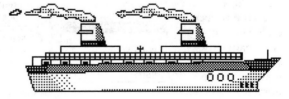

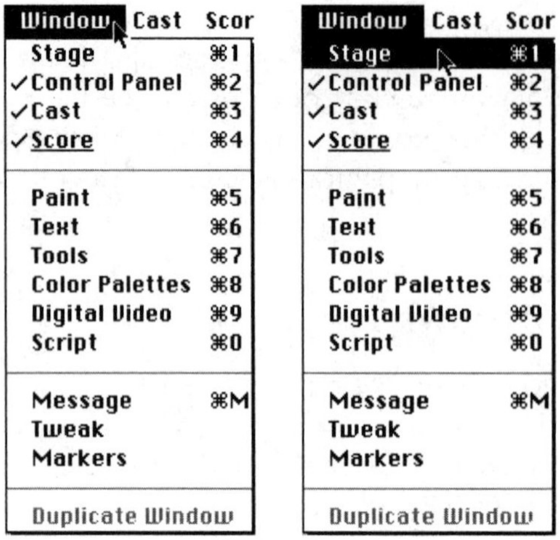

Figure 2.30
The Stage option
in the Window
menu lets you dis-
play the stage by
itself, with no
other windows.

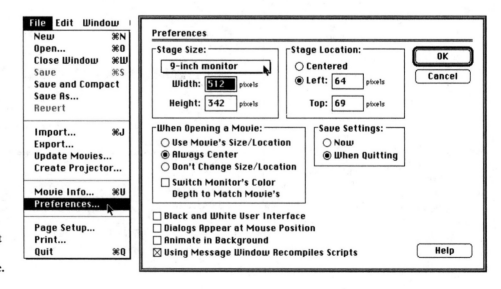

## The Stage Size

The size of the stage is important for several reasons. First, you must be able to display it on your computer. Second, it must fit on the display of those who receive your movie files for playback. If you pick a stage size larger than the displays commonly used, the recipients of your movies may not be able to play them. For this reason, many designers choose a stage size smaller or equal to the 13-inch display typical of so many Macintosh and Windows systems.

Set the stage size in the Preferences dialog box, which you activate by choosing the Preferences command in the File menu (Figure 2.31).

Director's Preferences dialog box provides a semipermanent method of altering the stage size and location. With this method, you can change the stage size and

Figure 2.31
The Preferences
dialog box lets
you change the
stage size and set
many other op-
tions for a movie.

location anytime you want, and set the stage automatically for everything in the movie.

Options are provided to automatically center the stage on the screen. Additionally, there are other options that allow you to adjust the stage size when opening a movie or document that has a different stage size. You should decide on your stage size before creating a movie, because the size of the stage has a direct bearing on how animations and PICT images will appear on the screen.

The movie we are examining uses a 9-inch stage size with the Center Stage window option. These options create a stage area that can display on any Macintosh or Windows system. The Center Stage window option is useful for playing movies created for the smaller Macintosh Classic screens.

You can display a movie's stage on multiple screens, and set the location of the stage in pixel measurements starting at the top left corner of the display. You can even specify a very small stage size and location, which is useful for creating digital video movies, or movies that play within another movie.

If you like a particular stage size and want to use it for all your movies automatically, you can set the option to save the settings now, or when quitting the program. For now, leave the stage size alone, so that you don't change the *Ocean Liner* movie. You can click the OK button to implement changes, or the Cancel button to cancel them.

## The Control Panel

If the screen is set to display the stage only, choose the Control Panel option from the Window menu (Figure 2.32) to display the Control Panel. Or, you may choose Stage again (from the Window menu) to turn off the stage display, and bring back the original windows, including the Control Panel. As a shortcut, you can press Command-2 on the Macintosh or Control-2 on the PC to display the Control panel.

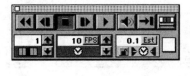

**Figure 2.32**
**The Control Panel.**

**Figure 2.33**
**The Control Panel**
**after playing the**
**movie** *Ocean Liner*
**stopped at frame**
**125, the last frame.**

The Control Panel controls resemble a VCR remote control: There are buttons for play, stop, and rewind that should be familiar. Play starts the animation, stop stops it, and rewind causes the next play to start from the beginning. There is also a step forward button for advancing through the movie frame by frame, and a step backward button for going backward frame by frame. There is no need for a pause button because the stop button functions as both a stop and a pause; just click play to resume from the current frame after stopping. Or press rewind to both stop the movie and rewind to frame 1, then click play to start from frame 1 again.

To see the *Ocean Liner* movie, click the play button in the Control Panel. At the end of the animation, the Control Panel switches automatically to stop, and shows the last frame number, which is 125 (Figure 2.33).

This means that the movie is 125 frames long. The movie played only once. The loop button, if turned on, plays the movie repeatedly until you click the stop button (or turn off the loop button). The movie advances to the last frame at the usual speed, then starts again at the beginning (performing an automatic rewind). The loop button is on by default, as shown in Figure 2.32. When you click it to turn it off, the loop button is replaced by the once-through button, as shown in Figure 2.33.

The sound control turns the sound on or off when you click it; the sound is on when the button is highlighted. The stage color chip changes the stage background from white to black, or back to white, on black-and-white displays, or to any color in the current color palette on color displays. On a color display, you can hold down the mouse button on the stage color chip, and a color pop-up menu appears (Figure 2.34).

**Figure 2.34**
**The Control**
**Panel's stage color**
**chip lets you**
**change the back-**
**ground color of**
**the Stage.**

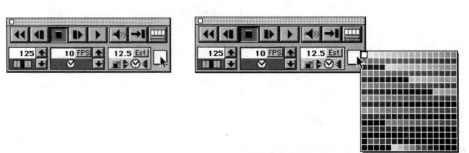

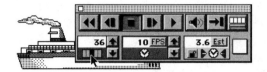

You can then drag the mouse to highlight any color to select it for the stage background color.

The frame counter displays the number of the current frame. If you click in the black rectangle underneath the frame counter and drag to the left or the right, you can jump to another frame. Dragging to the right increases the frame number, and dragging to the left decreases it (Figure 2.35).

As you change frame numbers, the frames appear in the stage area of the screen.

The tempo indicator, set to 10 FPS (frames per second, approximately) for this movie, lets you change the playback speed of the movie. You can use the up and down arrows to increase or decrease the speed. The number of frames per second in the tempo indicator is relative to the type of computer and the complexity of the animation. For example, animations generally run faster on a Mac Quadra 840 than they do on a Mac IIci. A movie with a lot of images and complex graphics will run more slowly than a movie with simple text and graphics. Along with the tempo indicator is a tempo mode button that lets you change the measure from FPS (frames per second) to SPF (seconds per frame). SPF displays the number of seconds, with fractional parts in milliseconds, of the duration of each frame.

The actual duration indicator shows the actual duration of the movie, estimated from the playing of the previous frame (while a movie is running). You can use this feature of the Control Panel to lock a movie to a certain time. However, it is possible for a movie to play more slowly than its designated time, due to computer performance variances. The actual indicator also has a mode button, which offers FPS and SPF (just like the tempo indicator mode), and the Est and Sum options. Sum displays a quick summary of elapsed seconds from the beginning of the movie to the current frame, while Est is a more accurate calculation (but slower to calculate) of elapsed time. Note that leaving the actual indicator in Est mode can reduce the playback speed due to the calculations, so you should change it to another mode.

The Control Panel is designed to give you control over the stage area. You can also control what happens on the stage from the Score window, by using the keyboard shortcuts for play, stop, and so on. Such keyboard shortcuts make it convenient for you to move the display into a position so that the audience sees the display, and to use the keyboard and mouse to control the movie. Here are some important keyboard shortcuts:

| *Macintosh* | | *Windows* |
|---|---|---|
| Command-P or Enter | Play | Control-P or Enter |
| Shift-Enter | Clear stage and Play | Shift-Enter |
| Command-period (.) | Stop | Control-period (.) or keypad 2 or 5 |
| Enter or keypad plus (+) | Toggle between Play and Stop | Enter or keypad plus (+) |
| Command-R | Rewind | Control-R or keypad 0 |
| Command-left arrow | Step backward | Control-left arrow or keypad 1 or 4 |
| Command-right arrow | Step forward | Control-right arrow or keypad 3 or 6 |
| Command-L | Loop | Control-L or keypad 8 |

In the following steps, we refer to the Macintosh keyboard shortcuts. If you're a Windows user, simply substitute Control for Command. (Note: The Command key is the key with an Apple symbol or a clover-leaf symbol found between the Option key and the space bar. The Control key is labeled Ctrl on some PC keyboards.)

If the Control Panel is still visible, select Stage from the Window menu (or press Command-1). Then press the following sequence.

1. Command-R, to rewind the movie to the beginning (in case the pointer is not already there).
2. Command-P, to play the movie.
3. Command-period (.) stops the movie at any time.
4. Command-P resumes playing the movie.

You can hold down the Shift key while clicking the play button, or use Shift-Command-P, to automatically switch to the Stage view and start playing a movie. Shift with the step forward button (or Shift-Command-right arrow) causes the movie to replay from the current position.

Another way of presenting a show to an audience is to use two display monitors: one for the audience, and one for the presenter. A Mac can support

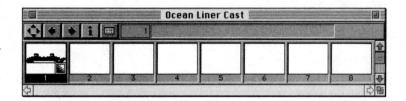

**Figure 2.36
The Cast window
for *Ocean Liner*
shows cast mem-
ber number 1.**

two or more displays (for example, a Mac with built-in video and a NuBus slot
can support a second video card in that slot, which drives another display
monitor). When you connect more than one monitor to a Macintosh, you can
specify in the Monitor Control Panel which display is the "menu" display, and
play the movie on that display.

## Introducing the Cast

The cast members make up the elements of your movie: text, graphics, images,
sounds, and digital video clips. In addition, an element that changes shape or
size can be represented by several cast members, one for each shape and size.
In some cases, if you use more cast members to represent a changing object
(such as a talking human face), the changes will be more subtle and realistic.

Cast members can include graphics, scanned images, pieces of graphics and
scanned images, text, individual letters, sounds, custom color palettes, and even
predefined animated sequences called *film loops*. The Cast window (Figure 2.36)
is a numbered list of elements.

You can have up to 32,000 cast members in a single movie, numbered from 1
to 32,000. In each cell is a thumbnail representation of the cast member.

The left and right arrows at the top left corner of the Cast window change the
selected cast member to the next or previous one. If you select cast member 1,
you can select the next cast member by clicking the right arrow (Figure 2.37).

You can also drag the window box in the lower right corner to change the size
of the Cast window and show more rows (Figure 2.38).

The *Ocean Liner* movie has only a few cast members, so you can keep the
Cast window showing only a few rows. The first cast member is the ocean liner
drawing, and the rest are steam clouds of different shapes and sizes. You place
these cast members on the Stage in different positions for each frame, creating
the illusion of a moving ship. The Score window shows how the cast members
are arranged in frames over time.

**Figure 2.37
Clicking the right
arrow to select
the next cast
member.**

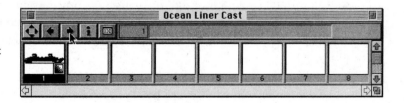

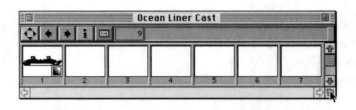

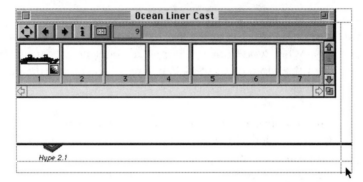

**Figure 2.38 Changing the size of the Cast window by dragging the box in the lower right corner of the window. You can scroll the Cast window with the scroll bar on the right.**

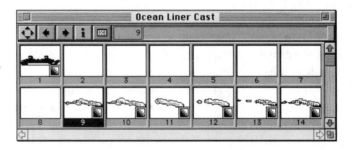

The Cast menu offers the Cast Member Info option, which displays a dialog box with information about the selected cast member (Figure 2.39).

You can also display this dialog box by clicking the "**i**" icon in the upper left corner of the Cast window. In the *Ocean Liner* movie, cast member 1 is a *bitmap* drawing in black and white. This means that it came from Director's Paint window (described in Chapter 4), or a painting program such as MacPaint. (*Bitmap* refers to the method of storing the graphical information as bits of pixels rather than as drawing instructions.)

You can use the Cast menu even if you are selecting cells in the Score window, or if no windows are open and you've clicked on the cast member on the Stage. The Cast menu is convenient for finding out about cast members in any of these locations.

You can create cast members by using tools in Director's Paint window, by typing text into the Text window, or by changing a palette in the Palette window.

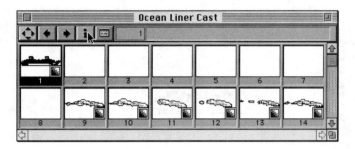

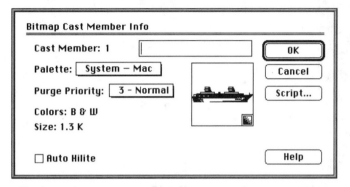

**Figure 2.39**
**The Cast Member Info dialog box, showing information about the selected cast member. You can get this box by choosing the menu option, or clicking the "i" icon in the Cast window.**

In addition, you can import elements, from many different types of files, into cast member positions with the Import command in the File menu.

Clicking inside a cast member cell selects the cast member, and you can select multiple cast members in a contiguous sequence by holding down Shift while clicking the last member in the sequence. By holding down the Command key while clicking, you can select multiple cast members that are not in a contiguous sequence. You can use the Cut Cast Members, Copy Cast Members, and Paste Cast Members commands, on selected cast members, to perform copy or cut-and-paste operations using the Clipboard.

Cast members created or imported through the Paint window can be edited in the Paint window. Double-click the cast member, and the Paint window appears, offering a variety of painting and drawing tools (Figure 2.40).

Chapter 4 covers painting and drawing. For now, close the Paint window by clicking the Close box in the top left corner of the window, select the Paint option in the Window menu, or use the Command-5 keyboard shortcut.

## Introducing the Score

The Score window describes the animation over time, using frames as units of time, and channels as layers of objects on the Stage. To open the Score window, use the Score command in the Window menu or type Command-4 as a shortcut. You can change the size of the Score window by dragging the resize box in the lower right corner (Figure 2.41).

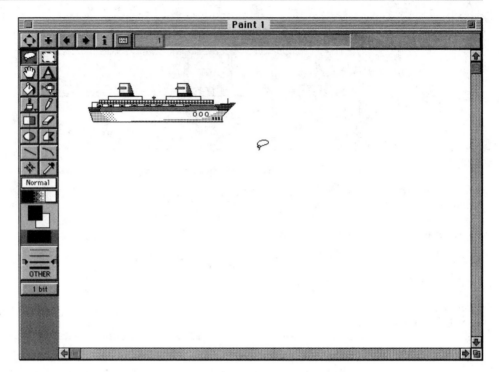

**Figure 2.40 After double-clicking a bitmap cast member, the Paint window appears with graphics tools for editing the cast member.**

In the Score window, channels appear as horizontal rows, and frames are vertical columns. The frame numbers appear along the top of the chart in multiples of 5 (that is, 1, 5, 10, 15, 20, and so on).

The active cells in the Score window typically show the number of the cast member in that frame and channel. When you select an active cell, a tiny representation of the cast member appears in the top left corner of the Score

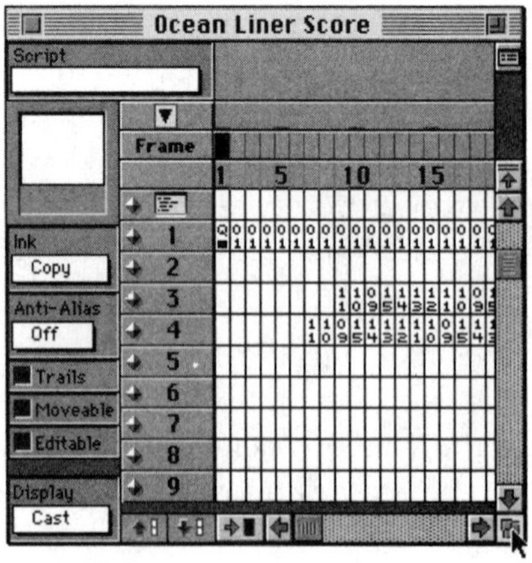

**Figure 2.41 Dragging the resize box to resize the Score window. The Score window shows channels as rows and frames as columns.**

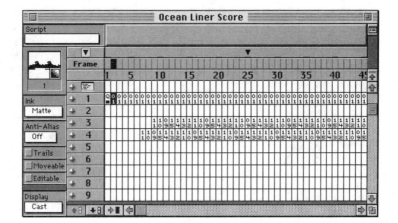

**Figure 2.42 Selecting the cell in frame 2, channel 1, which holds cast member 1 (indicated as 01).**

window. For example, click the cell in channel 1 of frame 2 (which contains the number "01"), and you'll see the representation of the ocean liner in the top left corner of the window (Figure 2.42).

A thumbnail image of the cast member appears in the upper left corner of the Score window.

You can select any cell in the score by clicking it (Figure 2.43).

You can scroll the Score window and move to other areas of the score. By scrolling along the horizontal scroll bar (Figure 2.44), you can move to the end of the score information, which is frame 116.

You can also drag the horizontal scroll box in the scroll bar, and a frame counter pops up to show you the current frame while dragging (Figure 2.45).

Scroll the Score window back to the beginning, frame 1, to continue with this lesson.

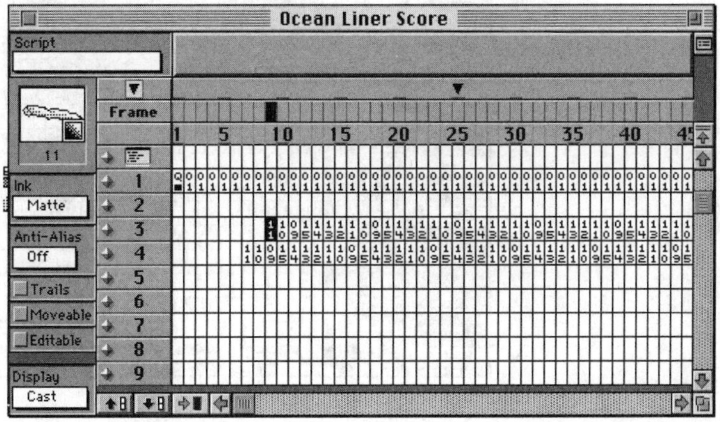

**Figure 2.43 The cloud cast member, number 11, is selected in channel 3, frame 9 of the score.**

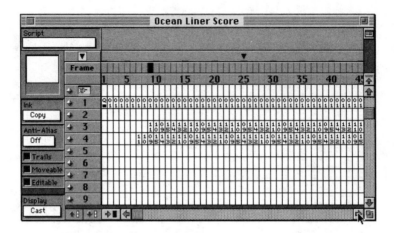

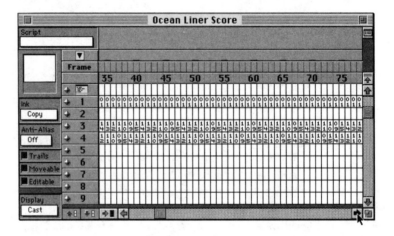

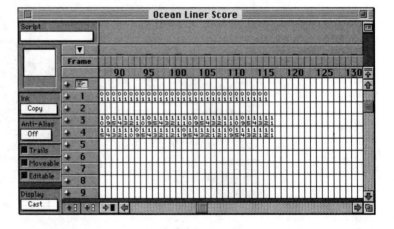

**Figure 2.44 Scrolling the Score window to see the end of this movie's score information, which is frame 116.**

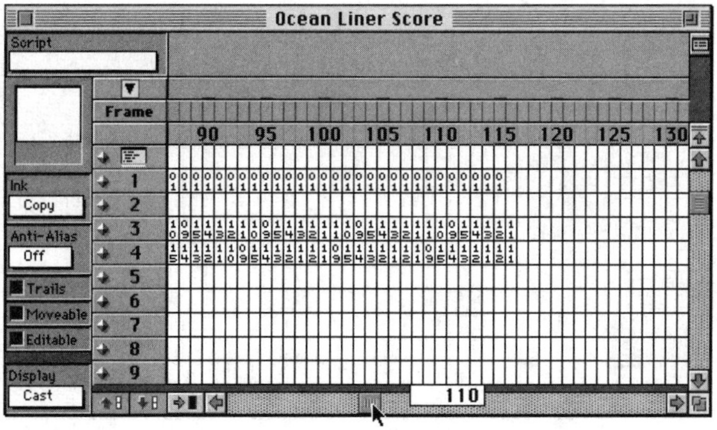

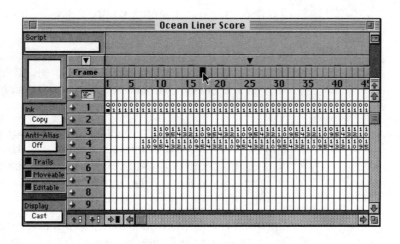

**Figure 2.45**
**A frame counter pops up to help you navigate the score when you drag the horizontal scroll box in the scroll bar.**

The black rectangle that appears in the row labeled Frame (above the channels and frame numbers) is the *playback head,* which indicates the frame displayed on the Stage (Figure 2.46).

You can drag this rectangle within this row (called the *scratch bar*) to move to a different frame quickly. The playback head moves in the scratch bar when the movie is playing. You can also click a frame in the scratch bar to move to that specific frame.

While the score can grow to be very large, it is not practical to have movies with many thousands of frames because it would be difficult to find things. However, it is quite common to have hundreds of frames. In fact, if you are creating animation for video that will be recorded frame by frame, you would use 30 frames for each second.

**Figure 2.46**
**You can drag the playback head to move to another frame in the movie. The playback head shows the current frame that appears on the stage, and it moves while the movie is playing.**

**Figure 2.47**
**The Jump to Top button displays the Score window from the top, showing the six special channels (Tempo, Palette, Transition, Sound 1, Sound 2, and Script), followed by the numbered channels.**

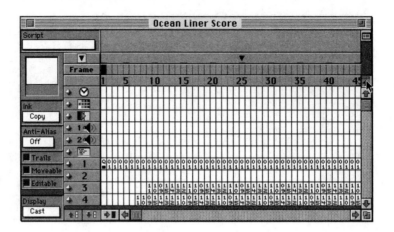

You also have up to 48 channels for cast members to appear in the same frame. For example, the ocean liner cast member (01) appears in channel 1 of frame 15, and the cloud cast members (12 and 10) appear in the same frame in channels 3 and 4.

The scroll bar on the right lets you scroll the Score window vertically. The Jump to Top button (Figure 2.47) scrolls the Score window to the top, exposing the six special channels. These are:

**Tempo**. This channel controls the movie's speed.

**Palette**. This channel controls color cycling effects and the color palette used for displaying in certain color modes (4, 16, and 256 colors on the Macintosh).

**Transition**. This channel controls special transition effects between frames.

**Sound 1**. This is a sound channel, which can play a stereo sound. A sound in this channel overrides the sound in a digital video movie, and must be turned off before starting a digital video movie sound.

**Sound 2**. This is the second channel, which can also play a stereo sound. On Macintosh models not equipped for multichannel sound, this channel is dimmed. A sound in this channel overrides the sound in a digital video movie, and must be turned off before starting a digital video movie sound.

**Script**. This channel contains scripts that execute as the movie leaves a particular frame, known as *frame scripts*.

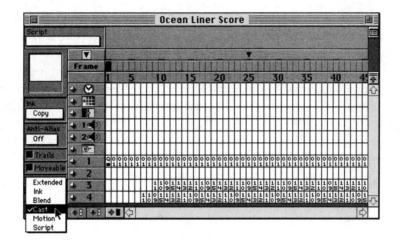

**Figure 2.48**
**With the Cast option selected in the Display pop-up menu, the Score window shows cast member numbers in each active cell.**

Below these are the animation channels numbering 1 through 48 for holding cast members. The stacking order of cast members depends on the channel number they are placed in. Channel 1 is the backmost channel, and channel 48 is the frontmost channel. Double-clicking a channel's number clears the contents of the channel; immediately use the Undo command in the Edit menu, or as a shortcut use Command-Z, to undo the clear operation. The active cells in the Score window can show the cast member numbers or other information, depending on the option set in the pop-up menu in the lower left corner of the window (Figure 2.48).

With this display, it is easy to see that channel 1 contains the same cast member throughout the movie, the ocean liner, cast member 01.

However, the ocean liner's position changes from frame to frame. You can see information about how the cast member changes position from frame to frame by changing the Display pop-up menu to Motion (Figure 2.49).

**Figure 2.49**
**Changing the Display pop-up menu to Motion to see motion information in the active cells rather than cast member numbers (the tiny arrows indicate direction of the motion).**

The tiny arrows indicate the direction of the motion, and the capital "B" in frame 2 of channel 1 indicates that frame 2 is where this particular bitmap cast member begins its appearance.

Switch the Display pop-up menu back to Cast, and look at the different cast members used in channels 3 and 4. Channel 3 starts with cast members 11, 10, and 09. In channel 3, click the fourth cast member (15), which is in frame 12 (Figure 2.50).

Then hold down the Shift key and click the cell in channel 3, frame 18 (cast member 09). You've just made a selection.

The selection you made highlights a sequence of cast members 15 down to 09, which repeats in channel 3 over and over across the entire length of the movie. The sequence also repeats in channel 4. The appearance of steam clouds

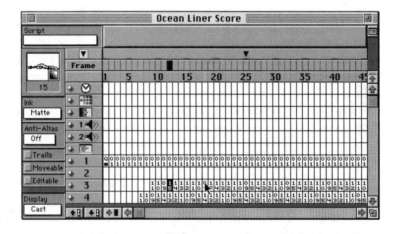

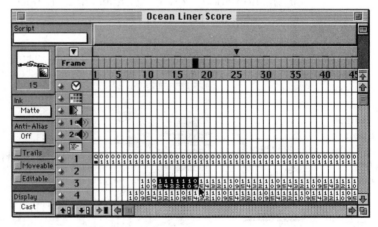

**Figure 2.50 Clicking one end, and shift-clicking the other end of an animation sequence involving cast members 9 through 15 in reverse order.**

rising from the ocean liner is actually a sequence of cast members (9 through 15) repeated in reverse order.

**Editing a Movie**

Working in the Score window is one of the best methods for copying pieces of animation. For example, you can create a second ocean liner with steam clouds, and have it start in a different position on the Stage. You can do this by copying the animation cells to new channels and changing the stage position of the cast members in the copied cells.

You can close the Cast window by clicking on the Close box, or selecting Cast from the Window menu, or using the Command-3 keyboard shortcut. You can also reduce the size of the Score window, so that you can see more of the stage area.

To create the second ocean liner, first double-click the channel number for channel 1 (Figure 2.51).

Then, holding down the Shift key, double-click the channel number for channel 4 (Figure 2.52).

The range of channels from 1 through 4 should now be selected. Since the entire ocean liner animation is stored in those channels, you have effectively selected the entire animation.

Next, scroll down the Score window so that the empty channels below channel 4 appear (Figure 2.53).

The scroll bar on the right side of the window works by dragging the small empty box up and down. The arrows at either end are for single-line scrolling up and down. Dragging to the right or bottom edge of the scrolling window auto-scrolls the window.

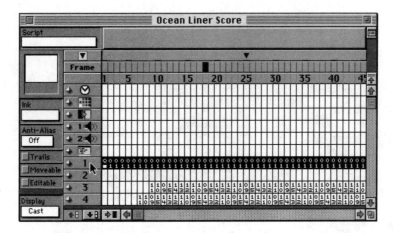

**Figure 2.51 Selecting an entire channel by double-clicking the channel number in the Score window.**

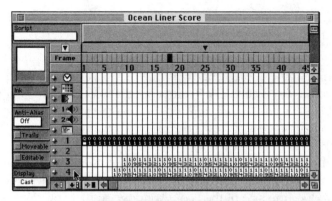

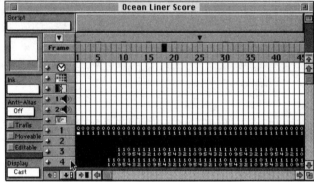

**Figure 2.52**
**Selecting the range of channels 1 through 4 by double-clicking channel number 1, and holding down the Shift key while double-clicking channel number 4.**

Since channels 1 through 4 are selected, you can choose the Copy Score command in the Edit menu to copy the Score information from those channels into the Clipboard for temporary storage (Figure 2.54).

Now you are ready to paste the copied cells (the ocean liner animation) in the Score in a new channel. Click in the first cell of channel 6, and choose the Paste Score command (Figure 2.55) to paste the contents of the Clipboard into the Score window at that location.

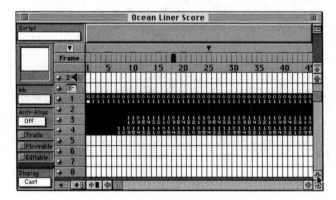

**Figure 2.53**
**Scrolling the Score window to see more channels.**

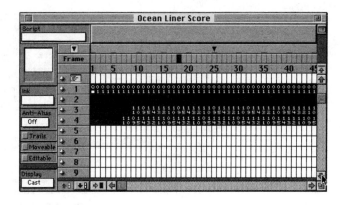
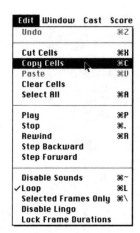

**Figure 2.54 Copying the selected cells in the score from the previous figure to the Clipboard.**

If you can't see the channels 6 through 9, scroll the Score window until you clearly see channels 6 through 9. After the paste operation, you should see the same score information in channels 1 through 4 repeated in channels 6 through 9.

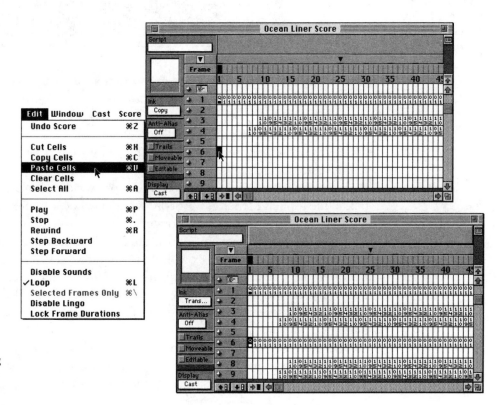

**Figure 2.55 Pasting the copied cells into the score starting at frame 1, channel 6.**

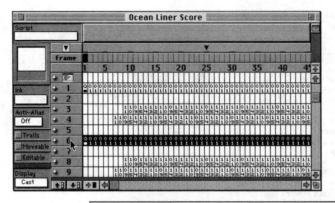

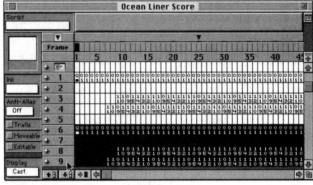

**Figure 2.56
Selecting channels 6 through 9 by double-clicking channel number 6, and then holding down Shift while double-clicking channel number 9.**

To select channels 6 through 9 as you did before with channels 1 through 4, first double-click the channel number for channel 6, then hold down Shift and double-click the channel number for channel 9. The range of channels from 6 through 9 should be highlighted (Figure 2.56).

Drag the playback head to a frame that shows the ocean liner in the middle of the stage (Figure 2.57).

To see the entire stage area, close the Score window by clicking on the close box in the top left corner of the Score window, choose Score from the menu, or use the Command-4 keyboard shortcut.

On the stage, the ocean liner and steam clouds appear selected. This is because they are still selected in the score (channels 6 through 9). Hold down the mouse button while pointing somewhere in the middle of the ocean liner, and drag downward and to the left. The ocean liner and steam clouds will move as you drag your mouse, exposing another ocean liner with another set of steam clouds underneath (Figure 2.58).

When you let go of the mouse button, the ocean liner and clouds stay selected so that you can continue to drag them until you get their position exactly the way you want it. If you click outside the area of the selected graphics, the cast

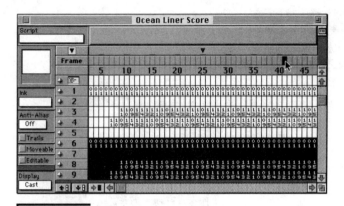

**Figure 2.57**
**Clicking the play-back head cell to move the play-back head to a frame in which the cast members are visible on the stage, then closing the Score window to see the stage. The pasted cells in the score are still selected.**

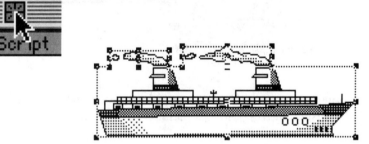

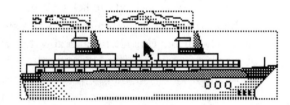

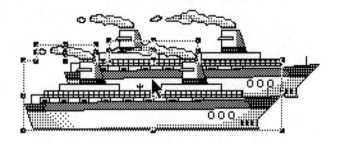

**Figure 2.58**
**Dragging the se-lected ocean liner and steam clouds to a new position on the stage.**

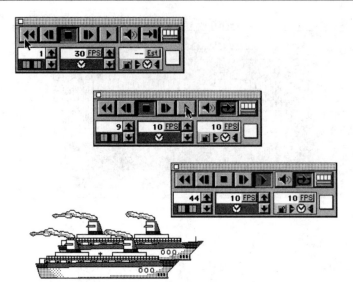

**Figure 2.59
Rewinding the
movie and play-
ing it.**

members are no longer selected and you can't move them again. When you are finished moving the cast members, click outside the graphics so that they are no longer selected.

Since multiple frames are selected in the score, you are moving the entire animation to a new position for all frames, not just for the single frame you are viewing.

Click the rewind button, and click the play button to play the movie again. This time, two ocean liners, with similar steam clouds, move across the display (see Figure 2.59). The second ocean liner is set off from the first one by the same distance that you moved the selected graphics in the previous figure.

Thus, you have just learned how to create animation simply by copying score information from one channel to another. You can also move the stage location of a particular segment of animation by selecting the score information for that segment and then dragging a piece of the segment to a new location.

The Score window's channels are similar to the layers of celluloid used on an animation stand in traditional cel animation methods. Each layer has a piece of artwork inked in a certain manner: black, color, transparent, or as the outline of a mask. This artwork appears in front of the layer below when viewed from the top through all layers.

Cast members in lower numbered channels always appear behind ones in higher numbered channels (Figure 2.60).

Thus, the ocean liner and clouds segment, occupying channels 6 through 9, runs in the *foreground* in front of the segment in channels 1 through 4, which are in the *background*.

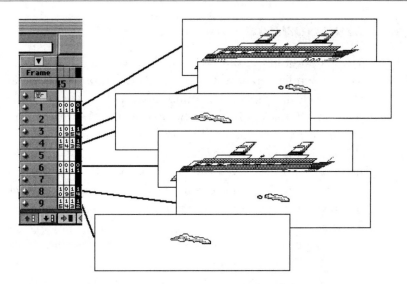

**Figure 2.60
A representation of the layering effect of channels in the Score; each channel is a separate layer, with objects in lower numbered channels appearing behind objects in higher numbered channels.**

When you start creating animation, it is natural to place elements first in the background, then in the foreground. With the Score window it doesn't matter where you start, because you can cut or copy and paste animation segments from one channel to another. You can fill a channel with automatic animations, as shown earlier in Lesson 1, or you can make up your own animation, as described in the next chapter.

## Using Clip Animation

Clip animation is available in the Freebies section of the CD-ROM that comes with this book. Movies and animated clips are also available on various other CD-ROMs and floppy disk clip libraries. You can use QuickTime movies and Director movies, PICS, AVI, and FLI, animation and video formats, as well as the still-image formats of PICT, MacPaint, EPS, TIFF, and BMP (DIB file sequence) files.

Clip animation is available for use without the need for you to ask permission. Sample movies, however, should not be used for commercial projects without permission, because they are protected by copyright.

This lesson has shown how you can use the Score window to keep track of animation, to copy animated sequences, and to reposition them on the stage. The Score window is where the action is catalogued, and once you've mastered the techniques of using it, there is no limit to the special effects and animations you can create. The Score window is also used for interactive scripting, which is described in Chapter 6.

In the next lesson, you'll learn how to add sound.

# Lesson 3: Using Sounds

The sound of music can be enthralling, jarring, provoking, soothing, or obnoxious, depending on how it is used and how it sounds. The reason for using sound must be clear. Appropriate sound is particularly important for business communication—the listener should be able to hear the narration, other sounds, and music clearly, without interference or unnatural distortion.

Narration is effective in all forms of training and educational applications. A narrator can be effective even if the quality of the sound is at least "voice quality" (a euphemism for telephone-line quality). Sound effects, such as a simple chime that plays during transitions, can be very useful to highlight graphics and to mark a change of topic.

There are several techniques for getting high-quality and voice-quality sound to use for Director movies, as described in Chapter 7. A sample folder of sound effects is supplied in the Extras folder supplied with Director 4, and in the Freebies section of the CD-ROM that comes with this book.

You can also include anything you can record and turn into digital form. The MacRecorder and Digidesign's family of sound cards are perhaps the most widely used sound digitizers for the Macintosh. Creative Labs' SoundBlaster 16, Media Vision's AudioSpectrum 16, and others are popular on the Windows platform.

With an appropriate sound card or digitizer, you can use Director's Record Sound command in the Cast menu, or use the software supplied with the sound card or digitizer, and save the sound in a file format that is compatible with Director. Formats include AIFF, Macintosh snd resources, SoundEdit files, and WAV files.

**Clip Sound**

To use a clip sound, supplied in the Freebies section of the CD-ROM part of this book, choose the Import command in the File menu (Figure 2.61).

It brings up a dialog box that lets you navigate through the Macintosh or Windows file system to find the appropriate folder or directory containing the file. When you get to that folder, use the Type pop-up menu to switch the file type to Sound.

You can play the sound before importing it (Figure 2.62) by clicking the Play Sound button in the Import dialog box.

The sound plays until you stop it by clicking the Stop Sound button, or until it ends. When you've found the sound you want, click the Import button to import it as a cast member. (Figure 2.63).

Director puts the sound in the next available cast member slot of the Cast window.

**Figure 2.61**
Using the Import dialog box to select a sound to import as a cast member, changing the Type pop-up menu to the Sound file type. The sound is from the clip sound folder on the CD-ROM.

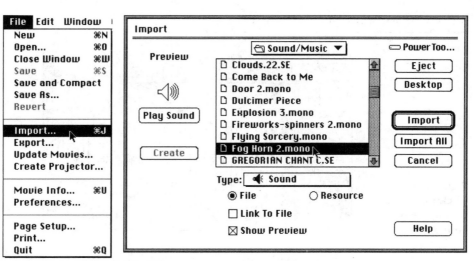

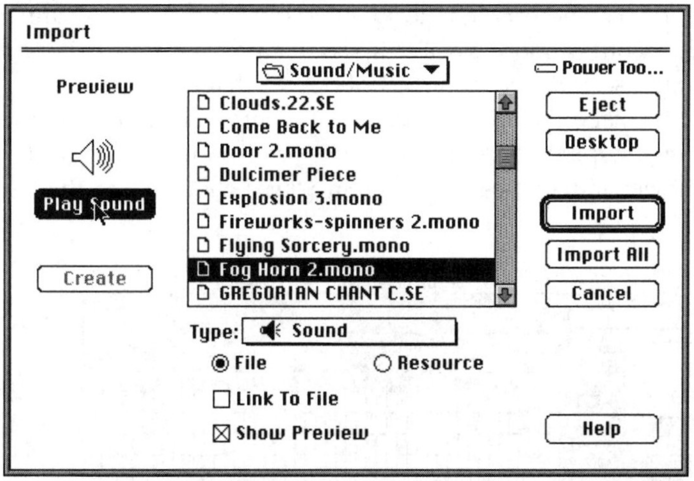

**Figure 2.62**
Playing the sound before importing it.

**Figure 2.63**
Clicking the Import button to import the selected sound file. Director automatically places the sound in the next available cast member slot of the Cast window.

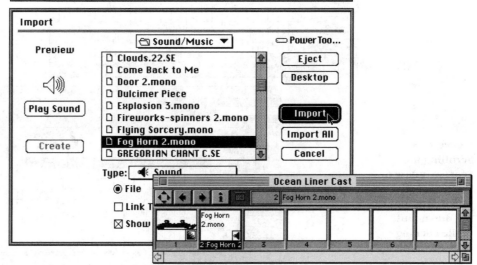

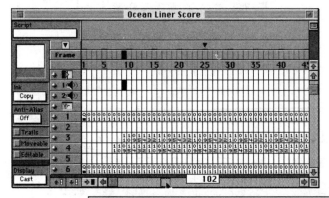

**Figure 2.64
Clicking the sec-
ond frame of
Sound channel 1.**

You can now assign the sound to one of the sound channels in the score. Open the Score window, scroll it up so that you can see the Sound channels, and click in the second cell (frame 2) of Sound channel 1 (Figure 2.64).

To make the sound play for the length of the movie, press Tab to reach the last occupied frame in the Score, or scroll the Score window to the end of the movie, and Shift-click the cell in Sound channel 1 in the last frame of the movie

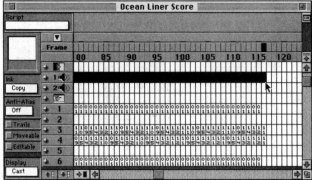

**Figure 2.65
Scrolling the
Score window to
the end of the
movie, and hold-
ing down Shift
while clicking
the last frame in
Sound channel 1.**

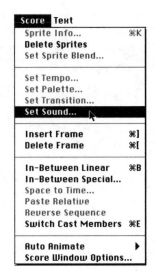

**Figure 2.66
Assigning a
sound cast member to the Sound
channel in the
score with the
Set Sound command in the
Score menu.**

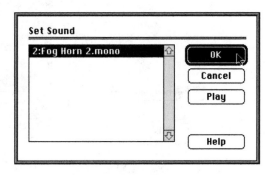

(Figure 2.65). To assign the sound to the Sound channel, choose the Set Sound command in the Score menu (Figure 2.66). A dialog box appears, letting you select different sound cast members. Select the sound (you can play it to test it), and click OK.

---

*Note:* If the Set Sound option in the Score menu is dimmed, Director is unable to find sound cast members. You must import sound cast members, or record them directly into the cast.

---

When you play the movie, the sound plays as well. This is true unless you have turned off the sound in the Control Panel. However, since the sound is short, it doesn't last for the entire movie. To make the sound repeat, find a location in the score where the sound has already stopped. For most systems, it stops before frame 70 (Figure 2.67).

Select the cell in frame 70, Sound channel 1, and use the Clear Cells command in the Edit menu to clear that cell. As a result, the sound will play the first time, then it will start playing again at frame 71.

## Recording a Sound

You can record a sound directly to the cast with the Record Sound command in the Cast menu. In order to use this command, you must first set up your sound input characteristics and sampling rate. For example, on the Macintosh, you would use the Sound Control Panel to set the sound input driver, and use the options or setup button to control the characteristics of the sound driver (Figure 2.68).

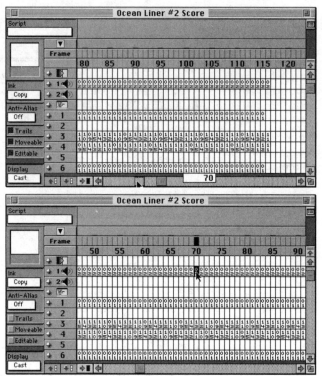

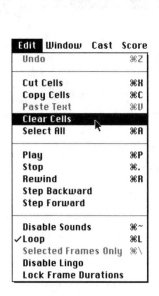

**Figure 2.67 Scrolling to frame 70 and clearing a cell in the Sound channel so that the sound plays again.**

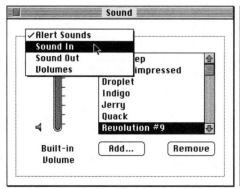

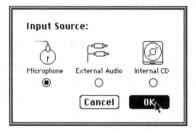

**Figure 2.68 Setting the sound input device for recording sound.**

**Figure 2.69
Recording a
sound directly
into the Cast win-
dow by using the
Record Sound
command in the
Cast menu,
which displays a
sound-recording
dialog box.**

The Record Sound command is dimmed if you do not have a sound driver for the Macintosh (which offers built-in sound input), or if you don't have a sound card on a Windows-based computer.

When you choose the Record Sound command in the Cast menu (Figure 2.69), it displays a sound-recording dialog box that offers record, stop, pause, and play buttons, and a speaker icon, which indicates the audio signal strength.

Click the record button to record a short sound (such as narration or ambient noise). For information about sampling rates and sound formats, see Chapter 7.

When you click Stop, and then Save to save the sound, Director stores the sound as an unnamed cast member in the next available slot in the Cast window (Figure 2.70).

You can name the cast member by clicking in the empty text field at the top right corner of the Cast window, and typing the name. It is a good idea to name the sound cast members so that their names appear in the Set Sound dialog box.

**Figure 2.70
The recorded
sound is stored as
an unnamed cast
member. You can
add a name by se-
lecting the cast
member, clicking
in the name field
on the right side
at the top of the
Cast window, and
typing a new
name.**

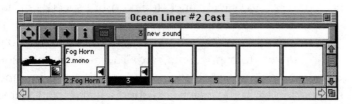

In addition to recording with Director, you can record into separate sound files with programs that specialize in recording sound, such as Macromedia's Sound-Edit 16, which can be test-driven and purchased directly from the CD-ROM accompanying this book. In such programs, you have more control over the sampling rate and format, and you can choose among several standard audio file formats. The list of formats, and more information about using sound, can be found in Chapter 7.

To create digital sound, you can record sound directly from audio equipment or with microphones, and use a sound card or digitizer to convert it to a digital format. You can also create digital sound with musical instruments and synthe-sizers that use the *Musical Instrument Digital Interface (MIDI)*. Digital sound is sound that is either created by the computer using synthesizer electronics, which is called *synthesizer sound,* or sound that is recorded in a digital format, which is called *sampled sound.*

The quality of sampled sound depends on the quality of the recording microphone and the ambient sound of the room in which you are recording. A good microphone can record sound more clearly and provide a dynamic presence that cheap microphones can't reproduce. Remember, also, that the audio portion of a multimedia presentation can be adjusted for volume when played back. If you record at too high a level, you may introduce distortion that can't be easily corrected.

Ambient noise in the room will most likely be picked up, as will noise from the next room. Don't record narration in an office cubicle surrounded by office workers who are moving around, talking, using typewriters, and so on, unless you want the noises to be heard.

The Macintosh is supplied with a microphone for recording that connects directly to the Macintosh sound-in port. Macintosh models with NuBus slots can be extended to digitize stereo CD-quality sound with cards such as the Audiome-dia card from DigiDesign. The newest Quadra and PowerMac AV models can digitize stereo CD-quality sound directly. For older Macintosh models with no slots, you can use Macromedia's MacRecorder, which connects into the modem or printer port. With two MacRecorders, you can record stereo music by connecting them to both the modem and printer ports.

The SoundEdit 16 software, supplied with the MacRecorder (and also available on the CD-ROM bundled with this book), can mix sampled sounds from separate sound channels into one channel, add a host of special effects and adjustments, and create sound files that can be used with Director.

To record sound in a Windows system, it must be extended with a sound card and sound drivers to support the card. The most popular sound cards are the Creative Labs SoundBlaster Pro and SoundBlaster 16, and Media Vision's AudioSpectrum 16. Turtle Beach also offers a high-quality sound card. The sound drivers for Windows are installed using the Drivers control panel to install the appropriate MCI drivers. After the drivers are installed, try playing .WAV (Windows standard format for digitally recorded sound files), .MID (MIDI sound format) files, or audio CDs using Microsoft's Media Player utility, to test the driver installation. You can also use .PCM format sound files in Director for Windows. You may also need to adjust the volume control on the sound card, and make sure the speakers are connected to the sound card properly. If your sound files are originating on a Macintosh, you can convert them to .WAV format using SoundEdit 16 on a Macintosh, before copying them to the Windows system.

The next lesson teaches you how to create a simple button that can be clicked by the user of your Director movie in order to jump to another movie. It is a simple example of interactivity.

## Lesson 4: Creating an Interactive Movie

If all we could create were animation and sound elements, this program would be quite useful. However, Director does much more: It lets you link these elements together to either form a linear narrative, or a nonlinear interactive presentation.

This lesson shows how easy it is to add a simple button to a movie that lets the user jump to another movie. It is a very common technique in just about every CD-ROM title and interactive presentation. Usually graphics are used rather than buttons, but the script is the same.

**Adding a Button**

To add a button to the *Ocean Liner* movie (now called *Ocean Liner #3*), scroll the Score window until it shows channel 11, which should be empty. Select the first cell in channel 11 (Figure 2.71), then close the Score window in order to see the stage.

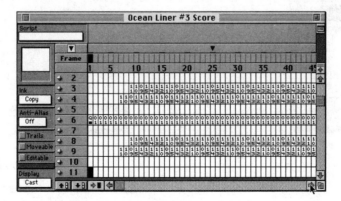

**Figure 2-71
Selecting the
score cell in
channel 11.**

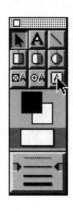

**Figure 2.72
Opening the
Tools window,
and selecting one
of the button
styles.**

Next, open the Tools window by selecting Tools from the Window menu (Figure 2.72).

The Tools window offers nine tools, two color chips, a pattern chip, and line styles. These are all described in Chapter 4. For now, select the button style that shows text inside the button. The cursor changes into a button placement cursor.

When you click the button placement cursor in the stage area, a button appears, ready for you to type some text. For now, just type the word **Information** (Figure 2.73), which should fit inside the button (you will learn how to resize buttons, and use graphics as buttons, in Chapter 6).

**Figure 2.73
Clicking the but-
ton placement
icon in the Stage
area to place the
button, and typ-
ing text into the
button.**

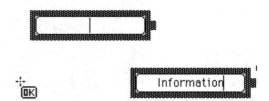

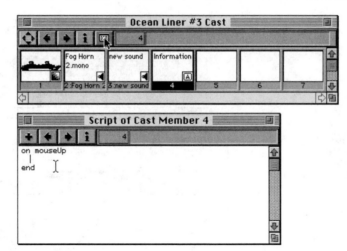

**Figure 2.74 Clicking the script icon in the Cast window for the selected button cast member, which displays the script window ready for editing.**

## Assigning a Script

The Cast window now shows a new cast member with the text Information that you should select. Then, click the script icon in the Cast window (Figure 2.74).

A script window appears for the cast member, with the text insertion bar blinking inside the on mouseUp script, ready for you to type an instruction.

(Note: we always use `this font` to denote actual script words when used in the context of a script.)

The instruction to type is the following:

```
Go to movie "EXAMPLE1"
```

When you are finished typing, the script window should have the following script inside (Figure 2.75):

```
on mouseUp
        Go to movie "EXAMPLE1"
end
```

Close the script window by clicking the close box in the upper left corner. The button now has a script assigned to it, and it is ready to use.

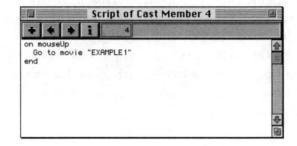

**Figure 2.75 Typing the instruction in the script window.**

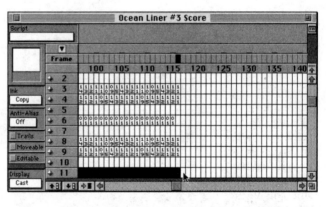

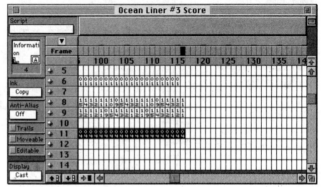

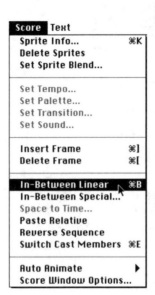

**Figure 2.76
Selecting the
range of cells in
channel 11 from
the first cell (al-
ready selected) to
the last cell.
Then choose In-
Between Linear
in the Score
menu, and Direc-
tor automatically
fills the channel
with the same
cast member
throughout the
selected range.**

---

**In-Betweening**

The final step is to extend the button in the score channel over the entire range of frames, so that it appears on the stage throughout the movie.

Open the Score window, and if the first cell in channel 11 is not already selected (the button cast member), select it now by clicking it. Scroll the window to the end of the movie (Figure 2.76), and hold down the Shift key, while clicking the last cell in channel 11. This is so that the range of cells from beginning to end is selected.

Now choose the In-Between Linear command in the Score menu, and Director automatically fills the range with the button cast member.

Close the Score window, click outside the button so that it is no longer selected, then rewind the movie and play it (Figure 2.77).

When you click the button, Director jumps to the movie *EXAMPLE1*.

This is your first interactive movie. Save it, so that after you've learned the sophisticated techniques in this book, you can come back to this movie and laugh about how simple it really is.

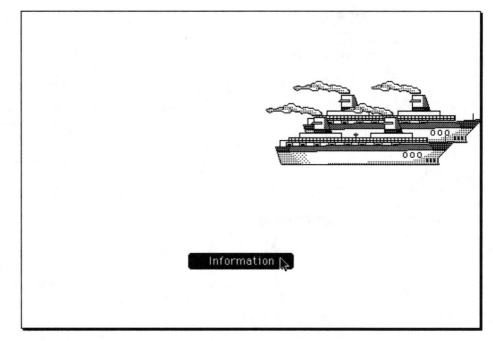

**Figure 2.77 Running the interactive movie. By clicking the button, the script is executed and the user jumps to the movie *EXAMPLE1.***

## *Lesson 5: Printing Movie Info*

In some projects it is useful to have a printed version of the Cast and Score windows, the scripts, and thumbnail or full-size images from movies. A thumbnail-sized print of each slide accompanying text is called a *storyboard*. A storyboard can be passed around and reviewed by a group to elicit new ideas or document changes. You can print a storyboard of a Director movie on any type of printer that can be connected to your computer.

This is only one reason to have the ability to print storyboards. In many cases, a presentation has more impact if you can provide printed handouts that match the slides to the audience. In such cases, the better the printing, the more professional you look. Therefore, a laser printer or a color printer should be used for presentation handouts.

You can produce black-and-white transparencies for an overhead projector by using a laser printer for paper masters and then using a copy service bureau or printing directly onto copier-certified film sheets. DeskTop color thermal-transfer printers make excellent color transparencies. These printers use a heating element to fuse a ribbon with a film of pigment or wax onto specially coated paper or transparency film.

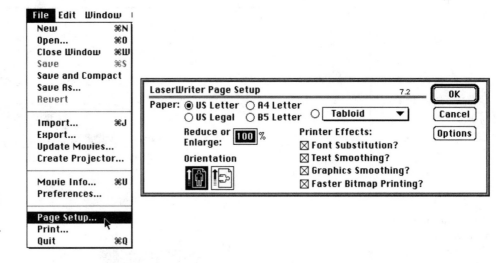

**Figure 2.78
Using the Page
Setup command
to set the paper
size and orienta-
tion.**

Director offers a variety of printing options so that you can print frames from your movies as slides to use as handouts, overheads, or storyboards. You can print all of the frames of a movie, or a group of selected frames.

Before printing a presentation, use the Page Setup command in the File menu (Figure 2.78) to:

- Set the paper size for your printer.

- Change the orientation of the image on the paper (portrait or landscape).

- Reduce or enlarge each page.

- Set printer-specific options.

Then, choose the Print command from the File menu, which displays the Print dialog box (Figure 2.79).

From this dialog box, you can choose all of the frames of a movie, or the current frame. Click the Options button for the Stage, and you can choose layout options for printing the stage area. The pages can include the date, file name, slide number, and custom footer. The frames can be centered or in a single-column format that leaves room for writing comments.

After choosing these options, click the OK button to return to the Print dialog box. Click Print to go to your printer-specific Print dialog box for specifying the range of pages, the type of paper feed, and so on (Figure 2.80).

Printing is accomplished automatically, and you return to Director as before.

You have learned how to create a movie from beginning to end in this chapter. Now you are ready for the basic animation techniques in Chapter 3. Don't forget to remember to save your file often! Choose Save from the File menu. Choose Save As from the File menu if you want to save it under a different name.

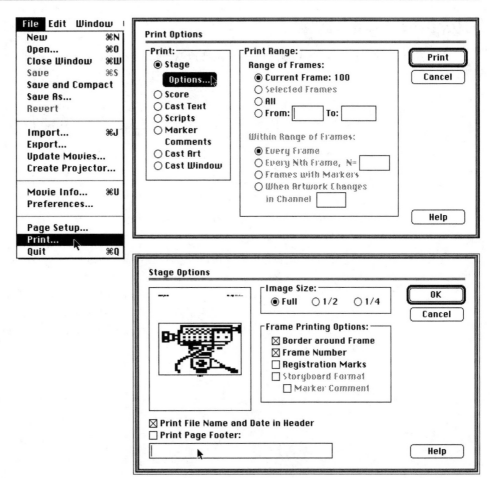

Figure 2.79. Using the Print command, and setting options for printing the stage area, including typing a custom footer. Click OK to leave the Options dialog box.

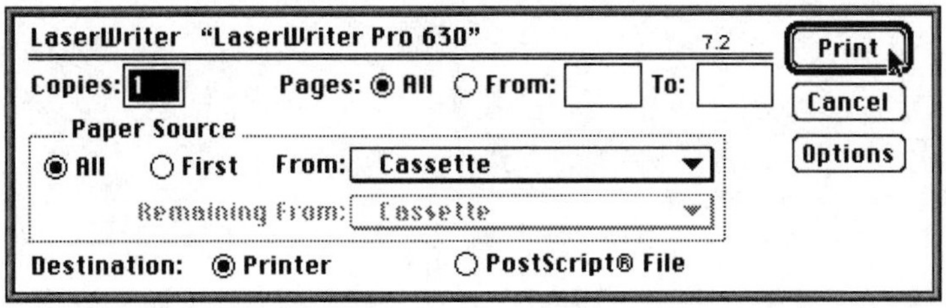

Figure 2.80 After clicking Print to print the movie, a printer-specific dialog box appears for setting the number of copies, the number of pages, the paper source, and so on.

# *Chapter Summary*

In this chapter, you learned how to use Director to:

- Create animated bullet charts, bar charts, and text effects.
- Set the Stage size for the audience of your movies.
- Navigate the Score and Cast windows, and use the Control Panel.

You also opened a simple movie and:

- Created cast members.
- Copied and pasted an animation sequence in the score.
- Used the In-Between Linear command to extend a stage cast member for many frames.

You also learned how to record sounds and use clip sounds and movies, and how to print frames from your movie.

We deliberately used only a few features of Director to show you how simple it can be to create interactive movies. These examples are in black and white, so that anyone with a monochrome Mac can follow along and learn simple methods for using Director.

# 3

# *Elementary Animation*

**I never needed Panavision and stereophonic sound to woo the world. I did it in black and white on a screen the size of a postage stamp. Honey, that's talent.**

Mae West

**H**ow do you start creating Director movies? You may think that graphics skill is required, and indeed, graphics skill is important. However, correctly judging how the audience will react to your vision is the most important skill of all.

The best kind of animation is the kind that stresses personality and strong impressions, not realism. Even in Disney cartoons, a duck did not always look like a duck, and artists would exaggerate gestures to present the point of the scene clearly.

Personality transcends all other aspects of animation, and the most important task is to communicate ideas. This is why an idealistic form of reality, such as animation, is so useful, even if it is looks crude. Effective multimedia presentations do not require painting and drawing skills as much as they require imagination. This is why Director is named Director. You need to be a Director more than you need graphic skills.

## *Creating Text and Graphics Elements*

The most important aspect of this process is visualizing the entire presentation, title, or work of art as a director might visualize a completed film. You need to develop a vision of the experience you want the audience to have.

Still, most animation projects start with visuals: graphics, images, or charts (storyboards). The first steps you take to create a Director movie are generalized below:

1. Develop an idea for the movie, and decide whether or not the movie must be capable of running on black-and-white (monochrome) displays and/or the smaller Macintosh Classic or 12-inch displays. (This decision limits the stage size, as well as the use of color and grayscale in graphics and patterns.)

2. Create, or import, artwork and images to serve as *cast* members.

3. Use various animation recording methods, such as in-between, real-time recording, step recording, and frame-by-frame recording, to record cast members on the stage.

4. Add special effects, such as transitions, and adjust the tempo in the Score.

The first example in this chapter, like the examples in the previous chapter, is simple enough for anyone to do. It starts with the creation of simple graphics and text objects to form an animated line graph. You can even create the example on a monochrome Mac PowerBook or Windows-based portable PC with minimal RAM (random-access memory). As with the previous chapter's examples, the purpose of the first example is to get you started with the program without requiring an expensive computer setup.

Subsequent examples are based on the works by multimedia artist Stuart Sharpe. Many of these require the use of a color monitor and at least 5 megabytes of RAM (8 recommended). This is because many of the techniques are better shown as color animation.

## Creating Graphics Cast Members

The development effort for a movie always begins with an idea. Our idea is to demonstrate the rise of air pollution, using a gritty-looking, black-and-white presentation that can be run on any Mac or Windows machine (even a 9-inch Mac Classic or PowerBook screen). Start this example by choosing New in the File menu to create a new movie file.

Throughout these tutorials we refer to Macintosh keyboard shortcuts for many functions. If you're using the Windows version of Director, simply substitute Control for Command. The Control key is labeled Ctrl on some PC keyboards.

Simple graphics are elementary to create in Director. You can use the Paint window and its tools to create any graphic image to use as an individual cast member. When you use that cast member in a movie, any change you make to it, in the Paint window, shows up in the animation. Therefore, if you create a crude-looking cast member for an animated sequence, you can always refine that cast member without having to redo the animated sequence.

The shapes and graphics for this particular animated line graph are easy to create in the Paint window. Open the Paint window by choosing Paint in the window menu or typing Command-5. Start by choosing a pattern for a background rectangle—the pattern pop-up menu appears when you click the box between the overlapping color chips and the line thickness choices (Figure 3.1).

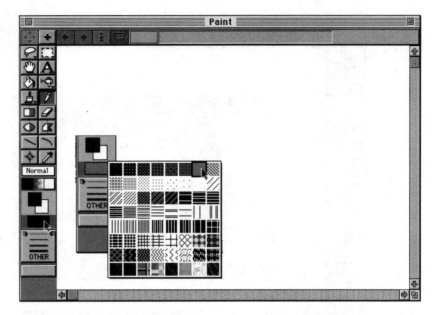

**Figure 3.1
Changing the default pattern in the Paint window (you can also choose Patterns in the Paint menu).**

An alternate way to change the pattern is to use the Patterns command in the Paint menu. Drag the mouse to select the mock-gray pattern, which provides the gritty backdrop that suggests air pollution.

Next, select the shaded rectangle tool, and then the one-pixel line (Figure 3.2).

As you draw the rectangle, the one-pixel line style is applied to the border, and the rectangle is filled with the selected pattern. This is because you are using

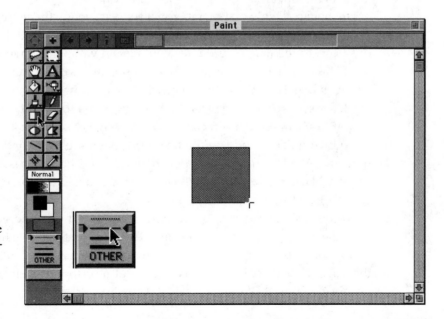

**Figure 3.2
Selecting the shaded rectangle tool and the one-pixel line thickness, and drawing a rectangle.**

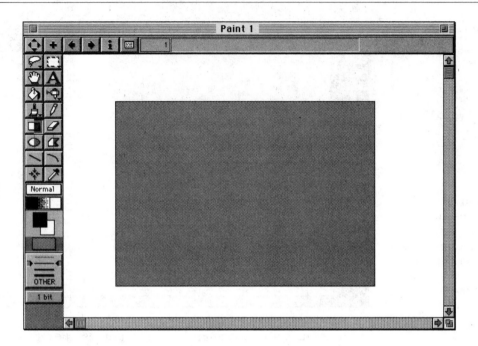

**Figure 3.3**
**The full-size rectangle with the mock-gray pattern.**

the shaded rectangle tool, rather than the blank-filled rectangle tool. Draw a rectangle that will occupy the space inside the line graph (Figure 3.3), and save the movie with the Save command. This graphic image automatically becomes cast member 1; you can see the cast member number at the end of the row of icons in the upper left corner of the Paint window.

The new rectangle cast member will serve to define the graph's x- and y-axes if we add text to it. However, the text will change from graph to graph, while this background may be used again and again without changing. Therefore, we leave this rectangle as a cast member by itself, and we will create text as separate cast members later. Close the Paint window for now (click the close box in the top left corner, choose Paint in the Window menu, or type Command-5).

Now you can place this rectangle on the stage to see how it looks, and to use as a visual guide for adding the text. First, open the Cast window (choose Cast from the Window menu, or type Command-3). The first cast member should show a black rectangle. Since this is a new movie, the frame indicator in the Control Panel should say frame 1.

Click inside the cast member rectangle and drag it onto the stage (Figure 3.4). With the rectangle on stage, it is much easier to set the text where you want it.

Now open the Score window, and resize it so that you can still see some of the stage. Note that channel 1 has a red dot next to it as well as a cast member occupying frame 1 of the channel (Figure 3.5).

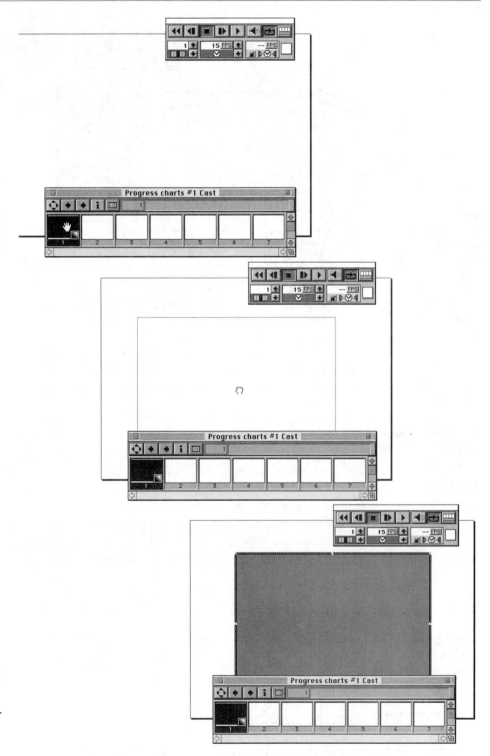

**Figure 3.4
Dragging the first
cast member, the
mock-gray rectan-
gle, onto the
stage.**

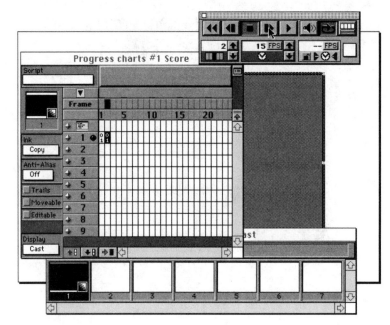

**Figure 3.5**
**The red dot next to channel 1 indicates that the stage is automatically recording in channel 1 (cast member 1). You can use the step button in the Control Panel to create the next frame.**

The red dot indicates that Director is recording something in that channel for the current frame. Click the Step button in the Control Panel to record the selected rectangle in frame 2. You now have the cast member recorded in two frames of the movie.

## Creating Text Cast Members

The next Step is to use the Tools window to create the text. To open the Tools window, select Tools from the Window menu, or type Command-7 (Figure 3.6). The Tools window contains a pointer tool, a text tool, a line tool, and three shape tools with blank and shaded options, which are described in Chapter 4. It also contains three button-creation tools, described later in Chapter 6, and the foreground and background color chips, described in Chapter 4 (we do not use them in this example). A pattern selector is provided, similar to the one in the Paint window, among the color chips and the line thickness selector.

**Figure 3.6**
**The Tools window, which offers a text ("A") tool for typing text directly onto the stage.**

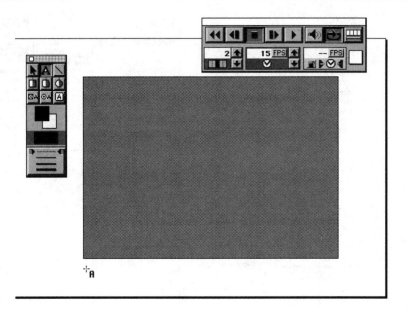

**Figure 3.7
Creating an insertion point for text with the text tool.**

The Tools window is especially useful for creating high-quality text that can be edited later. When creating text, the Tool window automatically saves the text in a cast member slot, so it is equivalent to using the Text window to create text (described later).

Click the text tool and then click in the appropriate place for the first horizontal axis label of the graph (Figure 3.7). The special pointer automatically changes to the text insertion pointer so that you can type.

Type the text for the label (Figure 3.8). You can use the Delete key to delete text while typing it (if you make a mistake), and you can use the Paste Text command in the Edit menu to paste text from the Clipboard.

A Text menu is available when editing text so that you can select the font, size, style, alignment, and border (Figure 3.9).

Set the text to *Geneva, 12 points, Plain style,* and *Left alignment.* The other options are described later in this section.

You can resize the text element holding the text by moving the mouse to the edge, where the pointer turns into an arrow, and dragging the edge in or out (Figure 3.10).

**Figure 3.8
Typing the text for the first label on the horizontal axis.**

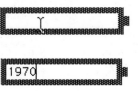

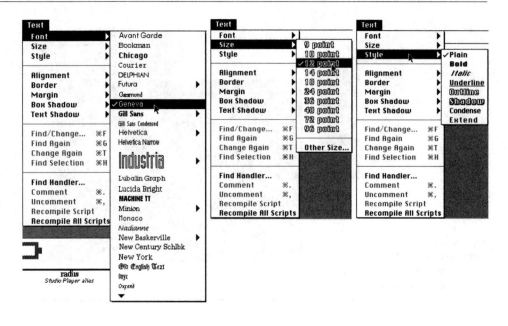

**Figure 3.9**
**The Text menu lets you set the text characteristics.**

**Figure 3.10**
**Resizing a text element by dragging its edges; the element's borders change, but the text stays the same size.**

Use the text tool to create text elements, and type the rest of the labels for the horizontal axis. Use the Return key to type more than one line in a text element or reshape the element to hold more lines by dragging its edges (Figure 3.11).

When all the text is created for the frame, open the Cast window to see that each text element has been entered as a separate cast member (Figure 3.12).

You can edit the text on the stage, or in the Text window, by dragging the text to edit, and retyping, or pressing Delete. You can also use the Cut Text, Copy Text and Paste Text commands in the Edit menu. To open the Text window, you can double-click any of the text cast members (Figure 3.13), or choose Text in the Window menu (or type Command-6).

**Figure 3.11**
**Resizing a text element to hold text in two lines.**

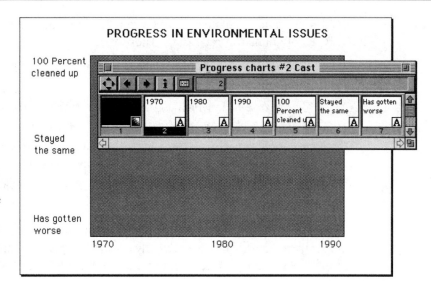

**Figure 3.12**
**Frame 2 now has all the text it needs for the line graph, and the text elements are automatically entered as cast members.**

With the Text menu you can set the text attributes (font, style, alignment, and so on). You can also use the Find/Change text command, which works like the find and replace commands that are typical of word processing programs.

## Recording Animation

So far you have created a simple graphic image and added text as separate cast members. You have learned how to record two frames of animation: frame 1, when you dragged the rectangle from the cast to the stage; frame 2, when you clicked the Step button in the Control Panel. This method of recording animation is called Step recording, because you use the Step button.

**Figure 3.13**
**The Text window for the selected cast member appears if you choose Text in the Window menu, or type Command-6, or double-click any text cast member.**

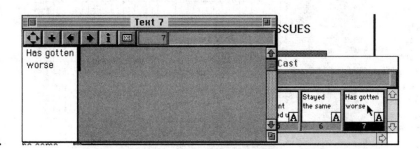

Besides the Auto Animate feature (which has limited use), Director offers four basic types of animation recording. They are:

- *Step recording*, in which you place a cast member on the stage in a frame, and step to the next frame while recording it.

- *Real-Time recording,* in which you drag a cast member on the stage while holding down the Control key and spacebar to record animation over several frames.

- *In-Betweening,* in which you select a beginning and ending cell in a range and have Director fill the range automatically, calculating the animation.

- *Score editing,* in which you edit cells in the Score window with commands such as Copy and Paste Score, Cast to Time, and Space to Time (described later).

It helps to know how to do all four types of animation recording. You will learn to rely on editing the score directly, as well as methods such as in-betweening, to make animations run smoothly and look professional.

**Extending a Scene with In-Between**

A look at the Score window provides a clear representation of what you have so far (Figure 3.14). As two frames are not enough, you need to extend the rectangle and text cast members to cover about 80 frames. The in-between method can do this for you automatically.

First, select the score cell in frame 2, channel 1 (Figure 3.15).

Then scroll the Score window to frame 80, hold down the Shift key, and select the cell in frame 80, channel 8 (which is the highest-numbered channel holding a cast member in frame 2). The result should be a selection of all the cells from frame 2 through frame 80 on channels 1 through 8 (Figure 3.16).

Next, select the In-Between Linear command in the Score menu (Figure 3.17). Director fills in the selected score cells with the same information from the first

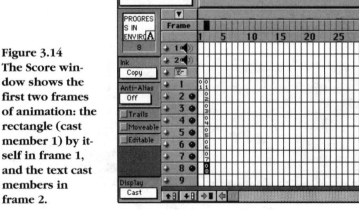

**Figure 3.14
The Score window shows the first two frames of animation: the rectangle (cast member 1) by itself in frame 1, and the text cast members in frame 2.**

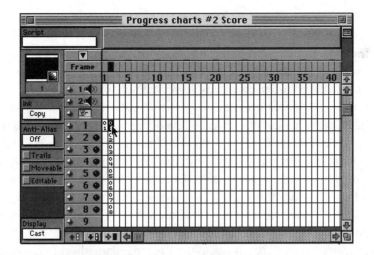

**Figure 3.15**
Selecting the cell in channel 1, frame 2, which contains cast member 1, then scrolling the Score window to frame 80.

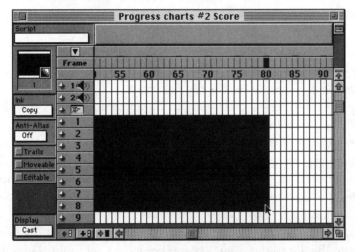

**Figure 3.16**
After holding down the Shift key and selecting the cell in channel 8, frame 80, the range of cells from frame 2 to frame 8, channel 1 through channel 8, are selected.

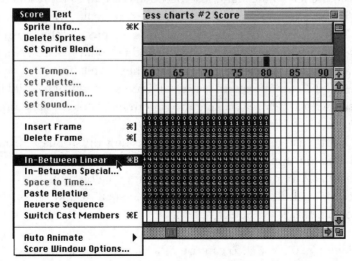

**Figure 3.17**
Choosing In-Between Linear to extend the score information over the selected frames.

frame (frame 2), so that the rectangle and text cast members remain on the stage for the duration of those frames.

You have just used a simple technique to create the background for many frames of animation. As long as the last frame of a selection is empty, the In-Between Linear command in the Score menu (Command-B) extends whatever is in the first frame of the selection, over the entire range of the selection. To see how it looks, run the movie by first rewinding it and then playing it.

If, however, the last frame of the selection has other information (such as a different location for the cast members on the stage), the In-Between Linear command can create animation for you. This technique is shown later in this chapter to create the steps of an animated sequence. For the next part of our example you will use the real-time recording method to create the first animated line of the line graph.

## Real-Time Recording

Sometimes the best way to test an idea for a movie is to try it. In such cases, any roughness is dismissed as part of the expediency of the moment—the quickest way to express the idea is the best way.

Director offers a quick way to do animation, called real-time recording. It is not as precise as the other methods, but is certainly one of the best for getting an idea down quickly. With real-time animation, you create frames of animation simply by dragging the mouse in real time. You drag an object, such as a cast member or group of cast members, from one location to another on the stage. Because you use the mouse, the animation may be a bit uneven, but it is recorded as you do it.

In this example you will create a brush stroke that moves across the graph from the left to the right, leaving behind a trail to represent a line in the graph. It is a simple brush stroke that anyone can create, with or without graphics skill.

First, create a cast member to represent a piece of the brush stroke by opening the Paint window and clicking the add (+) button. The Paint window automatically creates the cast member in the next available slot, which in our example is 9. If the current pattern is not solid black, change it to solid black (Figure 3.18) as described before (clicking the Pattern Indicator chip and dragging to the black square).

Next, change the brush size by selecting Brush Shape from the Paint menu. The menu appears whenever the Paint window is open (Figure 3.19). This command brings up the Brush Shape dialog box (an alternate way is to double-click the brush tool). Select the small round brush shape in the dialog box, and click the Select button.

Now use the brush tool to draw a thin horizontal brush stroke of solid black (Figure 3.20). You also can use other tools, such as the eraser tool, to refine the

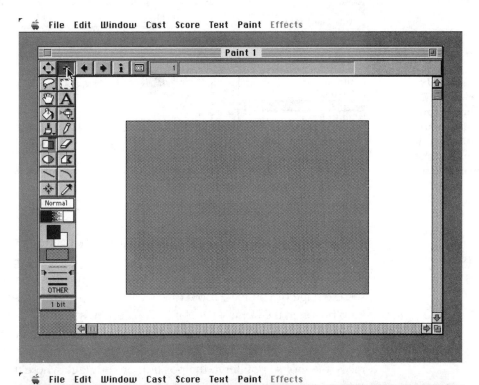

**Figure 3.18
Clicking the add
(+) icon to create
a new cast member in the Paint
window, and
changing the current pattern to
solid black.**

**Figure 3.19
Selecting Brush
Shape from the
Paint menu, and
choosing the
small round
brush shape.**

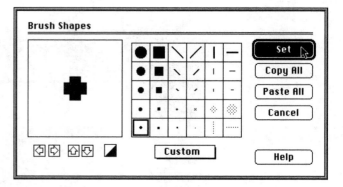

brush stroke so that it looks like our example. When you are finished, close the Paint window.

Open the Score window, and move the playback head to frame 2 by clicking the empty cell in channel 9, frame 2 (Figure 3.21). This is the frame and channel to start the real-time animation recording. You can now close the Score window in order to see the stage (if you have room to leave it open, you can do so). Also, turn off the loop button in the Control Panel if it is on. You may want to move the Cast window down to the bottom of the stage so that you can see the entire graph.

Click inside cast member 9 in the Cast window to select it (Figure 3.22). Then move the mouse pointer to the position on the stage where the animation should start, but don't press the mouse button yet.

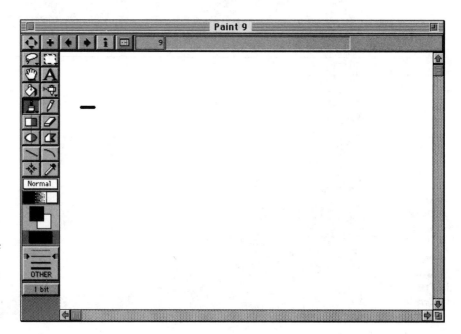

**Figure 3.20
Drawing with the
selected brush,
stroke a thin line
for use in real-
time animation
recording.**

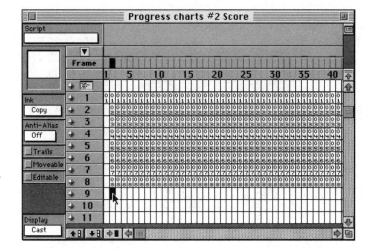

**Figure 3.21 Preparing for real-time recording: selecting the frame and empty channel to start the animation in the Score window.**

Now you are ready to record animation in real time. Hold down the Control key and spacebar, and drag with the mouse button pressed, to draw a path in a steady, smooth motion across the shaded rectangle, as shown in the example (Figure 3.23).

Director records the motion, and the cast member, in the selected channel of the score. You can see what channel is being used by noting the red dot in the

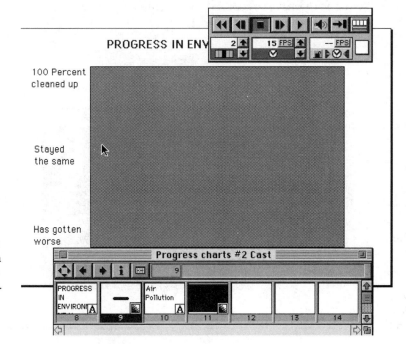

**Figure 3.22 Selecting the cast member to use in the recorded animation, and moving the mouse pointer to the starting location.**

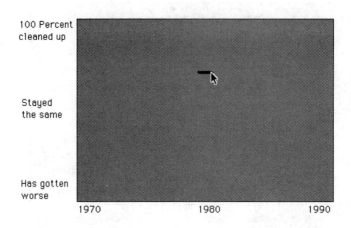

**Figure 3.23 Dragging the mouse along a path while holding down the Control key and spacebar to record the animation up to frame 80.**

Score window. Don't let go of the mouse button before frame 80 (the last frame), and continue dragging until frame 80 appears in the Control Panel frame indicator. You then can use rewind and play to play the animation (Figure 3.24).

Wouldn't it be nice if the animation left a *trail* of copies of itself, which could form a line of the graph? You can change one characteristic of this selected sequence so that a trail is left. First, open the Score window to view channel 9, which now contains cast member 9 and the score information for the entire sequence you just recorded. Select the sequence by double-clicking the cell in frame 2 of channel 9 (Figure 3.25).

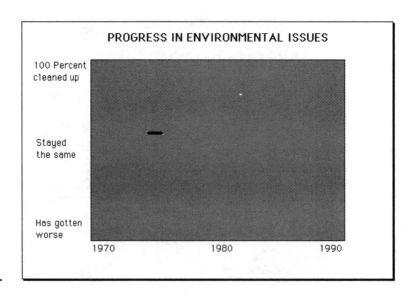

**Figure 3.24 Playing the movie to see the brush stroke move across the stage (PROGCH2A.DIR in the TUTORIAL folder/directory).**

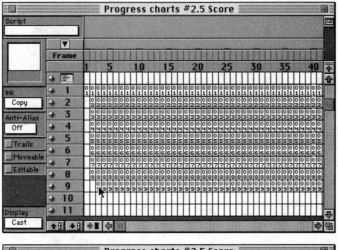

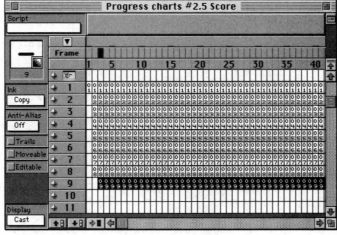

**Figure 3.25 Double-clicking the cell in channel 9, frame 2, in order to select the entire sequence recorded in real time in channel 9.**

On the left side of the Score window are three checkboxes: Trails, Moveable, and Editable. Click on the Trails checkbox so that a check mark appears (Figure 3.26).

Now close the Score window and play the movie to see the effect (Figure 3.27).

It looks good, but there are white spots surrounding the brush strokes. This is due to the *ink effect* used in the Score, which controls how the object appears on the stage. Usually the ink effect in use is Copy, which copies the cast member and a rectangle that defines the graphics' outside edges, called the *bounding box*. The bounding box surrounds the entire object and appears white because it, and its enclosed object (the brush stroke image), are both opaque.

You can change the ink in the Score window for any cell or selection of cells. Open the Score window, and the sequence in channel 9 should still be selected (if not, reselect it as described earlier). Change the ink effect by selecting a new

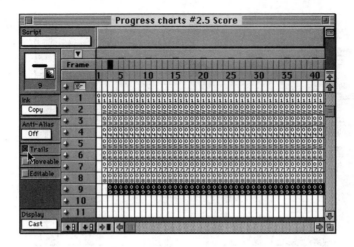

**Figure 3.26 Selecting the Trails checkbox in the Score window for the selected animation to add the trails effect.**

effect from the ink pop-up menu on the left side of the Score window. Choose the Matte ink (Figure 3.28).

The Matte ink outlines the black part of the cast member, leaving it opaque, and makes the bounding box transparent. Run the animation again to see the aftereffect of the Matte ink (Figure 3.29).

You have just learned how to record animation in real time. Now you will learn a more precise technique for recording animation in frames.

## Step Recording

When you record cast members in a certain position on a single frame, and then use the step button in the Control Panel (or Step Forward in the Edit menu) to move to the next frame, you are using a frame-by-frame recording technique called *step recording*.

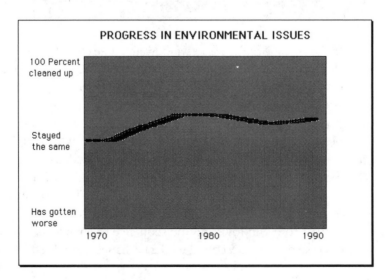

**Figure 3.27 The trails effect on the selected animated sequence causes the cast member to repeat itself for every position along the path, leaving a trail (PROGCH3.DIR in the TUTORIAL folder/directory).**

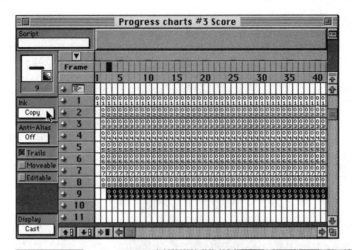

**Figure 3.28
Choosing the
Matte ink in the
Score window
for the selected
sequence in chan-
nel 9.**

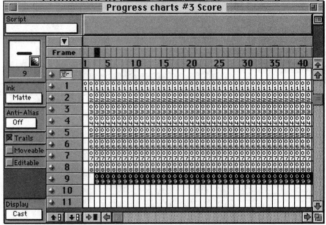

**Figure 3.29
The Matte ink
makes the bound-
ing box transpar-
ent around the
cast member so
that no white
shows around
the image
(PROGCH4.DIR
in the TUTORIAL
folder/directory).**

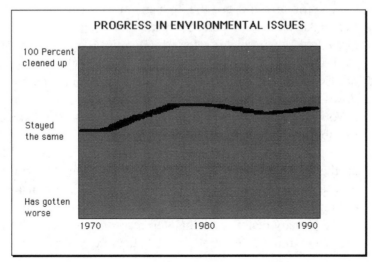

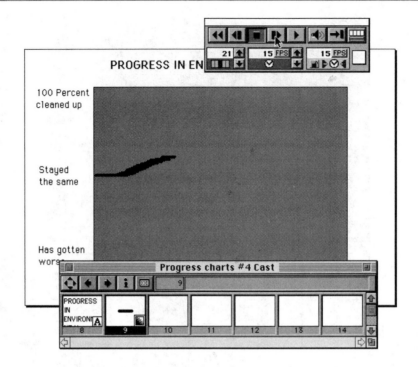

**Figure 3.30
Stopping on the
frame where the
label for the
graph line
should appear.**

For example, to place a label on the animated line on the graph, you can use the rewind and play buttons to view the movie up to a certain point. You then use the stop button to stop the movie on the frame, where you want the label to appear (Figure 3.30).

Open the Tools window to use the text tool to add text to frame 21 (Figure 3.31).

Type the text and use the Text menu to set the text to the Bold Style with Center Alignment, a 1-pixel Border, and a 2-pixel Box Shadow (Figure 3.32).

While the text remains selected, open the Score window (Figure 3.33).

The red dot in channel 10 indicates that the channel is recording. If the red dot is not on, you can activate it by clicking the channel number, while holding down the Option key.

You can now click the step button in the Control Panel to record the cast member in the next frame (Figure 3.34).

For each subsequent frame, the cast member is recorded for that frame. Step all the way to frame 80 to record the cast member—you can hold down the mouse button while clicking the step button to step quickly. At frame 80, click the rewind button, and play back the movie to see the result (Figure 3.35).

The primary benefit of using Step recording is to see all the cast members on the stage at any given moment. Additionally, you can make position changes,

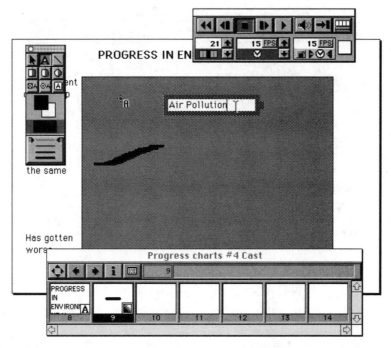

**Figure 3.31**
**Using the text tool in the Tools window to create text on this frame (a new cast member is automatically created to hold the text).**

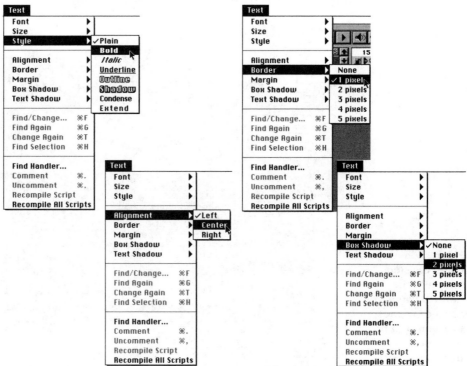

**Figure 3.32**
**Typing the text, and setting the text Style, Alignment, Border, and Box Shadow options.**

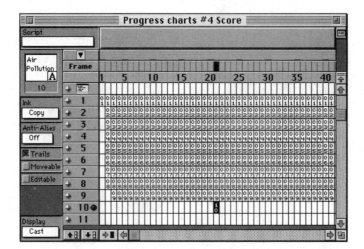

**Figure 3.33**
**The Score window indicates that channel 10 is recording (the red dot) in frame 21, ready for the step button, and the ink is set to Copy.**

cast member substitutions, or introduce new cast members as you wish, with the precision you need at the frame-by-frame level. You can then step to the next frame, rearrange, replace, or introduce new cast members, step to the next frame, and so on. You can do this from within the Score window, which is more convenient for many of these operations.

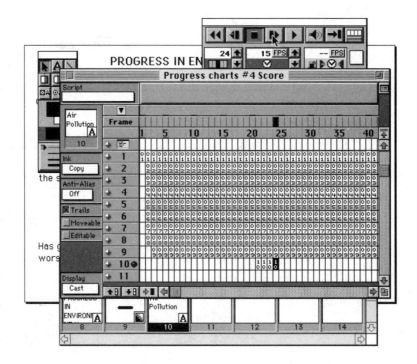

**Figure 3.34**
**Using the step button in the Control Panel to advance frame by frame and record the cast member in each frame.**

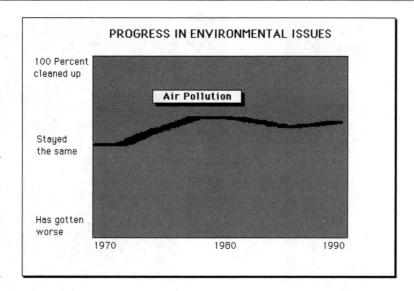

**Figure 3.35**
**After step-record-ing the text cast member to frame 80, you can play back the movie to see the result (PROGCH5.DIR in the TUTORIAL folder/directory).**

## Editing in the Score

You have now graduated to the rank of experienced Director user, and you can begin to use this tool in creative and imaginative ways. You have already learned how to do step recording by dragging a cast member onto the stage from the Cast window and using the step button in the Control Panel. You also learned how to do real-time recording by dragging a cast member over the scene while the movie plays to the last frame.

Now you are ready to make use of Director's productivity features for animation, such as switching cast members, using In-Between Linear and Special, using Space to Time, and so on.

You are also ready to use professional terminology. For example, rather than referring to *"the cast member used on the stage with effects or changes applied to it,"* we can use the term *sprite*. Sprite means an instance of the cast member on the stage. Think of the cast member as a kind of template for the sprite. You can change the sprite in many ways (ink, position on the stage, scale, trails effect, and so on) without changing the actual cast member. However, if you change the cast member, *every sprite based on that cast member will change accordingly.*

**Animating with Cast to Time**

One of the fastest techniques for arranging cast members over time, as sprites in the score, is to use the Cast to Time command with a selection of cast members.

See, for example, Figure 3.36, Stuart Sharpe's first-run *Red Silo d w/b&w stripes* movie (named REDSILOD.DIR in the TUTORIAL folder/directory of the CD-ROM), then look inside the score (Figure 3.37).

**Figure 3.36**
**The movie** *Red*
*Silo d w/b&w*
*stripes* **by Stuart**
**Sharpe**
**(REDSILOD.DIR**
**in the TUTORIAL**
**folder/directory)**
**features a danc-**
**ing figure.**

**Figure 3.37**
**The cast and**
**score for the**
**movie** *Red Silo*
*d w/b&w*
*stripes.* **The**
**dancing figure is**
**in channel 3.**

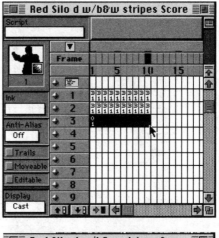

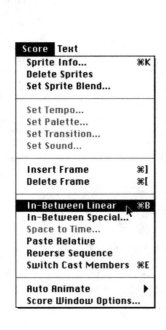

**Figure 3.38
Extending the
cast member to
create sprites
over frames 1
through 10 on
channel 3, using
In-Between
Linear.**

The dancing figure is formed by animation in channel 3. It was created by first extending a single cast member to create sprites over frames 1 through 10 on channel 3, using In-Between Linear (Figure 3.38).

Then, after selecting the range of sprites in channel 3, frames 2 through 10, and selecting a range of corresponding cast members in the Cast window, the artist used the Cast to Time to switch the new cast members for the sprites (Figure 3.39).

The Cast to Time command placed the cast members in the selected channel cells in sequential order by cast number. If you select a range of cells, it fills the range with enough cast members, but stops at the end of the range, even if there are more cast members selected. If you select only one cell, it fills out the channel for as many frames as needed to contain all the selected cast members.

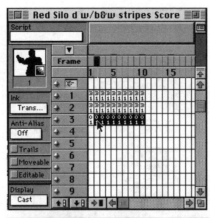

**Figure 3.39 Using the Shift key to select the range of sprites in channel 3, from frame 2 through frame 10, and selecting a range of corresponding cast members in the Cast window, then using Cast to Time to switch the new cast members for the sprites.**

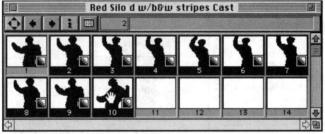

## Animating with In-Between Linear

You have already learned how to use the In-Between Linear command to extend a nonmoving scene over many frames at once. Although nothing changes in those frames, you have the control to change any particular frame by moving to it and then making changes directly to each sprite.

The In-Between Linear command is often used to extend the existing scene while building a new scene, or to extend a particular channel to line up with other channels in a frame. However, it can also be used to calculate the in-between frames for a moving object.

For an example, look again at the *Red Silo d w/b&w stripes* movie and its score. Channel 1 contains a white-filled rectangle, drawn with the Rectangle tool from the Tools window, and set to the Add ink effect (Figure 3.40).

To create a sequence of them, from one location to another, the artist used the Copy Cells command in the Edit menu to copy the first sprite in channel 1 (frame 1), the white-filled rectangle (Figure 3.41).

Then the artist clicked the empty cell in channel 1, frame 5, and used the Paste Cells command in the Edit menu to paste the copied sprite into that cell (Figure 3.42). The artist then moved the sprite in frame 5 to a new position on the stage. Thus, the first and last frames were defined.

To select the range for in-betweening, the artist Shift-clicked the sprite in channel 1, frame 1 (Figure 3.43).

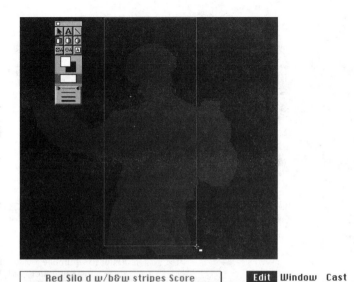

**Figure 3.40 Drawing the filled rectangle behind the moving figure in the movie *Red Silo d w/b&w stripes.***

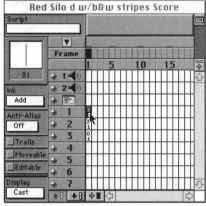

**Figure 3.41 Copying the first sprite in channel 1 (frame 1), the white-filled rectangle.**

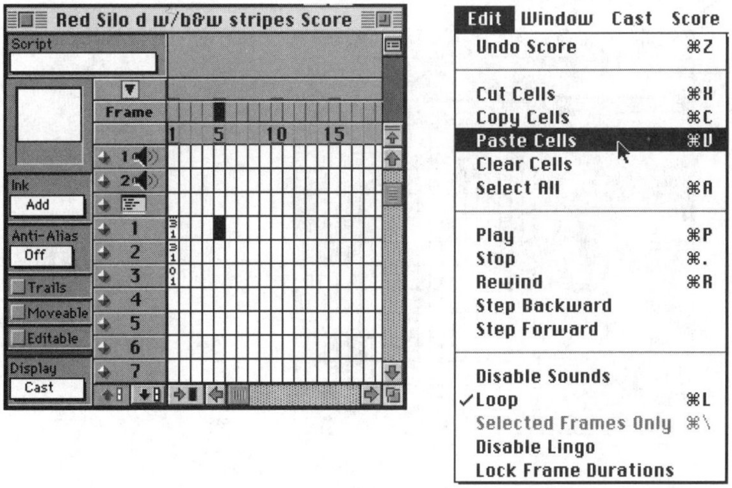

**Figure 3.42 Clicking in the empty cell in channel 1, frame 5, and pasting the copied sprite into that cell, then moving it to a different position on the stage.**

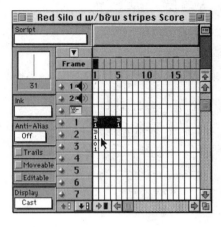

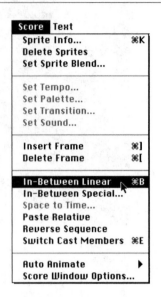

**Figure 3.43**
**Shift-clicking the sprite in channel 1, frame 1, to select a range of cells from frames 1 through 5, then choosing In-Between Linear.**

The artist then chose In-Between Linear to performing the *tweening*. The result (Figure 3.44) was that the in-between frames were automatically calculated. To see how the sprites are moved on the stage, change your view of the score to Motion by clicking the Display pop-up menu (now set to Cast) in the bottom left corner of the Score window (Figure 3.45).

A range of only a few frames, as in channel 1 in the above example, doesn't show off the power of In-Between Linear. However, the same movie offers another example of its use: channel 2, which has the same white-filled rectangle starting at one side of the stage and moving to the other.

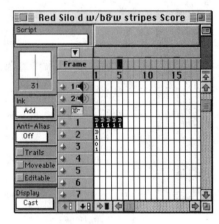

**Figure 3.44**
**The result of using In-Between Linear: the in-between frames are automatically calculated.**

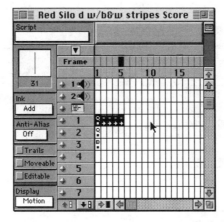

**Figure 3.45
Switching the
Score window
display to Motion
from Cast.**

---

*Note:* If you changed the movie while playing with it, you can always revert back to the last saved version of the movie by choosing Revert in the File menu.

---

In channel 2 (Figure 3.46), the white rectangle was placed on the left side of the stage in frame 1, and in frame 10, it was placed on the right side. The artist then selected the range as described before, and used In-Between Linear to automatically generate the frames in-between.

In-Between Linear is used mostly to extend scenes and to move a sprite in a straight line, as shown in the above example. It can also be used to show an object growing or shrinking smoothly, as described in Chapter 4.

**Figure 3.46
The sequence in
channel 2 was
created by In-Be-
tween Linear af-
ter placing the
sprites on the
stage in the first
and last cells.**

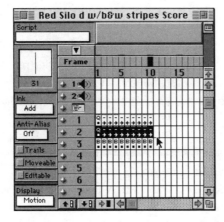
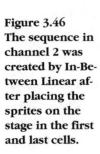

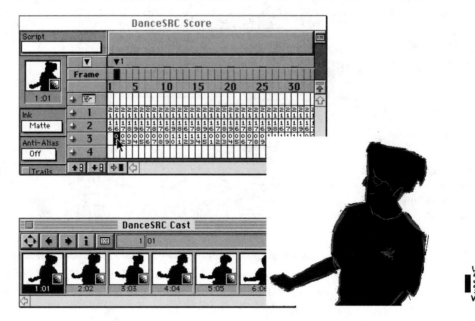

**Figure 3.47**
**The movie *Dance source* by Stuart Sharpe shows a dancing sprite in channel 3, starting with cast member 1 (DANCESRC.DIR in the TUTORIAL folder/director).**

## Switching Cast Members for a Sprite

One technique that comes in handy during step recording is to switch the cast member used for a particular sprite. You can line up one sprite over frames using one cast member, then switch the cast member for each sprite. This is done so that all the cast members line up properly in the same position on the stage.

For an example, look at Stuart Sharpe's *Dance source* movie and its score (filename: DANCESRC.DIR). Channel 3 in the score, which contains the dancing character (Figure 3.47), was created by placing the first cast member of the dancing figure in frame 2, then extending the cast member to frame 16 (Figure 3.48) with In-Between Linear. Then, for each sprite in channel 3, the cast member was switched. This was done by first selecting the new cast member in the Cast window, then selecting the sprite in the score, and choosing Switch Cast Members (Figure 3.49). The new cast member occupies the sprite position in channel 3.

This method lets you align cast members to their proper sprite positions on a frame-by-frame basis. You can then drag the sprite to a new location if you want, or leave it aligned.

> ***Note:*** For cast members to line up properly, their registration points must be set in the same place in the Paint window as described in the next chapter. When you Copy and Paste an image into another cast member slot, the registration point is the same for the copy.

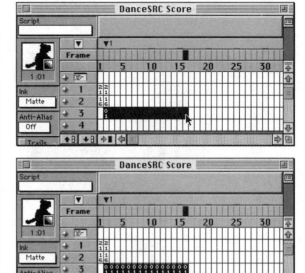

**Figure 3.48**
To create the dancing sprite, cast member 1 was placed in channel 3, and then extended out to frame 16 with the In-Between Linear command.

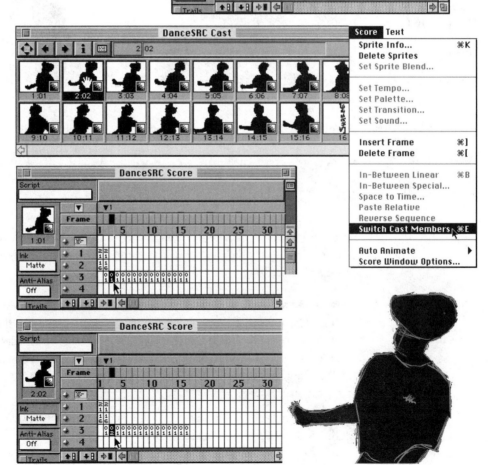

**Figure 3.49**
Selecting the second cast member for the dancing figure, selecting the sprite (channel 3, frame 3) to switch cast members, and then choosing Switch Cast Members.

**Figure 3.50
The first 16
frames of the
movie *Dance
source* represent
the core segment
of animation.**

## Using Copy and Paste Cells

To finish the dancing sprite, cast members 2 through 15 were switched for frames 3 through 16. The cast members for the sprites in channel 2 were also switched for these frames, and the sprite for channel 1 was moved slightly from frame to frame.

The result is a 16-frame animation (Figure 3.50), which represents the core animation segment. Select this range of cells (Figure 3.51) by clicking the last frame and channel (frame 16, channel 3) and Shift-clicking the first frame and channel (frame 2, channel 1) of the range. To copy the selected range to the Clipboard, choose Copy Cells from the Edit menu.

---

***Note:*** Copy, Cut, and Paste change their meanings depending on the active window. They apply to selected cells when the Score window is active. You can't use Copy, Cut, or Paste directly from the stage. You can make alterations to the stage by using these commands in the Score or Cast windows.

---

After copying, click the first cell in the score to receive the copied information (Figure 3.52), and choose Paste Cells.

**Figure 3.51**
**Selecting the range of cells for copying, and using Copy Cells.**

The empty cells are filled with the copied score information, and the movie is doubled in length. The artist used this technique several times to create a movie that runs out to frame 240 (Figure 3.53).

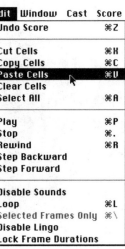

**Figure 3.52**
**Selecting the first cell in the score to receive the copied information, and pasting into that cell.**

**Figure 3.53
The Copy-Paste
cells technique is
used over and
over to create a
longer movie.**

## Animating with Space to Time

Another automatic way to put sprites in their proper stage positions over frames is a technique called Space to Time. You can place several cast members on the stage as sprites in one frame to see how they relate to each other in space. Afterwards you can spread them out over several frames using the Space to Time command in the Score menu.

To see how this method can be useful, look at an early version of the *Cartoon Walk* movie (filename: WALKMAN1.DIR). In this movie, the cast members that comprise the walking man were first arranged on the stage in one frame (Figure 3.54). They were dragged out from the Cast window one at a time and arranged in one frame from first to last as they would appear over time moving slightly to the left from center stage.

The sprites are now placed in separate channels in the same frame. However, the goal is to place them in the same channel across consecutive frames. First, select the range of sprites in frame 1 (Figure 3.55), and then choose Space to Time in the Score menu. This command presents a dialog box for specifying how far apart (in number of frames) the sprites should be over time. Click OK with the setting of only one frame apart. The result is that the sprites are arranged over time rather than in space.

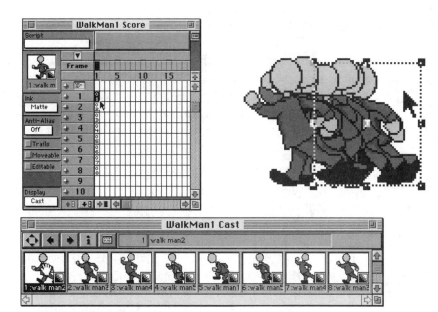

**Figure 3.54**
**An early version of the *Walking Man* movie (filename: WALKMAN1.DIR in the TUTORIAL folder/director) in which the cast members for the walking man were first arranged on the stage in one frame.**

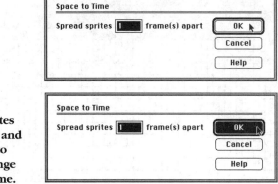

**Figure 3.55**
**Selecting the range of sprites on the stage, and using Space to Time to arrange them over time.**

129

The animated sequence of the walking man can now be saved as a film loop, which is described in Chapter 5. This is how the movie *Cartoon Walk* (in the ClipMedia Sampler) was created. Space to Time is a useful technique for comparing the positions of animated figures. It is similar to the *onion skin* technique in traditional *cel* animation in which the artist can see all the positions of a moving figure through transparent layers of drawing material.

## Animating with In-Between Special

The In-Between Special command makes it possible to create smooth movement for animation automatically, without painstakingly modifying each frame. You can set options to make an object move with accelerating speed at the beginning, and decelerating speed at the end, for more realistic motion.

For a very simple example, open the *Car Accelerating* movie (filename: CARACCEL.DIR) select the score information in channel 2 except for the very first frame (frame 1), and choose Cut Cells to delete them from the score. Then change the Score window display to Motion so that the score information is relevant for this animation method (Figure 3.56).

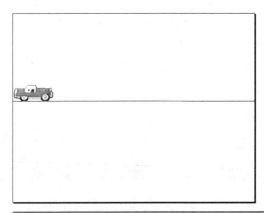

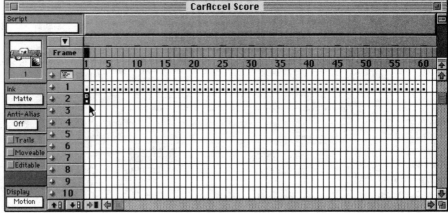

**Figure 3.56**
**An early version of the *Car Accelerating* movie (filename: CARACCEL.DIR in the TUTORIAL folder/directory), in which the car sprite occupies only the first frame of channel 2. The Score window is set to display Motion information rather than Cast.**

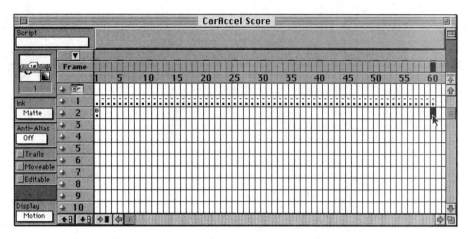

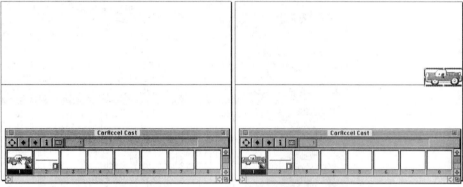

**Figure 3.57 Clicking the last frame of the sequence in the score, and arranging the sprite on the stage for the last frame, before in-betweening.**

With the car in position in frame 1, you now have to establish the ending position of the car in the last frame (frame 60). Click in the score in frame 60, channel 2 (Figure 3.57), and drag the car out to the stage position from the Cast window. If you can't see the stage, click first in the Score window (in frame 60, channel 2), and then close the Score window by clicking the close box or select it again.

Open the Score window again, and you should see a new sprite in frame 60, channel 2 (Figure 3.58). Hold down the Shift key and click the first sprite in this channel to select the range of cells for the in-between operation. Then choose In-Between Special from the Score menu.

This command presents a dialog box with various options for the in-between operation (Figure 3.59). You can *'tween* the location, size, foreground, background, and blend of the sprites. In this example, only the location is changing from the first to last frame, so the location parameter is the only one chosen. The Ease In and Ease Out options for acceleration and deceleration have pop-up menus for selecting the number of frames for these motion effects.

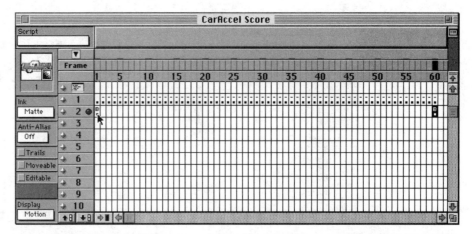

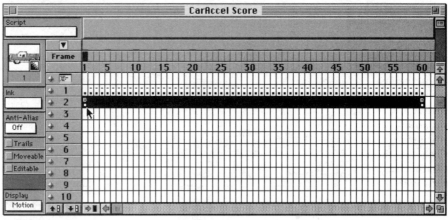

**Figure 3.58**
**Selecting the**
**range of cells for**
**the in-between**
**operation, start-**
**ing with the**
**newly arranged**
**sprite in frame**
**60, and Shift-**
**clicking the first**
**sprite in the**
**same channel,**
**then applying**
**the In-Between**
**Special com-**
**mand.**

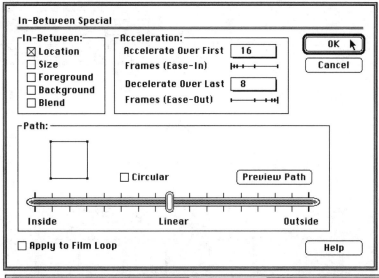

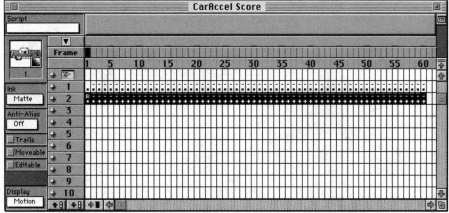

**Figure 3.59 Selecting options for in-betweening the location of two sprites, with acceleration and deceleration, in the In-Between Special dialog box.**

The result of the In-Between Special command is a channel filled with score information that '*tweens* the location of the sprite. Play the movie, and you'll see the car accelerate, move along at the same rate, then decelerate before coming to a stop (Figure 3.60).

The In-Between Special command can draw an imaginary curved path for animation between two locations, and provides a *slider control* for controlling the smoothness or sharpness of the curve. The curved path is defined by positions you set with sprites. You need to set at least three sprite locations on the stage to define a curved path.

To see how this works, open the movie *Moon Rise* (filename: MOONRISE.DIR). Once again Delete the cells in channel 2 (the moon sprite) except for the first cell, which contains the moon sprite at its starting location (Figure 3.61).

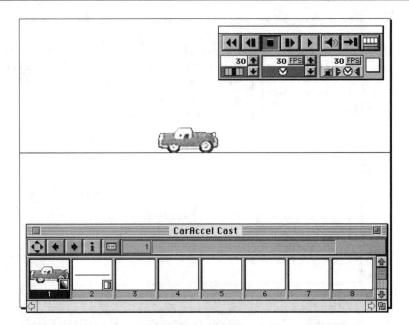

**Figure 3.60**
**The car moves across the stage, accelerating over the first 16 frames, then decelerating over the last 8 frames before reaching the end.**

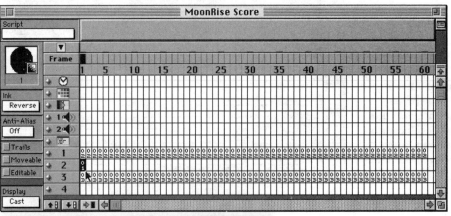

**Figure 3.61**
**Channel 2 of the *Moon Rise* movie (filename: MOONRISE.DIR in the TUTORIAL folder/directory) contains the starting point of the moon sprite in frame 1.**

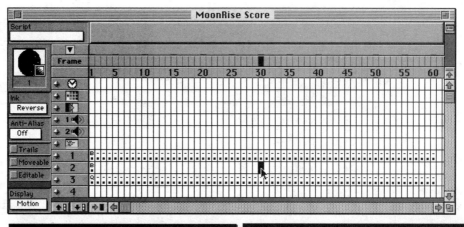

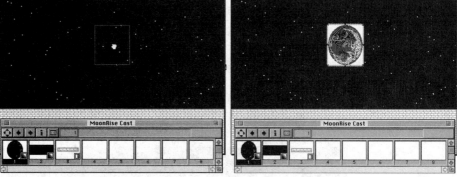

**Figure 3.62 After switching to Motion display, clicking in frame 30 and dragging the moon cast member out to the stage to set the midpoint.**

Switch the Display pop-up menu to Motion, and select frame 30, then drag the moon cast member out to the stage to set its midpoint position (Figure 3.62).

While the use of ink effects in the Score window are described later, right now you should use the Reverse ink for the sprite by clicking the Ink pop-up menu (Figure 3.63), and selecting Reverse. This ink effect turns the black moon into a white moon against the black background.

Next, arrange the last position of the moon by clicking in frame 60 (Figure 3.64), drag the moon cast member onto the stage, and, if the sprite's ink is not already set to Reverse, set the ink to Reverse.

Now you are ready to select the range for the In-Between Special operation. If the last cell of the range is not already selected, select it first, then Shift-click the first cell of the range to select the entire range (Figure 3.65).

Then choose the In-Between Special command, which brings up the dialog box you've seen before (Figure 3.66).

You have already used the acceleration and deceleration pop-up menus; set them back to 0 (zero) frames for this sequence. Then drag the slider control that determines the degree of the curves of the path. The center position, Linear,

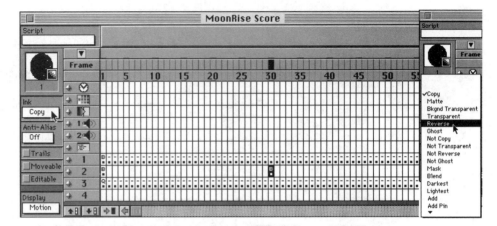

**Figure 3.63**
**Setting the ink of the sprite to Reverse.**

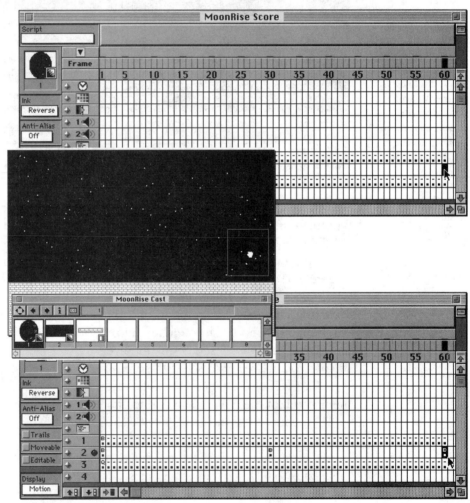

**Figure 3.64**
**Arranging the last position of the moon by clicking in frame 60, dragging the moon cast member onto the stage, and setting the sprite's ink to Reverse.**

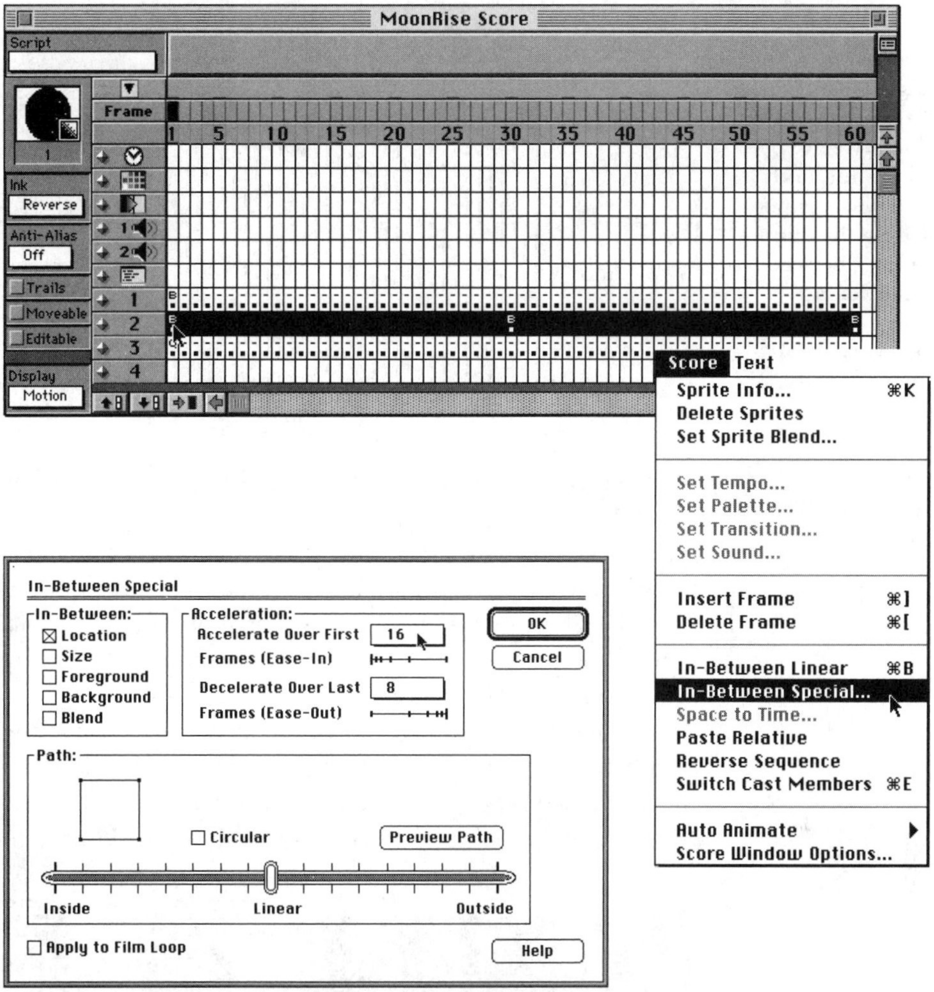

**Figure 3.65**
**Selecting the range of cells by Shift-clicking the first cell in the range; then using In-Between Special with the selected range.**

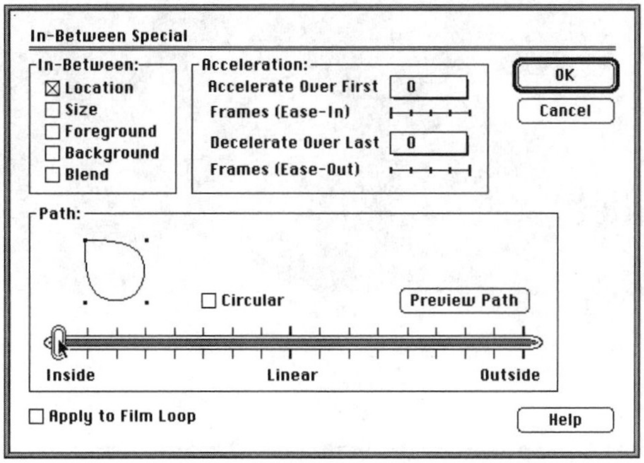

**Figure 3.66**
**The In-Between Special dialog box. First change acceleration and deceleration to 0 frames, then drag the slider to form a curve that is inside the control points to make the path very smooth.**

**Figure 3.67**
**The result of the In-Between Special command are new sprites filling the blank frames between the existing three cells that act as control points for the curve.**

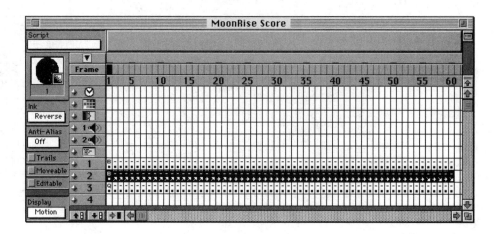

defines straight lines between the control points, which makes the path very sharp. Drag the slider to the right, and the path curves to the outside of the points; drag it to the left, and the path curves to the inside of the points. For now, drag the slider to the left (inside), and click OK to create the score cells (Figure 3.67).

In the Score window, the channel now should be filled with active cells containing new positions for the moon sprite. Play the movie to see how the animation looks (Figure 3.68).

The moon rises too low on the horizon. Let's change the In-Between Special dialog box to define a curved path that goes outside the control points. Select the sequence, choose In-Between Special again, but drag the slider in the In-Between Special dialog box to the right instead of the left (Figure 3.69).

**Figure 3.68**
**Playing the movie to see the animation.**

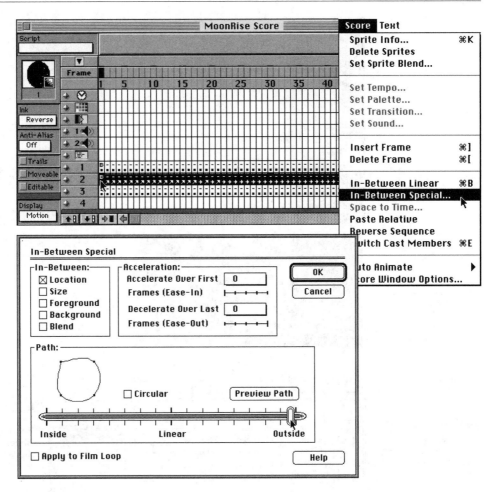

**Figure 3.69
Changing an in-
between se-
quence by
reselecting it,
choosing In-Be-
tween Special,
and changing the
options in the
dialog box.**

To change the sequence even further, you can select the control point sprite in frame 30, move it toward the top of the stage, and redo the in-between operation again (Figure 3.70).You can reapply new settings to a sequence that has already been created, to fine-tune the animation, which is one of the major benefits of In-Between Special.

There are many different kinds of paths that can be accommodated. If the beginning and ending points of the path are the same, the diagram in the In-Between Special dialog box is circular, indicating that the sprite's path is a circle. If you then check the Circular option, the sprite will go in a round circle without passing through the starting point, so that the circle will be as round as possible. You can see the path resulting from your choices in the dialog box by clicking the Preview button, which displays a path on the stage representing the in-between path.

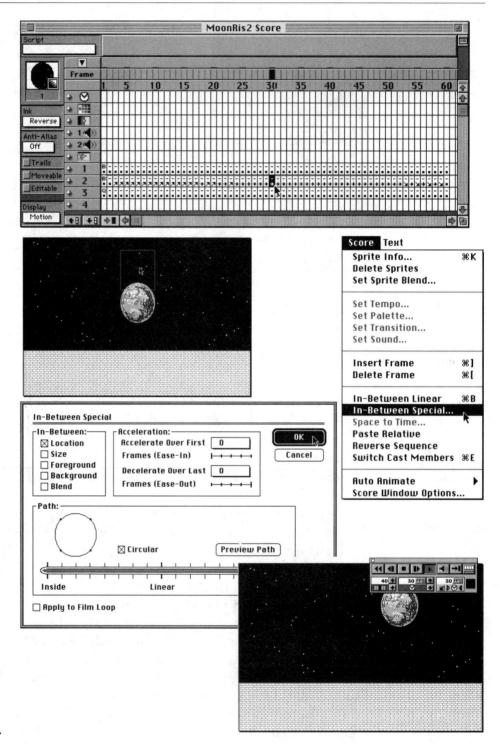

**Figure 3.70 Moving one of the control point sprites, then redoing the In-Between Special to change the animation in a later version of the _Moon Rise_ movie (filename: MOONRIS2.DIR in the TUTORIAL folder/directory).**

So far you have learned how to perform nearly every method of creating animation, though you haven't yet been introduced to all the tricks and techniques. You also have some experience with cast members, used as sprites, in the score, the channels of the score that act as layers, and the flexibility of using Copy, Cut, and Paste with score cells. You have also been introduced to the way in which a cast member's sprite is "inked" on the stage using the Copy, Matte, and Reverse ink effects.

## Understanding Sprites

Anything that appears on the stage that occupies a cell of the score (that is, in a single channel and a single frame) is a sprite. With 48 channels available in the current version of Director, you have the ability to display 48 different sprites on the screen in the same frame.

Think of a cast member as the *normal* or generalized version of a sprite. When you place a cast member on the stage, you are creating a single instance of the cast member, which is a sprite. This sprite can be placed anywhere on the stage, in front of or behind other sprites. This sprite, which is just a single instance of the cast member, can be resized and distorted on the stage. It can also be assigned different ink effects such as Reverse or Matte, without affecting the normal cast member, as it appears in the Paint window. However, any change to the cast member itself in the Paint window is immediately reflected in all instances all sprites based on that cast member.

This ability to change the appearance of many sprites, by changing the cast member, is as powerful in the graphics world, as are templates and style-sheets in the word processing world. The Paint window gives you full control over the appearance of each pixel in each bitmap cast member, and the Text window gives you full control over the appearance of each text element. If you resize, on stage, a sprite based on a cast member, it has no affect on the cast member (so that other sprites based on the cast member are not changed). If you change the cast member, it changes the appearance of any sprites based on it. The resized sprite on the stage is still resized the same way, but it is a different graphic image.

QuickDraw shapes, created with the tools in the Tools window, are also sprites on the stage, but they are not editable in the Paint window, only on the stage itself. QuickDraw shapes are useful as simple graphic objects that can be repeated over many frames. They can be resized, distorted, and styled with ink effects just like sprites derived from bitmap cast members. Text can be typed into a bitmap graphic cast member, or typed onto the stage as QuickDraw text. Each QuickDraw text element is saved as a separate cast member that can be edited in the Text window.

Perhaps the most popular technique of manipulating sprites is simply to arrange them properly so that some sprites are in front of others, providing a three-dimensional effect. The stage is actually a set of layers represented by channels in the score, and the way sprites appear on these layers is controlled by the ink effects.

## Arranging Sprites

When you are arranging sprites on the stage, you have many choices. The first sprite can go into any channel from 1 to 48. Channel 1 is the lowest layer and acts as the ultimate background; channel 48 is the highest layer and acts as the ultimate foreground. Sprites on channels between these two layers can be hidden or revealed by sprites in front of them (in higher-numbered channels). The ink effect chosen for a particular sprite determines whether any sprites on layers underneath are hidden or revealed. The cast member number has no bearing on the arrangement of cast members in the score.

Before dragging a cast member from the Cast window onto the stage, you can select a channel by clicking in a cell in the score to make sure that the cast member is placed on the appropriate layer.

You can select any sprite in the stage area. A regular dotted outline appears around the sprite, offering *handles* for resizing it, as described in the next section. Although you can select any sprite in the stage area, the Score window provides the greatest flexibility in selecting sprites on the stage. You can select any sprite in any channel, even if the sprite is hidden behind another one. Once a sprite is selected, you can move it anywhere on the stage. You can Shift-click another sprite to add it to the selection. Holding down the Shift key while dragging constrains your movement to straight horizontal and vertical directions.

To move one or more sprites precisely, use the Tweak window (Figure 3.71) to move in increments of a single pixel in any direction along the horizontal or vertical axes (x and y). When you click inside the box in the Tweak window, a line appears indicating the direction of the movement, along with the number of pixels. You can also use the arrow keys to move a sprite one pixel at a time.

## Stretching and Squeezing Sprites

An object bouncing off a wall, or floor, may stay the same shape in reality, but in animation, you can exaggerate the impact by temporarily changing its shape. Whenever you need to show exaggerated motion or pressure, such as moving tires on a car or bouncing balls, you can stretch or squeeze the sprites in specific frames without affecting the original cast members.

Selected sprites on the stage show small black squares called handles at the corners and sides of the selection. You can stretch or squeeze an object by dragging on one of these handles (Figure 3.72).

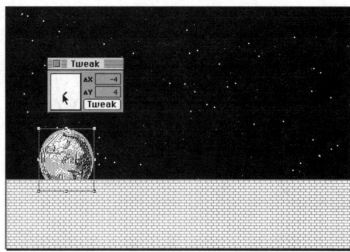

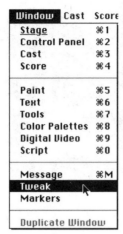

**Figure 3.71
Using the Tweak
window to move
one or more se-
lected sprites on
the stage by a spe-
cific number of
pixels in horizon-
tal and vertical di-
rections.**

With this technique you can distort the shape of an object over a few frames to simulate impact or gravity—or, in the case of the example, a moon sitting on the horizon.

You can make a sprite gradually stretch or squeeze over several frames by setting the first and last frame, and using In-Between Special with the Size parameter. For example, select the sprite in channel 2 in the last frame of the movie *Moon Rise* (filename: MOONRISE.DIR), and drag its handles to distort the shape as described above. Then select the entire range of sprites from frame 1 to the last frame in channel 2, and use the In-Between Special command with the Size parameter (Figure 3.73).

**Figure 3.72
Distorting the
shape of the
moon sprite in
the first frame by
dragging the se-
lection handles
on the stage after
selecting the
sprite.**

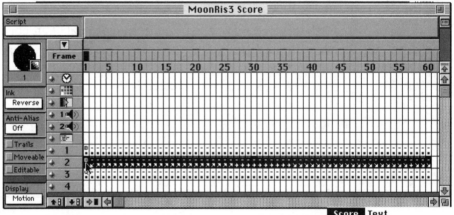

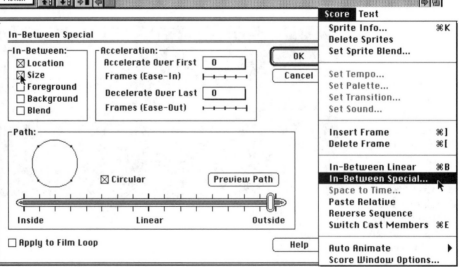

**Figure 3.73**
**After distorting the shape of the moon sprite in the last frame, selecting the range from first to last frame in channel 2, and using In-Between Special with the Size parameter.**

**Figure 3.74 Playing a new version of the *Moon Rise* movie (filename: MOONRIS3.DIR in the TUTORIAL folder/directory), newly 'tweened in size as well as location.**

The command *'tweens* the size as well as the location of the moon sprite (Figure 3.74).

The sprite may animate more slowly if it is a complex shape. Designed for faster animation, use the Auto Transform command in the Paint window, to create individual cast members representing each transitional shape.

Changing the shape of a sprite can help provide the illusion of three-dimensional space (Figure 3.75), with the sprite moving toward or away from you.

You can shrink or expand a sprite proportionately by holding down the Shift key while dragging a corner handle (Figure 3.76).

**Figure 3.75 Squeezing the object to exaggerate the feeling of impact; simply drag the handles of a selected object to stretch or squeeze the object.**

**Figure 3.76 Squeezing an object while holding down Shift to shrink it in proportion, so that it appears to move away from you.**

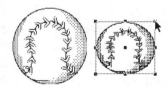

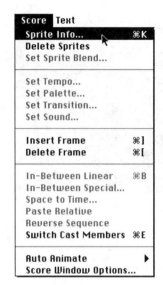

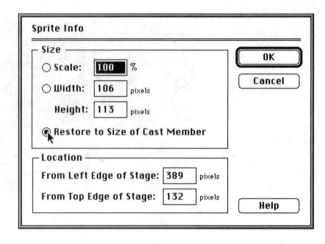

**Figure 3.77
The Sprite Info
dialog box,
which lets you re-
store a sprite to
the original cast
member size.**

You can always return a sprite to its original size by selecting it and choosing Sprite Info in the Score menu (the Score window must be open). This command (Figure 3.77) displays a dialog box with information about the sprite and the option to restore the sprite to the original cast member's size.

## Using Ink Effects and Trails

The ink effect chosen for a particular sprite determines whether any sprites on layers underneath are hidden or revealed. The Copy ink effect is essentially the *standard* ink effect. The image is copied as is to the stage, and the bounding box around the sprite is white. This is fine for sprites that appear against white backgrounds. However, most sprites are composited with backgrounds that are not white.

You have already used Matte and Reverse, which are ink effects that are useful in black and white and color. The Matte ink makes the bounding box transparent around the sprite so that no white shows around the image.

The Reverse ink has a different effect on black-and-white cast members: Reverse simply reverses the black and white. However, on color cast members, the results depend on the colors and the color palette, described in the next chapter.

Another useful ink effect is Bkgnd Transparent (Background Transparent), which does what it says: It makes the background transparent by turning any white pixels to transparent pixels. To see this ink effect, open the movie *SSJLVID* (filename: SSJLVID.DIR) and click the sprite in channel 2, frame 1 (Figure 3.78). The Bkgnd Transparent ink makes it possible to see the black background inside the hole in the letter (which would otherwise be white).

**Figure 3.78**
In the movie
*SSJLVID* by
Stuart Sharpe
(filename:
SSJLVID.DIR in
the TUTORIAL
folder/directory),
the sprite for the
letter "A" is set to
have the Bkgrnd
Transparent ink
effect.

The same movie offers another example of an ink effect. This time, it's the Lightest ink, used for a rectangle QuickDraw sprite to allow the white letter to show through the red fill of the rectangle (Figure 3.79).

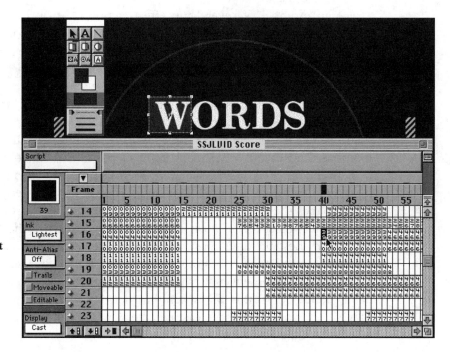

**Figure 3.79**
In the movie
*SSJLVID*, a filled
QuickDraw rec-
tangle sprite is
set to the Lightest
ink effect so that
the white letter
behind the rec-
tangle shows
through the rec-
tangle's red fill.

To create a color image
with a thermal wax printer,
the paper must pass in front
of the thermal head four times.

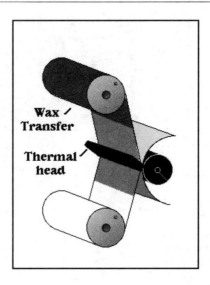

**Figure 3.80**
**The *Visualiza-***
***tion* movie**
**(filename:**
**VISUALIZ.DIR in**
**the TUTORIAL**
**folder/directory)**
**shows how a**
**color thermal**
**printer works.**

It is quite easy to hide one sprite behind another by moving the sprite to a lower-numbered channel so that it is on a layer beneath the other sprite. And with creative use of ink effects, part of the underneath can be revealed.

Another popular ink effect is Ghost, in which any black pixel in the foreground of the sprite is turned to white. Ghost works well in black and white, but has only limited use in color.

For an example of several ink effects working at once, look at the movie *Visualization* (filename: VISUALIZ.DIR). *Visualization* explains showing the thermal print head, how colors are applied to paper (Figure 3.80).

The moving color on the belt is accomplished with a series of sprites placed appropriately in channels (Figure 3.81).

The sprites representing the thermal print head, roller, and paper, are in higher-numbered channels and are set to Bkgnd Transparent or Matte ink effects. The Bkgnd Transparent effect shows whatever is underneath through the white portions. Underneath are parallelogram shapes filled with color (Figure 3.82).

Between these color shapes and the thermal print head image is a ghost image of the thermal print head, which is set to the Ghost ink effect. The underneath color shapes show through only where the ghost image shows white. The black parts of the ghost image do not show, as they are set to the Ghost ink effect. However, they act as a mask to prevent the underlying color shapes from appearing outside the edges of the thermal print head image.

Ink effects stay in effect after you've used them for cells in the Score window. Many people forget this, and when they drag another cast member out onto the stage, they wonder why the cast member looks weird. It may be due to an ink effect set in the Score window, so check there first.

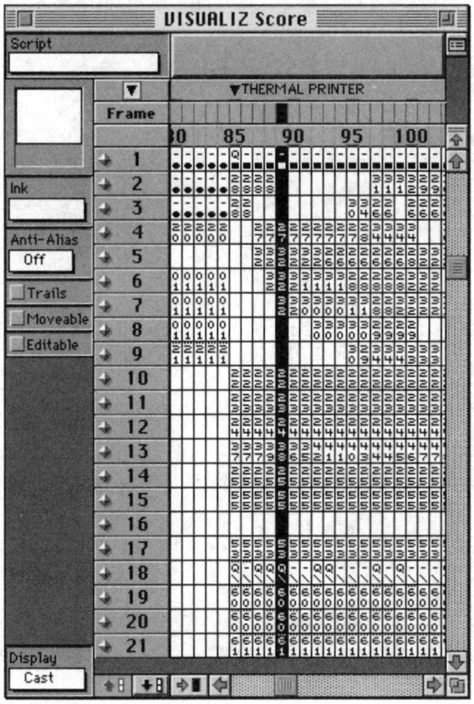

**Figure 3.81**
**The score for a single frame of the thermal print head animation, showing how cast members are arranged in channels.**

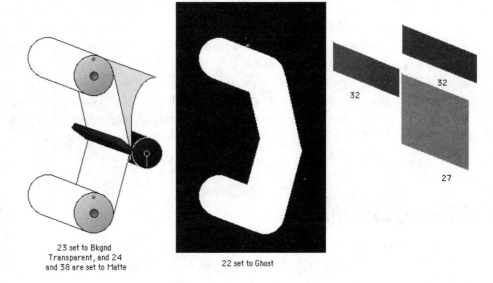

**Figure 3.82**
**The sprites shown apart, with the underneath shapes on the right in lower-numbered channels, and the images on the left in higher-numbered channels, separated by a ghost image acting as a mask.**

23 set to Bkgnd
Transparent, and 24
and 38 are set to Matte

22 set to Ghost

32

32

27

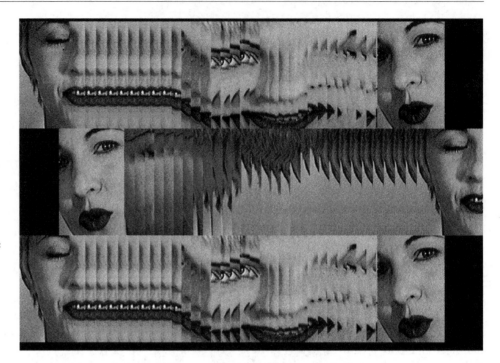

**Figure 3.83
A fragment from
the movie *Undo
Me prototype
(IM4)* by Stuart
Sharpe (filename:
UNDOIM4B.DIR
in the TUTORIAL
folder/directory)
shows how the
Trails effect can
be used effec-
tively.**

Ink effects are also available in the Paint window, and the next chapter provides a summary of all the ink effects, including color effects.

Trails are an exceptional case of an ink effect. The image leaves a *trail* of itself on the stage wherever it goes. You have already used the Trails effect in the example on real-time recording earlier in this chapter. Another excellent example of the use of trails is the movie fragment *UNDOIM4B* [from *Undo Me prototype (IM4)*]. In this example, sprites are set to have the Trails effect (Figure 3.83), and then the Trails effect is turned off so that the sprites can move back over their trails and erase them.

The Trails checkbox is on the left side of the Score window. To activate Trails, click on the Trails checkbox so that a check mark appears. The trailing images remain on the screen until the display changes. You can make the display change by adding a transition (described in the next section), or you can simply overlay another image.

## Understanding Frames

As you probably already know, Director creates animation by displaying frames of still images. Each frame is a representation of a *moment* in time, but it is not a strict representation because the program displays frames only as fast as the computer can process them.

Director is a frame-based animation program, which means that Director plays every frame of a sequence regardless of how much time it takes. By comparison, most digital video movies (such as QuickTime movies) are time-based, which means that some frames in the movie may be skipped in order to keep the duration of the movie accurate.

Since you can use digital video movies inside Director movies, or create time-based digital video movies from Director (by exporting the sequences), you can take advantage of both methods of animation.

Director provides transitions and tempo settings to help you control the display of frames. The transition setting controls how the frame will be introduced when displayed, and the tempo setting controls how fast the frame will be played (the upper limit on animation speed, but not the lower limit). You can also lock the playback speed of your animation so that it plays back at the same speed on faster machines.

## Inserting and Deleting Frames

The Insert Frame and Delete Frame commands in the Score menu give you the ability to add or delete frames. These are commands you will probably use frequently. For instance, say you decide to lengthen a short animation sequence or to insert something into the sequence, you can use the Insert Frame command to insert as many new frames as you need. Or you may need to delete a sequence; the Delete Frame command makes this operation easy (perhaps too easy—be careful!).

For example, we need to insert a new frame at the very beginning of the movie *Car Accelerating* (filename: CARACCEL.DIR), so that we can add a transition in the next section. To add the new frame, open the movie, click in any cell in frame 1, and choose Insert Frame from the Score menu (Figure 3.84).

The newly inserted frame is a duplicate of the frame of the cell you selected; it contains all of the same sprites. This makes it very easy to extend a scene without having to worry about extending each sprite. Eventually you will be accustomed to using Command-right bracket (Command-]) over and over to insert a lot of frames at once.

Deleting a frame is just as easy. Click in any cell in the frame to be deleted, and choose Delete Frame from the Score menu. If you select a range of cells across several frames, Delete Frame deletes only the last frame in the selection.

Another way of adding or deleting frames is to use the Paste Cells or Cut Cells commands in the Edit menu with an insertion point in the frame number. Click an insertion point (Figure 3.85) in the frame number itself, and a blinking line appears between the frames indicating the insertion point.

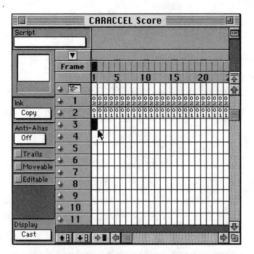

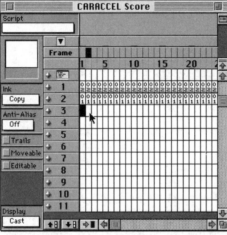

**Figure 3.84
Inserting a new
frame at the be-
ginning of the
*Car Accelerating*
movie (filename:
CARACCEL.DIR
in the TUTORIAL
folder/directory)
by clicking in a
cell in the first
frame and using
Insert Frame.**

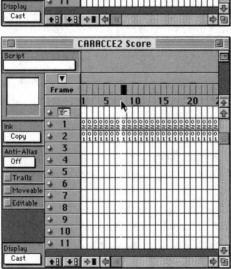

**Figure 3.85
Clicking an inser-
tion point in the
frame numbers
to insert or de-
lete frames.**

Just remember, if you don't see the blinking line, Cut and Paste will overwrite rather than Insert or Delete. If you select a cell before using Paste Cells, the paste operation overwrites the existing cell information rather than inserting new frames. The same is true for Cut Cells. If you select a cell before using Cut Cells, the cut operation does not remove the frames but only empties them.

## Adding Transitions

Transitions are easy to add to the score. A channel is reserved for them on a frame-by-frame basis. Transitions are most often used when a sprite makes its first appearance on the stage, and at the beginning of a movie. They are not necessary; some animators prefer to use a range of frames to define a very specific transition between sequences but the built-in Director transitions can often be convenient.

> **Note:** Professional animators recording individual frames of a Director movie to tape rarely use the built-in transitions.

Transitions can, of course, be used over the entire stage, but some of them can also be defined to affect only the changing area of the stage (leaving the stationary sprites alone). When a sprite makes its first appearance, the right type of transition effect can make the appearance dramatic, smooth, or subtle. Automatic transitions are often used to introduce a new sprite, and some transition effects can make it appear that the sprite by itself undergoes the transition while the background remains essentially unchanged.

For example, in a new version of the movie *Car Accelerating* (filename: CARACCE2.DIR), which has the additional frame inserted as described in the previous section, you can introduce the car sprite with a transition. First, delete the cell in frame 1, channel 2 (Figure 3.86) to remove the car from the first frame and prepare for the transition. The movie will henceforth start out without the car, but after a transition, the car will appear in frame 2.

Now, scroll the Score window using the Jump to Top button (Figure 3.87) or the vertical scroll arrows or scroll bar, so that the Transition channel is visible.

Double-click the cell in the Transition channel in frame 2, or single-click that cell and choose Set Transition in the Score menu, to get the Set Transition dialog box (Figure 3.88). In this dialog box, you can scroll the list of transitions and select one, then change the options.

For this example, the transition should apply, only, to the changing area However, you can leave the duration (set to 8 in $\frac{1}{4}$ second, which translates to 2 seconds) and the chunk size (set to 16, somewhere in between smooth and

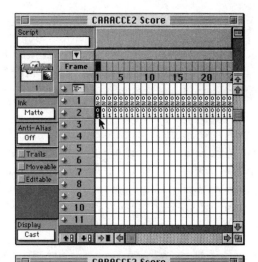

**Figure 3.86**
Clearing out the cell in channel 2, frame 1 (removing the car sprite from the first frame), to make ready for the transition.

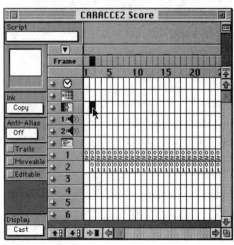

**Figure 3.87**
Double-clicking in frame 2 of the Transition channel (the frame in which the car sprite first appears).

**Figure 3.88**
**The Set Transi-**
**tion dialog box,**
**where you can**
**choose a transi-**
**tion and set it to**
**work only on the**
**changing area of**
**the stage.**

rough, but closer to smooth). The result is the use of the Cover Right transition that introduces the car from the right (Figure 3.89).

The reason why you put the transition in frame 2 rather than frame 1 is that the transition occurs when the playback head first reaches that frame. The playback head always starts from frame 1 to frame 2.

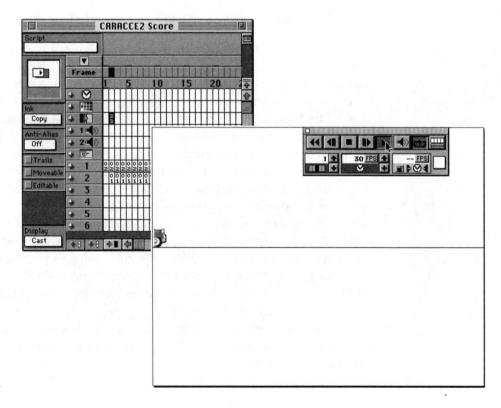

**Figure 3.89**
**The resulting**
**transition intro-**
**duces the car**
**sprite from the**
**right (the Cover**
**Right transition).**

> ***Future Tip:*** Serious movie developers will want to experiment with these
> settings while running movies on different computers to check performance
> differences. Read the section on synchronizing animation later on in this
> book. Also, some transitions are not appropriate for cross-platform devel-
> opment.

Director provides more than 50 transitions ranging from wipes and dissolves
to Venetian blinds. Most transitions can be grouped into the following categories:

- **Wipe**: A wipe drags the next frame on top of the current frame, completely
  covering the current frame (only the next frame moves).

- **Reveal**: A reveal moves the current frame to reveal the next frame behind
  it (only the current frame moves).

- **Push**: The next frame pushes the current frame off the screen (both frames
  move).

- **Strip**: The next frame appears as the current frame is taken away in strips.

- **Cover**: The next frame moves into place on top of the current frame.

- **Dissolve**: The current frame dissolves and the next frame gradually appears.

There are more transitions, such as Center, Edges In, Zoom Open or Close,
Venetian Blinds, Vertical Blinds, and Checkerboard, that comprise their own
category of *special* transitions. There are too many transitions to show examples
of every one, and it is easy to see how transitions work by experimenting with
them. The best way to see how a transition works is to place one between a
mostly white frame with black lines (or a text frame) and a mostly black frame.

The Chunk Size setting determines the number of pixels in each *chunk* of the
image that changes in a transition; thus, the greater the chunk size, the rougher
the transition. In all transitions, the Chunk Size is preset to default to the optimum
value, and you don't have to change it unless you want to (in some transitions
it is fixed and can't be changed, such as in Dissolve, Pixels Fast).

The Duration setting determines how long the transition should take, usually
in quarters of a second. You can change this setting as you want, although in all
transitions the duration is preset to an optimum value. In a few transitions, such
as Dissolve, Bits Fast and Dissolve, Pixels Fast, the duration can't be changed.

People often confuse transitions as needing to occur before a frame. Not so.
The transition occurs for the same frame in which it is placed. It occurs before
the frame itself displays. Director keeps track of transition stages as microframes,
and these microframes display before the main frame (no pun intended).

To change the characteristics of a transition already set in the score, simply select the cell, or cells, containing the transition in the Transition channel, and choose Set Transitions from the Score menu.

## Adjusting Tempo

The Tempo channel lets you change the tempo for one or more frames, and provides a more precise control over the timing of animation.

Tempo settings do not control the way transitions, sounds, or movie windows play the tempo settings. They merely control how fast Director will play the frame (and subsequent frames) until another tempo setting is encountered. Think of the tempo setting as the speed that Director is trying to achieve. A Director movie may run slower on a slower machine, but it will not run faster than the tempo setting. Remember also that moving large images around the screen, or using blends, can significantly slow things down no matter what your tempo setting is.

The tempo indicator in the Control Panel displays the tempo setting of the current frame. Although you can change the tempo in the Control Panel, this is for convenience in testing only. If you want to set the tempo of a movie, you should set it in the first frame (Figure 3.90). The tempo remains at that speed until you change it.

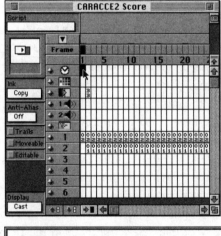

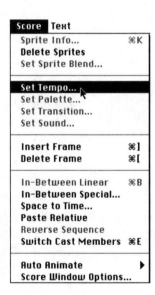

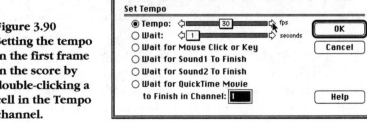

**Figure 3.90**
**Setting the tempo in the first frame in the score by double-clicking a cell in the Tempo channel.**

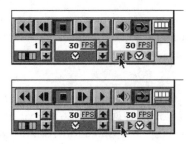

**Figure 3.91**
**The lock button**
**in the Control**
**Panel can be**
**used to lock the**
**animation to a**
**certain speed.**

The Tempo dialog box offers different types of control over time.You can set a delay of a few seconds, or a wait for a mouse click or key press. A wait for mouse click or key press is a useful way to set up a movie for a live presentation. You can also set the tempo to wait for sounds and digital video movies to finish. These options are described in Chapter 7 and 8.

## Locking Animation Speed

When designing movies that will run on different computers, you may want to confine the animation speed within a parameter, so that the movie looks the same on all these machines. To do this, however, you must slow the animation down to run on the slowest possible machine.

The Control Panel lets you lock the animation speed to the actual rate of the animation as it plays on a specific machine. The Control Panel can be used to estimate how long the movie takes to play (Figure 3.91). The Lock button can be used to lock the movie's speed. You can also use Lock Frame Durations command in the Edit menu.

However, if you want the movie to remain locked, you must relock it after making editing changes. There is no getting around the final step of locking the movie after all changes are made.

The Control Panel's actual duration indicator shows the actual duration of the movie, estimated from the playing of the previous frame (while a movie is running). The actual indicator has a Mode button, which offers FPS and SPF (just like the tempo indicator mode), but also offers the Est and Sum options. Sum displays a quick summary of elapsed seconds from the beginning of the movie to the current frame, while Est is a more accurate calculation (but slower to calculate) of elapsed time. Note that leaving the actual indicator in Est mode can reduce the playback speed due to the calculations, so you should change it to another mode.

To lock the animation speed, first rewind the movie to the first frame, turn off Looping in the Control Panel or Edit menu. If you've written any Lingo scripts, turn on the Disable Lingo option in the Edit menu, so the scripts are not in control.

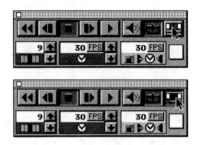

**Figure 3.92
The Selected
Frames Only but-
ton on the Con-
trol Panel lets
you play only the
selected frames
in the Score win-
dow. You can
then click the
lock button to
lock only the se-
lected frames
rather than the
entire movie.**

Play the movie through once. At the end, click the Lock button, or choose Lock Frame Durations from the Edit menu.

Either way, the lock icon appears in the Control Panel indicating that the movie is locked. At this point, the movie runs at the same speed on the same computer or player and on all faster computers and players; however, it will run slower on slower computers and players. The movie remains locked until you make any editing or tempo changes, although you can turn off the Disable Lingo option in the Edit menu without affecting the lock.

Locking the animation speed in this manner is more accurate than adjusting the Tempo channel yourself on a frame-by-frame basis. This is because transitions occur at different speeds on different machines. Even though you can set the tempo for the transition, the same rules apply: a high setting causes Director to try to achieve the tempo, and a low setting is usually too slow. The answer is to run the movie (with its transitions set to whatever makes sense) on the slowest possible machine, and then lock it.

The reason why you must disable Lingo scripts while locking is because Director can't measure the time if scripts are controlling the animation. When you play back the movie, the animated sequences should be locked, but your scripts can be put back into control.

You can also lock portions of a movie without having to lock the entire movie. First, clear all locks previously set by holding down the Option key while clicking the Lock button or choosing Lock Frame Durations from the Edit menu.

At this point, the Actual time display shows two dashes. Select the frames to lock, and click the Selected Frames Only button in the Control Panel (Figure 3.92). Click the Play button to the play the selected frames (this sets the actual duration). Then click the Lock button or choose Lock Frame Durations from the Edit menu.

Another way to lock a movie is to export sequences requiring rigid synchronization as digital video movies in formats such as QuickTime, which is automatically synchronized. You can then import the digital video movie and use it in another Director movie while retaining synchronicity. That technique is described with digital video in Chapter 8.

## *Chapter Summary*

In this chapter, you learned all about the standard animation methods in Director, including how to:

- Create cast members.
- Perform real-time recording.
- Use step recording of animation.
- Use the in-between features.

You were also introduced to quick animation techniques such as In-Between Linear, Cast to Time, and Space to Time. You learned how to switch cast members for sprites, use Copy and Paste Cells, and use In-Between Special for controlling the acceleration, deceleration, and path of an animation curve.

This chapter also introduced the concepts of sprite and frames. You learned about arranging sprites, stretching and squeezing sprites, and using ink effects and trails. You also learned how to insert and delete frames, add transitions, adjust the tempo, and lock the animation speed.

Most of the examples are in black and white, so that anyone with a monochrome (black-and-white) screen can follow along and learn simple animation methods in Director. The next chapter shows how to use Director's painting and drawing tools and graphic effects, including color, to create visually appealing artwork for animation.

# 4

# *Painting Techniques*

**Computers are useless. They can only give you answers.**

Pablo Picasso

**N**early all multimedia projects begin with graphics. As you have seen in the previous chapters, you do not need graphics skill to put together an effective presentation, but it sure helps. You can acquire graphics from many third-party sources, but sooner or later you will probably need to create something unique for your presentations and multimedia projects.

Painting and drawing tools for the Macintosh are invaluable for bringing out the creative side of individuals who have never drawn or painted before. You can work with scanned artwork (as long as you acquire the copyrights) and create collages with little or no drawing or painting skill. An abundance of digital clip art—artwork you can use without obtaining permission—is available for use with desktop media applications. Macromedia provides sample clip art with Director, and volumes of clip art on floppy disks and CD-ROMs are available, including those collections represented on the CD-ROM accompanying this book.

With a little practice you can learn how to manipulate and change clip art into custom artwork using Director's painting and drawing tools. You can also learn how to paint and draw original artwork and to change copies of artwork to create different cast members.

This chapter introduces Director's Paint window and painting and drawing tools. It also explains how you can use other painting and drawing programs to create art for Director documents. By the end of this chapter you will know how to create and edit graphics for special effects in Director.

## Learning About Graphics

A dramatic saving in time and cost comes with the ability to create graphics in electronic form and use them in other projects by copying the digital information.

You can scale digital graphics in equal or unequal proportions, rotate and skew them across an axis, and transform them by a variety of special effects. You can use pieces of one image to create a new one. In fact, you can use almost anything from the outside world: sketches, hand drawings, photographs, etc. by simply converting it to electronic form with a scanner.

The extensive painting and graphics transformation tools in Director can create several cast members to form a sequence of frames for animation. Some artists prefer to work entirely within Director. Others prefer to use other painting and drawing programs. Director for Macintosh can paste graphics copied through the Clipboard from other programs. Director can also import a variety of graphics file formats. The Macintosh version can import PICT and MacPaint files directly into the Cast window. Director for Windows can import the following graphics file formats: .BMP (Windows bitmaps), .WMF (Windows metafiles), .PNT (MacPaint files), .PCT (Macintosh PICT files), .TIF (TIFF files), .EPS (Encapsulated PostScript files), .PCX (PC Paintbrush files), .PCD (Photo CD files), and.GIF (GIF files).

Painting and drawing programs are popular for freestyle painting and artwork because the programs are easy to learn and very flexible, and digital graphics can be copied and altered to fit any shape or context. These programs also are used by commercial artists, designers, architects, and engineers because they offer greater precision than hand tools, perfect geometric shapes, and graphic objects that can be moved, transformed, cloned, and grouped with other objects. Rotating elements of a drawing or painting and creating mirror-image graphics is easy to do. Skewed shadow versions of graphic objects add a touch of realism. You can retouch and prepare photorealistic gray and color images for use in Director documents.

## Painting and Drawing

There are two kinds of graphic images: *paint-type* (also called *bitmap* graphics) and *draw-type* (also called *object-oriented* graphics). Each is created and manipulated in a different way.

Paint-type bitmap images are created from individual dots that correspond to screen pixels. You use painting tools to create them; such tools give you the power to directly change individual pixels or groups of pixels. Painting tools typically include:

- An electronic pencil for painting single-pixel lines.

- Different types of brushes for painting wider strokes.

- An Airbrush tool for simulating an airbrushed effect with pixels.

- A selection tool for selecting a group of pixels.

- An eraser tool for deleting pixels from the image.

On the other hand, object-oriented graphics, rather than consisting of arranged pixels, are created with a series of drawing commands in a graphics language (although as a user, you never see the language). Drawing tools create geometric shapes, straight lines, and curves. The images or pieces of images you draw with these tools are referred to as "objects" when you create and manipulate them. The commands are issued by the program when you use a drawing tool, such as a straight-line tool, a rectangle tool, an oval tool, and so on. The commands tell the computer where to place the pixels to display the image. The language used to describe drawn objects is, in most Macintosh programs, the QuickDraw language, and in a few other programs, the PostScript language (a standard for printing and publishing applications). Windows drawing and painting programs also use the PostScript language. In addition, Windows programs can use the PC Paintbrush (.PCX) bitmap format, TIFF bitmap format, Graphics Interchange Format (.GIF, bitmap file format created by CompuServe), Windows bitmap format (.BMP), and the Microsoft Windows metafile format (.WMF), which contains both bitmap and object-oriented (aka vector) image data. The Windows version of Director can also import Macintosh MacPaint (bitmap) and PICT (QuickDraw) files.

As a Director user, you need to know the difference between painted bitmap images and drawn objects because you can animate bitmap images faster than drawn objects. Director lets you create or import both types of graphics, and you can use Director to convert a drawn object into a bitmap image to make it animate faster. Director offers a full set of painting tools in the Paint window to create bitmap graphics; there is a set of drawing tools in the Tools window (including a text tool) to create drawn graphics. Bitmap graphics are limited in resolution to the display you are using. Drawn objects usually are not limited to the resolution of the screen. They may look a certain way on-screen, but they invariably look better when printed with a higher resolution laser printer. However, if the primary medium is the screen or videotape, bitmap graphics are invariably easier to work with and provide the greatest flexibility.

Another major difference between bitmap graphics and drawn graphics is how they can be manipulated with tools. Drawn graphics are usually made up of distinct objects you can edit and move separately. A bitmap graphic image is generally made up of a single layer of pixels—the "objects" in the graphic cannot be manipulated independently. (However, a new generation of bitmap programs featuring independent layers, including Fractal Design Painter X2, Specular Collage, and Adobe Photoshop 3.0, have now come to market.) The advantage of bitmap programs is that they give you direct control over each pixel, including the ability to colorize each one.

You can place pieces of a bitmap image on the stage as individual cast members, and move each one around as an object that is distinct and separate from other objects on the stage. This is because Director treats each cast member (painted or drawn) as a separate layer on the stage.

One major reason for using bitmap images is faster animation (due to the fixed resolution), and the ability to create special effects easily and to colorize pixels individually. High-resolution (greater than screen resolution) images, as well as drawn QuickDraw or PostScript objects, have to be transformed into the screen resolution in order to be displayed, and this extra computation can slow down animation.

You can make Bitmap images with a scanner, which breaks down an image into a set of dots with corresponding gray or color values. Such images are at the scanner's resolution setting. However, this setting may be much higher than the screen resolution (such as 200 or 300 dots per inch, compared to 72 or 75 for the display). As we will describe later in this chapter, you can scan images at a higher resolution for publishing and photographic slide-making, but reduce them to either 72 or 75 dpi for use in Director. Scanned images stored in high-resolution format (such as 300 dpi) use more disk space and are usually only necessary for printing. So you can save disk space, if you intend to use the images only for animation or video, by reducing the resolution to 72 or 75 dpi (sometimes called "down-sampling" the image).

## Using Text

When creating animation, you should consider text as a highly intricate form of graphics, since there are so many graphical effects to use with textual characters. For example, you can create text with three-dimensional block letters and shadows, with gradually changing patterns, gray shades, or colors on the letters. You might want titles to gleam, or throb with pulsating light, or flicker with sparkles.

When creating text to use in animated sequences, you have greater control over graphical effects by creating the text as bitmap graphics in the Paint window. The animation moves faster, and you can style the text in any font and then save it as a painted image. This way you no longer need the font information stored in the system. You can create drop shadows with text, rotate text to any angle, and use textual characters as part of patterns, as well as create gradually shaded characters (called *gradients* and described later in this chapter). To change painted text, however, you have to change the individual pixels or simply erase the text and type it again.

Sometimes it makes sense to create the text with the text tool in the Tools window, or directly in the Text window. Then you can edit it whenever you wish, even after you create the animated sequences. Text created with the text tool in the Tools window or in the Text window becomes a cast member in the Cast window.

In addition, text created with the Tools window's text tool or in the Text window stays in a resolution-independent (Macintosh QuickDraw) format, which is useful when printing the individual scenes on a printer. Nevertheless, you have less control over special effects, and animation with drawn text may run slower than painted text. In addition, the font information for the chosen font must exist in the System folder, either as a screen font in the System, or an Adobe font (when using Adobe Type Manager).

Text effects created with the Auto Animate command (Score menu) are bitmap graphics. For most graphical applications of text, bitmap text offers the most flexibility and the fastest performance with animation. For applications in which text is used in a simple, nongraphical way, text cast members are usually more flexible because you can edit them quickly without affecting their positions on the stage.

## Using Colors and Grays

Resolution is not the same thing as color depth, which is the number of different colors or gray shades you can assign to each pixel. The realism you can achieve is limited by painting or drawing in black and white. However, you can create images with enough gray shades or colors to make them look as good as or better than video.

The standard 8-bit color graphics circuitry (built into some machines or provided on a separate card in other models), can display 256 colors or different shades of gray, including black, for each pixel. This is because 8 bits can hold 256 different combinations.

The vast majority of personal computers have color screens that use an 8-bit color card (or built-in circuitry) and a 13-inch or 14-inch color display. Most presentations are designed for this type, or for 9-inch displays. QuickTime movies are often designed for even smaller windows, and Director provides an automatic setting for the standard QuickTime window for software-only playback.

Color images created in Director can have as many as 24 bits (16.7 million possible colors) or as few as 4 bits (16 possible colors) of color information per pixel. Gray images can have as few as 1 bit (black and white) or as many as 8 bits of gray information (256 shades) per pixel. However, real-time playback of animation is impractical with 24-bit and 32-bit images. These images are best for backgrounds, linked to the original file rather than imported into Director. Most machines can play back 8-bit color images, and animation in real time is much smoother with 8-bit and 4-bit images.

The Macintosh models that are capable of supporting display cards can display up to 32 bits of color information per pixel. In practice, 24 bits are used for color information (providing 16.7 million different colors per pixel), and the extra 8 bits are reserved for special effects. Continuous tone color images scanned at full

24-bit color depth look like photographs on screen, and 24-bit graphics are often used as overlays on video or as photorealistic animations for videotape. Director supports the recording frame by frame of 24-bit images to videotape, as described in Chapter 7, for extremely realistic animation.

No matter what color depth your hardware is set to, Apple's System (with its 32-bit QuickDraw module) is capable of assigning any of its 16.7 million possible colors to an image. Thus, with an 8-bit display card, the 256 colors you can assign to an image can consist of any 256 of the possible 16.7 million colors available. The System uses a color palette to determine which colors to use. It is therefore possible to display a photorealistic 8-bit image if you (or the System) choose the appropriate colors for the palette. You can use Director to convert a 24-bit image into an 8-bit image, and you can define and use custom palettes to display 8-bit and 4-bit images.

To handle 8-bit gray and color images, you need:

- At least 40 (and possibly 80) megabytes of hard disk space.

- A grayscale or color desktop scanner that can scan up to 256 levels of gray or color (to bring in photographic material or outside drawings).

- At least 5 megabytes of RAM for Macintosh computers (preferably more), and 8 megabytes of RAM for Windows computers (preferably more).

The extra disk space and RAM are necessary because 8-bit gray and color images take up far more disk space than 1-bit black-and-white images. Twenty-four-bit color images take up far more disk space and RAM than 8-bit images—approximately three times more space. A 32-bit image that uses all 16.7 million possible colors would require approximately 67 megabytes of RAM to display all the colors simultaneously.

SuperVGA-equipped PCs can display at least 8 bits of color information per pixel (depending on which display mode the PC is set to). Although Director supports 24-bit and 32-bit cast members (the images are not changed), on Windows systems these cast members are displayed using the closest-matching 256 colors in the currently active palette. VGA display–equipped PCs can display only 4 bits of color information per pixel. On VGA display–equipped Windows machines, 24-bit and 32-bit cast members are displayed using the closest-matching 16 colors in the currently active palette.

Bitmap graphic images are created in the Paint window, which you access by choosing Paint from the Window menu, or by typing Command-5. Images from other programs can be imported into the Cast window and the Score. You can access the Paint window to edit a particular cast member by double-clicking the cast member in the Cast window.

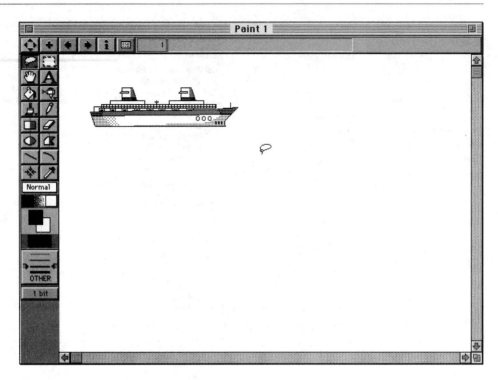

**Figure 4.1**
**The Paint**
**window.**

## Using the Paint Window

The Paint window (Figure 4.1) provides access to Director's entire paintbox of tools and an electronic easel and white background for your painting. Along the left side are icons representing tools and line styles, and pop-up menus for tool options, patterns, and colors. You can zoom into a magnified view of the artwork you are creating, or importing, by selecting the Zoom In command (or typing Command-plus or Command-=), or zoom out again with the Zoom Out command (Command-hyphen, Command-minus, or Command-underscore).

The area in the Paint window in which you can paint new artwork or view already painted artwork is called the drawing area or easel. The easel has scroll bars on the right and bottom sides so that you can scroll across or down a large image. You can also drag with the hand tool to scroll the image in any direction within the easel.

On a black-and-white display (or a display set to black and white in the Monitors Control Panel), the easel is set automatically to a color depth of 1 bit per pixel. On a color display the color depth is set to 8-bits per pixel. You can change the color depth of selected cast members with the Color Depth setting in the Transform Bitmap dialog box. The color depth is displayed when you select the Transform Bitmap command from the Cast menu, and when you double-click the Color Resolution Indicator (Figure 4.1). You can paint in color

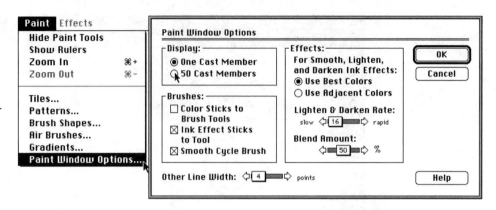

**Figure 4.2**
**Selecting the Display 50 Cast Members option in the Paint Window Options dialog box available from the Paint menu.**

or shades of gray only if the color depth is greater than 1, which is the setting for black and white. Setting the color depth to 1 for a color image is a simple way of changing color images to black and white images.

You can color black-and-white images with the foreground or background color pop-up menus in the Tools window. However, you can't color black-and-white images in the Paint window: You color them by selecting them in the score, and use the Tools window color pop-up palette choices for foreground and background colors. The cast member will still be black and white, but it appears as a colored sprite on the stage.

When you first use Director, the Paint window is set to display one easel the size of the entire window. With this single-easel display you can see only one cast member at a time. If you want to paint a cast member while simultaneously looking at another cast member, you can choose to display multiple easels. Select the Paint Window Options command from the Paint menu, and select the Display 50 Cast Members option instead of the One Cast Member option (Figure 4.2).

With the 50 Cast Members option, the Paint window can display up to 50 cast members simultaneously, each in a different easel (Figure 4.3). The currently active easel displays with a thicker border than the other easels. You can drag its title bar and move the active easel around the Paint window to view easels underneath; resize an easel by dragging the handle in the lower right corner of the easel's frame.

To see images blocked by a larger image, use the previous and next cast member buttons above the drawing area to scroll through all of the cast members. Even if you have hundreds of cast members, in your movie you may display them 50 at a time.

You can still Copy and Paste from one easel to another. However, by viewing many easels at once, you can create a sequence of the same image with minor alterations, such as a perspective change, or a rotation. Then use the sequence to create animation.

**Figure 4.3**
**With the Display 50 Cast Members option on, the Paint window displays all of the cast member easels (50 at a time). You can move them around inside the window and resize them as needed.**

The Paint window previews animation, creates original art, and edits imported art. To see how this works, first switch back to single-easel viewing by selecting Paint Window Options again from the Paint menu, and clicking the One Cast Member option. Next, open the document *THEN GO* (Figure 4.4).

Click in or open the Cast window of the document, and show two rows.

**Figure 4.4**
**The Cast window of *THEN GO* by Stuart Sharpe (filename: THENGO.DIR) showing the first two rows, which contain cast members for the image of a swirling word (THEN).**

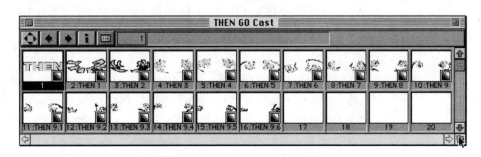

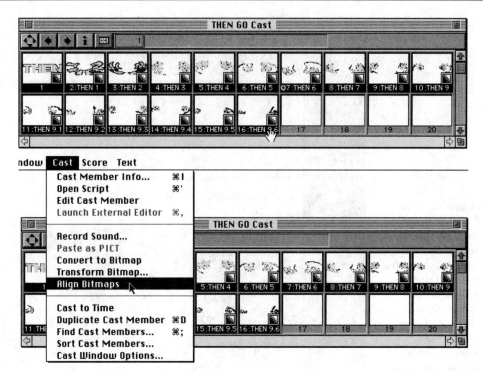

**Figure 4.5**
**Shift-selecting all**
**the cast members**
**for the movie,**
**and using the**
**Align Cast option**
**in the Cast menu.**

Select cast member 1, and hold down the Shift key and select cast member 16, so that you select all of the intervening cast members (Figure 4.5). Then choose the Align Bitmaps Command in the Cast menu.

This option places the selected cast members in alignment with each other in the Paint window according to their registration points, so that you can preview the animation by flipping through the cast member images.

Open the Paint window to see the first cast member (1), and select the Registration tool, which is the snowflake-looking icon in the lower left corner of the tool box. This tool displays the registration point as a crosshair on the Paint window easel (Figure 4.6). The registration point aligns a series of cast members so when they appear on the stage in succession, they are aligned to this point. Director automatically defines a registration point in the center of each cast member you create or import in the Paint window. You will learn how to set and change registration points later.

Next, click the right arrow to advance to the next cast member. Hold down the mouse on this button in order to quickly flip through cast members. You can see that the selected cast members align to a registration point that does not move.

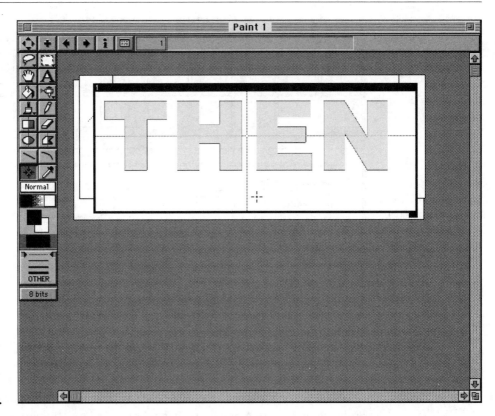

**Figure 4.6
Displaying the
registration
point for the first
cast member in
the Paint window.**

You can click another tool, such as the selection Lasso or Rectangle at the top of the tool box, to flip through the cast members without seeing the registration point.

The Paint window is where you create most of your artwork and edit imported artwork. All of the artwork created in the Paint window, including text typed with the A tool in the Paint window, is saved as a bitmap cast member. You can paint or draw any shape in the Paint window, and the image automatically becomes a bitmap cast member. Each created or imported cast member can be a separate bitmap image on the stage.

After typing text with the A tool in Paint window, the text becomes part of the image once it is deselected, and can't be edited or styled again without erasing it and then retyping. You can only drag to reposition it in the Paint window, or change the font, size or style, immediately after you type it, while it is still selected. Drag inside the text box to move the text. Once you click outside the text box, the text is deselected. To create text that you can edit later, use the Text tool in the Tool menu.

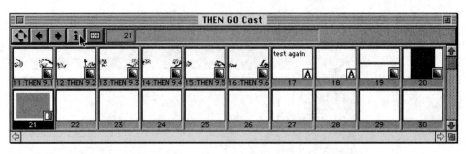

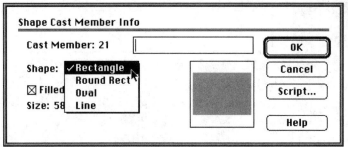

**Figure 4.7**
**Using the Info button in the cast window displays the Shape Cast Member Info dialog box, where you can access the Shape pop-up menu.**

## Using the Tools Window

The Tools window contains tools for creating text and for drawing shapes instead of bitmaps. You can type text, draw lines, rectangles, rounded rectangles, and ovals; the shapes can be with or without patterns inside them.

When printed, these drawn graphics appear smoother than bitmap graphics, and take up less memory. However, when animated, bitmap graphics move faster and more smoothly than drawn graphics.

One benefit of using drawn shapes is that they store in the cast as algorithms rather than as bitmaps, so they occupy less memory. Selected shape cast members can be further refined without having to change the animation or the Score. Use the Info button in the cast window to access the Shape pop-up menu in the Shape Cast Member Info dialog box (Figure 4.7). You can also select the cast member in the cast window, then either the Cast Member Info Command (Command-I) or the Edit Cast Member Command from the Cast menu, and use the Shape pop-up menu.

Since shapes can be resized easily by dragging a corner, the Tools window is quite useful for creating a rectangle, line, or oval for the stage background. You can also draw a line or shape that changes size from frame to frame.

The Text window and Tools window are also useful for typing text you can manipulate as a separate object and edit later as text rather than a bitmap image. Unlike graphics created by tools in the Tool Window, text elements made by the Text tool are stored as cast members, and can be converted to bitmaps using the Convert to Bitmap Command.

The Tools window offers basic drawing facilities, but you can use tools in the Paint window to draw the same types of shapes. The difference between them is that with the Paint window, drawings become bitmaps that move faster. However, they occupy more disk space and can have ink effects applied. Shapes drawn from tools, in the Tools window, store as shapes in the cast window. You can quickly edit them on the stage by dragging handles after you select the object. They do not appear in the Paint window, and you can't use Paint Window tools to change them.

# The Paint Window

Director offers painting tools that will be familiar to you if you have used other Macintosh or Windows painting programs, such as MacPaint, SuperPaint, or PC PaintBrush. You can use Director for any type of painting or drawing.

The controls for the Paint window are in boxes along the top and left side of the Window (Figure 4.1). At the top are the cast member buttons (Place, Add, Previous, Next, Info, Script), a box with the cast member number, and a box with the cast member name. Press and drag the Place button to drag a selected cast member to the cast window, to the stage or to the score. Click the Add button (or type Command-Shift-A) to create a new cast member to insert in the cast window. Choose Previous (or Command-Shift-Left arrow) and Next (or Command-Shift-Right arrow) to switch cast member easels. Click the Cast Info button (or Command-I) to display the Cast Member Info Dialog box for a selected cast member. Click the Script button (or Command-') to open a new script window, or the script window for a selected cast member. (If you select more than one cast member, the script window for the first of the selected cast members opens.)

**Painting Tools**

Below the cast member buttons is the boxed set of painting tools, also called the Paint tool palette.

In the first row of painting tools, Director offers the lasso and rectangle selection tools used for selecting an area of the graphic image. Dragging in the easel with these tools can shrink, or tighten, the selection around a regular shaped or an irregularly shaped object (tracing the edges). Use the Option, Shift, or Command keys in combination with these tools to constrain a selection. (On Windows PCs, substitute the Control key for the Command key, and the Alt key for the Option key.)

Press the Option key while dragging the lasso tool to draw a straight line parallel with the edge of an object. Option-click the lasso to anchor a point and draw another line, repeat as necessary; double-click to end the selection. Drag the selection to a new location, or drag only a copy.

If you press and hold down the Option key before you start dragging a selected object with the lasso, you drag a copy of the selection, and the original remains where it was. You must press the Option key before you start to drag the object, not after. Click the mouse immediately and select Undo (Edit menu) if you need to start again. Drag the selection (as you hold down the Option key), then click the mouse when you have dragged a copy of the object to its new location. If you continue to hold down the Option key, you can drag another copy of the object to a third location, etc., clicking whenever you wish to place a copy of the object.

You can further constrain the movement of objects selected with the lasso by using the Shift key to constrain movement to either a vertical or horizontal direction. First, depress and hold down the Shift key, and then drag the selection. If you drag the selection up or down while holding down the Shift key, you constrain the object to vertical movement only. Holding down the Shift key and dragging left or right constrains the object to horizontal movement.

Additionally, if you click and hold down the mouse button when you select the lasso tool from the paint tool box, the lasso pop-up options menu displays. The lasso tool options are Shrink, No Shrink, and See Thru. Shrink, the default option, causes the lasso to tighten around the selected object, unless the selection contains more than one color. When a selection contains more than one color, all portions of the selection the same color as the first pixel, are excluded from the selection when you pick the Shrink option. To choose everything inside a selection, use the No Shrink option. The See Thru option makes the selection transparent (so that objects behind the selected object show through), like applying the Transparent ink effect (see ink effects described later in this section).

Like the lasso tool, the selection rectangle tool has a pop-up options menu. Shrink, the default option, causes the selection rectangle to tighten around the selected object. To select everything inside a selection rectangle, use the No Shrink option. You can choose the Lasso option for the selection rectangle, after first using the Shrink or No Shrink option. The Lasso option then tightens around the selection, like the lasso tool. It is also color-sensitive and will exclude the color of the first colored pixel at the center of the crosshair. The See Thru Lasso option tightens the selection and makes the selection transparent, like the lasso tool's See Thru option.

To select the whole Paint window, or all of the pieces of the active cast member, when the Paint window is set to the 50 Cast Members option, double-click the selection rectangle tool.

Use the Option, Shift, or Command keys in combination with the selection rectangle tool to constrain a selection. (Note to Windows users: Substitute the Alt key for the Option key, and the Control key for the Command key, in these instructions.) If you hold down the Option key before dragging with the selection rectangle tool, you can move a copy of the selection leaving the original untouched. Click to place the copy, then continue to hold down the Option key to move another copy, click to place it, etc. Pressing the Shift key before starting to drag a selection with the selection rectangle tool constrains the selection to either horizontal or vertical movement. To cut (clear) a selection, made with the selection rectangle tool, press the Delete or Backspace key.

Using the Command key combinations with the selection rectangle tool allows stretching and copying of a selection.

- Press Command to stretch the selection when you drag.

- Press Command-Shift and drag to stretch the selection proportionally.

- Press Command-Option and drag to copy and stretch the selection simultaneously.

 In the second row, you will find the hand tool to scroll the image in the Paint window, and the "A" text tool for adding text to the bitmap image (the text remains in bitmap form suitable for on-screen display). The hand tool can be used temporarily while using any other tool (except the text tool) by pressing the spacebar key. This is a convenient method for quickly seeing hidden parts of a large image. The image does not change its position on the stage, but your position in the window relative to the artwork changes when you use the hand tool.

Text can be typed, selected, colored, and styled using the text "A" tool in the Paint window. However, it becomes part of the image once it is deselected, and can't be edited or styled again without erasing it and then retyping. You can only drag to reposition it in the Paint window, or change the font, size, or style immediately after you type it, while it is still selected. Drag inside the text box to move the text. Once you click outside the text box, the text is deselected.

 In the third row, you will find the paint bucket tool, which fills a closed area with the specified pattern or color, and the airbrush tool, which sprays a definable pattern of pixels simulating a real airbrush.

The paint bucket's fill color can be changed using the options in the Ink effects pop-up menu. If the area that you are filling is not a closed area, and paint leaks out, immediately select Undo Bitmap (in the Edit menu) to undo the spill and the fill. Fix the area to be closed before filling again.

There are no zoom tools in the Paint window toolbox. You can choose the Zoom In command (or type Command-+), from the Paint menu, to examine in detail an area that is not completely enclosed, but appears closed at actual size. You can zoom in up to three levels of magnification, make repairs, then zoom back out to actual size using the Zoom Out command (or type Command- –).

Double-clicking the paint bucket tool opens the Gradients dialog box. Use this as a shortcut instead of choosing the Gradients command from the Paint menu (described later).

Double-click the air brush tool, or select Air Brushes from the Paint menu, to open the Air brushes dialog box. The air brush tool also has a pop-up menu of ink effects, called AIR 1, AIR 2, etc. up to AIR 5, that are accessed by a single click on the air brush tool. You can control the air brush tool's spray size, dot size, flow rate, and shape. Using the Air Brushes dialog box, you can define five different types of air brush settings that remain in the pop-up menu until you change them. First choose the pop-up item you want to assign, then choose Air Brushes from the Paint menu. Select the size of spray, dot size, flow rate, and brush shape, then click the Set button. Do this for each of the pop-up items. You will be able to choose one of the five pop-up options, instead of having to always select the Air Brushes option from the Paint menu, or the air brush tool.

The standard paintbrush and pencil tools are in the fourth row. The pencil paints a single pixel at a time, or, if you drag it, a line that is a single pixel in width. The paintbrush paints with a brush stroke. You can paint with the active color, ink effect, or fill pattern, and make several brush shapes available, while painting, then select them (Brush 1, Brush 2, etc. up to Brush 5) using the paintbrush pop-up menu.

The pencil tool draws in black and white in a 1-bit mode (black dots on a white background, and white dots on a black background), or in the currently selected color in 8-bit mode. The foreground color is used, but if you are using the pencil to draw on pixels that are already in the foreground color, then the background color is used.

Double-click the pencil tool (or depress the Command key and click the mouse button) to magnify your view, centering the view on the last point clicked. Use the scroll bars, or the hand tool, to move around, or click on the reduced view in the top right of the paint easel to return to actual size. The pencil tool allows only one zoom level, similar to the FatBits feature of MacPaint. You can use the Zoom Out command (Command- –) to return to actual size. As with the paint bucket and other paint tools, you can use the pencil tool while you are Zoom(ed) In.

The paintbrush can be set to one of several brush shapes and sizes, which you can change at any time, by double-clicking the paintbrush tool to display the Brush Shapes dialog box. Additionally, if you click and hold down the mouse button, a pop-up menu appears that stores five brush settings (Brush 1–Brush 5). Use the five default brush settings, or modify them to frequently used brush settings. This saves time since you do not have to use the Brush Shapes dialog box each time you wish to change a setting.

To define the five brush settings, select one of them, and use the Brush Shapes command, in the Paint menu, to display the Brush Shapes dialog box. Select either a standard or custom brush setting for the brush size and shape you want and click the Set button to store your settings.

The standard brush settings can be edited if you click the Custom button. Use the arrows to reposition the pixels on an existing brush shape. Or, click on any area of the screen (you can even click outside the Paint window) to copy any block of pixels to use as is or to edit, or create a brand new brush shape, clicking to turn a pixel (black) on, or turn it (white) off, by clicking it again. Clicking the button with the black-and-white triangles will instantly reverse the pixels (black to white, and white to black) for any brush shape you are viewing. You can store many custom brushes in the Scrapbook, and up to five in the paintbrush tool pop-up menu. Custom brushes are also stored to disk in the Director 4.0 Preferences file.

Use the Copy All button in the Brush Shapes dialog box to copy a custom brush pattern to the Clipboard. Then click the Cancel button to close the Brush Shapes dialog box. Select Scrapbook from the Apple menu, and Paste from the Edit menu (Command-V), to paste the custom brush shape into a Scrapbook. Using this method, you can store a large number of custom brush shapes, to use on different projects.

To retrieve brush shapes stored in a Scrapbook, open the Scrapbook file, select the shape you want, and select Copy from the Edit menu (Command-C). Then, in Director, select the Brush Shapes command to display the Brush Shapes dialog box. Click the Custom button, then the Paste All button to paste the custom brush shape into the set of custom brush shapes.

The paintbrush tool (like the pencil tool) uses the current colors, ink effect, and fill pattern settings. Change these to the desired settings before you begin to draw with the paintbrush or pencil, and change them again when you are drawing to achieve any desired effect..

The half-empty, half-filled rectangle shape in the fifth row of tools represents the rectangle tool. If you click in the empty side, you can draw a blank rectangle with an outline (border) in the foreground color. If you click in the shaded side, the rectangle is automatically filled with the foreground and background colors, and current ink effect and pattern. To change the width of the border, use the line width selector (at the bottom of the toolbox) to change the setting before you draw. Hold down the Option key, while drawing, if you want the border of the rectangle to be filled with the current pattern. (Note to Windows users: Substitute the Alt key for the Option key.) You can create a rectangle of any size and shape. If you want to draw a perfect square, hold down the Shift key, while dragging with the rectangle tool.

Double-click in the shaded side of the rectangle, as a shortcut to open the Gradients dialog box (described later).

Next to the rectangle tool is the eraser tool, which clears anything in its path when you drag it across the image. You can erase everything in the visible area of the easel by double-clicking the eraser tool (which is the same as using the Clear Bitmap command in the Edit menu).

 In the sixth row of the Painting tools box, you will find the ellipse (for ovals and circles) and polygon tools, which have empty and shaded sides just like the rectangle tool. The left side of the ellipse tool draws an outline (border), and the right side draws a shaded ellipse using the current foreground and background colors, pattern, and ink setting.

When using the ellipse tool, you can draw a perfect circle by holding down the Shift key; without Shift you can draw an oval of any size and shape.

To change the width of the outline (border), use the Line Width Selector (at the bottom of the toolbox) to change the line width setting before you draw. Hold down the Option key, while drawing, if you want the border of the ellipse to be filled with the current pattern. (Note to Windows users: Substitute the Alt key for the Option key.)

With the polygon tool you can draw a polygon of as many sides as you wish. Just as the rectangle tool, the shaded side fills the polygon or circle with the foreground and background colors, the current ink effect and pattern. The thickness of the outline is defined by the active line style. Hold down the Option key, while drawing, if you want the border of the polygon to be filled with the current pattern. (Note to Windows users: Substitute the Alt key for the Option key.)

Double-click in the shaded side of the ellipse or polygon tool as a shortcut to open the Gradients dialog box.

In the seventh row, you will find the line and arc tools.

The arc tool draws curved arcs of any angle and size; these are one quarter of a circle (or ellipse) in size.

Ordinarily, the line tool can draw a straight line in any angle. However, if you hold down the Shift key, you can constrain the angles to 45-degree increments, with the direction of the line depending on the direction in which you start to drag.

The thickness of a line or arc is defined by the active line style, and the line or arc is drawn using the current foreground color and ink effect.

Hold down the Option key, while drawing, if you want the line or arc to be drawn with the current pattern. If you are using the Windows version of Director, hold down the Alt key, while drawing, if you want the line or arc to be drawn with the current pattern.

In the last row of the painting tools box you will find the registration tool and the eyedropper tool.

You can use the registration tool to display and change the registration point for a cast member. By default, the registration point for a bitmap cast member is in the center of the artwork. (Shapes, text, and button cast members have a registration point default on the upper left corner of the object.) For bitmap cast members, click the registration tool, and crosshairs appear in the Paint window easel for the current cast member. The registration point for the cast member is the intersection of these crosshairs. To change it, click the new point you want in the Paint window easel, or click and drag the crosshairs to reposition the registration point.

Double-click the registration tool to reset the registration point to the center of the artwork for a selected easel. (As described earlier, you can also use the Align Bitmaps command from the Cast menu to reset the registration points of a selected number of cast members all at once. Using this technique, you can use the arrow keys in the Paint window to scroll through all of the cast members.)

The registration point of cast members is the key to animation control. You need to manage the registration points of images to properly position cast members on the stage. For a turning wheel, the registration point would be the center of the cast members. For a running man, you might choose a point in the same place on the ground ahead of him as the registration point for each cast member.

The eyedropper tool is used to match a color on the easel. The color clicked with the eyedropper tool becomes the foreground color. Using this tool can save you time in reusing a color without opening the color palette, and you are assured of a color match. On a Macintosh, you can access this tool, while using any other tool, by holding down the Control key when using the other tool. On a Windows machine, you can access this tool by clicking any other tool with the right mouse button.

## Ink Effects

The Ink effects pop-up menu (Figure 4.8), above the gradient color selector in the Paint window, affects the way your drawing tools create objects. It is not the same menu that you were introduced to in Chapter 3, in the Score window. The Paint window ink effects are used once to render an image in the Paint window. Further manipulation of the object's inking can be done in the Score window, as described in the next chapter.

The Ink effects are selected by clicking and dragging to the desired effect in the pop-up menu. Normal is the default ink effect.

To use an ink effect in the Paint window, click on a tool that will use it, such as the brush or a filled shape. Then choose an effect from the Ink effects pop-up menu. From that point on, every time you use that tool, the same ink effect will

**Figure 4.8**
**The Ink effects**
**pop-up menu in**
**the Paint win-**
**dow, for use with**
**painting and**
**drawing tools.**

be associated with it. (You can turn off this automatic effect by clicking the Ink effect sticks to tool option in the Options dialog box.)

Some ink effects have different consequences when painting in color, rather than black and white. Some effects work well with patterns, and others work better with solid colors. Monochrome display users have access to the first six effects only; the rest require support for color.

The default **Normal** ink effect uses the current foreground color and pattern to paint with opaque ink (ink that obscures any objects behind the object colored with Normal ink). It works with all the Paint tools.

The **Transparent** ink setting makes the background color in a pattern invisible (that is, only the foreground color is visible). However, objects underneath show through when the background color is in a Normal ink effect setting. This ink effect works with all Paint tools except the pencil, eyedropper, and paint bucket tools.

The **Reverse** ink setting affects new shapes that overlap existing artwork. Formerly white pixels become transparent pixels (the artwork beneath shows through), and black pixels are changed to the background color.

For example (Figure 4.9), a black filled box with white stripes bordered in white becomes a white filled box with black stripes, bordered in black. In areas where the art overlaps, the white pixels become transparent (the black shows through), and the border changes from black to white with white pixels reversed

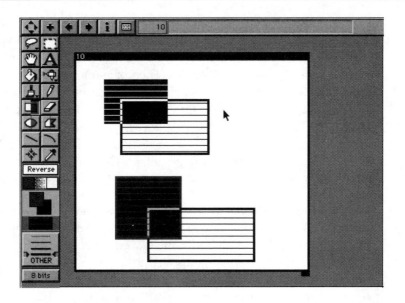

**Figure 4.9
The effects of
painting with the
Reverse ink.**

to black. A blue filled box with red stripes, bordered in red, becomes a white
filled box with black stripes, bordered in black. In areas where the art overlaps,
white pixels become invisible, and the border changes from black to white, with
white pixels invisible. This ink effect works with all Paint tools except the
eyedropper and paint bucket tools.

The **Ghost** ink setting uses the background color, instead of the foreground
color, for the fill, pattern, and outline color. It also makes the foreground color
transparent (invisible), so that objects below show through. In black and white,
Ghost creates an invisible object that only appears when placed over a black
background. This ink effect works with all paint tools except the pencil,
eyedropper, and paint bucket tools. Ghosts are best with solid black, or with
color patterns.

The **Gradient** ink setting is used to paint gradient fills, using the text, paint
bucket, paintbrush, and outline and filled rectangle, ellipse and polygon shape
tools. The starting color for a gradient is the foreground color, and the ending
(or destination) color is set in the gradient color bar. Other parameters for
blending the starting and destination colors are set in the Gradients dialog box,
selected from the Paint menu, or displayed by double-clicking the Gradient color
bar. (See Gradient color bar description that follows this ink effects description.)
For black-and-white gradient fills, in-between color steps are rendered in shades
of gray. This ink effect does not work with the pencil, eyedropper, arc, line, and
airbrush tools.

The **Reveal** ink setting is especially useful for creating mask effects, with the
air brush tool, for multiple cast members. First create the color effects you want

for one cast member using the air brush tool. Then create an area large enough to fill an object. Next create a second cast member in which you will define the shape of the object. Select the Reveal ink effect, and then the paintbrush, or shape (rectangle, ellipse or polygon) tool. Then paint or draw a filled shape, which will be painted using the air brush pattern of the first cast member.

The **Reveal** effect erases white areas to show the artwork in the immediately preceding cast member position. Reveal is used to merge the previous cast member with the current cast member. Reveal is often used to merge a random pattern painted with the air brush tool with a specific shape. You can paint with the paint brush tool and reveal portions of the other cast member as you paint.

***Note:*** The paint bucket also works with the Reveal ink effect, but because it simply creates a duplicate of the first cast member, it's not useful. This ink effect is more useful when applied to a shape that changes from frame to frame, but for which you want the background color and pattern to be the same for all the cast members. In addition to the air brush, this effect works with the paintbrush, paint bucket, outline and filled rectangle, ellipse and polygon shape tools, and the text tool. It does not work with the pencil, eyedropper, arc, or line tools.

The **Cycle** ink setting only works with solid colors and patterns, and the air brush and paintbrush tools. The colors change as you draw, cycling through the colors in the current palette, depending on which colors you have chosen for foreground and gradient destination colors. (You can set the gradient destination color in the gradient color bar by clicking the destination color chip and dragging it to the desired color in the pop-up palette. You can also double-click the Gradient color bar, or use the Gradients command to display the Gradients dialog box to change colors and/or palettes.)

If you are using the standard palette, use white as the foreground color and black as the destination color to cycle through all the colors in the palette. For instance, if you choose white as the destination color, and the foreground color is set to white and the background color is set to black, you will only be able to paint with white, using the Cycle ink setting.

Patterns and solids both work with this effect. This effect does not work with the text, pencil, eyedropper, paint bucket, arc, line, outline and filled rectangle, ellipse and polygon shape tools.

On Windows machines, this ink effect works with the air brush only in the 256 colors setting (8-bit color resolution).

The **Switch** ink effect changes any foreground-colored pixels as you paint over them to the gradient destination color. This effect works only with color and the paintbrush tool. This effect does not work with the text, pencil, eyedropper, paint bucket, arc, line, outline and filled rectangle, ellipse and polygon shape tools. On Windows machines, this ink effect works with the paintbrush only in the 256 colors setting (8-bit color resolution).

The **Blend** ink effect blends a background object's color with a foreground object's color to create a translucent color ink. This effect does not work with the pencil, eyedropper, and paint bucket tools. Use the Paint Window Options command to display the Paint Window Options dialog box. Then use the Effects settings to specify a blend percentage, to control the ink's translucency (its darkness or lightness). Patterns and solids both work with this effect. This effect works with the text, air brush, paintbrush, arc, line, outline and filled rectangle, ellipse and polygon shape tools. On Windows machines, this ink effect works with the text, air brush, paintbrush, arc, line, outline and filled rectangle, ellipse and polygon shape tools only in the 256 colors setting (8-bit color resolution).

The **Darkest** ink effect works with solids and patterns, and is useful for colorizing black-and-white artwork, using the text, paintbrush, air brush, line, arc, outline and filled rectangle, ellipse and polygon shape tools. Using solid colors, the Darkest setting paints so that the darkest color shows through, and blends with all the other colors that overlap it. When you paint, or use a pattern, with this effect, the darkest colors remain the same, while the lightest colors are changed. If, for example, you are painting a pale beige onto a black-and-white image, the black stays black, while the white turns to pale beige.

This effect does not work with the pencil, eyedropper, and paint bucket tools. On Windows machines, this ink effect works with the text, air brush, paintbrush, arc, line, outline and filled rectangle, ellipse and polygon shape tools only in the 256 colors setting (8-bit color resolution).

The **Lightest** ink effect works with solids and patterns, and is useful for colorizing black-and-white artwork, using the text, paintbrush, air brush, line, arc, outline and filled rectangle, ellipse and polygon shape tools. Using solid colors, the Lightest setting paints so that the lightest color shows through, and blends with all the other colors that overlap it, lightening them (Figure 4.10). The Lightest ink effect is the opposite of the Darkest ink effect: The lightest colors remain the same, while the darkest colors are changed.

This effect does not work with the pencil, eyedropper, and paint bucket tools. On Windows machines, this ink effect works with the text, air brush, paintbrush, arc, line, outline and filled rectangle, ellipse and polygon shape tools only in the 256 colors setting (8-bit color resolution).

The **Darken** ink effect works only with the paintbrush tool on patterns and solid colored inks, and makes ink darker (more black and less bright) each time you pass the paintbrush over an area. You must first release, and then reclick and drag the mouse button, for each individual pass. As long as you continue to

**Figure 4.10**
**A dark pink**
**square shows the**
**effects of Darkest**
**(top left) and**
**Lightest (bottom**
**right) ink effects**
**when over-**
**painted with or-**
**ange rectangles.**
**Because the**
**white back-**
**ground is lighter**
**than the orange**
**paint, the bottom**
**right of the or-**
**ange rectangle**
**does not appear.**

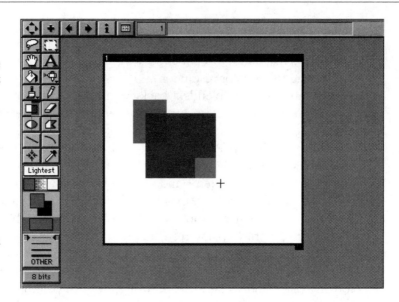

hold the mouse button down, you are still only making a single pass over the area, even if you paint on top of the same spot. Release the mouse button, then click and drag over the area again to make a second pass, and use the same technique for subsequent passes.

With each pass, the ink overlays your color or pattern with a darker shade of gray, until the area becomes solid black. The color darkens the more you brush with the Darken effect. It is the same as reducing the color's brightness with the controls in the Color Palettes window, only you don't actually change the color in the Color Palettes window. You can vary the effect in the Paint Options dialog box. Use the Paint Window Options command to display the Paint Window Options dialog box to vary the rate for this effect from slow (1) to fast (255), for 8-bit palettes. On Windows machines, this ink effect works only with the paintbrush tool in the 256 colors setting (8-bit color resolution).

The **Lighten** ink effect works only with the paintbrush tool on both patterns and solid color inks. It makes ink lighter (lightens grays and blacks to increase a color's brightness) each time you pass the paintbrush over an area that has been previously darkened with the Darken ink effect. On Windows machines, this ink effect works only with the paintbrush tool in the 256 colors setting (8-bit color resolution).

As with the Darken effect, you must first release, and then reclick and drag the mouse button. As long as you continue to hold the mouse button down, you are still only making a single pass over the area, even if you paint on top of the same spot. Release the mouse button, then click and drag over the area again to make a second pass; use the same technique for subsequent passes. With each pass, the ink overlays your color, or pattern, with a lighter (brighter) shade of color, until the area becomes solid white.

Use the Paint Window Options command to display the Paint Window Options dialog box to vary the rate for this effect from slow (1) to fast (255), for 8-bit palettes.

Note that in bright areas of color, which do not have any gray or black in the starting color, the Lighten ink effect will not seem to work. To further lighten such areas, use the Darken ink effect, to add some gray to the color, then use the Lighten ink effect to add white to the color.

The **Smooth** ink effect works only with the paintbrush tool and solid colors and patterns, to blur the edges of shapes and colors. On Windows machines, this ink effect works only with the paintbrush tool in the 256 colors setting (8-bit color resolution). This ink effect allows you to erase hard or jagged edges, where light and dark areas of color appear side by side.

With each pass of the paintbrush, the sharp edges of dark colors are blurred and softened, similar to the Smear ink effect. However, the Smooth ink effect blurs edges evenly, with no fade in or out over the length of the stroke.

Dark thin lines can be diffused with multiple passes of the paintbrush (you must click before dragging to begin each new pass) until they disappear into a white background. This ink blurs colors only at the edges of colored and patterned objects, and has no effect on solid color areas (those with no edges).

Lighter colors that contain white are blurred (smoothed) to be brighter (with less white) where they meet darker colors, and to be whiter where they meet white areas. The number of passes the paintbrush makes determines how much the colors blur. The Paint Window Options settings have no effect on the rate of smoothing.

The **Smear** ink effect works only with the paintbrush tool on solid colors and patterns, to mix colors in already painted cast members, fading in and fading out over the length of the stroke. For example, starting with a dark ink, the paintbrush smears first dark, and then lighter shades. Starting with a light (or white) ink, the paintbrush smears first light (or white), and then less light (or less white) shades of ink. The smearing effect is spread in the direction you drag.

Just as with real pigments on a canvas (such as painting with watercolors), the smear fades as you drag further from the starting point. Subsequent passes can be used to drag more ink, to mix colors further, and extend the length of the smear.

Note that the foreground, background color settings have no effect on this ink effect, since it only mixes already painted colors. On Windows machines, this ink effect works only with the paintbrush tool in the 256 colors setting (8-bit color resolution).

The **Smudge** ink effect works only with the paintbrush tool on solid colors and patterns, to mix colors in already painted cast members. On Windows machines, this ink effect works only with the paintbrush tool in the 256 colors setting (8-bit color resolution). It is similar to the Smear ink effect, but instead of colors fading in and fading out slowly over the length of the stroke, in the Smudge ink effect the colors are mixed faster. The colors fade faster as they are spread away from the original area. Using the example of pigments on canvas, this is like having wetter or more paint on the brush for each brushstroke. As with the Smear ink effect, subsequent passes can be used to drag more ink, to mix colors, and extend the length of the Smudge ink effect.

The **Spread** ink effect works only with the paintbrush tool on color and black and white easels, on artwork already created. (However, you must set the color depth to 8 bits before using this effect. It can't be used on 1-bit black-and-white images, until you set the Paint window color depth to the 8-bit setting.) You can get many different effects, depending on the shape of your paintbrush, what color pixels you click on, and the direction in which you drag.

The Spread ink effect with the paintbrush tool works like the eyedropper tool in that it picks up whatever colors are under the brush. While the eyedropper can pick up only a single pixel, the paintbrush picks up as many pixels as are included in your brush shape, including multiple colors, patterns, adjacent colors, etc. For example, using a round brush, if you click the point of intersection of two colors and drag away in a straight line, you spread equal parts of both colors. Dragging to the left or right spreads more of one color, depending on the brush shape, and the angle of the direction in which you drag. The colors are spread evenly as you drag the brush (they do not fade or darken).

The **Clipboard** ink effect works only with the paintbrush tool on both color and black-and-white easels. (However, you must set the color depth to 8 bits, before using this effect. It can't be used on 1-bit black-and-white images.) It uses the active settings of the Clipboard as the brush pattern. The direction in which you drag may vary the effects of the painting strokes, as do the brush's shape, colors, and patterns.

## Gradients and Color Chips

The **Gradient** color selector bar is located below the Painting tools box, and under the Ink effects pop-up menu.

The color chips below the Painting tools box, under the Ink effects menu (and below the Gradients color selector bar), indicate which colors are the foreground and the background colors. The chip in front is the foreground color, and the partially obscured chip is the background color.

The Gradient color selector bar displays three color chips. The left chip is the foreground color, the middle is a blend of the foreground color and the destination color, and on the right is the destination color. The colors you select

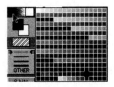

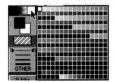

here from pop-up color palettes for the foreground and destination colors are used for the Gradient, Cycle and Switch ink effects, for both color and black-and-white inks. As a shortcut, you can hold down the Option key and press the up or down arrow keys to cycle through the color choices available in the current palette. (Note to Windows users: Substitute the Alt key for the Option key.) To switch palettes, double-click in the Gradient color selector bar to display the Color Palettes window. You can also open the Color Palettes window by choosing the Color Palettes command from the Window menu (or type Command-8).

Select a palette from the pop-up menu, or create a new palette or edit an existing palette, using the Palette menu commands that are available when the Color Palettes window is active.

Note that the middle color blend chip is always shown as a blend of color from left to right, no matter the direction of gradient you select. Select Gradients to display the Gradients dialog box, where you can change the direction of the gradient and other parameters to use.

The color chips below the Painting tools box, under the Ink effects menu (and below the Gradients color selector bar), indicate which color is the foreground and which is the background. The chip in front is the foreground color, and the partially obscured chip is the background color. On a black-and-white Macintosh, or a display set to 1-bit, the default foreground is black, the background is white.

On a color monitor, the foreground color is displayed on both the foreground color chip, and as the color on the left side of the Gradients color bar. The foreground color is affected by the settings for the pattern and ink effects you have chosen, unless you use the default pattern (solid) and the Normal ink effect.

On a color monitor, the background color (the chip partially obscured by the foreground color chip) is displayed and used as the second color for patterns. It is also affected by the ink effect setting. For example, the Transparent ink setting makes the background color in a pattern invisible (only the foreground color is visible), and objects underneath show through where the background color would be with a Normal ink effect setting. The Ghost ink setting uses the background color instead of the foreground color for the pattern and outline color, and makes the foreground color transparent (invisible), so that objects below show through.

To change the foreground or background color setting, click on the foreground or background color chip, and hold the mouse down as you drag to the new color in the pop-up color palette. As a shortcut to changing the foreground color, press the up or down arrow keys to cycle through the foreground colors in the color palette. To cycle through the background colors, hold down the Shift key and the up or down arrow keys.

Double-clicking the foreground or background color chip (or the gradient color bar) opens the Color Palettes window, so you can switch palettes or change the colors in the current palette. You can also open the Color Palettes window by choosing the Color Palettes command or type Command-8.

## Pattern and Line Styles

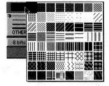

The pattern chip is located below the Painting tools box, and immediately below the foreground and background color chips.

The line styles appear in the line width selector below the pattern chip.

The pattern chip displays the pattern currently selected from the pop-up pattern palette. The default pattern is a solid pattern that uses the foreground color. To change the pattern, click the pattern chip and drag to the new pattern you want to use in the pop-up pattern palette.

As a shortcut, if you hold down the Option key (or Alt key on Windows machines) before clicking the pattern chip, the default pattern choices displayed are changed to shades ranging from the background color to the foreground color. This change of patterns will remain the same until you press the Option (or Alt) key again before clicking the pattern chip to display the default pattern choices. Use the Option (or Alt) key in this manner to toggle between the two pattern palettes.

To edit patterns or select new sets of patterns, double-click the pattern chip (or select the Patterns command from the Paint menu) to display the Patterns dialog box.

The thickness of the outline (border) drawn by the shape tools (rectangle, ellipse, polygon, line and arc) depends on the line style chosen. The line styles appear in the line width selector below the pattern chip. The styles include a dotted line, three standard line thicknesses, and an Other line style that can be defined to be thicker than the standard settings. The dotted line setting draws filled shapes without borders, or hairlines in the foreground color (when using the line or arc tools).

To set a thicker line, double-click the line width selector box to open the Paint Window Options dialog box, or select the Paint Window Options command from the Paint menu.

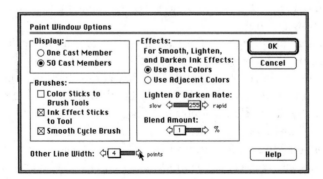

**Color Resolution Indicator**

Below the line width selector is the color resolution indicator. Double-clicking the color resolution indicator displays the Transform Bitmap dialog box, which enables you to change the resolution of the currently active cast member to be 1, 2, 4, 8, 16, or 32 bits.

Increasing the resolution of a cast member increases the amount of disk space required to store it, and increases the file size of your movie.

You can reduce a color cast member from 32 bits to 8 bits, or from 8 bits to 1 bit (black and white) to save disk space and to reduce file size. When you choose to reduce the number of colors (resolution) for a cast member, you can choose to either dither or remap the colors. (The Transform Bitmaps dialog box also allows you to change the size of the cast member, as described later.)

After reducing a color cast member to be black and white, you can colorize it using the Tools window foreground and background color palettes. It will be stored as a black-and-white cast member, which takes less space, but will appear as a color sprite on the stage. Use this trick to import black-and-white cast members, and then color them for the stage.

> **Note:** You can't apply the colors from the Colors Palette, or the foreground and background colors from the Paint window, to a 1-bit cast member, unless you first increase the resolution of the cast member in the Paint window to be more than 1 bit. You select the 1-bit cast member in the Score window, when it is on stage and called a sprite, to apply foreground and background colors using the Tools window.

The painting tools described so far do not make you an artist, but they help prepare artwork much more effectively than manual drawing tools. Perfect circles and squares can be drawn, as well as ovals and polygons of any shape, then transformed into other shapes. Director's Effects menu options are available, after you use the selection rectangle to select artwork, which enable you to scale, rotate, flip, invert, and otherwise transform cast members. (Note that the resolution of your monitor must first be changed to match the resolution of the cast member in the Paint window before the Effects menu commands are available.) You can create any kind of image with these tools and effects, and refine the image by zooming in and changing the pixels individually.

## Basic Painting

Perhaps the greatest benefit of painting and drawing by computer is the ability to be precise to the pixel. Copying bitmaps and duplicating objects is made simple, because the Lasso and Selection tools offer a level of precision you cannot easily attain using manual tools. You also have precise controls over Paint Brush and Airbrush shapes and sizes, and Director lets you zoom into the Paint window to see an enlargement of the easel.

## Zooming into View

The Zoom In command in the Paint menu (or type Command-+) enlarges the view by 2X at first. Use the command again to enlarge the view to 4X, and again to enlarge it to an 8X view. You can also double-click the pencil tool to zoom in to an 8X view, or Command-click in the area you want to enlarge, using any painting tool. The Paint window shows the enlargement of a letter N and includes a window showing the actual size of the enlarged area (Figure 4.11). The Paint window allows four levels of magnification in all, including actual size, 2X, 4X, and 8X views.

To move the image in this view, use the hand tool or the scroll bars. You can temporarily change from any tool to the hand tool by pressing the space bar. The pencil tool is the best tool to use in the 8X enlarged view, because it can turn a white pixel black and a black pixel white, or turn any pixel into a different color.

You can quickly return to normal size by clicking inside the normal size window, while in an enlarged view. You can also choose Zoom Out in the Paint menu, or type Command- – (minus), Command- - (hyphen), or Command-_ (underscore). By using the Command key when clicking in an area of the easel, you can jump to an enlarged view, and by Command-clicking again you can jump back to the normal view.

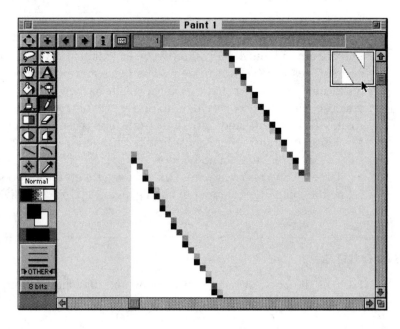

**Figure 4.11**
**After using Zoom In to enlarge the artwork to an 8X view, you can move around with the hand tool or scroll bars and still see a normal-sized representation in a window.**

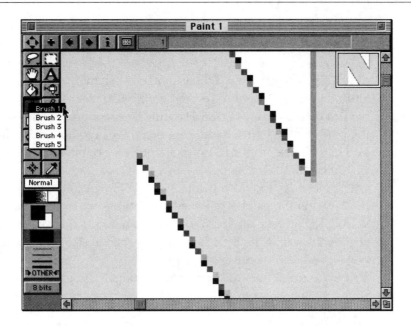

**Figure 4.12
Selecting a brush
shape for the
paint brush tool
in the custom
window.**

## Using Brushes

The paintbrush paints with the current foreground color, or black, if the color depth is 1 bit, and the ink effect is set to Normal. It uses the current fill pattern and ink effect, which are set to solid, Normal ink unless you change them. The paintbrush paints with a wider stroke than the single-pixel stroke of the pencil.

You can edit the brush shape by double-clicking the paintbrush tool. A dialog box appears with different brush shapes to choose from, and a magnifying window for customizing the pixels of the brush shape (Figure 4.12). You can customize the shape by adding pixels (Figure 4.13). Just click in the window in a white space to add a black pixel, or on a black pixel to turn it white.

Below the magnified shape window are arrow buttons for moving the brush shape one pixel to the left, to the right, up, or down. The button on the lower

**Figure 4.13
Customizing the
brush shape by
adding pixels in
the custom win-
dow.**

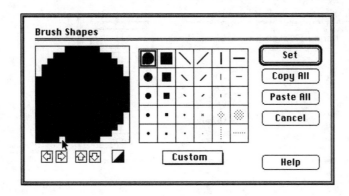

right corner turns all black pixels to white and all white pixels to black. You can also pick up a shape to use for a brush by clicking outside the dialog box, anywhere on the screen.

Once you have defined a custom brush shape, you can click the Set button and return to the easel to use the paintbrush tool. The shape you set becomes the first defined shape (Brush 1) for the Brush pop-up menu by default. To access the pop-up menu, click in the paintbrush tool and hold down the mouse button. You can choose from five brush shapes, or double-click the paintbrush tool to customize these five shapes.

The air brush tool also paints with the foreground color (or black for a 1-bit display), but the paint is "sprayed" onto the easel to simulate a real airbrush. By double-clicking the air brush tool you can access the Air Brushes dialog box to change the size of the area the spray covers, the size of the dots in the spray, the flow speed, and more (Figure 4.14).

Use the scroll bars to change the settings. The gray circle in the dialog box shows the spray area, and the white circle (centered in the gray circle) shows the spray's dot size.

After clicking the Set button, you can return to the easel to paint with the air brush tool. Experiment with the settings to get what you want. You can always use Undo to undo what you do. The Normal setting sprays uniform dots, and the Speckle setting sprays with random dots. You can also spray in the shape of the current paintbrush by selecting the Brush Shape option in the Air Brushes dialog box.

The air brush settings are saved as the first air brush type (Air 1) for the Air brushes pop-up menu by default. To access the pop-up menu again, click in the air brush tool and drag. You can choose from five air brush shapes, or customize them.

**Figure 4.14**
**The Air Brushes dialog box for customizing the "spray" of the air brush tool. You can set the size of the spray area, the size of the spray dot, the flow speed, and more.**

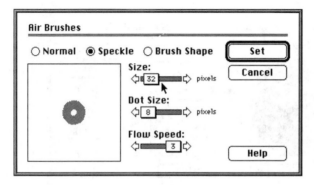

**Making
Selections**

The trick of electronic painting and drawing is to make good selections before moving, copying, or applying transformations on them. The selection rectangle and lasso tools are designed to make the job of selection easy and precise. Both tools have pop-up menus to further refine their actions.

The lasso is for selecting irregular areas of the image, and the rectangle is for selecting rectangular areas. With the lasso you can select areas to Cut, Copy, or Clear, as well as move by dragging. With the rectangle, you can select areas to Cut, Copy, Clear, move by dragging, or to transform using any command in the Effects menu.

Both tools offer shrink to outline of the objects within. To see how this works, paint an irregular shape, or open the *Chicago* movie (available on the accompanying CD-ROM; filename: CHICAGO.DIR), open the Paint window, and use the right arrow button to advance to cast member 3, the image of a sailboat. Click the lasso tool and drag it to the right to open the pop-up menu, select the Shrink (default) option. Then drag the lasso around the area to be selected. A solid line appears when you are dragging the lasso, but disappears once you let go of the mouse. The selection shrinks to the outline of the object, leaving out the surrounding white background. The selected objects blink to indicate that they have been selected.

If you use the No Shrink option, the area you drag around is literally whatever is inside your imaginary lasso. The See Thru option makes the white areas of the selected object transparent, so that you can drag the selected object over other objects without obscuring the other objects.

The rectangle selection also offers Shrink and No Shrink options. Click in the rectangle selection tool and drag to the right to show the pop-up menu, and choose No Shrink.

Drag the rectangle selection tool diagonally across the area you want to select. A moving dotted outline, called the marquee, is displayed in the shape of a rectangle around the image area. When you let go of the mouse, the entire area within the marquee is selected.

Try it again, this time with the Shrink option: Click the rectangle selection tool, drag to and select Shrink, then select the same area of the paint easel. The marquee shrinks as close as it can to the actual outline of the objects, while keeping a rectangular shape.

You can use the rectangle selection tool with the Lasso option to surround an object and have it shrink to the actual irregular outline, as if you were using the lasso tool with its Shrink option. You can also choose the lasso See Thru option with the rectangle selection tool to simulate the use of the lasso tool with the See Thru option.

**Copying Bitmaps**

There are several ways to duplicate a graphic object in the Paint window. Depending on your project, you may want to copy part of a bitmap as part of a single cast member, or duplicate a cast member to create another cast member. In the former case, you are modifying an existing cast member, and in the latter case. you are creating or *cloning* new cast members. We describe cloning later.

In the *Chicago* movie, there are two cast members representing one sailboat. Open the movie, then the Paint window, and click the right arrow button to show cast member 3.

Cast member 3 shows this sailboat in one position, and cast member 4 shows the same sailboat in a slightly different position (the obvious change is the shape of the flag). To preview the animation that takes place with these two cast members, select them in the Cast window. Next, choose the Align Bitmaps command from the Cast menu, so that their registration points line up (Figure 4.15). Now you can preview the animation by clicking the arrow buttons in the Paint window from one cast member to the other.

To create a second sailboat, you can duplicate both graphic objects that represent the first sailboat. Rather than creating another cast member and defining its animated sequence, you can change the two cast members 3 and 4 to represent two sailboats rather than one. By doing so, you automatically change the animation so that two sailboats sail across the screen rather than one sailboat.

Before copying a bitmap, it is wise to think about what parts of the object you want to duplicate and select only those parts. For example, if you select the object

**Figure 4.15** Using Align Bitmaps to line up the registration points for cast members 3 and 4, in order to preview the movement of these two cast members and to see them in the same locations for painting operations.

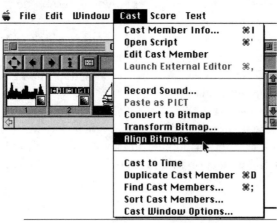

**Figure 4.16
Selecting the
graphic object
with the rectan-
gle selection tool
set to the Lasso
option, so that
the rectangle tool
acts like a lasso
with the Shrink
option.**

with the rectangle selection tool, with the No Shrink or Shrink options, the tool
will still select white space around the image, because it shrinks to a rectangular
selection. If you used the rectangle selection tool, with the lasso See Thru option,
the white space will be transparent. However, this is not what you want, because
in this case the duplicated sailboat must be positioned right next to the first one,
and any white space in the boat's sail and the boat itself would be transparent
and show the other boat behind it.

Therefore, to select the first object, either use the lasso selection tool with the
Shrink option, or use the rectangle selection tool with the Lasso option (Figure
4.16). If you use the rectangle selection tool, with the Lasso option, you may
notice that the selection tool changes automatically to the lasso tool after selecting
the object. This is because using the rectangle selection tool, with the Lasso
option, is simply a convenient way to get the same effect as using the lasso tool
with the Shrink option. However, you don't have to draw a lasso around the
object; instead you draw a rectangle and it shrinks to a lasso. Otherwise, the
function is exactly the same as using the lasso tool with the Shrink option.

Now, to copy this selected bitmap, simply hold down the Option key, click
inside the selected object, and drag. An exact copy is created (Figure 4.17). Leave
the duplicate bitmap slightly below, but overlapping the original bitmap. Repeat
this procedure for cast member 4.

**Figure 4.17
Dragging the ob-
ject with the Op-
tion key held
down to create a
duplicate object
as part of cast
member 3, and
performing the
same operation
for 4.**

**Figure 4.18 Running the *Chicago* movie (filename: CHICAGO2.DIR) after duplicating the objects in cast members 3 and 4, effectively creating a second sailboat to sail alongside the first one.**

Close the Paint window, rewind *Chicago* and click the Play button. Two sailboats should now sail across the screen in place of the single sailboat (Figure 4.18). Since you duplicated the sailboat bitmap, both sailboats have exactly the same ink effect, so they pass behind the larger boat just as the single sailboat did previously.

You can see how this technique can be useful for professional animation. First you can create a dummy cast member with a certain ink effect, then put it through animated sequences. You can then modify the dummy object to create real artwork, and that artwork is automatically used in the animation. You have just learned the basic principle behind "object-oriented" animation, which is a new form of traditional cel animation. Each cast member is not only an object that occupies its own layer, it is also an object that can be revised at any time, without having to recreate the animation.

When you use the drag-Option key combination with the rectangle selection tool, it is similar to using Copy Bitmap and Paste Bitmap (in the Edit menu). However, it is faster for duplicating an object and manipulating the duplicate to be positioned close to the original object. If, on the other hand, you needed to duplicate an object to place in another cast member's space (to add to another cast member), use Copy Bitmap to copy the image into the Clipboard. Then you would move to the other cast member's space and use Paste Bitmap.

## Duplicating Cast members

You could use Copy and Paste to make a copy of a cast member, but there's an easier way. Display the appropriate cast member in the Paint window, and then use the Duplicate Cast Member command in the Cast menu. This command creates a new cast member in the next available cast member position that is an exact duplicate of the displayed cast member. The Paint window switches to the new cast member, so that you can begin to make alterations.

Although cast member names are optional, you might want to give a new duplicate cast member a name. Select the cast member you want to name (use the next, or previous, arrow buttons). You can either click in the cast member name field (next to the cast member number) in the Cast window, or in the Paint window, to type a name for the current cast member. Or, you can choose the Cast Member Info command, from the Cast menu (or Command-I) to display the Cast Member Info dialog box, and type a name for the cast member, next to the cast number.

Each duplicate's registration point is exactly the same as the original cast member, which makes it easy to use a clone as a starting point for creating a mask. *Masks,* and other advanced art techniques, are described later in this chapter.

In addition, cloning is useful when performing distortions, or using the Auto Distort command (in the Effects menu). You can create a new cast member, and accomplish several distortions, without affecting the original cast member.

## Distorting Objects

Director offers extensive features for distorting bitmap text and graphics to create special animation effects, such as rotating objects, reversing the perspective, and stretching and distorting an object for perspective drawing, slanting, and edge tracing. Distortions can be repeated and performed automatically, creating new cast members for each intermediate step to set up an animated sequence.

Distortions are used whenever an animator needs a graphic image to go through a change in shape, size, or perspective. If something should look like it is turning or rotating, you use the Rotate commands from the Effects menu to make several cast members representative of the visible positions of the object. Distortions are also useful for creating original artwork, because you can draw perfect squares, circles, and rectangles, and then distort or slant them into other shapes.

You can perform all of the distortions in the Effects menu, if you select an image area with the rectangle selection tool. Only the Reverse and Fill Effects are available if you use the lasso tool (or the rectangle selection tool with the Lasso options).

---

**Note:** You can't use the Effects menu if your cast member is a 1-bit cast member. Change it to 8 bits using the Transform Bitmap command in the Cast menu.

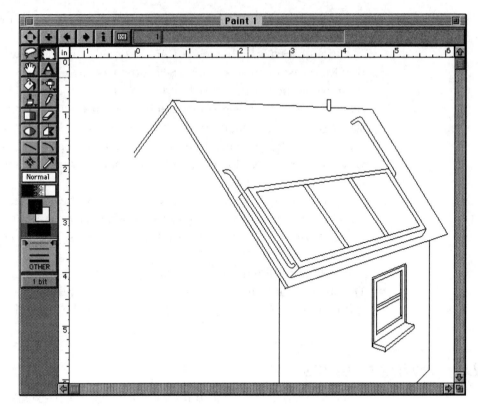

**Figure 4.19**
**The roof of the house and the solar collector shapes and window shape were created from geometric shapes using Slant and Distort transformations (*Solar Heater* movie, by Stuart Sharpe—filename: SOLARHTR.DIR, courtesy of Macromedia).**

## Slanting and Perspective Drawing

Using simple distortions, such as this slant, you can draw artwork as complex as the house in the *Solar Heater* movie. The house in cast member 1 (Figure 4.19) was drawn with geometric shapes, then distorted with Slant and Distort. After selecting the object with the rectangle selection tool, choose Slant or Distort, then drag the corner handles of the selection.

You can also stretch and squeeze a graphic image that is selected with the rectangle selection tool by dragging any corner point.

Many of these techniques become even more useful when you need to create a dozen or more cast members to represent an object that is changing its shape, size, or perspective. The Auto Distort command (from the Effects menu) can create the cast members automatically for a particular distortion. You can also repeat any distortion you just performed by selecting Repeat Effect from the Effects menu (or use Command-Y).

The Perspective effect distorts a graphic image to simulate a third dimension for perspective drawing. To make artwork appear to vanish in the distance, you would choose Perspective and bring the handles at the top of the selection together, and move the bottom handles apart.

**Figure 4.20**
**The baseball re-**
**volves as it flies**
**across the city**
**in** *Chicago*
**(filename:**
**CHICAGO.DIR)**
**(created with**
**eight cast mem-**
**bers in different**
**positions set**
**with rotation**
**transformations).**

## Flipping and Rotating

The Flip Horizontal effect turns an image into a mirror image of itself horizontally. The Flip Vertical effect creates a mirror vertical image. These are simple to try: Select anything with the rectangle selection tool, and choose them from the Effects menu.

Rotate Left and Rotate Right effects are provided to automatically rotate the selected image area by 45 degrees to the right or left. These distortions do not create mirror images; they create a new image based on the original image, rotated by 45 degrees. Director also offers the ability to rotate the selected image to any angle. You can choose Free Rotate, which displays handles on the selected image. Drag the selection handles to rotate the image.

Rotations are used to show objects revolving as they move through space. For example, in the *Chicago* movie (filename: CHICAGO.DIR in the TUTORIAL folder/directory), a baseball flies across the city and revolves as it flies (Figure 4.20).

To accomplish this effect, artist Roy Santiago used one image of a baseball and seven more duplicates, with a different rotation angle for each clone. Open the Cast window and look at cast members 17 through 24 to see them (Figure 4.21).

**Figure 4.21**
**The eight cast**
**members for the**
**revolving base-**
**ball.**

Although Director provides the ability to precisely rotate each cast member, you may be in a hurry. You can let Director create the cast members for you with the Auto Distort command.

## Auto Distort

Director can automatically generate the cast members that would logically be "inbetween" an original image and the result of a distortion (a rotation, a perspective change, a slant, or a distortion). You can set a single distortion of an original image, then create any number of cast members to be images that would come between the original and the distorted image.

To try it, select the baseball (cast member 17 in *Chicago*) with the rectangle selection tool set to Shrink, and use Copy Bitmap to copy it to the Clipboard. Select New from the File menu to create a new movie. After selecting inside the new movie's Paint window, or cast member 1 in the Cast window, use Paste Bitmap to paste the baseball image into cast member position 1. It should remain selected and ready to transform (Figure 4.22).

Use the Rotate Right command twice, to rotate it 90 degrees (Figure 4.23).

Then select the Auto Distort command in the Effects menu, and type 4 for the number of cast members to create (Figure 4.24).

The cast members are created automatically, and you can see them by opening the Cast window (Figure 4.25).

> **Note:** When you distort a bitmap cast member, the registration point used for distortions is always the center of the original image.

To distort bitmap cast members, and be able to use a different registration point, create a temporary dot for registration that you can use as a guide to change the registration point for each new cast member. In the Paint window, create a

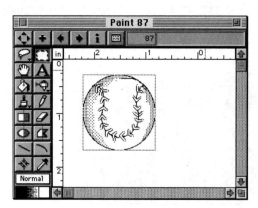

**Figure 4.22
The original base-
ball image before
transforming it
with the Auto Dis-
tort effect.**

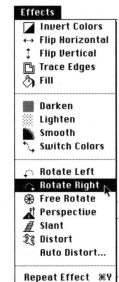

**Figure 4.23**
**Transforming**
**the baseball**
**twice with the Ro-**
**tate Right com-**
**mand to rotate it**
**90 degrees.**

**Figure 4.24**
**Using the Auto**
**Transform com-**
**mand, and set-**
**ting it to**
**generate four**
**new cast mem-**
**bers between the**
**original and the**
**transformed im-**
**ages.**

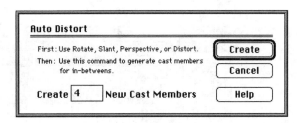

**Figure 4.25**
**The Cast window**
**shows the origi-**
**nal image and**
**the four new im-**
**ages created by**
**Auto Transform.**

visible dot at the new registration point of the starting image. Select the image, distort it to create a final image, then select Auto Distort from the Effects menu to create the in-between cast members. Select each cast member one by one, and use the Registration tool to position a new registration point in place of the dot, and then test the animation before you delete or re-color the temporary dot. Select all the cast members and use the Align Bitmaps command in the Cast menu to reposition them for animation. You can then use the next (right arrow) and previous (left arrow) buttons to preview the animation in the Paint window, to test the registration points, before you delete or re-color the temporary dot in each image.

What do you do with a sequence of automatically generated cast members that form a complete distortion? One popular technique for adding them to the score is to use the Cast to Time command in the Cast menu, after selecting all of the cast members in the Cast window. These, and other animation techniques, are described in more detail in Chapter 5. You can see the result of the Cast to Time command by scrolling the Score window for *Chicago* out to frames 315 to 322 and looking in channel 17 for the repeated sequence of cast members 17 to 24 (Figure 4.26).

Using Auto Distort with colored images can provide powerful special effects in an instant. This is because you can use Director to generate cast members that fall between certain colors, as well as certain shapes and positions.

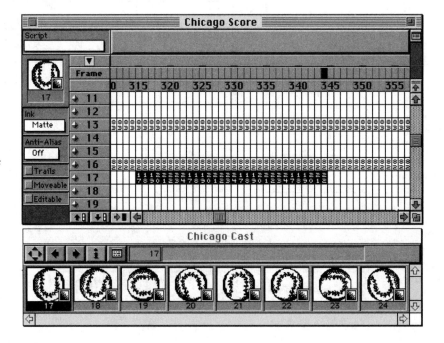

**Figure 4.26 The Score for the flying baseball in *Chicago* (filename: CHICAGO.DIR) was created with the Cast to Time command used with the previously transformed baseball images.**

# *Introducing Color and Resolution*

Until now we have shown mostly black-and-white examples, in deference to those readers who are using black-and-white systems. Professional results can be obtained with black-and-white graphics, but color provides a new dimension of expression. Director offers extensive color facilities, color painting effects, and animation effects.

Color requires the use of a color display and possibly a display adapter. With the capability to display 8-bit color, or shades of gray, the number of colors or shades of gray that can be displayed at one time are 256 out of a possible 16.7 million colors. This is usually enough for most real-time animation projects for the Mac platform, and it is the upper limit for projects designed for Windows.

The Mac offers the capability to expand your color range to include all 16.7 million colors simultaneously, but this requires storage of 24-bits per pixel of the image, and this much data is not ideal for real-time animation on current Mac models, although fine for still images. You can create 24-bit photorealistic animation with Director animations by recording frame by frame onto videotape.

When using 8-bit color images, a *palette* is stored for each image that contains the particular set of 256 colors to render that image. Before you create an image, the active palette is set to the System palette. When your display is set to 24-bit (or 32-bit) color depth, Director ignores palette settings or changes. Therefore, you must set the display to 8-bit or 4-bit color depth to use palettes.

> ***Note:*** Director's performance is affected by three levels of resolution settings: the monitor and display card's capability (maximum playback resolution), the monitor's current resolution, and the resolution of cast members.

To find out the maximum resolution for your monitor and display card on the Mac, use the Control Panel's Monitors command from the Apple menu (256 colors is for 8-bit displays, Thousands is for 16-bit displays, and Millions is for 24- or 32-bit displays). The largest number of colors shown determines the maximum resolution for your display. The highlighted selection in the Monitors control panel tells you what the current resolution setting is for your display card and monitor. The current resolution setting of the monitor determines the resolution in which your movie will be saved.

In addition, individual cast members in the movie can have their own resolution settings that are different from the resolution setting of the movie. These resolution settings determine palette color choices.

Using Windows, you can select Windows Setup from the Main window to see the maximum number of colors available on your display. The movie's color depth setting only has an effect when the movie is played on a Macintosh. For cast members, the color depth can be 1 bit, 4 bits, 8 bits, 16 bits, or 24 bits, resulting in black-and-white, 4-color, 16-color, 256-color, 32,768-color, or 16.7 million-color images. However, Director displays only 256 colors at a time on the stage. Therefore, 16-bit and 24-bit images are displayed using the colors in the active 256-color palette that most closely match the cast member's colors. (Note that the cast member's palette is not changed, and the original colors of the cast member are preserved.) To edit or create cast members in the Paint window, using the Windows version of Director, you must first set the Windows display driver to 256 colors. You can improve performance in the Windows version of Director by using the black and white User Interface setting in the Preferences dialog box (in the File menu). This setting saves time because Director doesn't have to update its color user interface to switch palettes.

You can use a graphics program, such as Director, to define custom palettes for creating images, or for applying them to scanned images. You can store palettes separately and use a custom palette with more than one image or movie. Director supplies several standard palettes you can use for images, including System-Mac, System-Win (for SVGA PCs), Rainbow, Grayscale, Pastels, Vivid, NTSC (for video images), Metallic, and VGA (for VGA PCs).

You can see the currently active palette for a movie when you click the foreground or background color chip in the Tools window. Click the foreground or background color chip in the Paint window to see palette choices for a cast member (Figure 4.27).

You can drag to select any color in the palette. You can click on the foreground color chip to set the foreground color (for pencil, brush strokes, and outlines), or click on the background chip to set the background color (for shades,

**Figure 4.27**
**The currently active color palette showing 256 colors out of a possible 16.7 million colors, available by clicking the foreground or background color chip in the Paint window or Tools window.**

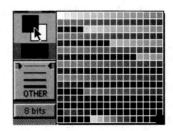

background fills, and so on). The colors in the palette are arranged as a single array that start in the upper left corner and proceed from left to right down to the lower right corner.

---

*Note:* The Paint window color palette color choices depend on the resolution to which the cast member is set. Change the current cast member's resolution (and palette choice) by double-clicking the color resolution indicator (located immediately below the line width indicator) to display the Transform Bitmap dialog box.

---

Manipulating color palettes is a trick you can use for special effects with color animation. For example, when you import a PICT image into Director, you can use the color palette (stored with the image). Or, you can remap the most important colors from the image palette to another palette, in order to use the palette for more than one image.

Imported palettes can be defined by name, and you can blend colors within them to create a smooth color transition, reverse the order of colors in a palette, and sort colors by hue, saturation, and brightness. Every frame of the Score can use a different palette, though in practice it is often better to use one optimal palette for all images. This avoids the need for color palette transitions between frames. You can only display one palette at a time in 8-bit graphics display mode.

Director offers gradients, which are blends of colors used mostly for backgrounds, shading, surfaces, and highlights. A gradient blend, from one color to another, can be rendered within an object in a particular direction, such as top to bottom, or left to right, or from the center, such as a shape burst or sun burst.

In the Paint window you can choose the foreground color for an object or pattern, which is the color you paint with; the background color, which is the secondary color in a pattern; and the gradient destination color for use with gradients.

## Using Gradients

A gradient is a blend of two colors that fills an enclosed shape. Director uses a process called *dithering* to mix the dots of different colors in a pattern to create a blend from one color to another. Director offers several dithering choices, as well as patterns for blending between colors or shades of gray. You can also blend from any color or gray to white or black.

A gradient is a special ink that can be used in the Paint window to fill an enclosed shape with the paint bucket, filled shape tools (rectangle, ellipse, and polygon), paintbrush, or bitmap text created (and still selected) with the text tool. Gradients also can be used to cover small areas painted with the Paintbrush tool.

The starting color for a gradient is the foreground color, which you can choose at any time for painting or for setting up a gradient. The second color is the destination color. The blend can be defined by the colors that are in between these two colors in the palette, or by the colors between these two colors. You can assign both colors in the Paint window using paint tools, or you can assign them while defining other gradients settings in the Gradients dialog box (select Gradients from the Paint menu to display the Gradients dialog box).

Artists often test gradient characteristics before actually using them. The gradient you set in the Gradients dialog box (Figure 4.28) remains in effect until you change it. The Gradients dialog box provides a preview display of a rectangle shape with the selected gradient.

The foreground and destination colors can be defined by clicking on the gradient destination selector. Click on the left side to bring up the palette to select the foreground color. Clicking on the right side brings up the palette for the destination color (Figure 4.29).

You can also define the foreground color by clicking on the foreground color chip, beneath the destination selector. The pattern for the gradient can be set in the pattern selector (Figure 4.30).

The Direction pop-up menu specifies the direction of the gradient—Top to Bottom, Bottom to Top, Left to Right, Right to Left, and so on. The Sun Burst starts at the edges and gradually changes to the center with concentric circles. The Shape Burst direction gradually changes to the center following the shape of the area to be filled or painted.

Directional gradients can be set, which allow you to decide which direction to run the gradient, when you use the filled shape or paintbrush tools. A directional line appears when you use the tool, and, when you click in a certain direction, the gradient is created in that direction.

**Figure 4.28**
**The Gradients dialog box with its gradient preview window is used to set up a gradient ink effect, which can be used with the text tool, filled shape tools, paint bucket, and the paintbrush tool in the paint window.**

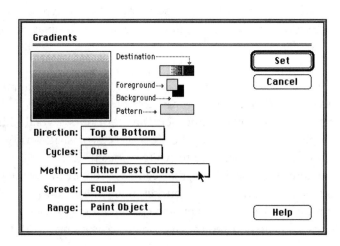

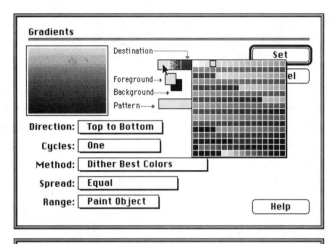

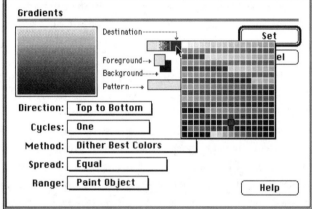

**Figure 4.29
Defining the fore-
ground and desti-
nation colors of
the gradient in
the Gradients dia-
log box.**

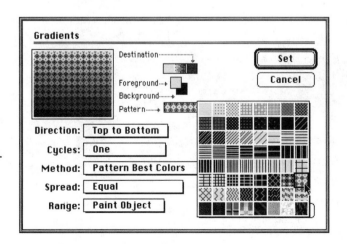

**Figure 4.30
Setting the pat-
tern for the gradi-
ent, which can
produce differ-
ent results de-
pending on the
Method chosen.**

In nearly all cases, the chosen pattern and/or method affects the result as well as the direction. The Method pop-up menu specifies whether to use the selected pattern, or a dither pattern generated by the computer.

For example, the Pattern Best Colors and Pattern Best Colors See Thru options ignore the order of colors in the palette, and use colors that would logically form a continuous blend. The Pattern Adjacent Colors and Pattern Adjacent Colors See Thru options, on the other hand, use the colors that are in between the two colors in the palette to form blends, and in the latter case, white pixels are treated as transparent.

The dither options ignore the selected pattern and create their own dither patterns. Dither Best Colors ignores the order of the colors in the palette and uses colors that form a continuous blend. Dither Adjacent Colors uses only the colors that are between the foreground and destination colors in the palette.

The Dither Two Color option uses only the foreground and destination colors when it forms its blending pattern. Dither One Color fades the foreground into white with a dither pattern (Figure 4.31). Both are useful when creating gradients for black-and-white displays, which offer only 1 bit per pixel.

The Standard Dither and Multi Dither options ignore the colors between the foreground and destination, and add several blended shades (of the foreground and background colors) in a smooth dither pattern. The Multi Dither option uses a randomized dither pattern to make the smoothest possible gradient.

The Cycles pop-up menu specifies how many complete gradients are to be created within one filled, or brushed, area. For more than one gradient, you can specify smooth or sharp cycles. Smooth goes from the foreground to destination and then back to foreground in an automatic reverse for each gradient. Sharp goes from foreground to destination for each gradient.

The Spread pop-up menu allows you to distribute colors in the blend with larger amounts of the foreground, destination, or middle colors by choosing those options. For example, the *Solar Heater* movie (filename: SOLARHTR.DIR in the

**Figure 4.31**
**Using the Dither One Color option with black as the foreground color for a gradient that will display on monochrome displays.**

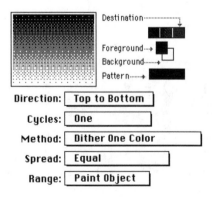

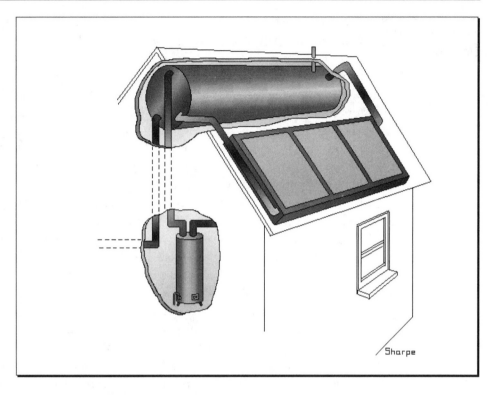

**Figure 4.32 The movie *Solar Heater* (filename: SOLARHTR.DIR) shows how distributed gradients can be used. The existing water heater shows the More Destination option with Two Smooth cycles, and the insulated storage tank shows More Foreground.**

TUTORIAL folder/directory) uses gradients that are distributed with more colors closer to the destination color for the existing water tank, and more colors closer to the foreground color for the insulated storage tank (Figure 4.32).

The Range pop-up provides greater control over how the gradient is created relative to the cast member's position on the stage, or in the Paint window. The options are Paint Object, Cast member, and Window.

Paint Object paints the full gradient as the fill or brush stroke of the object, regardless of the object's location in the Paint window. Cast member paints the full gradient with respect to the size of the cast member. Window paints a full gradient only if the object is the length, or width, of the entire window. Otherwise, it paints a partial gradient corresponding to the object's location in the window.

The Cast member option for Range is useful for touching up objects that already contain gradient fills, becaause the area you change will have a gradient range as if it filled the entire cast member.

The look of a gradient depends a great deal on the colors you've chosen for the foreground and destination, especially the colors that come between the two. You can edit a palette, and save custom palettes, for use with special gradient effects, as well as for color palette management.

**Using Color Palettes**

A palette is stored for every color image you scan, or create, with a graphics program. The palette contains the particular set of 256 colors to render that image in an 8-bit color display system. Before you create an image, the active palette is set to the System palette. If you never change this palette, the image you create uses the System palette. You can see the active palette, when you click the foreground, or background, color chip and drag it to the right to select a color. The selected color has a thicker outline than the rest of the color rectangles.

You can use any graphics program, including Director, to define custom palettes for creating images or to apply to scanned images. Director provides the ability to remap a cast member's colors to a new palette, or to import a cast member with its palette. Palettes can be stored separately, and a custom palette can be imported and used with more than one image or movie. In addition, Director supplies several built-in palettes you can use for images, including System-Mac, System-Win, Rainbow, Grayscale, Pastels, Vivid, NTSC (for video images), Metallic, and VGA (for consistent mapping of colors to 4-bit 16 color VGA Windows displays).

To switch to another palette, double-click the foreground or background color chip in the Paint window, or the gradient destination selector. You can also choose Color Palettes from the Window menu or press Command-8. The current palette is displayed and can be enlarged (click the zoom box in the upper-right corner of the window to display the palette full-screen size, or drag the size box in the lower-right corner to create any size window) so that you can see the colors to edit the palette, and you can choose from among the stored (and any imported) palettes in a pop-up menu (Figure 4.33).

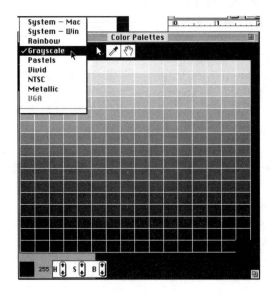

**Figure 4.33
The Color Palettes window allows you to switch palettes and manage the use of color among cast members.**

It is helpful to stay with the System palette as much as possible, or to use one palette for all cast members, as the need to change palettes between frames of a movie can slow it down. In fact, only one palette can be in effect for a given frame of animation, and all the cast members in that frame must share the same palette. A cast member may have its own palette, assigned in the Paint window, but when it is on the stage, the cast member is displayed using the colors of the active palette. The Palette channel in the Score determines which palette is active for a particular frame of the movie. (Note that everything displayed on the screen uses the active palette, including the Mac's Finder, and Windows Desktop, etc.) This is because you are limited to using an 8-bit color display mode, which is currently the ideal mode for animation. However, Director offers a Palette channel to facilitate switching between palettes from frame to frame, and special effects for blending one palette into another during animation.

When you switch to a new palette, the colors change based on their positions in the palette. The index number in the lower left corner of the Color Palettes window identifies each color position in the palette from zero to 255. If you switch the palette for a particular cast member, the cast member's colors change to the new colors that inhabit the same positions in the new palette. For example, if an image contains a sky blue color that is in position 144 in the System palette, switching to the Rainbow palette changes that color to bright yellow-green.

If you have created, or imported, cast members with different palettes, and you want to only use one palette for all of these cast members, you can avoid this direct replacement of colors by *remapping* cast members (changing the color grid) to the current palette, or create a new optimal palette, and remap the cast members to it. With remapping, Director chooses the best colors in the currently active palette and matches them to the cast member's original palette, regardless of the different color positions in palettes. The colors may not be identical, but they will be close.

If you are importing an image to the Paint or Cast windows, and the original palette for the image does not match the active palette, you are given the choice to remap (with dithering or not) (Figure 4.34), or to install the image's palette as a separate cast member, for storing and using multiple palettes in a movie.

Director has an automatic remapping facility, so you don't have to specify remapping, when importing graphics. You can set the option Remap Palettes when needed (Figure 4.35) in the Movie Info dialog box.

You can remap a cast member to another palette by selecting the cast member (or range of cast members) and using the Transform Bitmap command in the Cast menu (Figure 4.36).

You can remap all of the cast members that use a certain palette, using the Find Cast Members command in the Cast menu (Figure 4.37) to select them all,

**Figure 4.34**
**The bitmap (an imported PICT image) was created with a palette different from the one currently active, so you are given the choice to remap the bitmap's colors to the current palette or to store the bitmap's entire palette as a separate cast member.**

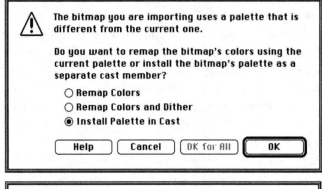

**Figure 4.35**
**The Movie Info dialog box has the option Remap Palettes when needed.**

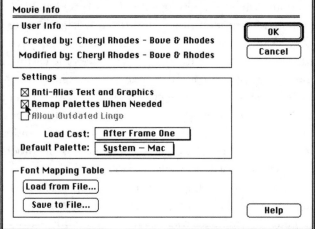

**Figure 4.36**
**Using the Transform bitmap dialog box to remap a cast member to a new palette.**

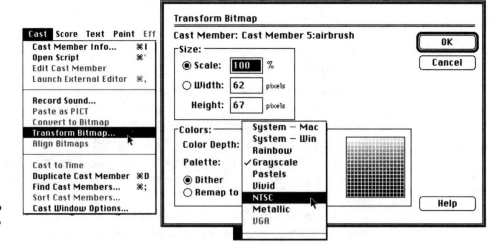

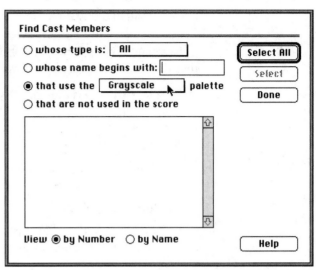

**Figure 4.37
Using Find Cast
Members to se-
lect all cast mem-
bers that use a
particular palette.**

then use the Transform Bitmap command to remap all the selected cast members at once to another palette.

If the Dither option is selected, it dithers the colors that are not available in the new palette, using whatever colors are available in the new palette for the dither pattern. Dithering usually provides the best results—it approximates the color by using a pattern of dots of other colors—but Director provides the option of turning it off. If the Dither option is not selected, colors are not dithered, but replaced with close choices. With solid colors (such as bar charts), it may be better to turn dithering off.

If you are not sure that the remapped image will look right, perform the operation on a clone (duplicate) of the cast member, so that the original cast member and its palette are preserved.

You do not have to remap cast members that are in black and white, because all palettes should contain a black and white that are fixed to the starting and ending cells of the palette. However, most gray-shaded images will have to be remapped when using a different palette.

## Creating a Common Palette

Custom palettes can be created by editing the colors in the Color Palettes window, and by copying and pasting colors from other palettes. One reason to create a custom palette is to create an optimal, common palette for use by all images (in case the System palette is not optimal). Another is to use a standard palette, but with some replacement colors. Director provides the tools to directly edit palettes.

You can also select the actual colors used in each of several cast members' original palettes, and clone a palette to build a new one that contains the right colors for all of the cast members (known as a *common palette*). Using the Palette menu you can automatically select the colors used by the particular cast member.

To create a common palette for a group of images, start with a cast member that does not use every color in its palette.

### 1. Select the used colors.

To see how many colors in the palette are used, select the cast member in the Cast window, and open the Color Palettes window. Choose Select Used Colors from the Palette menu, which displays a dialog box for selecting the colors used by the cast member. Click Select to select the colors. In the Color Palettes window, the selected colors are highlighted.

### 2. Clone the palette.

When you've found an image that uses only a few of the colors in its own palette, choose Duplicate from the Palette menu, and give the palette a new name.

### 3. Reposition the selected colors in the new palette.

Switch to the newly cloned palette (using the pop-up menu in the Color Palettes window), and choose the hand tool in the Color Palettes window. Then drag the selected colors to a new location in the palette. With the hand tool you can drag a single color to another location, or grab a selection of colors and move them to the top or bottom of the palette (or to any position). You can select a range of colors by dragging the hand across colors, before they are selected. Once you've selected one or more colors, dragging the hand moves the entire selection. If you drag a noncontiguous selection of colors to a new location, the selection is reorganized to be contiguous. (Command-click lets you select individual noncontiguous colors to add to the selection.) With the selected colors organized into a group at the top of the palette, you are ready to modify the palette.

### 4. Invert the selection to select the unused colors.

Choose Invert Selection from the Palette menu in order to reverse the selection (the color cells that were not selected are now selected).

### 5. Blend the unused colors to identify them.

Choose Blend from the Palette menu, so that the unused colors change into an identifiable blend. These are the colors you will replace with groups of colors from other palettes. (Creating the blend is an optional step that simply makes it easier to see the colors you want to replace.)

### 6. Pick colors from other palettes.

Switch to another cast member by clicking in the Cast window; its palette should also appear in the Color Palettes window. Select the used colors by choosing Select Used Colors from the Palette menu. Hold down the Command key while clicking color cells to deselect certain colors, if too many are selected. Select only the representative colors. The total number of colors, from all other palettes, can't exceed the range of unused colors in the optimal palette.

You can also select the colors directly, with the help of the eyedropper tool. You can click anywhere in the stage area with the eyedropper tool, and the color of the pixel you clicked on is selected in the Color Palettes window. (Clicking the arrow tool simply changes your pointer to the arrow.) To select a contiguous array of colors, click the first color in the range, and hold down the Shift key and click the last color in the range. To include, in one selection, colors that are not in a contiguous array, hold down Command while clicking the color.

With the colors selected, choose Copy Colors in the Edit menu. Switch back to the common palette, and select a range of color cells in the unused portion (the blended area) equal in number of cells to the copied range (or larger). Choose Paste into Palette in the Edit menu. The pasted selection replaces the original colors, starting from the position you clicked in the optimal palette.

Repeat this step for each cast member to be remapped to the common palette. Avoid copying the same colors from different palettes—if the color is already represented in the optimal palette, choose other colors that are not represented.

**7. Clone the cast members before remapping them.**

When you've finished building the optimal palette, choose the cast members to be remapped, and use the Copy Cast Members and Paste Cast Members commands to make clones of each. Or select all of the cast members and use the Duplicate cast member command in the Cast menu (Command-D) to duplicate them all at once. Select the clones, then use the Transform Bitmap command in the Cast menu to remap them to the common (optimal) palette.

## Editing Palettes

You can't change any of the standard palettes, but you can duplicate them and change the cloned versions. The best way to create a new custom palette is to start with an existing palette, duplicate it, and edit the color cells (or Copy and Paste color cell groups from other palettes). When you try to change a color in a standard palette, Director asks you to name a new palette, so that the standard palette is preserved.

The Color Palettes window offers hue, saturation, and brightness controls (HSB) for changing the color in any specific palette position.

**Figure 4.38**
**The Apple Color Picker can be displayed for changing any color in the Color Palettes window; it offers red, green, and blue controls as well as hue, saturation, and brightness.**

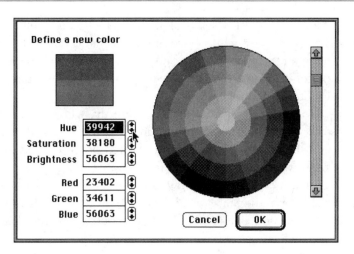

Hue is a color created by mixing two primary colors (resulting in six possibilities—three primary hues and three secondary hues). Saturation measures the amount of white mixed with a particular color. Full saturation produces vivid colors (no white mixed in), and less saturation produces pastels, or shades of gray (white mixed in). Brightness controls how much black is mixed in. Bright colors have little or no black, and as brightness is reduced, the color gets darker. A brightness value of zero produces total black, no matter what the hue and saturation values are set to.

You can change a single color in the palette by selecting Set Color from the Palette menu, or double-clicking a color in the palette. In the Macintosh version, the Apple Color Picker appears (Figure 4.38). Each of the 16.7 million possible colors can be selected using the Color Picker's red, green, and blue controls. Or, you can use the hue, saturation, and brightness controls, or point at a color in the wheel (use the scroll bar to change the brightness). When you click OK, you return to the Color Palettes window.

You can change a selection of colors by using the HSB controls. For example, you can select a group of colors, reduce their brightness or saturation in one operation, or cycle through hues. You can also change a group of colors, into a single color, by selecting the group, then choosing Set Color from the Palette menu, to bring up the Color Picker (or use the arrow tool to double-click any color in the Color Palettes window). The new color you choose occupies all the positions in the palette.

Other features of the Color Palettes window include:

- The **Blend** command to create a gradient between two colors in the palette.

- The **Reverse Color Order** command to reverse the position of a contiguous selection of colors, so that the first color becomes the last.

- The **Rotate Colors** command to shift colors by one position.
- The **Sort Colors** command to sort colors in the palette by hue, saturation, or brightness.
- The **Invert Selection** command to deselect all selected colors in the Color Palettes window and select all previously unselected colors.
- The **Reserve Colors** command to reserve colors, so that they are not used in Gradients.

However, gradients that use adjacent colors will use all colors in the gradient's color range, including any reserved colors, and in Smear, Smooth, and Cycle ink effects. Reserved colors are not available (they appear with stripes) in the Paint window, or Color Palettes window, or when Director is remapping a cast member. Select the colors you want to reserve in the Color Palettes window, and then use the Reserve Colors command, in the Palettes menu, to reserve the colors you want to use for color cycling, so that all other objects on the stage remain colored and are not affected by the color cycling.

The Blend command is particularly useful for preparing a fine gradient where you can control every color step of the gradient. The Reverse Color Order command can turn an image into a negative of itself by reversing each color with the color in the opposite position of the selection. You can also use the two together to reverse a blended selection.

Now that you understand the palette and how color can be assigned to objects, you are ready to try special effects such as custom patterns, brush shapes, image tiles, and ink effects.

## *Using Patterns*

To provide nearly every conceivable effect that could be useful to an animator, Director provides ink effects (described earlier), sets of different patterns, and the capability to edit patterns. In addition, a pattern called a *tile* can be created consisting of repetitions of a cast member.

**Using and Editing Patterns**

The Clipboard ink effect is used to define a pattern for the brush. To use the Clipboard effect on black-and-white images, you must transform them into 8-bit images.

To use the Clipboard as a pattern, copy some artwork to the Clipboard. It is usually necessary to select artwork with the lasso set to Shrink, or with the rectangle selection tool set to Lasso, so that the image used does not contain a white outline. Then, after clicking the paintbrush tool, select the Clipboard effect from the pop-up menu of Ink effects. Now, when you click the paintbrush tool,

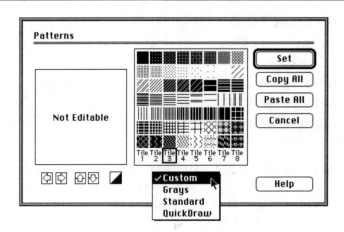

**Figure 4.39**
**The Patterns dialog box allow you to choose the current pattern set for the pop-up menu from among four built-in sets of patterns.**

the Clipboard image appears. You can click the paintbrush tool a number of times to add more images. If you drag with the paintbrush tool, you get the equivalent of the image dragged with the Slide effect. The Clipboard effect makes it easier and faster to make multiple copies of a particular image.

You can choose a pattern from a pop-up menu by clicking the pattern selector chip under the foreground and background color chips. The patterns displayed in the pop-up menu are the current set of patterns (using the active palette) for use as area fills, geometric shape fills, and paintbrush strokes. Double-clicking the pattern chip displays the Patterns dialog box, where you can edit existing patterns, or select new sets of patterns.

Director offers four sets of patterns (Grays, Standard, QuickDraw, and Custom), and you can view them, and define the current pattern set for the pop-up menu, by opening the Patterns dialog box and selecting Patterns from the Paint menu, or double-click the pattern selector. The Custom palette is the same as the Default palette until you change it by editing patterns in the Patterns dialog box to create a Custom palette.

The Patterns dialog box (Figure 4.39) provides a pop-up menu to choose from among four different sets of patterns. The Grays, Standard, and QuickDraw sets contain patterns that cannot be edited.

The Custom set, however, provides patterns that can be edited (Figure 4.40). Clicking a pattern in the Custom set displays the pattern, enlarged, in the pixel editing window. You can click any pixel to change it from black to white (or, when working in color, from the foreground color to the background color). You can also shift the pattern up or down, or side to side with the arrows below the editing window. The diagonal black-white icon reverses all of the pixels in the pattern (creating a negative of the pattern).

When you click outside the Patterns dialog box, the pattern in that area is copied to the editing window, so you can incorporate it into the Custom pattern

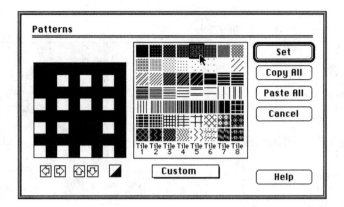

**Figure 4.40 Using the Custom pattern set, in which individual patterns can be edited in the pixel editing window.**

set. You can copy the patterns of the other three sets by selecting the pattern set (for example, the QuickDraw patterns) and using the Copy All button. Then, select the Custom set, and use the Paste All button. This button is also useful if you've edited one or more patterns in the Custom set, but you want to undo the editing. Use Copy All to copy the current set of patterns, then edit, then use Paste All if you need to reset the patterns to their original form.

To store more than one set of custom patterns on a Macintosh, use the Scrapbook. Edit the Custom palette in the Patterns dialog box, click Copy All, then click Cancel and Paste the Custom palette into the Scrapbook. To replace the current Custom palette with one from the Scrapbook, open the Scrapbook, select the Pattern palette, Copy it, then use the Paste All command in the Patterns dialog box to replace it. The current Custom palette is stored in the Director 4.0 Preferences file.

When you click on the pattern selector in the Paint window, the current pattern set is displayed and you can select any pattern. If you hold down the Option key while clicking the pattern selector chip, the patterns are replaced by shades starting with the foreground color and blending to the background color. On a black-and-white display, these shades are the same as the Grays pattern set. The current pattern set stays as shades, until you hold down the Option key again, when clicking the pattern selector chip to switch back to the default patterns.

You can create patterns that use the foreground and background colors, but to use more colors in a pattern, you need to create a *tile*. A *tile* is a repeating image created from artwork and used as a building block for a custom pattern.

**Creating Tiles**

The bottom row of patterns in the Standard and QuickDraw pattern sets are reserved for tiles 1 through 8. Director offers eight default tiles. You can create more tiles from cast members. Tiles can be used as a pattern with the Paint tools in the Paint window, and with the shape tools in the Tools window. However,

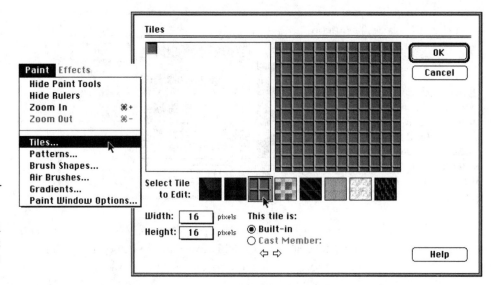

**Figure 4.41**
**The Tiles dialog box allows you to start from a default tile or from the image of a cast member, and to define a height and width for the tile.**

tiles can only be edited/created in the Paint window on Macintoshes and Windows machines set to a color depth greater than 1 bit. The foreground and background color settings do not affect the color of tiles, but the color of tiles is affected by palette changes.

A tile can be as small as 16 by 16 pixels, or as large as 128 by 128 pixels. Each tile appears in the patterns pop-up selector. When you use tiles, the background and foreground colors have no effect, unless you combine the use of tiles with a particular ink effect. However, if you switch palettes, the tiles are affected.

To create a tile, choose the Tiles command from the Paint menu. You can start with a default tile, or a cast member, by clicking one of the radio buttons (Figure 4.41). To select a default tile, click one of the tiles displayed. You can set the width and height in pixels. The tile you clicked is the one replaced by the newly modified one.

If you choose to start with a cast member, left and right arrows appear to cycle through the cast members. Cast members that are greater than 1 bit deep in color resolution can be used to make tiles. If the Cast Member radio button is gray, all the cast members in your movie are 1-bit (black-and-white) cast members, and can't be used to create a tile. If you are working on a color Mac or Windows machine, start with the desired 1-bit cast member displayed in the active easel in the Paint window. Then use the Transform Bitmap command to convert the 1-bit cast member to 8 bits, before attempting to create a tile from it. The selection rectangle, positioned over a portion of the cast member displayed in the Tile dialog box, can be adjusted by dragging it to show different parts of a cast member, including white space, for creating the tile (Figure 4.42). The size of the

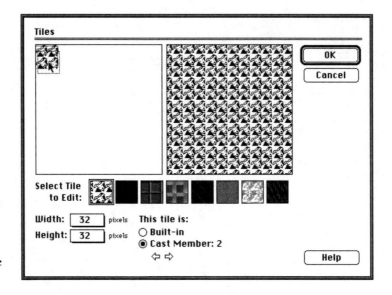

**Figure 4.42 Starting from a cast member and selecting part of the image and part of the white space to form the tile.**

selection rectangle is determined by the Width and Height settings. When you click OK, this new tile replaces one of the eight default tiles, depending on which one was selected. The tiles you create are saved with the Director document (movie file), unlike patterns, which are saved in Director's Preferences file.

Tiles can be effective as fills and brush strokes, and they are often used in conjunction with masked cast members to obtain unusual effects.

## *Chapter Summary*

This chapter addressed many of the details of using Director's Paint window to create and modify bitmap graphics. It also described the differences between bitmap graphics and QuickDraw objects.

This chapter explained how color can be used, and how color palettes control what colors are displayed on 1-bit, 4-bit, and 8-bit graphics displays. You learned about painting with brushes, and transforming images by flipping, rotating, slanting, and distorting them. You also learned how to use Auto Distort to create intermediate cast members between two shapes.

The next chapter shows how ink effects in the Score window are used with layered cast members, to merge the cast members smoothly and create sophisticated animations.

# 5

# *Animation Techniques*

**It's all in the mind.**

George Harrison, Beatle, *Yellow Submarine*

**P**rofessional animators have many techniques at their disposal for creating realistic animation and the illusion of three-dimensional space. The most successful cartoons are those that make the audience believe that the characters are real, and that space and time are accurately portrayed. Even more effective are those which manipulate perspective and visual imagery to suggest human emotion and pathos.

The same principles used by professional animators can be highly effective when put to use in a multimedia presentation. However, it is not enough to use whizzy graphics and colorful images—you should also pay attention to how and when animation elements are presented, and which style or effect is most appropriate for your subject, concept, and audience. For example, in many cases a caricature of a person is more effective at communicating an idea than a scanned image.

Director provides a collection of tools and features for manipulating animation so that you can make it look exactly as you want. However, you have to know what you want. There is no substitute for training in visualization, graphic design, and animation.

In this chapter, you'll learn some of the techniques used by professional animators and multimedia artists. You'll also learn important methods for managing multimedia projects, such as combining several movies into a presentation, managing the use of cast members for several projects, and adding comments to the score to be used as markers for scripts and for editing and updating.

## Film Loops

You have already learned how to create movies using standard animation methods involving text, automatic animation, transitions, and simple graphic images. You've also explored the basics of painting and drawing with Director. Now we'll show you how to use both facilities to create more realistic animation and special effects.

One important animation technique is to create a repeating sequence, called a *film loop*, and use it as a cast member for sprites in other sequences. You can create film loops for a variety of tightly designed animated sequences and use them over and over in several different movies. A walking animal or human figure is a fine example of the use of a film loop.

The benefit of using a film loop over other methods of encapsulating animation is the use of Director's In-Between Special feature. You can in-between a film loop from one point to another, and it will be animated through all the frames. For example, if you in-between a walking man film loop, the man walks from one point on the stage, to another, automatically.

There are other ways to encapsulate animation and then use it as a canned sequence in other movies. You can, for example, save the sequence as a Director movie and import the movie into another movie as a cast member. You can also play a Director movie as a window within another Director movie, which is a technique described in Chapter 9, "Tips and Advanced Techniques," and requires a bit of knowledge about Lingo scripting (see Chapter 6, "Elementary Scripting").

Another way is to export a selected sequence (or an entire movie) as a QuickTime movie. QuickTime offers time-based synchronization with sound, and is supported by a variety of editing programs. Another way is to export it as a PICS file, a frame-based format that can be imported into Director's Cast window. QuickTime is the preferred format, since you can edit a QuickTime movie in Director's Digital Video window, or in other editing programs such as Adobe Premiere. These techniques are described in Chapter 8, "Using Video."

Why are there so many different ways? Each has its own set of limitations and advantages. Film loops, for example, can't have cast member or sprite scripts attached to them, and you can't apply ink effects to a completed film loop—you must set the ink effects first, then define the film loop. For more script flexibility, try using movie-in-a-window. For completely synchronized sequences, try Quick-Time. However, if you are animating a walking or flying character, film loops might do the trick nicely.

## Creating a Film Loop

A film loop is a sequence you intend to repeat continuously, which can be saved as an independent cast member. A film loop is created using step recording techniques using different cast members, and then copying from the score and pasting into a cast member position. You can also create one simply by importing

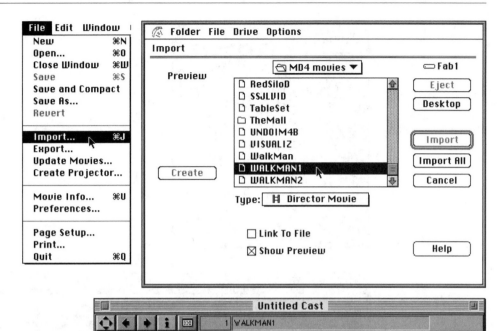

**Figure 5.1**
**The Import dialog box for importing a Director movie to use as a film loop; the film loop's name is the movie name.**

a Director movie because when the movie is imported, it's converted to a film loop.

Film loops are often created to show a running or walking character, a flying bird, or some other animated creature whose motions must be repeated in a certain sequence to simulate movement.

To create a film loop, you must first create the animated sequence to be repeated. You created one earlier, when you used the Space to Time command in Chapter 3 in an early version of the *Walking Man* movie (filename: WALK-MAN1.DIR), in which the cast members for the walking man were first arranged on the stage in one frame, then automatically animated with the Space to Time command.

The easiest way to use this movie as a film loop is to import it into a new movie. Choose New from the File menu, and then choose Import. The Import dialog box lets you change the file type (Figure 5.1) to Director Movie and select a movie to import. The result is a film loop and the cast members that comprise it.

Another way to make a film loop is to select a sequence in the score, apply the Copy Cells command, then Paste into an empty slot in the Cast window; or

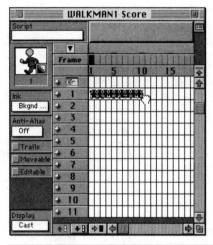

**Figure 5.2**
**Pasting (or drag-**
**ging) a score se-**
**lection into an**
**empty slot in the**
**Cast window to**
**define a film**
**loop and give it a**
**name.**

you can simply drag the selected sequence into an empty slot in the Cast window. The sequence can be any size and any number of channels, and you can include sound channels. A dialog box appears asking you to name the film loop (Figure 5.2). Director stores the film loop in the cast member position.

Although the film loop is stored as a cast member, you still must keep the original cast members in their original Cast positions for the film loop to work properly. If you move any of the cast members to other positions, the film loop will not work.

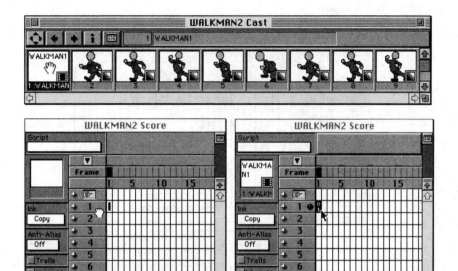

**Figure 5.3
Dragging the film loop cast member to the Score window in order to place it directly into a sprite channel in the score in the first position.**

## In-Betweening a Film Loop

The film loop is now ready to use in the movie. While you do this, you can learn yet another way to place a sprite on the stage in a frame. Drag it from the Cast window to a cell in the Score window. Drag the film loop cast member directly to the cell in channel 1, frame 1 (Figure 5.3).

You've recorded the first position of the film loop sprite. You may want to adjust the position of the film loop sprite on the stage before proceeding.

Now scroll the Score window to frame 60, and drag the film loop cast member from the Cast window into the score directly to the cell in channel 1, frame 60 (Figure 5.4). Move that sprite into the destination position on the stage.

Now, select the range of cells in channel 1 from frames 1 through 60 (click one end, and Shift-click the other). Use the In-Between Special command, and set the Apply to Film Loop option (Figure 5.5). The 'tweened frames now contain different cast members representing the sprite, as they were defined in the film loop, so that the loop animates as it moves across the stage.

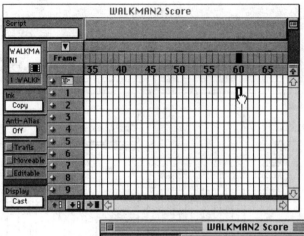

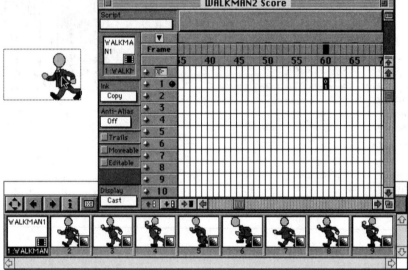

**Figure 5.4
Dragging the film
loop cast mem-
ber to its last po-
sition in the
Score window,
then moving the
sprite into posi-
tion on the stage.**

You can also use real-time recording techniques (described in Chapter 3) to
record a film loop. However, this method can be imprecise. It is usually better
to arrange the sprites at the beginning and end of the sequence as we did above,
and use the In-Between Special command to fill out the sequence.

With In-Between Special, you can set the path of the film loop's movement to
go inside or outside the defined points by dragging the slider that defines the
curve. To define a more accurate curve, you can drag more film loop cast
members to their score positions as described above, and use In-Between Special
again to re-'tween them.

You also can choose options from the pop-up menus to accelerate over the first
few frames, and decelerate over the last few frames, so that the movement is realistic.

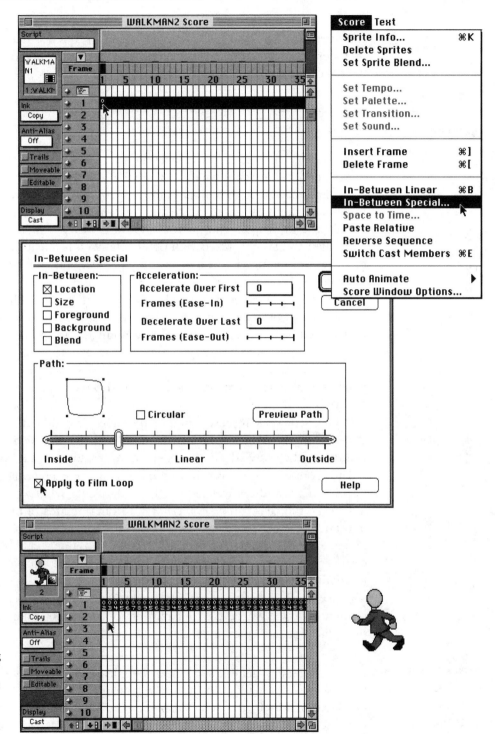

**Figure 5.5
Selecting the
range of cells by
clicking one end
and Shift-clicking
the other, then
using In-Between
Special with the
Apply to Film
Loop option.**

The most powerful feature of film loops is the ability to treat a film loop as a cast member. You can, for example, define a sequence that uses another cast member, then switch the film loop for the other cast member to use the same animation path.

# Score Techniques

Nearly every technique for animating in Director involves some editing of information in the Score window. Everything in a movie is controlled either by Score information or by scripts. Almost anything in the movie can be changed by direct manipulation of Score information, except for the content of cast members and scripts. The Score window is where all frame-based action is controlled and synchronized with other actions. It is like a spreadsheet detailing the action of the movie, with each cell representing a unit of time on a layer of animation.

The Score resembles a musical score in that it charts the appearance and characteristics of instruments (in this case, cast members as sprites) over time, moving left to right. Cast members are arranged as sprites in horizontal rows called channels, which are layers containing a graphic or text object and its appearance over time. Additional elements, such as sounds, transitions, color palettes, timers, and script instructions, are also recorded in the score in separate channels.

Vertical columns represent frames of time. The unit of time measurement depends on the speed, expressed in frames per second, which is set by the Tempo channel of the score (defaulting to the tempo setting in the Control Panel).

The score can be viewed in one of several ways, controlled by options in a pop-up menu at the lower left corner of the Score window. In any view, score information in cells can be copied or cut from one area of the score and pasted into another area. Score information can also be cut or copied and pasted into other movie documents, or into a cast member position as a film loop as described earlier. Selected score cells can also be dragged from one location in the score to another, and to the Cast window.

Other score techniques include using Paste Relative to paste a copy of a sequence down where the original left off, and using Reverse Sequence to duplicate a sequence in reverse.

**Adding Marker Labels**

If you are creating generic sequences to be used in other movies, it helps to have these sequences marked in the score with markers so that you can find them quickly. Markers in the score also serve to locate specific frames for editing purposes, and they are indispensable as labels for scripts (described in Chapter 6).

In the second-to-left column of the Score window above the word Frame is a down-arrow symbol called the *marker well*. If you drag from this symbol well to the right, a marker appears in its own channel (Figure 5.6). You can use this marker to mark sections of the score for various reasons, such as adding a label to the score and adding comments to explain the labels.

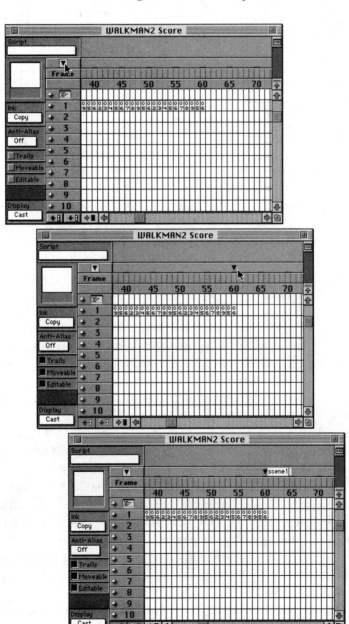

**Figure 5.6
Dragging from
the marker well
to add a marker
label, then typing
a label.**

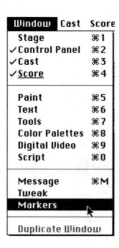

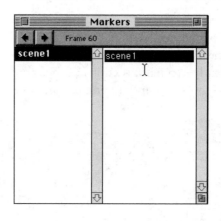

**Figure 5.7
Double-click a
marker or use
the Markers com-
mand in the Win-
dows menu to
bring up the
Markers window,
which lets you as-
sign comments
to markers.**

Marker labels, also known as *frame labels,* are used for identifying particular
frames for adding scripts as described in the next chapter. For example, you might
add the capability to play different segments of a movie, or different movies, by
clicking on a button or cast member that executes a "go to" instruction to start
playing the movie from a particular frame. With a frame label, you can specify
the label rather than the exact frame number, so that if you insert or delete frames
later on, your scripts still work properly. Using labels also makes your Lingo
scripts easier to read.

You will most likely want to create a marker label for the starting frame of any
important animated sequence. It is helpful to use a single memorable word as a
label, rather than a lengthy phrase (although you can type anything as a label).
This way, the label does not extend too far beyond the actual frame it describes.
A short label is also more useful than a long one when using labels in scripts.

Double-click the marker on top of the frame, and Director opens the Markers
window (Figure 5.7). The Markers window can help you navigate through a
complex movie, such as Stuart Sharpe's *Sketch Book Source* (filename:
SKETCHBK.DIR), found in the TUTORIAL folder/directory of the accompanying
CD-ROM.

Open this movie, and use the Markers command to see how many labels there
are (Figure 5.8). The left and right arrows above the labels in the Markers window
allow you to advance from one label to the next in a score. You can also click
the labels to move directly to those sections of the score.

You can drag as many markers as you wish to create labels. When the Markers
window is open, the Text menu becomes active, and you can set the font, size,
and style of the text.

As you will learn in the next chapter, Lingo scripts can refer to labeled frames.
Scripts can also refer to frames by frame number, but if you insert or delete frames,

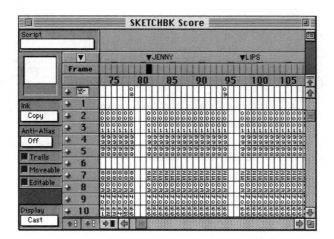

**Figure 5.8
In Stuart
Sharpe's *Sketch
Book Source*
(filename:
SKETCHBK.DIR),
you can jump to
score sections by
clicking the
labels.**

the scripts may end up referring to the wrong frame. Thus, labels are extremely useful for scripting because the label stays attached to the frame it describes. If you add or delete frames, the label still points to the correct frame, no matter what the frame number is. You don't have to change your scripts every time you insert or delete a frame.

## Copying Cells to Other Movies

One major benefit of using the digital medium for creating graphics is that the graphics can be copied from one document to another without any loss of information or quality. If you can copy digital graphics to and from documents, why not copy complete animated segments?

Actually, many of the Director techniques you use to create movies involve borrowing from other movies. It may not be simple to create animated sequences with special effects. However, once they are created, they can be used again and again in other movie documents simply by using the Copy Cells and Paste Cells commands.

Suppose you wanted to use a particular sequence from another movie. Scroll the Score window to the marker for the end of the sequence. Select the cells in the sequence, and use the Copy Cells command in the Edit menu to copy the score information to the Clipboard (Figure 5.9).

Open another movie or choose New in the File menu. If you have just performed the copy operation, the selected area of the score will remain selected as you open the new movie (or existing movie). You can paste directly into this selection. If, however, there is no selection, you can select the cell in the first open channel of the first empty frame.

When you choose Paste Cells in the Edit menu, the score information is copied into the channels. If you are pasting into another movie, the cast members are automatically copied to the first open positions in the Cast window (Figure 5.10).

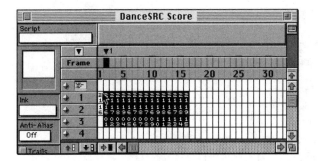

**Figure 5.9 Selecting and copying cells to the Clipboard. Cast member information is automatically copied along with score information.**

There are two important rules to remember when using Copy and Paste. First, before using the command, check to see what it says. Copy Cast performs a different action (copying a cast member) from Copy Cells, which copies score information that could include several cast members. You use Copy Cast to copy the artwork of a cast member to another cast member position or to another movie. You use Copy Cells to copy the actual position or positions of one or

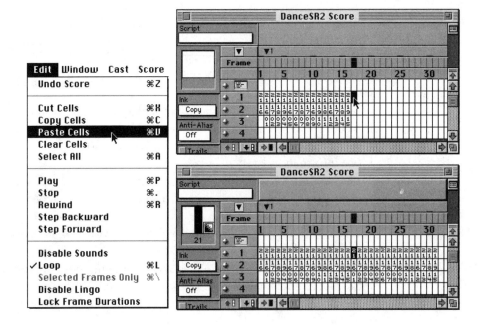

**Figure 5.10 Pasting cells from the Clipboard into the score.**

more sprites on the stage over one or more frames, and their cast members. Copy Cells copies both the cast member(s) and the sprites, including position, ink effect, and so on.

The second rule is a general one for nearly all programs. Whatever you copy to the Clipboard must be pasted somewhere else before you use any other Copy command, because the Clipboard is wiped clean every time you use a Copy command. Its contents are completely replaced by the newly copied item.

Essentially the actions of the Copy and Paste commands depend on which window is currently the active window. The active window is the one with horizontal lines and a close box in the title part of the window, and only one window can be active at a time. You make a window active by clicking within it.

The actions also depend on the type of data that is currently stored in the Clipboard. For example, if you use Copy Cells to copy score information to the Clipboard, then switch to the Cast window and select a cast member position, the Paste Cells command is active because score information is what is stored in the Clipboard. If you then use the Paste Cells command to paste score information into the cast member position, you create a film loop.

Score information can be copied to the Clipboard and then pasted into the Scrapbook for temporary storage. You can copy and then paste animation clips into the Scrapbook in order to use the same clips in different movies. The Scrapbook acts as a database of animation, containing all the score information you need to use the clip in another movie.

The stage is not a window, and Copy and Paste commands can't be used with objects on the stage. When you click on objects in the stage area, the score information for the selected object for that frame is automatically selected in the Score window. You can use the Sprite Info command in the Score menu to see information about that sprite. You can also delete a sprite from the stage with the Delete Sprites command in the Score menu. You can even switch to the Score window, where you can select the Score information for one or more frames and use Cut Cells.

## Various Ways of Selecting Cells

The actions of the Copy Cells and Cut Cells commands are different depending on the area of the Score window you have selected. If one cell is selected, only one cast member and its sprite (score information) are copied or cut from the Score. If a range of cells is selected, all cast members used as sprites in that range are cut or copied.

There are various methods of selecting cells. You can click in a single cell, or drag across a range of cells—but be careful not to drag the contents of those cells to a new location! It is best to hold down the Shift key and click to establish the ending of a range of cells. You can also hold down the Shift key and click more contiguous cells to add to a selection.

To add discontiguous channels to a selection, hold down the Command key and click the last cell of the sequence in the alternate channel. The same range of cells selected in the first channel are also selected in the alternate channel.

By double-clicking the channel number, you can select all the cells in a channel from the beginning of the movie to the end. By double-clicking and dragging down from a channel number, you can select a range of contiguous channels. You can achieve the same effect by Shift-clicking the last channel in the range of contiguous channels.

With all these methods, if you select less than all of the channels of the selected frames, the Cut Cells command simply removes the information from the space, and leaves empty cells behind. The Paste Cells command in such cases simply replaces whatever is in those cells—you click the starting cell, and it fills in the rest starting from that cell. In both cases the movie's length is not affected.

If, on the other hand, you select all the channels in a frame or range of frames, and you use the Cut Cells command, the frames are removed and the movie is shortened. The easiest way to select all of the channels in one or more frames is to drag across one or more frame numbers (Figure 5.11).

As we saw in Chapter 3, if you click a single frame number and make a frame insertion point, the frame's inner line starts to blink. The Paste Cells command

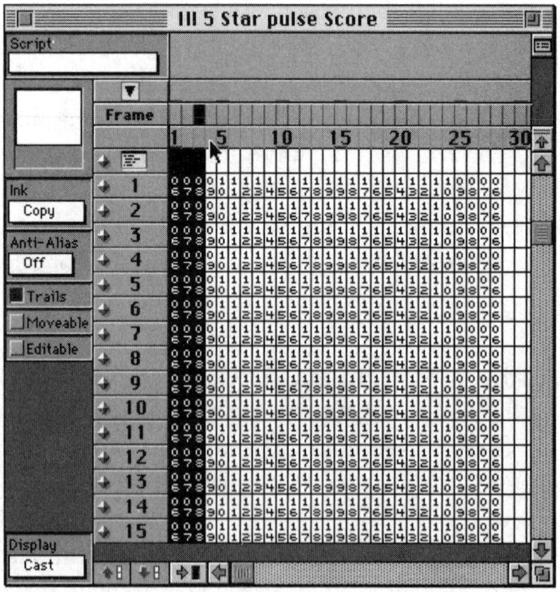

**Figure 5.11
Dragging across
frame numbers
to select all of the
channels on
those frames.**

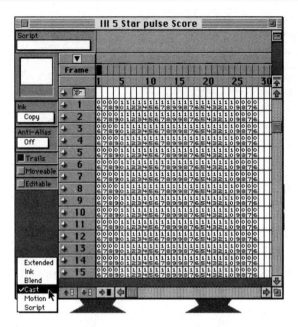

**Figure 5.12
The pop-up menu for selecting different views of the score, which is currently set to showing cast member numbers.**

will then insert new frames rather than replace the contents of existing frames. When you use Paste Cells after setting a frame insertion point, the movie is lengthened by the number of frames you are pasting from the Clipboard.

Another way to add or subtract frames is to use the Insert Frame and Delete Frame commands in the Edit menu, as described in Chapter 3. Delete Frame simply takes the selected frames out of the movie. Insert Frame adds frames and repeats the contents of the frame at the insertion point (the current frame).

No matter how you are selecting cells in the Score, it helps to know what is in those cells. Director offers several views of score information, including an expanded view offering score notation for all the information.

## Understanding Score Notation

The pop-up menu in the lower left corner of the Score window lets you change your view of the Score. When it is set to Cast (Figure 5.12), you see the cast member numbers in the cells.

Director offers other settings for viewing the score with the Score Window Options dialog box available from the Score menu (Figure 5.13). You can add color to cells for easy identification, and you can magnify cells to see them better on large displays.

The pop-up menu provides the quickest way to change score information. You can change this menu to the Ink notation (Figure 5.14). It shows a single-letter abbreviation for the ink effect (such as M for Matte or C for Copy), and a dotted

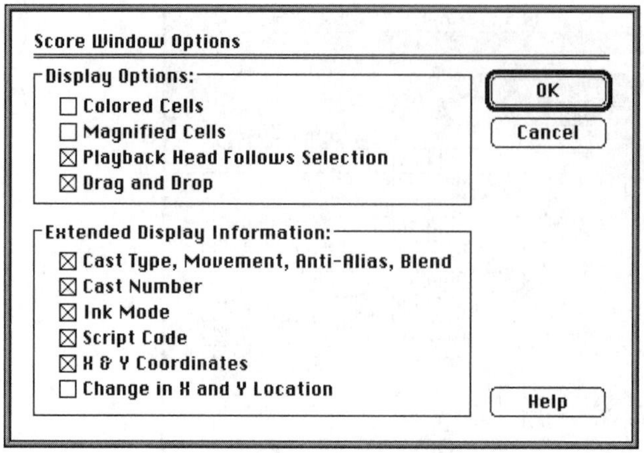

**Figure 5.13**
**The Score Window Options dialog box.**

line for the Trails effect, in the lower part. The upper part shows a symbol indicating one of the following:

- A drawn object (Q).
- A bitmap cast member (B).
- A PICT cast member (P).
- A text cast member (T).

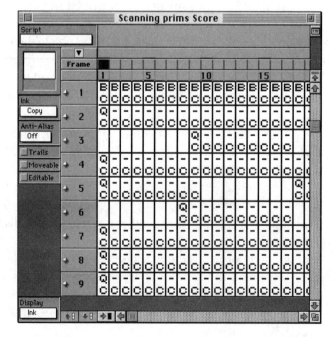

**Figure 5.14**
**Ink notation, which shows the type of ink effect, type of cast member, and use of the Trails effect (the Score is magnified with the Magnify option).**

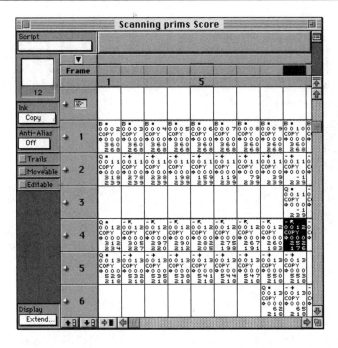

**Figure 5.15**
**The Extended notation, showing cast member type and number, ink effect, X and Y coordinates on the stage, and the change in the X and Y coordinates from the previous frame.**

The Motion notation shows arrows indicating motion as the lower symbol. The Script notation shows only zeroes in movie documents that contain no scripts, or it shows the number of the script. Scripts are described in Chapter 6.

The Extended display shows all of this information, plus more (Figure 5.15). The X and Y coordinates are the screen coordinates of the position of the cast member. You can add information about the change in the X and Y coordinates from the previous frame, which is relative to the previous cast member in that channel. Just select that option from the Score Window Options dialog box.

The score information can be quite useful, especially when combined with frame labels. Knowing how to edit the score opens up many possibilities for creating sequences. A variety of animation techniques are based on the ability to directly manipulate scenes by switching cast members in the score.

## Using Paste Relative

With Paste Relative you can link sequences into a continuous motion, so that a sequence of cast members forming one animated object can move in a controlled path on the stage.

First, create one complete sequence of cast members to represent the animated object. Then select the sequence, use Copy Cells to copy it to the Clipboard, then use Paste Relative to paste a copy back into the score. However, rather than starting the copy at the same place as the original, Paste Relative starts the copy at the position where the original stops. This feature makes it easy to lay down a set of sequences that form a continuous motion across the stage.

**Figure 5.16 The movie *Chicago* (filename: CHICAGO.DIR) demonstrates how Paste Relative could be used to make the rotating football sailing through the goal post sequence.**

For example, the movie *Chicago* (filename: CHICAGO.DIR), found in the TUTORIAL folder/directory of the accompanying CD-ROM, has a rotating football sailing through the air and between the twin poles of a field goal post (Figure 5.16). This path could be set using In-Between Special with a film loop. However, for more tight control, Paste Relative works better.

First, the cast members for the rotating football are created in the Paint window (using one football image and several clones rotated to the proper position). Next, one sequence of the rotating football is created. This sequence is selected, and copied to the Clipboard with the Copy Cells command. After selecting the next cell in the same channel, use Paste Relative to paste the copied sequence into the channel (Figure 5.17). You repeat this procedure until the object reaches its ending point of the motion.

A pause sometimes occurs between sequences when using Paste Relative. To avoid this pause, create the original sequence to include the first position of the next sequence (one extra frame). Then select this extra frame and use Paste Relative to replace this frame and subsequent frames. The goal is to use the same cast member at the beginning and end of a sequence, and overlap that ending cell with the first cell of the copy.

## Reversing Sequences

Another useful Score menu command is Reverse Sequence, which takes a selected sequence in the score and turns it around to be the reverse of what it was. This technique is used to make moving objects that go from one position to another and then back to the original position.

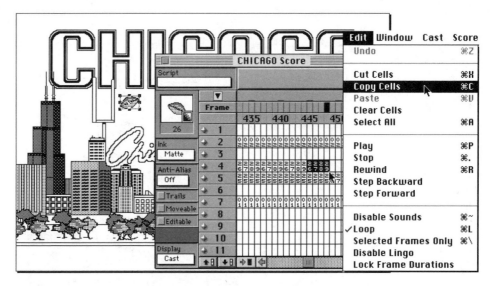

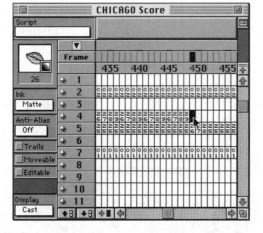

**Figure 5.17**
**The football sequence is selected, copied to the Clipboard, and then placed with Paste Relative in the same channel after the original sequence so that the copied sequence starts where the original sequence left off.**

For example, the movie *Radar & Satellite* (filename: RADARSAT.DIR), found in the TUTORIAL folder/directory of the accompanying CD-ROM, uses reversed sequences to animate the satellite dish (Figure 5.18).

First you create a sequence that defines the animated object going in a certain direction. Then select the sequence, copy it to the Clipboard, use Paste Cells to paste it into the score, and finally select the sequence and use the Reverse Sequence command to reverse it (Figure 5.19).

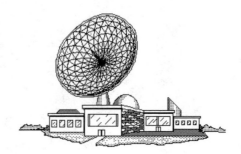

**Figure 5.18
The animated sat-
ellite dish in the
*Radar & Satellite*
movie (filename:
RADARSAT.DIR).**

The movie *Factory* by Stuart Sharpe (filename: FACTORY.DIR), found in the
TUTORIAL folder/directory of the accompanying CD-ROM, shows extensive use
of the Reverse Sequence command with the robot arms that move in one direction
and then reverse their movements (Figure 5.20).

Each robot arm is a combination of cast members in a sequence that runs in
regular order and then in reverse (Figure 5.21). The alternating regular and
reversed sequences help provide the illusion of a connected arm.

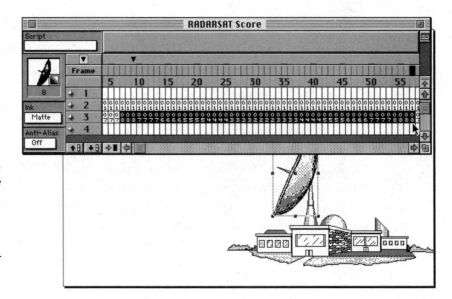

**Figure 5.19
The score for the
*Radar & Satellite*
movie (filename:
RADARSAT.DIR)
shows how one
sequence is used
over and over, al-
though reversed
each time.**

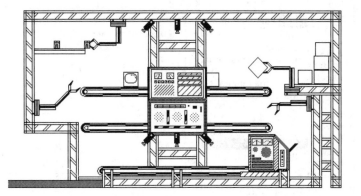

**Figure 5.20**
**The movie *Factory* by Stuart Sharpe (filename: FACTORY.DIR) demonstrates how reversed sequences can be used to show movement backwards and forwards (the robot arms).**

## Compositing Images

One of Director's greatest strengths is its ability to combine various images in a single frame, with great speed. Director can create *composite* images by combining cast members. You can then turn those composites into single cast members to use in other animation sequences.

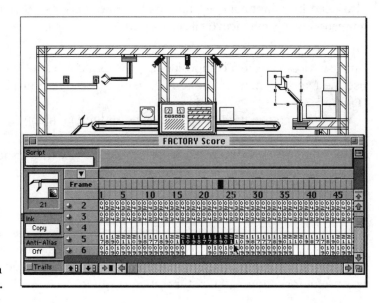

**Figure 5.21**
**The Score of the movie *Factory* with a robot arm selected, showing the different cast members in forward and then reverse sequence.**

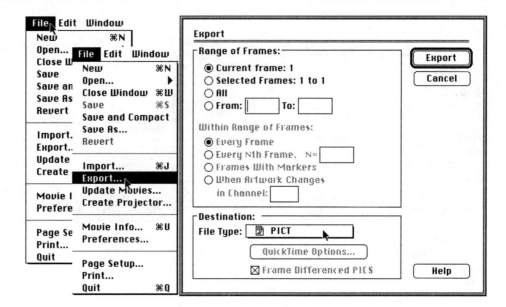

**Figure 5.22 Exporting a single frame as a PICT file to create a composite image of several elements.**

There are a number of tricks you can do with compositing. For example, you can go beyond the 48-channel capacity of the score by compositing some of the objects into one object that occupies a single channel.

Compositing images is a tradeoff. Replacing multiple cast members with one composite cast member is a good idea, especially if they need to have the Matte ink effect. This reduces the amount of memory required to run the animation. On the other hand, the composite image may occupy too much memory if you also need its components in the Cast for other reasons, such as using them for animation or for interactive click-on sprites.

## Copying the Stage to a File

An easy way to create a composite image is to put its elements on the stage, and use the Export command in the File menu to export an image file of the stage (Figure 5.22).

You can then use the Import command in the File menu to import the image as a separate cast member.

When compositing images, it helps to know a few tricks, such as how to use the Mask ink effect, and how to create backgrounds for text characters that are composited with graphics.

## Using Masks

A *mask* is a cloned cast member or graphic image in a cast member position immediately to the right of the original cast member. It directly affects the way the original cast member appears on the stage in relation to other cast members. It is useful for setting up a cast member to either:

- Be transparent and opaque in different places.

- Show a pattern or tiles in certain areas of an image.

- Show a cast member through another graphic image without showing an outline.

You would use a mask if you have a graphic image that contains a lot of white areas and patterns where white is the background color. You want some of the white areas to be transparent so that the artwork behind the image shows through. Also, some of the areas should be opaque so that if you move the image, it does not show the underlying artwork.

For a simple example, take a look at the *Cursors* movie (filename: CURSOR), found in the Tutorial folder/directory of the accompanying CD-ROM. The pointer cursor has a mask that is just like it, only slightly larger, due to an extra line of black pixels around it (Figure 5.23). That extra line of black pixels masks to white when the pointer cast member is placed on the stage with the Mask ink. The pointer cast member would otherwise nearly disappear into a black background with the Matte ink effect, since it is also black.

**Figure 5.23**
**The arrow cursor in the *Cursors* movie (filename: CURSORS.DIR) has a mask in the next higher numbered Cast slot that allows the white edge of the arrow to appear when the arrow is composited with a black background.**

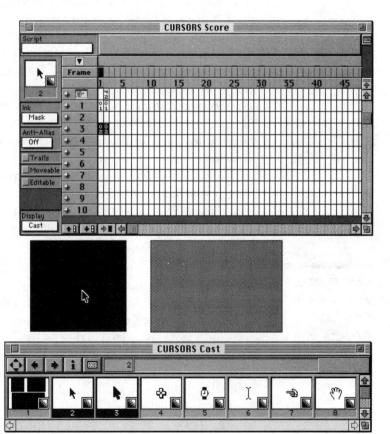

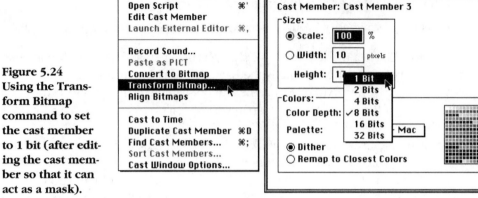

**Figure 5.24**
**Using the Transform Bitmap command to set the cast member to 1 bit (after editing the cast member so that it can act as a mask).**

Another example of how you might use the Mask ink effect is to show a moving car with a see-through window. If you want the white background of the window to be transparent and the white background of the car exterior to be opaque, create a mask of black areas for the car exterior and white areas for the insides of windows. The black mask blocks the transparency effect, leaving masked areas opaque in the image; the white areas of the mask remain transparent.

To create a mask of an image, use Copy Cast Members to copy the image. Use Paste Cast Members to paste the image into the next higher-numbered Cast slot, so the copied cast member is exactly the same. Then the areas of the cloned cast member with solid black that you want to remain opaque. Any black areas on the mask remain opaque, and white areas remain transparent, when you use the Mask ink effect in the Score window.

Finally, use the Transform Bitmap command in the Cast menu (Figure 5.24) to bring up the Transform Bitmap dialog box, and change the Color Depth of the copied mask image to 1 bit. In the current version of Director, any cast member to be used as a mask must be a 1-bit image.

# Creating Titles with Special Effects

In Director, text is a more complex form of a graphic image. You can type text directly onto the stage using the text tool in the Tools window. Alternately, you can choose the Text window from the Window menu and type text directly into a cast member position. Then drag the text cast member onto the stage. In both cases the text can be edited, either on the stage or in the Text window, even after placing it on the stage and using it in an animated sequence.

Text also can be created in the Paint window. One difference between text created in the Paint window, and text created with the Text tool in the Tools window, is that Paint window text can be manipulated at the pixel level to change individual pixels. You can create graphical effects, such as shadows, gradients

**Figure 5.25
At the end of the movie *Bell Tour* by Stuart Sharpe (filename: BELLTOUR.DIR), individual words of a title are animated separately at first, and brought together to form the title.**

inside characters, and special inks. To change the text itself, you must erase the pixels to make room for typing new text. This is because text in the Paint window does not exist as a text cast member—it is simply part of the bitmap graphic image that occupies a cast member position.

Use the Text window or the Text tool in the Tools window to create the text as a text cast member. However, if faster animation is your goal, create the text in the Paint window as a bitmap cast member, because text cast members animate more slowly than bitmap cast members.

The Auto Animate feature offers several text effects, but you can create your own with a little imagination. One popular technique for animating a title is to create separate cast members for each word of the title. Thus, you can control the movements of each word separately in the score, as in the *Bell Tour* movie (Figure 5.25) by Stuart Sharpe (filename: BELLTOUR.DIR), found in the TUTO-RIAL folder/directory of the accompanying CD-ROM.

You can adjust the positions horizontally while keeping the words lined up by dragging the words while holding down the Shift key. It helps to create a composite cast member for the completed title so that you can substitute the completed title for the title bits once they've been assembled to represent the completed title.

A subtle effect to obtain with text is a background shade that provides the illusion of three dimensions—as if the title were floating on top of its background. To do this, copy the cast member representing the completed title to another slot in the Cast window, and fill the characters with black (leaving white the holes in the characters). Place this shadow title cast member behind the actual title by placing it in a lower-numbered channel (Figure 5.26). Then, offset the shadow title slightly so that the edge of it appears to the right and underneath the title. Set this shadow cast member to have the Bkgnd Transparent ink effect so that the colored background shows through the empty areas of the characters.

**Figure 5.26**
**In the movie**
***Bell Tour* by**
**Stuart Sharpe**
**(filename:**
**BELLTOUR.DIR),**
**the "Telecommu-**
**nications" subti-**
**tle has a black**
**shadow, which is**
**a separate cast**
**member placed**
**in a lower num-**
**bered channel,**
**filled with black,**
**and set to have**
**the Bkgnd Trans-**
**parent ink effect**
**so that the back-**
**ground shows**
**through the**
**empty areas in**
**the text.**

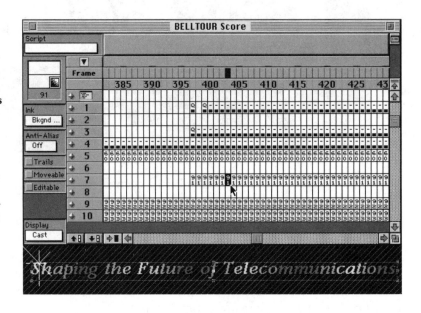

A popular embellishment for a title is to add one or more sparkles to the characters to capture attention (Figure 5.27).

This is easy to do. First, create cast members for the different types of sparkles you want (Figure 5.28). Then, use a sequence of different sparkles, over a period of frames, on a single character of the title. This effect makes it appear that the sparkle grew in size and originated from the character itself. Duplicate this sequence in other channels for other characters, so that the title sparkles in several

**Figure 5.27**
**Sparkles on the**
**text at the end of**
**the movie *Bell***
***Tour* by Stuart**
**Sharpe**
**(filename:**
**BELLTOUR.DIR).**

**Figure 5.28**
In the movie
*Bell Tour* by
Stuart Sharpe
(filename:
BELLTOUR.DIR),
sparkles were
created as sepa-
rate cast mem-
bers, then placed
with the Ghost
ink effect in se-
quence over sev-
eral frames on a
character to give
the illusion that
the sparkles
"grew" from the
character; the se-
quence can be re-
peated for other
characters in
overlapping
frames.

places at the same time (overlapping frames). Use the Ghost ink effect for the sparkles if you are using a black or colored background.

For the greatest flexibility with text characters, make each character a separate bitmap cast member, as Stuart Sharpe did in a credit screen for the movie *A Nice Easy Turquoise* (filename: ANETTEXT.DIR), found in the TUTORIAL folder/directory of the accompanying CD-ROM. Each character can then have its own ink effect and position on the stage (Figure 5.29).

Besides creating text in the Paint window, you can create bitmap versions of text by typing the text with the text tool or typing into the Text window to create the text cast member. Then select the cast member and use Convert to Bitmap in the Cast menu. This produces a bitmap cast member with the text the same as if you had typed it into the Paint window.

## Simulated 3-D

Although Director does not provide three-dimensional modeling tools, you can use a variety of 3-D (three-dimensional) programs including Macromedia's MacroModel to create three-dimensional objects. You can then prepare instances of these objects at difference sizes and perspectives, and import each instance into Director as a separate cast member.

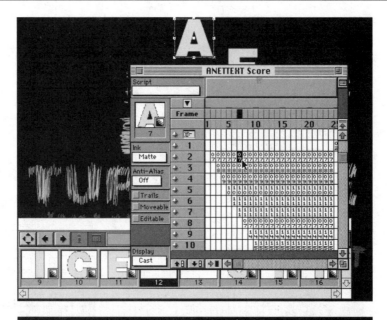

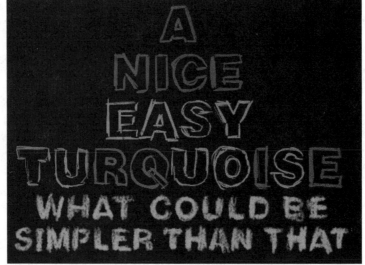

**Figure 5.29
The title screen
for the movie *A
Nice Easy Tur-
quoise* by Stuart
Sharpe
(filename:
ANETTEXT.DIR)
animates each
character (con-
verted to bitmap)
of the text.**

For example, in the *Bell Tour* movie (Figure 5.30), a rotating Earth is created
by importing a three-dimensional model of the Earth as separate views into
separate cast member positions (Figure 5.31).

To provide a three-dimensional effect, animated objects should be larger when
they move closer to the viewer and smaller when they move away. Other
three-dimensional techniques, such as changing the viewer's perspective, are
useful for animated as well as static objects.

**Figure 5.30
The movie *Bell Tour* by Stuart Sharpe
(filename: BELLTOUR.DIR)
features a rotating Earth with a simulated 3-D effect.**

Some programs, such as Macromedia Three-D, can render complete photo-realistic images to PICT files that can be used in Director for animation. Three-D can also render an animated sequence into the PICS format to record 3-D animation directly into Director's score, where it can be manipulated further. For instance, look at Stuart Sharpe's movie fragment (Figure 5.32), *Brixxx* (filename: BRIXXX.DIR), found in the TUTORIAL folder/directory of the accompanying CD-ROM, from the MediaBand CD-ROM (Canter Technology). This movie consists of a sequence of 23 cast members recorded as 3-D animation in Three-D, then imported into Director, where the sequence is repeated and eventually integrated with other Director animations and movies. The sophistication of the 3-D rendering (there are many moving images within the main image) is state-of-the-art for desktop multimedia.

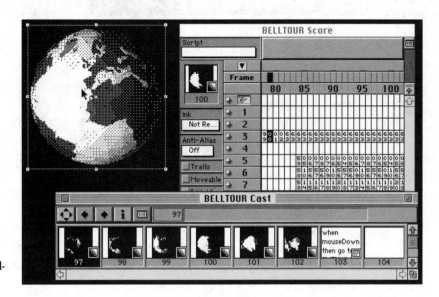

**Figure 5.31
The turning Earth in the *Bell Tour* movie is composed of separate images from a three-dimensional modeling program.**

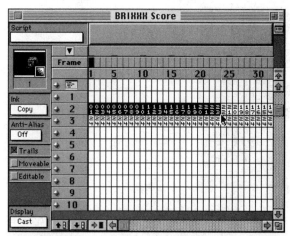

**Figure 5.32 Stuart Sharpe's *Brixxx* (filename: BRIXXX.DIR) from the Media-Band CD-ROM (Canter Technology) was created with 3-D animation recorded in Three-D, then imported into Director. The main sequence shown in the score is repeated in reverse.**

Most 3-D rendering programs can save each view as a separate image file. When importing such images, be sure that the registration points of the cast members are aligned (as described in Chapter 4), or else the animation may jump all over the stage.

It is possible to create the illusion of three dimensions by shrinking or expanding an object directly on the stage, as explained before. However, for complex, exaggerated animation such as *KEY3D* by Stuart Sharpe (filename: KEY3D.DIR), found in the TUTORIAL folder/directory of the accompanying CD-ROM (Figure 5.33), the best results are achieved in the Paint window, creating cast members for each shape (Figure 5.34).

A 3-D effect can be achieved by distorting a bitmap in the Paint window to represent different views, such as the movie *STURN* (filename: STURN.DIR) by Stuart Sharpe (Figure 5.35), found in the TUTORIAL folder/directory of the accompanying CD-ROM.

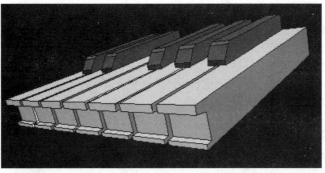

**Figure 5.33**
The *KEY3D* movie (filename: KEY3D.DIR) by Stuart Sharpe demonstrates how perspectives can be exaggerated for simulating three-dimensional space.

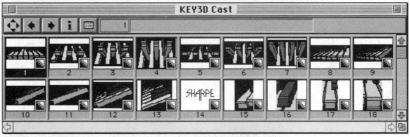

**Figure 5.34**
The *KEY3D* movie cast with 3-D image cast members.

**Figure 5.35**
The movie *STURN* (filename: STURN.DIR) by Stuart Sharpe shows how distorting bitmaps in the Paint window is one way to create 3-D animation.

The two-dimensional cast members were "tortured" in the Paint window with Distort in the Effects menu, before being placed in sequence in the score. Perspective and Distort, both useful for simulating three dimensions, are available in the Paint window's Effects menu when a rectangular selection is made. 3-D distortion and perspective exaggeration are probably the most popular techniques in animation.

## *Animating with Color Palettes*

Some of the most sophisticated graphics effects with Director can be accomplished simply and easily by cycling through colors in the palette, or by switching palettes. The palette contains the particular set of 256 colors to render an image in an 8-bit color display system. (In a 4-bit display mode, there are only 16 colors in the palette.)

The currently active palette is usually set to the System palette when a movie begins. You can switch to any other palette for any frame by specifying a new palette in the Palette channel, as you will see below. You can also change the palette that the movie should begin with, by changing the Default Palette setting in the Movie Info dialog box (use the Movie Info command in the File menu).

Once you've changed the palette, the new palette remains in effect until you change it again. The reason for switching the palette in a movie is usually to display a new image that looks best with its own palette. Also, you can create a stunning graphic effect by changing the colors in an image. All of the images on the stage are affected by a palette switch.

The ability to cycle through the colors of a palette over time is an excellent method of showing pulsating or flowing colors. The cycling occurs as fast or as slow as you wish, without the need to switch palettes. You can cycle colors on any palette and choose the color range for cycling through.

**Switching Palettes**

You change the palette by selecting a palette transition in the Palette channel of the score. You can do this by selecting a frame cell in the Palette channel and choosing the Set Palette command in the Score menu, or by double-clicking a cell in the Palette channel. A dialog box appears with a pop-up menu of palettes to switch to (Figure 5.36). Several built-in palettes are always available: System-Mac, System-Win, Rainbow, Grayscale, Pastels, Vivid, NTSC, and Metallic. You can also choose the palette of a particular cast member.

Palette transitions can occur in one frame, or over several frames, if you select the frames in the Palette channel, and click the Over time option in the Set Palette dialog box. When a palette transition occurs in just one frame, all animation stops while the palette changes colors. You can see how the palette changes colors by

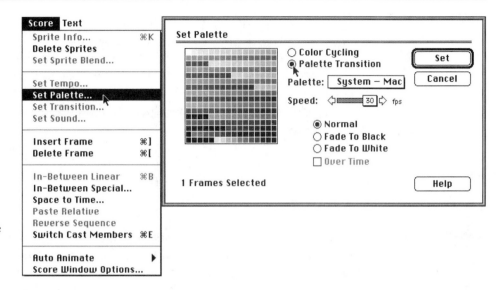

**Figure 5.36
Setting a palette
transition for the
frame in the Set
Palette dialog
box.**

leaving the Palette window open as the transition occurs. You also have control over how long the transition should take, by adjusting the Speed slider control in the Set Palette dialog box.

For a demonstration of switching color palettes (Figure 5.37), open the *Tie Dye* movie (filename: TIEDYE.DIR), found in the TUTORIAL folder/directory of the accompanying CD-ROM. In this movie, one image is shown with different palette transitions—some at full speed and some at slower speeds.

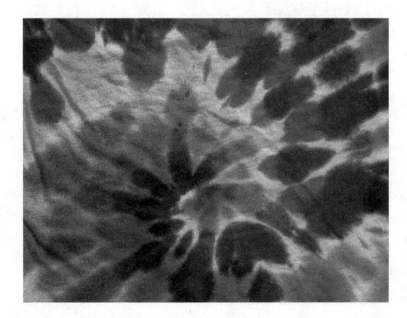

**Figure 5.37
The movie *Tie
Dye* (filename:
TIEDYE.DIR)
demonstrates
color palette
switching.**

When you have cast members that use different palettes, and you are switching from one to the other while also performing a palette transition, you may see the first cast member change colors before disappearing. To hide this effect, you can use a transition in the Transition channel, or the Fade to Black or Fade to White options in the Set Palette dialog box, to hide the flash of color. The last frames of the movie *Tie Dye* use a slower speed and the Fade To Black and Fade To White options.

The best transitions for hiding palette changes are ones that happen quickly over the entire screen, such as Dissolves, Venetian Blinds, Checkerboard, and so on. The Fade to Black or White options are the best choice if you want to completely hide the flash of color.

## Cycling Through Colors

You can cycle through a range of colors in a palette to produce an effect that is similar to rotating color positions in the palette—colors tend to pulsate or flow. An excellent example of color cycling is in the *Solar Heater* movie (filename: SOLARHTR), found in the Tutorial folder/directory of the accompanying CD-ROM. As the animation runs (Figure 5.38), any object that uses a color in the selected range changes colors as the cycling occurs.

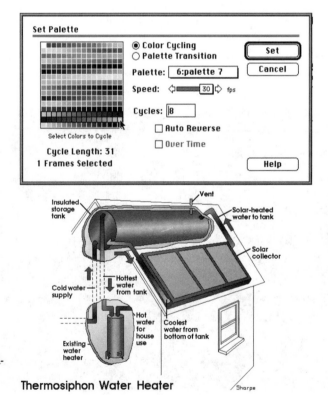

**Figure 5.38 The movie *Solar Heater* (filename: SOLARHTR.DIR) by Stuart Sharpe contains an excellent example of color cycling.**

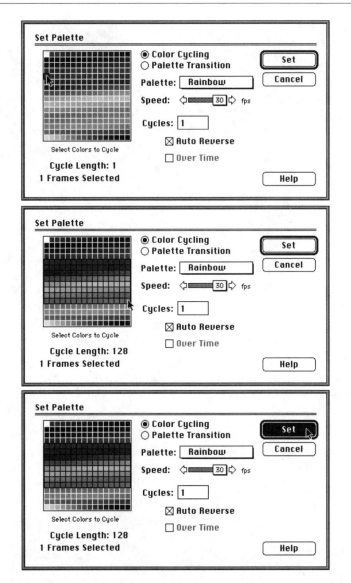

**Figure 5.39**
**Selecting a range of colors for a color cycling effect.**

You can set color cycling to occur over a range of frames in the Palette channel rather than in a single frame. The color range is set by dragging across the colors in the palette displayed in the Set Palette dialog box (Figure 5.39).

You also can set the range by clicking one color as the beginning and Shift-clicking the ending color. The Cycles option determines how many cycles are run through (one complete cycle is once around the range of colors). The color cycle can be set to reverse its direction after each cycle, which provides even more of a pulsating effect.

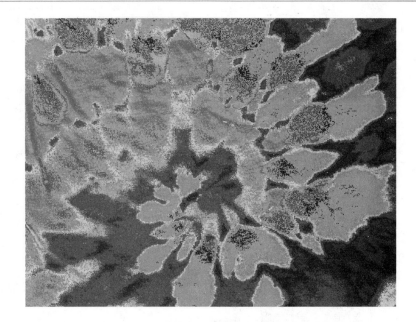

**Figure 5.40
The movie *Tie Dye2* (filename: TIEDYE2.DIR) demonstrates various color cycling effects.**

An example (Figure 5.40) is the movie *Tie Dye2* (filename: TIEDYE2.DIR), found in the TUTORIAL folder/directory of the accompanying CD-ROM.

In frames 6 through 9, the color cycling is set to occur over time (Figure 5.41). This is done by first selecting the cell range in the score, then choosing Set Palette and setting the Over Time option in the dialog box. In addition, color cycling and palette switching can be combined so that a palette transition occurs and then the color cycling begins.

The color effects you can achieve with these methods are limited only by your imagination. The best way to see how these features work is to experiment with them. Leave the Palette window open while you experiment so that you can see how colors cycle and what colors change when you switch palettes.

## *Managing the Cast*

As we've discussed, the cast represents all of the elements involved in a movie—text, graphics, video images, sound, film loops, and palettes. The cast also represents the largest volume of space occupied by the movie, either on disk or in RAM. The score information is a very small part compared to the cast, which can be enormous. The largest data types are sound and 24-bit images, and to a lesser extent, 8-bit images.

You will want to manage cast members so that you can easily locate them, make them more efficient in using disk space, and make them animate faster.

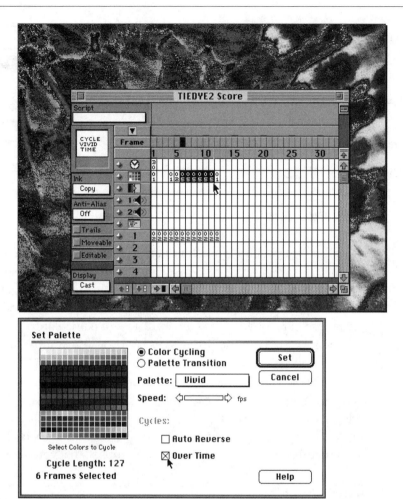

**Figure 5.41
Frames in the
movie *Tie Dye2*
demonstrate
color cycling
over time, which
is an option set
in the dialog box.**

The Cast menu offers several commands for managing the use of cast members. In addition, Director lets you drag cast members around the Cast window into different slots, and keeps track of them in the score.

Memory management—the loading of cast members into RAM from disk or CD-ROM—is the single most important factor in saving memory space and increasing animation speed. There are various techniques, including managing the loading of cast members, and sharing cast members among several movies.

**Locating
Cast
Members**

The Cast Info command, available in the Cast menu, displays vital information about the selected cast member (Figure 5.42). For instance, it displays its type, size in kilobytes, color depth (1 to 24 bits), and the color palette, with a pop-up menu to choose another palette.

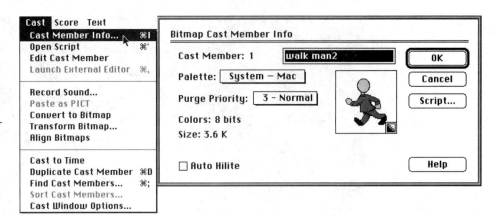

**Figure 5.42**
**The Cast Member Info dialog box provides information about the selected cast member, including size, color depth, and palette.**

This information is helpful for many reasons, including the ability to search for cast members that use a certain palette. The Find Cast Members command in the Cast menu opens a dialog box (Figure 5.43) that lets you choose various options for the search. For example, you can choose to find all unused cast members, or only those bitmapped cast members that use a particular palette. The latter choice is useful for subsequently using Cast Info or Transform Bitmap to change the palette used by the selected cast members.

In addition to dragging a cast member to a new location in the Cast window, you can drag a group of cast members, simultaneously, to a new location by selecting the group with Shift-click. The cast members at the point of insertion move forward to make room for the inserted cast members. The score automatically adjusts to the new cast member positions so that your movie doesn't change.

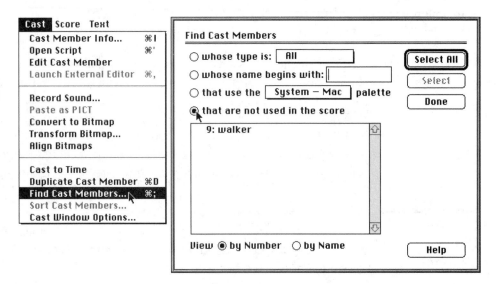

**Figure 5.43**
**Finding a cast member by using Find Cast Members. You can click on any name to select a cast member, or search to create a new list with options on the search, such as searching for all unused cast members.**

However, any Lingo scripts that refer to specific cast member numbers have to be changed. (Scripts are described in Chapter 6.)

## Reducing Space

When working on a large movie, it is also common to have unused cast members. One feature of the Find Cast Members command is the ability to find and select all cast members that are not used in the score. Then you can view them and decide what to do with them. For instance, clear them with the Clear Cast Members command in the Edit menu.

Deleting or clearing unused cast members will free up trapped space in the cast portion of your Director movie and make the file smaller. When you use the Save and Compact command in the File menu, Director stores the cast members in consecutive order for faster loading from CD-ROM, and compacts the file to be smaller. Since Director movies need enough memory to fit in order to run, this operation also increases the likelihood that a computer with less memory can run the movie.

However, if you delete cast members not used in the score that contain Lingo scripts (described in Chapter 6), you may inadvertently delete scripts that refer to cast members used in the score, such as puppet sprites.

Another way to reduce the space occupied by cast members is to reduce their color depth if they do not use color. When creating graphics with a color display, often you create black-and-white graphics without color as well. The black-and-white cast members can be changed to have a color depth of 1 bit, because 8 bits are not needed. An image with a color depth of 8 bits occupies eight times more memory and disk space than 1 bit. The Transform Bitmap command lets you increase or decrease the color depth.

Conversely, if you need to add more than one color to a black-and-white image, you must first change its color depth from 1 bit to at least 4 bits (16 colors) or 8 bits (256 colors). A 1-bit cast member can be set to a color other than black by changing the color chip in the Tools window when placing the cast member on the stage.

Other ways to reduce space include importing a link to external sounds rather than importing the sound itself, keeping your animations (relative to overall screen size), and your movie file, small. Use Lingo scripts (as you will see in Chapter 6) to call other movies, rather than putting all the animation into one big movie file.

## Memory Management

If you are distributing Director movies to others, it may be unwise to assume the customer has a lot of RAM, and you may need to manage the use of RAM. Indeed, control over the loading and unloading of cast members is essential for professional title production. This can be controlled by various options.

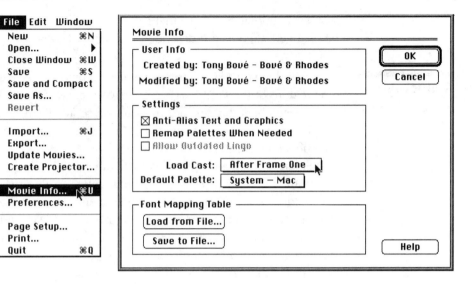

**Figure 5.44
Opening the
Movie Info dialog
box to set op-
tions for the load-
ing of cast
members.**

When Director (or a projector file) runs out of RAM, cast members that have already been used are discarded from memory so that new ones can fit. Director discards first the cast members that haven't been used in a while. However, if Director needs to reload a cast member, a pause may occur.

You can distribute the loading of cast members to reduce the demand on RAM by opening the Movie Info dialog box (Figure 5.44), and choosing When Needed for the Load Cast pop-up menu. This option tells Director to load cast members only when they are required and not currently available in memory (if there is enough RAM, Director loads all cast members). Another useful option is After Frame One. It loads all the cast members after first loading frame 1 for display. This is useful because you can display an opening screen, and perhaps start a sound, before loading all the other cast members.

In addition to setting the loading time, you can set the *purge priority* for each cast member, which determines how quickly Director will discard the cast member if it runs out of RAM.

The purge priority is set in the Cast Member Info dialog box (Figure 5.45) and offers these options:

- The Normal setting means that the cast member will be among the first to go (as necessary).

- The 2-Next setting means that it is next to last to go (the Normals go first).

- The 1-Last setting means that it is the last to go (Normals and 2-Next cast members go first).

- The 0-Never setting means that it will never be purged—the cast member remains in RAM as long as the movie itself does.

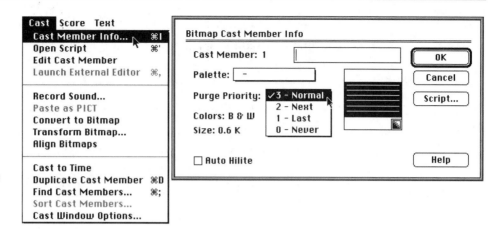

**Figure 5.45**
**Setting the purge priority in the Cast Member Info dialog box.**

---

*Note:* A good formula for calculating the amount of RAM used by a cast member is the number of bytes of an image in memory is equal to the image's height in pixels, multiplied by the width in pixels, multiplied by the color depth in bits, divided by 8.

---

An easy way to see how much memory is occupied by a movie is to use the About Director command (in the Apple menu on the Macintosh, or in the Help menu on Windows-based PCs). It displays a bar graph showing how much memory is used (Figure 5.46). It shows:

- The total memory available to Director.
- The total used by your movie, and the file size of your movie.

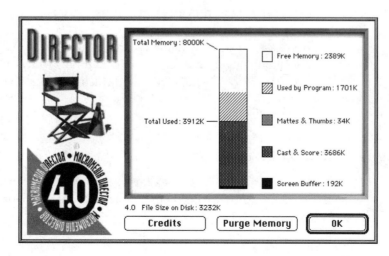

**Figure 5.46**
**The About Director command opens the memory chart. You can purge unnecessary items from memory to gain a bit more RAM for playback if you need it.**

- The amount of free memory and amount used by the program.

- The amount used by cast members that use the Matte ink in the score, and by thumbnails in the Cast window.

- The amount used by the cast members and the score notation.

- The screen buffer, used as a temporary image storage area while Director is animating.

You can click the Purge Memory button to remove all unnecessary items from RAM, in order to gain a bit more RAM for playback when you need it.

(While you are visiting the About Director dialog box, don't forget to click the Credits button to see who brought you this software.)

## Sharing Cast Members

If you use the same cast members in several movies, you can store them in one movie, and share them without keeping duplicates in the other movies. This cuts down on loading time (cast members are loaded into RAM with the first movie that needs them).

To share cast members, they must be stored in a movie named SHARED.DIR that exists in the same folder (subdirectory) as the Director movies that use them. Create this movie by starting with a new movie and naming it SHARED.DIR.

One important caveat: Place the shared cast members in the SHARED.DIR movie, in Cast window slots that are high enough in number so they don't conflict with cast members in movies that share them. This is because Director must load the shared cast members on top of the actual cast members in the movie when it loads the movie. The rule of thumb is to put the shared cast members in higher numbered slots, leaving enough room to accommodate any and all movies that need them. You may even want to put them in slots numbering 1000 and up.

The shared cast members' names appear in italics when they show up in the Cast window of the other movies. You can use these shared cast members just like other cast members.

The shared cast remains in memory until you open a movie in a folder or directory containing either another SHARED.DIR file (which replaces the shared cast in memory), or no SHARED.DIR file (which removes the shared cast from memory).

## *Increasing Animation Speed*

There are many tips and techniques for increasing animation speed, or making animation smoother. Most of them involve managing memory properly, as described above.

Essentially, movies play back faster or slower depending on the complexity and size of the changing area of the screen. A movie with many sprites that move at the same time will be slower than a movie that moves its sprites at different times. Large cast members animate more slowly than smaller ones, and stretching and changing the size of sprites on the stage also slows down animation.

Bitmap graphics generally move faster than draw object graphics created with tools in the Tools window. This is also true of text created as part of a bitmap graphic image, as compared to text object cast members. One of the best methods of speeding up animation is to convert object text to bitmap cast members with the Convert to Bitmap command in the Cast menu.

Once converted, the text will move faster on the screen, but you can't edit it as text. You can alter each pixel with painting tools in the Paint window, including deleting any part with the eraser tool. To change the text of bitmap text, you must completely erase it and retype the new text with the text tool in the Paint window. Another way is to create another text cast member with the text tool in the Tools window (or in the Text window), and convert it again to bitmap graphics with the Convert to Bitmap command.

Another advantage, besides speed, with converting text object cast members to bitmap graphics is that you no longer need the font used for the text. You can pass the movie around to other users who don't have that particular font in their System folders, or on their Windows system.

Director offers the Export command to export a sequence as a set of image files or as a digital video file such as a QuickTime file. If you export animation into a QuickTime file, you can re-import the QuickTime file and make it run as fast as possible by loading the entire QuickTime file into RAM. (Set the option in the Cast Member Info dialog box.) This is explained in Chapter 8. This method provides the fastest speed for moving images, outside of using Director itself.

## *Chapter Summary*

In this chapter you learned some of the techniques of professional animators, including the use of film loops, marker labels, and other score techniques. This chapter explained score notation and various ways to select score information. It also showed how you can create animation with Paste Relative and Reverse Sequence, and showed how to composite images to a file and then import them back into Director. Masks, text titles, and 3-D techniques for text and graphics were also introduced. In addition, you learned how to switch color palettes and perform color cycling for special color graphics effects.

This chapter covered the essentials for managing cast members, reducing space for movies, controlling the loading of cast members into memory, sharing cast members among movies, and increasing the speed of animation. All of these techniques are essential for moving on to the next step: scripting interactive movies with the Lingo language, described in the next chapter.

# 6

# *Elementary Scripting*

**Because something is happening but you don't know what it is...**

Bob Dylan, *Ballad of a Thin Man*

Y ou may know a thing or two about Director by now, but do you know how they make the movies interactive? Can you put buttons on the screen for the user to click that can change the movie? Whether you consider yourself a programmer or not, scripting is essential to the process of authoring. Even if those scripts are hidden behind easy-to-use dialog choices, you will find that the choices themselves are not easily understood unless you learn something about scripting.

You have already learned the basics about creating multimedia presentations using text, graphics, recorded sound, and animation. You have also been introduced to various animation methods, painting and drawing techniques, cast management, and using the score. All of this information is a prerequisite for understanding how to effectively prepare interactive media projects with Director.

Interactive media has the potential to be far more effective than any other type of media. The power lies in your ability to understand the methods of interaction, such as menu choices, dialogs, links, and browsing tools. These are used to develop learning experiences, persuasive presentations, reference tools for accessing information, demonstrations of concepts and products, entertainment, and so on. The goal of many interactive media projects is to provide a relationship between information and people so that the people can interact with, and navigate through, the information in various ways.

This chapter presents examples of using Director and its underlying scripting language, Lingo, to create interactive media projects. It explains the design techniques you should acquire, and the production methods you should adopt. It explains the concept of scripting, which is similar in many respects to scoring an opera, and in some respects to directing a film. After reading this chapter, you will be ready to start interactive media projects. You will know:

- What skills are required.

- What interactive features of Director are best for the types of applications you are doing.

- What to expect with the design and production process.

## *Understanding Interactive Media*

Some of the examples presented in this book in the previous chapters were drawn from interactive media projects. For example, the movies *Undo Me prototype (IM4)* and *Brixxx* by Stuart Sharpe (Figure 6.1) are part of an interactive music and entertainment CD-ROM, produced by Canter Technology, called *MediaBand* (filenames: UNDOIM4B.DIR and BRIXXX.DIR, in the TUTORIAL folder/directory).

**Figure 6.1. Excerpts from the interactive music and video title, *MediaBand*, by Canter Technology (animation by Stuart Sharpe).**

**Figure 6.2**
**The movie** *Bell Tour* **by Stuart Sharpe (filename: BELLTOUR.DIR) is a teaser for a comprehensive interactive presentation on Bell-South's communications products.**

Entertainment is not the only application for interactive movies. The *Bell Tour* movie (Figure 6.2) is a small part of an interactive presentation of communications products that used colorful images and original music. They also used navigational aids and menus for selecting parts of the presentation.

Director is a popular authoring tool for creating games and *environments*. Reactor's *Spaceship Warlock*, Drew Pictures/Spectrum-Holobyte's *Iron Helix*, Time-Warner's *Hell Cab*, and Electronic Arts/Pop Rocket's *Total Distortion* are just a few examples. Director is also popular for creating music-related titles with video and animation, such as David Bowie's *Jump* (ION) and Bove & Rhodes' *Haight-Ashbury in the Sixties*.

One reason Director is such a popular authoring tool for creating these titles is that animation is required for a lively interface. One of our favorite examples (Figure 6.3) of a lively interface is Stuart Sharpe's *Table Set* movie (filename:TABLESET.DIR), found in the TUTORIAL folder/directory of the accompa-

**Figure 6.3**
**The interactive movie** *Table Set* **by Stuart Sharpe (filename: TABLESET.DIR) demonstrates an environment where everything can be clicked on.**

nying CD-ROM. It shows how you can be creative about the way a user might interact with objects. We wish our Mac desktops were as much fun as *Table Set*.

## Applying Interactive Media

There are as many different applications of interactive media as there are human experiences that need to be learned.

At the top of the list are applications in the art and entertainment worlds, including CD-ROM titles, such as games and music-related reference titles. The interactive medium offers new possibilities for an art form that changes with audience interaction. For entertainment, there is a constant need for new games with interesting visual and audio elements.

However, entertainment is not the only area that deserves attention. Learning experiences, such as topical video, animated brochures, and product demonstrations, can be designed to enable users to browse through information in different ways. With them, you can interrupt a presentation on one particular topic and jump into another topic, or subtopic.

Reference tools, such as employee directories, product information databases, research databases, and catalogs, can be built to hold information linked to other data, through the use of hyperlinks. These are scripted tasks that are activated by clicking a *hot zone* that may be a button, one or more words, or graphics. In Director, any cast member can be defined to execute a script. A script can be used to:

- Take the user to a new screen of information.

- Display a footnote or image.

- Play a sound.

- Play another Director movie.

- Do almost anything that is allowed in the Lingo language.

Visualizations, such as simulations and prototypes, can be used to communicate an abstract idea, or process. This category can include new kinds of simulations never done before, such as business plans, that simulate business activities and computer models for manufacturing.

Self-paced training presentations can enable trainees to explore areas of interest, and try simulated exercises. Expert systems can demonstrate processes, explain concepts, respond to user queries, and monitor user responses.

Many of today's businesses rely on instructor-led training courses, and published materials, to communicate everything from how to use a phone system, to product or support information. Such methods can be cumbersome and expensive to produce, compared with interactive presentations on a CD-ROM or information distributed over a network from a server. Electronic training materials can be prepared by those who really know the content, and can be updated more quickly than printed manuals.

## Designing Interactive Media

Interactive media involves nonlinear exploration, self-paced learning without any supervision, and an experience that combines text with rich graphics and sound. This type of learning implies the creation of a rich environment, in which a learner interacts with the information.

The combination of recorded music, sounds, graphics, carefully worded text, animation, and hyperlinks can provide an invigorating learning environment. The key ingredient is a plan that enables the content provider to associate different pieces of information in a logical way, so that the hyperlinks attract users down their paths to new information. Incorporating text, sound, images, animation, and video have a strong impact on both memory and learning.

The goal is an application that transparently facilitates the user's relationship with the content, and is obvious and effortless to use. It's not enough to only use graphics to enhance text, or to be cute. Graphics can be used to provide context, and to create visual landmarks. A compelling application often involves a high level of meaningful interactivity, and user control.

The most compelling applications are those that incorporate techniques from the worlds of animation, film, video, graphics, typography, music, entertainment, advertising, and communications. The major difference between applications that are successful, and those that are not, lies in the ability of the content developer to understand and effectively use the media. Training in video techniques may help, but the most important activity is visualizing the entire presentation as a director would visualize a completed film.

Today, an interactive media project team may have members with the following skills.

- A director or general architect, who designs the structure of the information and the navigational routes.

- A production manager, who organizes the project and assigns work to various artists.

- A visual, or graphic designer, with one or more computer graphics artists.

- One or more Director specialists, who can do the scripting.

- One or more writers/editors with considerable knowledge of the subject matter.

In rare cases, one person fulfills many, or all of, these roles, but a team approach is usually best.

Every project requires a detailed analysis. Before launching into a project, it is important to define the content approach. In the case of a business, or training presentation, it is the problem to be solved, or the question to be answered. After this important goal has been identified, the audience, and subject matter, should become clearer, as well as how that subject matter will be created or collected. You will also want to consider how the audience will use the subject matter in the real world.

After this analysis, take a broader perspective, and develop a vision of the actual experience you want the user to have. Take into consideration games, television, films, books, courses, and so on, to create a rich and seductive environment. Think about real-world models that may apply to your content.

As you develop an application, think of a metaphor that will work for both the audience, and the content, and a plan of routes for users to navigate through the information. You can use Director to create a prototype, or just a thin slice, of this environment so that you can determine whether it is practical and effective from a technical standpoint as well as for the audience. Then you will want to test this prototype with actual users. This phase of designing, and testing prototypes, is iterative. Your plans will change based on feedback from real-world usage.

If you are designing content that will be delivered on CD-ROM discs, keep in mind that CD-ROMs are not as fast as hard disks when retrieving information. The layout of the information can be changed to optimize performance. When designing an interactive presentation for CD-ROM, you must design with a read-only environment in mind: The software must be able to function without having to write anything to the original disc. If a portion of the presentation must accept new data, store that portion in a separate file on a separate read-write disk (or instruct users to copy a particular file to their read-write disks).

There are many more things to know when authoring for CD-ROM. They are described in Chapter 9, "Tips and Advanced Techniques."

## Learning Lingo

Director's scripts, written in the Lingo language, are added directly to the score of a movie, or to individual cast members.

The Lingo language evolved from Director's precursor, the VideoWorks Interactive Toolkit, which was used to create a variety of interactive presentations in the very early days of multimedia computing.

The interactive features of Director are similar to other authoring tools that offer the ability to click on buttons, or defined hot spots. However, in Director, any object can be *hot* and have a script attached to it. The Lingo language in its simplest forms looks identical to HyperCard's HyperTalk, a well-known scripting language for the Mac. So if you know HyperTalk, you should be able to learn Lingo very quickly.

**Figure 6.4**
**The** *RollOver*
**movie (filename:**
**ROLLOVER.DIR)**
**demonstrates**
**simple interac-**
**tive elements.**

In Director, scripts can be viewed anytime in the Script window. The sequence of actions can be determined by viewing the score, which shows information over time (including scripts), from left to right. Director also recognizes events and actions, such as mouse and key clicks, so that you can direct your scripts to perform tasks based on these events and actions.

## Finding the Scripts

One of the best ways to learn about scripting is to take a close look at sample movies provided in the Tutorial folder/directory on the accompanying CD-ROM. For example, open up a simple movie (Figure 6.4) that demonstrates some common interactive techniques, like *RollOver* (filename: ROLLOVER.DIR).

The first place to look for script activity in a movie file is the Score window. You can change the view to Scripts, by changing the display pop-up menu (Figure 6.5).

**Figure 6.5**
**Using the Score**
**window's Dis-**
**play pop-up**
**menu to switch**
**to the Script dis-**
**play, which**
**shows script**
**numbers in the**
**cells, or 00 if**
**there is no sprite**
**script attached to**
**the cell, or + is**
**there is a cast**
**script.**

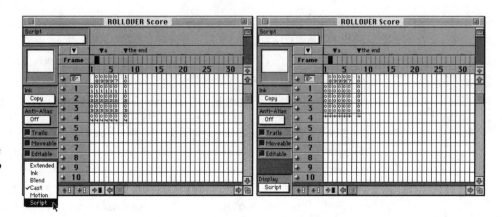

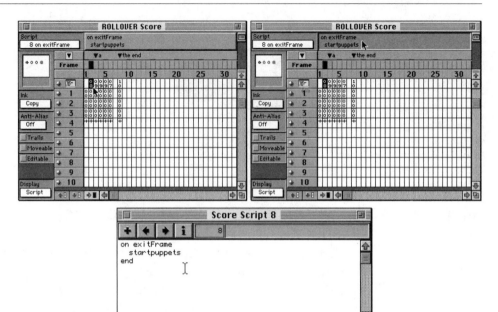

**Figure 6.6
Clicking an occupied cell in the Script channel displays the script in that cell in the script entry area. Click inside the entry area to display the Script window.**

Cells without scripts are displayed as 00 and cells with scripts have some other number, or a plus (+) sign. Select a single cell containing a script, such as the cell in the Script channel in frame 2 (Figure 6.6), and you will see the script in the entry area above the score information. Click inside the entry area to display the Script window.

The script you see is the following:

```
on exitFrame
     startpuppets
end
```

This script defines a *handler,* which is a code fragment that handles a specific task. The task, in this case, is to do something called startpuppets, when the frame is exited. The on exitFrame statement defines the beginning of the handler, and the end statement defines the end. The handler does just one thing: It executes another handler, called startpuppets.

So, how do you find the startpuppets handler? The Text menu contains the Find Handler command, which lets you click on the handler name to find it (Figure 6.7). A Script window appears with the handler displayed.

The handler is defined by on and end statements, with Lingo statements between them. The lines beginning with dashes (--) are comments for understanding the script, not executable script expressions. A handler typically starts

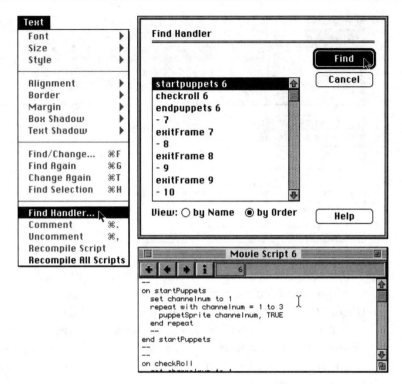

**Figure 6.7**
**Using the Find Handler command to find a handler by name.**

with a blank comment—a blank line starting with dashes (--), followed by the on statement.

Don't expect to be able to understand the scripts right away. Most handlers are defined in a script cast member, so they are easy to find and edit. In the above example, the `startpuppets` handler is defined in a movie script (Movie Script 6), which is a script cast member. It is not attached to any other cast member, but exists by itself as a cast member.

## Understanding Different Types of Scripts

*Movie scripts* are the most common form of scripts for defining handlers, because they can be easily copied from one movie file to another with Copy Cast Members and Paste Cast Members. You can define all of your handlers in one **movie script** cast member, or divide them among several movie script cast members. The **Script editing window** is like any text editing window. You can select text and copy it to the Clipboard, then paste it elsewhere.

In addition, other cast members (text, bitmaps, sounds, movies, etc.), can have scripts attached to them, called *cast scripts*. The cells in the Score window in Script view with plus (+) signs indicate that the cast members in those sprite channels are controlled by cast scripts. Cast scripts are activated when the user clicks the mouse on the cast member.

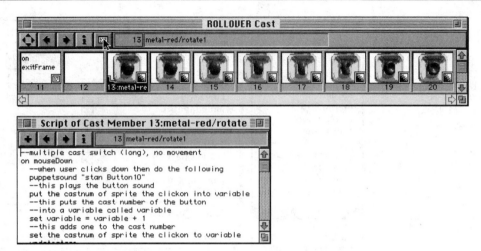

**Figure 6.8
Clicking the
Script icon to
open the Script
window of the
cast member con-
taining the cast
script. You can al-
ternatively use
the Open Script
choice in the
Cast menu.**

To find the **cast script** of a cast member, select the cast member in the Cast window, and click the script icon in the upper left corner next to the "i" icon (Figure 6.8). You can also use the Open Script choice in the Cast menu.

Cast scripts start with the on `mouseUp` or on `mouseDown` handler, which defines what action to take when the cast member is clicked. A mouse down condition is when the button on the mouse is pressed down. This condition registers immediately in Director.

A mouse up condition, in this case, is a full down and up mouse click—Director waits for the button to be released up. Thus, if the user presses down on the mouse button over this cast member, but then drags the mouse pointer to another location, the script is not executed (no mouse-up occurred).

In addition to movie scripts and cast scripts, you can also attach scripts directly to cells of the Script channel, as shown before. These are typically handlers, such as on `exitFrame`, or on `enterFrame` that execute when Director exits, or enters, the frame. Script-channel scripts are called *frame scripts,* because they are attached to a particular frame of time in the Score. They belong to a class of scripts called *score scripts,* because they are assigned to cells in the score.

As you already know, a *sprite* is an object on the Stage, a cast member in a certain position, size, and ink. Sprites are referred to in scripts by the channel number. For example, `sprite 4` refers to the sprite in channel 4 (whatever cast member object occupies that channel is the sprite for that frame). The properties and movements of a sprite can be controlled from scripts in a handler; such a sprite is called a *puppet sprite.*

A script attached to a sprite, occupying a cell position in the Score, is called a *sprite script*, which is another example of a score script. A sprite script is only activated if you click on the sprite to which it is attached. Sprite scripts override any cast scripts that would otherwise be activated by clicking on that sprite. Sprite scripts typically start with the on `mouseUp` or on `mouseDown` handler, which defines what action to take when the sprite is clicked on.

You can see a portion of any score script for a cell by selecting that cell and looking at the field above the score markers. As you create score scripts, they are numbered sequentially, and stored in a pop-up list, to make it easy to select a score script for selected cells in the score. You can choose from this list of the entered scripts, by selecting one or more cells, and choosing the script from the script pop-up menu (Figure 6.9).

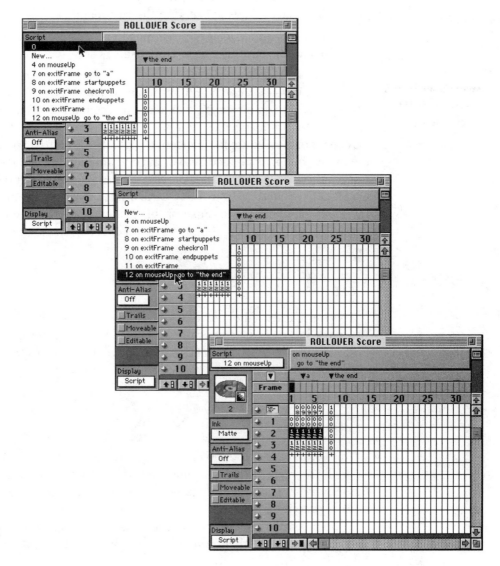

**Figure 6.9**
**Using the Script pop-up menu to assign a score script to the sprite in channel 3, frame 8.**

As you learn more about using movie scripts, score (frame and sprite) scripts, and cast scripts, you will also learn the order in which Lingo executes instructions. For now, simply remember the following.

- Movie scripts control the action of the entire movie and events, such as time-outs. Most handlers are stored in movie scripts.

- Score scripts in the Script channel (also called frame scripts) are used to control what happens at each frame of animation.

- Score scripts in other numbered channels (also called sprite scripts) are used to control what happens when the user clicks on a sprite. Score scripts override cast scripts attached to the cast member for that sprite.

- Cast scripts are attached to cast members, and are activated when the user clicks on the cast members when used as sprites.

## Using Go to and Labels

The most often-used command in the Lingo language is the Go to command. You can use it to go directly to another frame, start another movie, or start playing another movie at a specific frame.

A common procedure for interactive presentations is to display animation, until the mouse button is pressed, and then go to another frame and start playing from there. The movie from the previous example, *RollOver* (filename: ROLL-OVER.DIR), found in the TUTORIAL folder/directory of the accompanying CD-ROM, demonstrates the use of this technique. When the user clicks on the sprites in channels 2 or 3, the presentation executes the following Lingo handler:

```
on mouseUp
    go to "the end"
end
```

This script causes the movie to jump to the frame marked by the label the end when the mouse button goes up, after it is clicked on the sprite.

Meanwhile, if no sprite is clicked, the movie proceeds to frame 6, where there is the following frame script in the script channel.

```
on exitFrame
    go to "a"
end
```

This script causes the movie to jump back to the frame marked by the label "a" in the score. By scripting a jump back to this frame, you define a loop, because the movie proceeds again to frame 6, where it jumps back again, over and over until a sprite is clicked.

In both scripts, the Go to command is used to move the frame counter to another frame. The other frame is defined by a label. The Go to command can be used with a specific frame number, or, as in the above scripts, with labeled markers called frame labels. Note that in scripts, you can mix and match upper- and lowercase characters, since Lingo is not case-sensitive.

As you learned in Chapter 5, "Animation Techniques," a marker can be dragged to a specific frame in the Score window, and you can type an identifying label for it. You can then use that label in a `Go to` command, such as `Go to "the end"`. Frame labels are easier to use than frame numbers, because they are more descriptive and make scripts easier to understand. Even more important is the fact that frame labels stay attached to their appropriate frames, even if you edit the movie's Score. Using frame labels keeps you from having frame number reference problems with existing scripts when you insert, or delete, frames.

Using labels, rather than specific frame numbers, helps make scripts more readable. They also make it easier to continue editing the movie frames. If, for example, you insert, or delete, frames, and the frame number changes, the scripts referring to that specific frame number would be incorrect.

The `Go to` command can also be used with movie names, so that you can go directly to a different movie. The command

```
Go to movie "NewMovie"
```

starts running the movie *NewMovie* from the first frame. You used this type of `Go to` script in Chapter 2 with your first interactive movie. Alternatively, you can jump to a specific frame of another movie by typing the frame number, or label, such as in the command

```
Go to frame MENU of movie "Bell Tour"
```

As in the above examples, the `Go to` command is often used with handlers defining events such as on `mouseDown`. The idea is to create a branch to another frame, or movie, when a key, or the mouse button, is pressed. You can also use the `Go to` command to continually repeat a sequence—to go back to a previous frame. Between this previous frame, and the frame with the `Go to` command, you might put other scripts to branch elsewhere depending on which item is selected on the screen.

One of the most interesting examples of an animated, entertaining menu is Stuart Sharpe's prototype for the *MediaBand* CD-ROM (Canter Technology), *Undo Me prototype (IM4)* (filename: UNDOIM4A.DIR), found in the Tutorial folder/director on the accompanying CD-ROM. In this movie, various sequences are laid out over frames, so that you can view some of them in sequence up to the final menu sequence (Figure 6.10). Sound plays on all these sequences. If you click a sprite, the movie jumps immediately to another sequence, and the new sound plays. This complex-looking animated menu was implemented *entirely* with the use of `Go to` statements!

Figure 6.10
In the movie
*Undo Me proto-*
*type (IM4)*
(filename:
UNDOIM4A.DIR),
the menu se-
quence contains
many sprites that
have sprite
scripts attached
that go to an-
other sequence
immediately
when the mouse
button is pressed
down over the
sprite. (Click the
"eye" or the im-
age of static to
exit.)

So it is possible to create very professional-looking, interactive movies with the skills you've learned in the previous chapters and this chapter. You don't necessarily have to learn much Lingo to create compelling applications, because a great deal of interactivity can be programmed with simple Go to statements.

Another way to use the Go to command is with the *marker* function. A *function* is something that calculates and returns a value. The marker function returns the number of the next, or previous frame marker (whether the marker has a label or not). When used with the Go to command, Go to marker (1) jumps to the next marked frame, Go to marker (0) jumps to the currently marked frame (the closest marked frame before the current frame), and Go to marker (-1) jumps to the previous marked frame (before the currently marked frame).

For example, in the *Table Set* movie by Stuart Sharpe (filename:TABLESET.DIR), the marker function is used for the TV segment to change channels (Figure 6.11).

When the up-arrow sprite is clicked, the movie jumps to the next marker, and when the down-arrow sprite is clicked, the movie jumps to the previous marker. The marker function is also useful for implementing "next" and "previous" buttons.

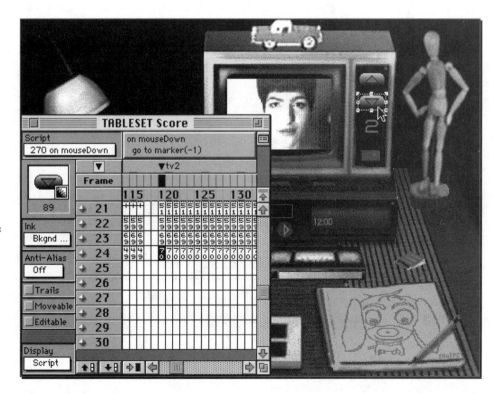

**Figure 6.11**
In the "Table Set" movie by Stuart Sharpe (filename: TABLESET.DIR), the marker function is used with the go to command for the up-arrow and down-arrow (selected) sprite to change the TV channels.

**Figure 6.12**
**The Tools window offers three standard button styles: the standard click button (Start), the on/off radio button (Audio On/Off), and the on/off checkbox (Include intro).**

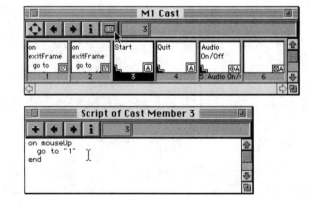

## Creating Buttons and Hot Spots

You have already been introduced to the Tools window, and the simple interactive button (see Chapter 2, "Your First Movies."). The Tools window offers three button-making tools (Figure 6.12). They are:

1. The check box, which shows an "X" check mark when clicked.

2. The regular button, which inverts (white turns to black, black turns to white) when clicked.

3. The radio-button, which inverts inside a tiny circle, within a circle (a filled dot) when clicked.

After selecting a button, click in the stage area to create the button, and stretch it, or resize it, by dragging the selection handle. Then type the text for the button. The button shows up in the next available channel in the Score window, and in the next available cast member position in the Cast window. It also remains selected, so that you can click the button's script icon in the Cast window (Figure 6.13), and type its script into the Script window. You can always resize the button by dragging the selection handle while it is selected on the stage.

**Figure 6.13**
**Clicking the button's script icon in the Cast window in order to type the cast script into the Script window.**

The regular button's activity is typically handled with an on mouseDown, or on mouseUp, handler. Regular buttons invert automatically.

Radio- and checkbox-buttons, however, do not invert, and they are handled with property settings. A *property* is some attribute of the object, whether the object be a cast member (as in this case with a button), a sprite, a field, and so on. The hilite property of cast members determines whether the radio- or checkbox-button cast member is *true* (filled dot for the radio-button, check mark for the check box) or *false.*

You can write scripts to execute based on testing these conditions with an if-then-else statement, such as the one for the Audio On/Off radio-button.

```
on mouseUp
      if the hilite of cast "Audio On/Off" = TRUE then
            set the soundLevel to 7
      else
            set the soundLevel to 0
      end if
end
```

This script checks to see if the hilite property of the button is set to TRUE (highlighted with a filled dot). If it is, then the script sets the sound level to 7 (turning the volume up on the computer's sound output or speaker). This happens the first time the user clicks this button. Originally, the button is set to FALSE (unfilled dot), but when the user clicks the button, the hilite property is set to TRUE, and the sound level is set to 7. The next time the user clicks this option (or the next time the movie starts from the beginning), the button will be changed to FALSE, and the sound level set to zero (no volume). The checkbox-button works the same way as the radio-button—the check mark appears (TRUE) or disappears (FALSE).

These are not the only kinds of buttons you can have, of course. Any sprite on the stage can act like a button. You simply attach a script to the sprite that uses the Go to command to move to another frame if the sprite is clicked with the mouse. Alternatively, you can attach a similar script to the cast member itself, so that you can copy the cast member to other movies with Copy Cast Member and Paste Cast Member, and use the cast member in the same way (with the same script) in the other movies.

For example, in the movie *MM1* (filename: MM1.DIR in the TUTORIAL folder/directory), the graph sprite has a sprite script attached to it in the score. This script causes a jump immediately—on mouseDown—when the graph itself is clicked (Figure 6.14).

The use of sprites as buttons is evidenced throughout the interactive movie examples included on the CD-ROM with this book.

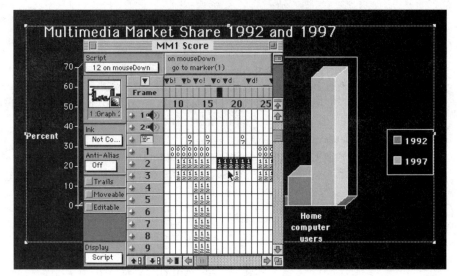

**Figure 6.14**
**In** *MM1* **(filename:**
**MM1.DIR), the en-**
**tire graph sprite**
**in channel 2 is**
**used as a button:**
**It has a sprite**
**script attached to**
**it that executes**
**when the mouse**
**button is down.**

If you want your cast member to automatically highlight (white turns black, or black turns white; colors are reversed according to palette position) when clicked as a sprite on the stage, choose the Cast Member Info option from the Cast menu, or click the " i" icon in the Cast window for the Bitmap Cast Member Info dialog box (Figure 6.15). This box offers the Auto Hilite option for setting the highlight.

## Understanding Event Handling

One reason why Director is easy to use for scripting animated interactive movies is that you always know the sequence in which scripts will be activated. This is known as the *execution flow*. You know what happens first, what happens next, and so forth, because the score is arranged over time.

You have already seen how the on `mouseDown` and on `mouseUp` handlers can be used as sprite scripts or cast scripts, and that on `exitFrame` and on `enterFrame` handlers are appropriate for frame scripts. These, and other kinds of handlers, are called *event handlers*. They can also be defined in movie scripts.

**Figure 6.15**
**The Bitmap Cast**
**Member Info dia-**
**log box, which of-**
**fers the Auto**
**Hilite option for**
**setting the high-**
**light of the cast**
**member when it**
**is clicked as a**
**sprite.**

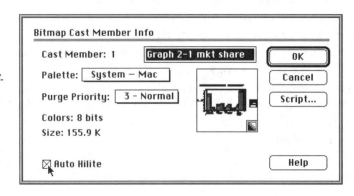

Events can also be generated by scripts, or by time-outs. The start of a movie and the end of a movie are events. Entering a frame and exiting a frame are events.

The following is the execution flow for events in Director.

1. When an event occurs, a message is sent first to the primary event handler, if one exists. This handler can be created along with other handlers in a movie script cast member (or by itself). A primary event handler is defined with one of the following expressions.

```
keydownScript
mousedownScript
mouseupScript
timeoutScript
```

For example, you could set the script for a keyDown event to the command Go to frame 30 with the following statement:

```
set the keydownScript to "go to frame 30"
```

You could put this statement in a startMovie handler, so that it applies throughout the entire movie.

```
on startMovie
set the keydownScript to "go to frame 30"
        .
        .
        .
end startMovie
```

The startMovie handler is always recognized first when a movie starts running. You can put many statements inside a startMovie handler, which should be created as a movie script cast member.

To turn off a primary event handler, you would use this statement:

```
set the keydownScript to EMPTY
```

2. If there is no primary event handler for the particular event that occurred, then the message continues to the next type of script depending on the type of event:

- Movie scripts receive the idle, stopMovie, and timeOut messages.
- Score scripts (sprite or frame scripts) receive all other messages, such as enterFrame, exitFrame, keyDown, keyUp, mouseDown, and mouseUp.

The message stops when it finds a handler with the same name, such as on mouseDown for the mouseDown event.

3. If there is no handler for the message at the level described above (2), the message continues to the next level:

- Movie scripts receive enterFrame and exitFrame messages, if there is no handler in a score script.

- Cast scripts receive keyDown, keyUp, mouseDown, and mouseUp messages, if there are no handlers in sprite scripts. If there are no handlers in the cast scripts, then the message passes to frame scripts, and from there to movie scripts.

The event can be tested with if-then-else statements. You can also test when the mouse has been moved across a location on-screen, called the rollOver function. The function is TRUE, if the mouse is currently over the area specified by the sprite number. An example in Chapter 9 shows how to use rollOver.

While you can define sprites to be *moveable* (so that the user can move them on the stage), and text fields to be *editable* (so that the user can input text) in the Score window with the Moveable and Editable options, you can also set these properties from within scripts. This makes it possible to constrain the movements of moveable sprites, and turn on and off these properties from a handler. There are many different applications for these features.

## Tracing Script Execution

The Message window is useful for tracing the execution of scripts, especially if you use handlers or macros.

Bring up the Message window by choosing it from the Window menu, or by typing Command-M. Click the Trace checkbox to activate the trace feature in the Message window (Figure 6.16).

All of the scripts that execute appear in the Message window in the order of execution. You can interact with the movie (it runs slower in trace mode) and

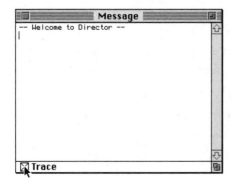

**Figure 6.16**
**The Message window has a Trace option for tracing the execution of scripts.**

see how scripts are activated by clicking sprites. The Message window scrolls with the entire transcript of the trace. You can read it there, or select the text and copy it to the Clipboard, and into a text file using a word processor.

You should turn off the Trace option when it is not needed, because it really slows down the animation.

You can also use the Message window to try out proposed Lingo statements, before making them part of a script. Type the statement in the Message window. It executes immediately when you press the Return key. If it doesn't work as planned, you can edit the statement in the Message window, and try it again.

Director makes it easy to type Lingo commands without having to memorize them, or look them up. The Lingo menu lists every command, function, keyword, operator, constant, and property in the Lingo language. The menu is organized alphabetically, so you can pick the appropriate expression. As you select an expression, Director displays the script in the Script editing window, or Message window (depending on which is active), and highlights the next part of the script for you to fill in.

## Compliance with Earlier Versions of Director

Earlier versions of Director used slightly different syntax for some things, and different statements for others. Director 4 automatically updates some of the older expressions and syntax, when opening an old movie file. However, you are encouraged to switch to the new syntax as soon as possible.

You can use the Allow Outdated Lingo option in the Movie Info window (File menu) for the movie to allow the use of some older Lingo syntax. However, if you edit this movie, new scripts must use new syntax.

Director 4 now requires explicit on mouseUp or on mouseDown handlers for sprite scripts, and on enterFrame and on exitFrame handlers for frame scripts. The new handlers offer more specific control. The older scripts, however, should work with the Allow Outdated Lingo option.

The use of handlers in movie scripts is considered a good modular programming technique, and makes it easier to read scripts, as long as you use descriptive handler names. You can also call a single handler from many different scripts, which makes your movies easier to program and debug.

# Using Puppets

Lingo offers an extensive set of commands, functions, and special effects. Some of the properties and movements of a sprite can be controlled from a script; such a sprite is called a *puppet sprite*. A script can control a puppet sprite's location on the screen, as well as its line style, color, ink effect, height, width, and other properties.

You can also define a tempo, transition, or palette as a puppet to be controlled by a script. Once declared as a puppet, a sprite, tempo, transition, or palette are no longer controlled by the score, but by scripts.

Puppets are useful for setting up sprites to be moved around the stage by the user, or to quickly switch cast members for a sprite when it is clicked, or to change a sprite's property when an event occurs, and so on. There are an infinite number of applications. The goal with using puppets is to control animation, or interaction, directly from scripts, rather than by moving the playback head to new frame locations. The result can be a much simpler score that performs a lot of functions in scripts.

## Puppet Sprites

Puppet sprites can vastly simplify the methods used to create moveable sprites, and sprites that change appearance as a result of scripted actions or interactions.

The movie *RollOver* (filename: ROLLOVER.DIR) illustrates this through the use of the rollOver function, which can detect whether the cursor is directly on top of a particular sprite. Move the cursor over the objects and watch them change inks. Then look at the score (Figure 6.17): the second frame executes a startpuppets handler, and the next three frames execute a check roll handler.

These handlers are defined in the Script window for the movie script in cast member slot 6 (Figure 6.18). The first handler, startpuppets, defines the channels to be used as puppet sprites. When you define a channel to be a puppet sprite, anything you put in that channel is controlled by the script referring to that channel, rather than by the score. The handler sets a channel number variable to one, then uses a repeat with loop to repeat the definition for the range of channel numbers. The loop is defined by an end statement.

The second handler, checkroll, uses the rollOver function in a similar repeat with loop. A function is a Lingo word that returns a value of some kind without changing anything. Different functions return different types of values. A logical function may return the value TRUE or FALSE, depending on the *arguments* (values passed to the function as parameters to operate on), or the current state of the system. The rollOver function returns the value TRUE if the pointer is currently over the bounding rectangle of a particular sprite. (The bounding rectangle is an imaginary rectangle that would fit around the entire object.)

If the rollOver condition is TRUE for a particular channel, the script changes the ink of the sprite in that channel. The if-then-else construct is the most widely used logical conditional test in programming. Like all constructs in Lingo, if-then-else is defined by an end statement.

Once you've declared a sprite to be a puppet sprite, you can change any sprite property, such as its size, shape, location on the stage, color ink, and so forth.

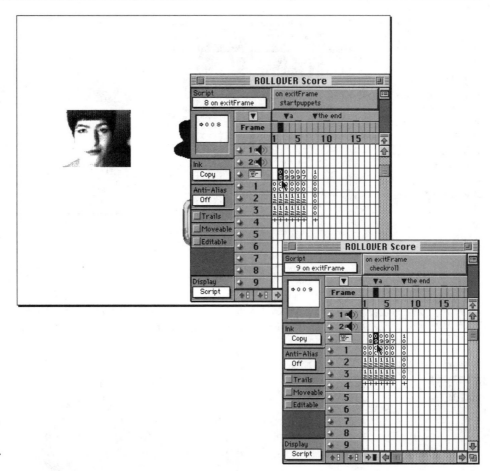

**Figure 6.17**
The movie *Roll-Over* (filename: ROLLOVER.DIR) shows how puppet sprites can be used with the rollOver function.

**Figure 6.18**
The Script window of the movie script cast member shows the handler definitions.

```
--
on startPuppets
  set channelnum to 1
  repeat with channelnum = 1 to 3
    puppetSprite channelnum, TRUE
  end repeat
  --
end startPuppets
--
--
on checkRoll
  set channelnum to 1
  repeat with channelnum = 1 to 3
    if rollover(channelnum) then
      set the ink of sprite channelnum to 4
      updateStage
    else
      set the ink of sprite channelnum to 8
      updateStage
    end if
  end repeat
  --
end checkRoll
--
--
--
```

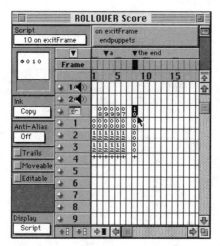

**Figure 6.19
The score shows
the endpuppets
handler used in
the Script chan-
nel in frame 8.
The handler's
definition is in
the Script win-
dow for movie
script cast mem-
ber 6.**

To turn off a puppet sprite, and return control over the sprite to the score, use a statement that identifies the sprite by its channel number and declares it to be FALSE. In the movie *RollOver* (filename: ROLLOVER), frame 8 contains the frame script endpuppets, which turns off the puppet sprites (Figure 6.19).

## Puppet Effects

Transitions, sounds, tempos, and palettes can be set from within scripts through the use of puppets. You can, for example, change the palette, or play a sound, depending on an event that occurs, without having to jump to a new frame.

With the puppetSound expression, you can override the sound channels of the score and play a sound. For example, the following handler plays the sound "NUMBER9" when the mouse is clicked.

```
on mouseUp
        puppetSound "NUMBER9"
end
```

If the above handler was attached to a button cast member, then whenever a user clicks that button, the sound plays.

To turn off the sound, use the puppetSound 0 command. This command gives control back to the score's sound channels. For more information on sounds, see Chapter 7.

In much the same fashion, you can also set the tempo with the puppetTempo command, such as puppetTempo 30 (set the tempo to 30 frames per second).

A puppetTransition command can be used to control transitions between frames. The syntax of the puppetTransition command follows.

```
puppetTransition whichTransition{, time}{, chunkSize}
{, changeArea}
```

The first argument, *whichTransition*, is a code number from 01 to 52 representing transitions (such as 01 for Wipe right, 02 for Wipe left, and so on, as listed under "puppetTransition" in the Lingo Dictionary supplied with Director). The subsequent arguments—*time*, *chunkSize*, and *changeArea*—are optional, but must be separated by commas as shown (the brackets indicate optional).

The *time* is in units of one-fourth of a second (minimum 0 for fastest, maximum is 120, or 30 seconds). The *chunkSize* is the number of pixels in each chunk of the transition (minimum 1, maximum 128). You get smoother, but slower, transitions with smaller chunk sizes. The *changeArea* should be FALSE to have the transition occur over the entire stage. If not specified or set to TRUE, the transition occurs only over the areas that change from one frame to the next.

For example, here is a puppetTransition that takes 4 seconds, uses a chunk size of 8 pixels, and occurs only in the areas that change from one frame to the next:

```
puppetTransition 24, 16, 8, FALSE
```

The puppetTransition command works only on the frame in which the command is encountered. Follow the puppetTransition command with the updateStage command:

```
updateStage
```

This command updates the stage with the new information, in this case, a transition, and refreshes the stage without having to advance a frame.

The puppetPalette command operates the same way: It requires arguments that define the palette to switch to, the speed, and the number of frames for palette switching across multiple frames.

```
puppetPalette whichPalette{, speed}{, number-of-frames}
```

For example, you might want to switch the palette to Grayscale over 10 frames, at 15 frames per second, after switching a puppet sprite's cast member:

```
puppetPalette "Grayscale", 15, 10
updateStage
```

When the puppet palette is on, subsequent changes to the Palette channel in the Score window are ignored. You have to turn off the puppet palette with the following command.

```
puppetPalette 0
```

This command returns control to the Palette channel. Palette effects work only in 256-color displays.

Puppets help you control the properties of sprites, or effects (palettes, transitions, tempos, sounds), without having to jump around and create new sequences of frames. However, be sure to turn off puppets whenever you use them; otherwise the display can be unpredictable. Don't forget to use the `updateStage` command to update the stage after a puppet effect.

## Using Moveable Sprites

An excellent interface technique is to give the user an object to drag with the mouse to another location. For example, in Stuart Sharpe's *Table Set* movie (filename: TABLESET.DIR), you can drag the CD on top of the CD player (Figure 6.20), which opens to receive it. You can also drag the video cassette into the VCR.

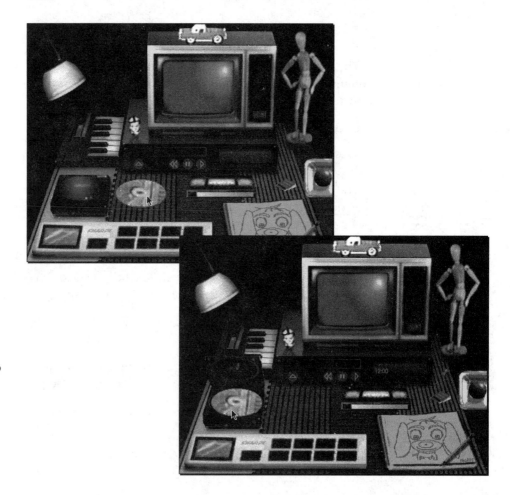

**Figure 6.20 Dragging the CD sprite on top of the CD player sprite in Stuart Sharpe's *Table Set* movie (filename: TABLESET.DIR).**

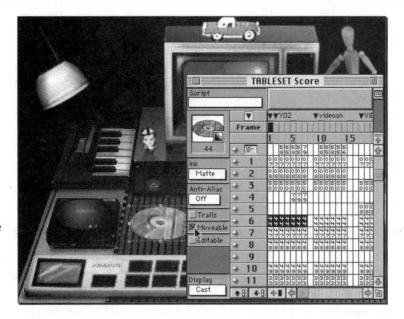

**Figure 6.21**
**The CD disc sprite is set to have the Moveable property in the score, so that the user can drag it.**

Both sprites are set to be moveable in the score with the Moveable property. To set a sprite to be moveable, simply select it and choose the Moveable option on the left side of the Score window (Figure 6.21).

However, setting a sprite to be moveable is only half the job. To have the CD player accept the CD, you have to test to see when the moveable sprite is within a certain range of the CD player sprite. In *Table Set* the following script opens the CD player to accept the CD object, when you drag the object to the player.

```
if (sprite 6 within 3) then
go to frame "CD OPEN"
end if
```

This script uses the `sprite ... within` operator to compare the position of two sprites. The syntax is:

```
sprite sprite1 within sprite2
```

You substitute the actual sprite numbers for *sprite1* and *sprite2*. The comparison is TRUE if the bounding rectangle of *sprite1* is entirely inside the bounding rectangle of *sprite2*. If both sprites are set to have the matte ink effect, the outlines of the sprites are used in this comparison operation, rather than the bounding rectangles. A sprite's outline is defined by nonwhite pixels that make up its border.

Another operator you may want to use is the `sprite ... intersects` operator, which also compares the positions of two sprites. The syntax is:

```
sprite sprite1 intersects sprite2
```

The comparison is TRUE if the bounding rectangle of *sprite1* touches the bounding rectangle of *sprite2*. Again, if both sprites are set to have the matte ink effect, the outlines of the sprites are compared, rather than the bounding rectangles.

If you want to compare sprites that are close to each other, but not touching, you may want to define one sprite's bounding rectangle to be larger or smaller.

The `spriteBox` command sets the bounding rectangle for a sprite using coordinates based on the sprite's registration point. You can set the left, top, right, and bottom sprite properties of a sprite directly using this command. Here's the syntax.

```
spriteBox whichSprite, left, top, right, bottom
```

Substitute a sprite number for whichSprite, and use coordinates for *left*, *top*, *right*, and *bottom*, which are based on the registration point. The registration point should be set to the upper left corner of the cast member in the Paint window. A sprite's coordinates will change based on the registration point of the sprite's cast member.

## *Making and Distributing Projectors*

Director lets you freely distribute movie files, so that the movie files can be run on other machines without Director itself. To do this, you must create a *projector* file that contains at least the first movie file. That first movie file can, in turn, use `Go to movie` or `Play movie` statements to run other movies. All movies can be interactive.

Although there are rules about the use of projector files in commercial projects, as of this writing the distribution of projector files is free. Macromedia does not charge a royalty.

You can use a simple projector file to start a large presentation of many Director files. First, create a Director movie that calls another movie (and the other movie, in turn, calls one or more other movies, and so on). The starter movie can be contained in a projector, and you can then distribute the projector and the folder of movies, and the recipient can run the movies simply by double-clicking the projector.

To create the projector, use the Create Projector command in the File menu (Figure 6.22). This command brings up a dialog box, in which you can select the movie file to be added to a projector.

What Create Projector does is create a projector file that contains the movie you added, plus the code required to play all movies. When you start running a

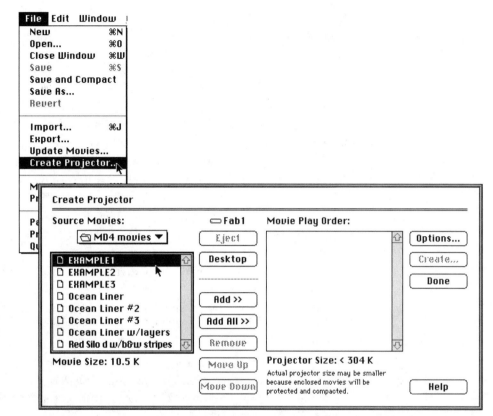

**Figure 6.22**
**Using the Create**
**Projector com-**
**mand to add the**
**startup movie to**
**a projector file to**
**distribute movies**
**to others. The**
**startup movie**
**has its own**
**script to run**
**other movies.**

projector file, the movie it contains can call other movies, which can be played without Director, because the projector's code remains in memory.

Click the Option button to see the Options dialog box (Figure 6.23). The Play Every Movie option plays the entire list of movies in sequence; if there is only one movie in the projector, you don't need this option to be checked.

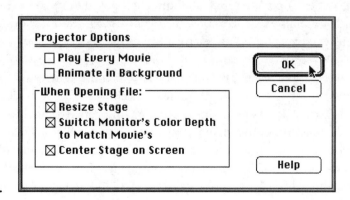

**Figure 6.23**
**Click the Option**
**button in the Cre-**
**ate Projector dia-**
**log box to set the**
**projector options.**

The Animate in Background option lets a movie play in the background, if the user clicks outside the movie's stage. This option is useful, if your Director movie is sending AppleEvents to other programs, or is used in conjunction with other programs. If it is not checked, the movie stops playing when the user clicks outside the stage size.

The Resize Stage option changes the stage size when a movie that uses a different stage size is opened; if not checked the stage size remains the same.

There is also an option to switch the monitor's color depth to match the movie in the projector's play list. This is a convenient way of assuring that the monitor is set to the right color depth. You can also set an option to center the stage on the screen, so that movies with smaller stage sizes will play in the center.

When you have set the options you need, click the Create button to create the projector file, give it a name, and store it on disk. Click the Done button in the Create Projector dialog box to return to Director.

Note that if you want to be able to open the movie file, or files included inside a projector with Director, you must keep the movie files, because you can't open a projector with Director. Projector files are simply for playing, and can't be edited or changed.

Keep in mind that in order to create a projector file, which will run on Windows systems, you must use Director for Windows to create the projector. However, the movie files can be used on any system, provided that certain conventions (such as filenames) are followed. To create a projector for Macintosh systems, you must use Director for Macintosh.

## *Learning More About Lingo*

As a media scripting language, nothing is as extensive as Lingo, with commands, functions, key words, constants, and operators with cross-platform performance. Lingo offers a complete set of arithmetic, logical, and comparison operators for building complex expressions. You can test for the location of sprites and for certain system properties, such as the monitor's color depth, or the amount of time passed since a mouse or key click.

Lingo supports the use of variables, which are temporary holding places for values. In fact, Lingo offers a flexible choice of global, local, and instance variables, as well as lists, which can contain property variables. Global variables can be referenced and changed by any script, handler, or macro; local variables can be changed only by the handler, or macro, that contains them.

Director 4 offers some amazing new Lingo features described in Chapter 9, "Tips and Advanced Techniques," including the ability to embed one interactive movie in a window inside another interactive movie. Another feature, explored in Chapter 9 is how to use QuickTime movies for interactive buttons.

Lingo also provides object-oriented programming methods, including a parent/child relationship that can be established between objects, and a construction known as a *factory,* which is used to create objects that are invested with certain properties and controlled by certain methods, which are macrolike scripts. Instance variables are used within these methods. It is beyond the scope of this book to provide details of object-oriented programming, other than the techniques and tips in Chapter 9.

Director offers an *object-sensitive* help facility. Simply press the Shift and Option keys simultaneously and click on any object, or any Lingo word in the Lingo menu, and a help message appears explaining that item.

For all of its power and flexibility, Lingo and Director provide the most useful paradigm for developing multimedia presentations with interactivity. The Score window shows the action as it is occurring, with a symbolic representation that enables you to cut and paste animated sequences into frames as well as synchronize sounds and transitions to frames. Scripts can be attached to score cells, cast members, or the movie itself, by entering text into the Script window. Handlers let you to condense complicated scripts into single-word commands that other scripts can use.

The Lingo language can be used to make decisions based on actions, events, timing, and even the horizontal and/or vertical location of the mouse itself (without clicking). You can use Lingo scripts to make similar objects, which have their own inner logic of constrained movement, child objects with a relationship to a parent object. If there is any interactive multimedia authoring system that can create the illusion of human actors leading you through a labyrinth of information, it is Director. There is no limit to the kind of interactive presentations you can create with it.

Chapter 9 contains a set of tips and techniques for using Lingo. Each technique is explained fully, so that you can use it without having to learn all of the details of using the Lingo language. However, this book can only scratch the surface of what is possible with Lingo, and it would take another book to delve into the details of using Lingo for complex scripting tasks. Fortunately, the Lingo Dictionary supplied with Director covers all aspects of Lingo scripting, including every Lingo keyword.

## *Chapter Summary*

In this chapter you learned how to add scripts to your movies to make them interactive. You were introduced to the Lingo scripting language and to applications of applying interactive features to movies. You also learned how to design movies for interactivity.

The most common script instructions were introduced in this chapter. You learned about frame scripts, sprite scripts, and cast scripts, and how to link animated sequences with variations of the Go to command with labels, markers, and frames.

You also learned about puppet techniques, including puppet sprites, puppet sounds, puppet transitions, puppet tempos, and puppet palettes. Moveable sprites were also covered.

The Create Projector facility was explained. It is a facility that lets you create a projector for a movie, which can call other movies, and all the movies can be distributed for playback on other systems without Director.

The next chapter combines all the information you need about using sound, including recording from audio devices, and using sound in your movies.

# 7

## *Using Sound*

**I'll play it first and tell you what it is later.**

Miles Davis

**Y**ou have learned the basics about creating interactive movies using text, graphics, and animation. You also have been introduced to scripting in Director's Lingo language. Learning about Lingo is a prerequisite for understanding how to prepare interactive projects using special audio and video equipment, and how to use various digital formats for audio and video.

Applications for sound as part of multimedia presentations, are everywhere—business communications, training, education, art, and entertainment are the major categories. Applications include narration, voice-overs, music, and sound effects, along with any kind of animated sequence or transition. Interactive presentations can be built around music as the content, or music can be used to enhance the content. Sound effects can also be very useful to highlight visual aids, and navigation controls in interactive presentations, for instance, a click when you activate a button, or a simple chime that plays during transitions between frames.

This chapter describes various uses of sound in movies. It describes the differences between using prerecorded audio on conventional compact discs, and audio recorded in digital form and stored on digital media. It explains how digital "sampled" sound is recorded, and how you can get the best quality from sound digitizers. It describes how to measure sound and minimize distortion to get a clear recording. In addition, it shows you how can connect musical instruments directly to the Macintosh to create, and play back, music.

After reading this chapter, you will have learned the basics of digital sound recording, and you will understand the methods and techniques for using sound with Director.

# Different Types of Sound

You already know that compact discs hold prerecorded high-fidelity sound. You also know that your personal computer can play sound. The difference between the two types of digital sound—high fidelity, and PC quality—can range from none to too much, depending on the sound capabilities of your computer.

Most multimedia-capable PCs and Macs can play high-fidelity sound right out of the box. Some can also record sound into a digital file without any additional hardware. Other computers require additional hardware for both functions.

There are basically three forms of sound.

- *Analog sound*, which exists as wave forms and is recorded with conventional analog recording equipment.

- *Digital sampled sound*, which exists as a digital file representing the aforementioned wave form.

- *MIDI (Musical Instrument Digital Interface) sound,* which exists as a digital file of instructions for a sequencer operating a synthesizer.

## Analog Sound and CD Audio Tracks

Analog sound can't be used with Director unless it is part of a videodisc or videotape used with a device controlled by Director, as described in Chapter 8. Analog sound is typically converted to digital sound before use with Director.

Sounds that are stored on conventional audio compact discs, or on audio tracks on a CD-ROM, are digital in format. However, they are used with Director in the same way as analog audio, by controlling a playback device. Conventional audio CDs can be played in most CD-ROM drives and controlled by Director through Lingo scripts. This use of CD audio tracks lets you present CD-quality recorded music, without overly burdening hard disks or creating pauses in your animation. This is because you are playing the sounds from the CD-ROM directly through the CD-ROM drive's sound output jack without using your computer processor. Computer performance is not affected, and disk accesses in the computer do not cause the sounds to pause.

However, because the sounds played with this method are not brought into the computer, you cannot freely edit, manipulate, or copy them without first digitizing them. Also, you cannot hear the sounds on the computer's built-in speaker as you can with digital sound stored in a computer file (except on AV Macs). Usually, you must rely on compact disc audio tracks, which are expensive to manufacture. Furthermore, prerecorded music is usually copyrighted.

## Digital Sound

Multimedia-capable computers, including all Macintosh models, have the capability to play digital sound at varying levels of quality.

Digital sound recorded into the computer can be edited, altered in various ways, and copied, with absolutely no loss in quality. It can also be heard on the computer's internal speaker (as well as on a speaker system connected via the computer's miniplug outlet).

To create digital sound, you can record sound directly from audio equipment, or with microphones, and use a sound digitizer to convert it to a digital format. The quality of the digital sound that the computer can record, depends on many factors, including the throughput of the computer system. Computers with built-in or additional DSP (digital signal processing) hardware, can usually record, and digitize to disk, stereo music at high fidelity without problems.

Many computer speakers are designed for voice-quality narration and sound effects, but not for high-fidelity music. Multimedia-capable PCs and all Mac models offer sound output jacks to connect the computer to conventional stereo systems, or to special desktop speakers with built-in amplifiers. You can also use headphones with the computers.

## MIDI Sound

In the world of professional and amateur music, MIDI (Musical Instrument Digital Interface) is the standard way to connect synthesizers, keyboards, and other musical instruments to computers.

If you have a synthesizer and a sequencer, you can purchase MIDI songs for your presentations. You can open a MIDI sequence, adjust it to fit the occasion and your synthesizer's configuration, and edit it. MIDI music sequences are available from a number of sources, usually priced at about $10–$30 per song.

Director does not offer control over MIDI devices, but you can issue commands to a MIDI sequencer through the use of third-party extensions to Director. QuickTime 2.0 allows you to embed MIDI in QuickTime Digital Video files.

On the Macintosh, XObjects are an extension mechanism. XObjects are external code resources used to control external devices, and to add functionality to Lingo such as independent windows, pop-up menus, and other interface elements. A number of XObjects are provided for your use in the Freebies folder/directory on the accompanying CD-ROM.

On Windows PCs, the Media Control Interface (MCI) offers control over media devices, and Director can be extended through the use of DLLs (Dynamic Link Libraries). For details on the Media Control Interface, see Chapter 9, "Tips and Advanced Techniques."

## Using Digital Sampled Sound

Sound that is recorded from the real world via microphone, or analog signal into a digital format, is called *sampled sound*. This is because a process called *sampling* is used to store the sound information as digital bits and bytes. Different sampling rates and different bit depths for each sound byte (no pun intended) offer different quality.

Every multimedia-capable PC and Macintosh model is capable of playing back digital sound at the rate of 22 kHz (22,000 cycles per second), or lower, in an 8-bit format (8 bits of information are used to store each sample byte). This is also the upper limit for playback on older Macs and PowerBooks (without requiring additional circuitry or an add-in card), and MPC Level 1 models.

While all these computers can play 8-bit, 22-kHz digital sound, with no additional hardware, 8-bit sound is not as high in fidelity as 16-bit sound at 44.1 kHz, which is the same quality as audio compact discs. MPC Level 2 models and Macintosh Quadra AV and PowerMac AV models can record and play 16-bit sound at rates up to, and sometimes above, 44.1 kHz. In addition, there are third-party cards for upgrading either PCs, or Macs with a NuBus slot, to 16-bit sound.

When playing sound from a digital file, the computer's internal speaker may not be enough to convey the quality of the sound. There are many speaker systems that can be attached directly to the computer via the stereo audio out jack (typically a minijack). You can also connect the computer to a conventional stereo amplifier, receiver, or headphone. Cambridge SoundWorks offers the Ensemble speaker system with two subwoofers that can be hidden under a desk or table. It also has two smaller speakers that can be placed on top of the desk or table, providing excellent high-fidelity sound.

## Recording Digital Sound

Most Macs, including PowerBooks, offer the capability to record and digitize at 22 kHz in 8 bits per sample, which is only medium quality for music, but is suitable for voices and sound effects. The AV-model Macs can record and digitize high-quality music at 44 kHz in 16 bits per sample. Multimedia-capable PCs with 16-bit sound cards are also capable of this high-quality rate, while 8-bit sound cards offer only medium quality.

For older Macs, Macromedia offers the MacRecorder Sound System Pro kit, which includes the MacRecorder recording/sampling device for 22-kHz, 8-bit sound. You can use one MacRecorder that connects directly to the Mac's modem, or printer ports, or use two MacRecorders, and connect to both serial ports for stereo sound. The MacRecorder can record sounds through its microphones, or directly from an audio source, such as an amplifier/receiver, tape deck, or high-quality microphone repeater. The MacRecorder is limited to recording only the amount of sound that can fit in RAM at any one time.

The CD-ROM accompanying this book has a demo version of another Macintosh audio capture program, Disc-To-Disc, specifically designed for recording sound from audio CDs. Maufactured by Optical Media International, it is capable of recording 8- or 16-bit sound at 11KHz, 22KHz, or 44KHz. The demo on the disc lets you record up to 10 seconds of audio.

The AV-model Macs can record and digitize 16-bit, 44-kHz sound directly to hard disk, and play back the same high-quality sound directly from hard disk, or CD-ROM. With other Mac models that have at least one NuBus slot, you can do the same with a professional digital audio recording and sampling card, such as DigiDesign's Audiomedia card and Deck program. DigiDesign offers a range of 16-bit coprocessor cards for sound recording and editing, and playback cards for NuBus-model Macs, with variable sampling rates, including the compact disc standard 44.1-kHz rate.

With most 16-bit sound cards on PCs, such as Creative Labs' SoundBlaster 16, you can also record and digitize high-quality sound directly to hard disk, and play it back from hard disk and CD-ROM. MPC Level 2 machines are capable of digitizing and playing back 16-bit, 44.1-kHz sound.

The storage requirements for digital sound are enormous. You need 22 kilobytes to store 1 second of 22-kHz sampled sound without compression. You can reduce the amount of memory and disk space required to hold sounds, by *downsampling* the sound: reducing the sampling rate to 11, 7, or 5 kHz. Although the sound remains stored with 8 bits per sample, there are fewer samples to store, so typically the sound file is reduced by half. However, downsampling reduces the frequency range (for example, the range for an 11-kHz sample is from 0 to 5 kHz). Downsampling, therefore, is more useful for recording speech than for music. Monaural voice narration can be recorded at a low sampling rate.

You can use a 5-kHz sampling rate for telephone-quality sound; 7 kHz for AM radio sound; 11 kHz for television sound and medium-quality music; 22 kHz for higher-quality music, and 44.1 kHz for high-fidelity music. (Examples you can hear are available on the accompanying CD-ROM.)

After you have recorded the basic sounds, you may want to add special effects. Some effects can be added in the sound editing program and fine-tuned to match the sounds already recorded. For example, SoundEdit 16 for the Macintosh, supplied with the MacRecorder, or available separately, lets you mix sounds from separate channels into one channel. Various programs are available for the Windows system.

## Importing Digital Sound into Director

You can use sampled sounds with Director in two ways: internal sounds (stored in the Director file), or external sounds (stored in external sound files). You have several choices in file formats that are recognized by Director when importing files.

- On a Mac, you can save the sound as a SoundEdit file that can be imported into a Director movie as an internal cast member. You can then use the cast member in one, or more, of the score's sound channels. With this method, the entire sound segment must be loaded into memory before it is played, but the sound segment can have predefined loops.

- On a Mac, you can save the sound, as an snd resource, in a resource file. You can import snd resources from other files into Director as cast members. Again, with this method, the entire sound segment must be loaded into memory before it is played.

- On a Mac, or a Windows PC, you can save the sound as an AIFF file, then import it as a cast member, but with the Linked option. This lets you play the sound directly from disk. The sound file is played continuously, directly from disk, without a significant memory requirement.

- On a Windows PC, you can save the sound as a WAV file, then import it as a cast member, but with the linked option, which lets you play the sound directly from disk.

One AIFF or WAV file can be shared by an unlimited number of movies. You can also play AIFF or WAV external sound files using Lingo commands. If you don't use the linked option, the information in the AIFF or WAV file is stored in the Director file like any other internal sound that is loaded and played from memory.

To import a sound, use the Import command in the File menu, and pick Sound in the pop-up menu for the type of file (Figure 7.1). You can import SoundEdit, AIFF, WAV, and AIFC files, and snd (8-bit) resources in other Macintosh files.

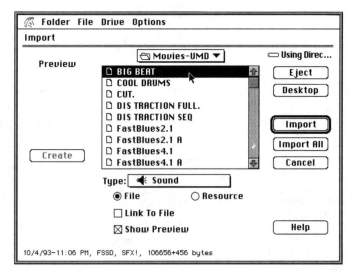

**Figure 7.1 Importing a sound as a cast member.**

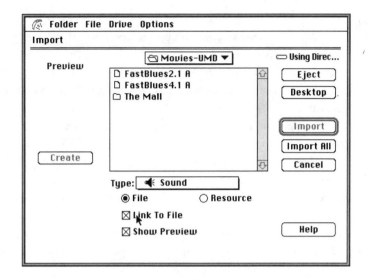

**Figure 7.2
Using the "Link to" option to establish a link to an AIFF external sound file.**

If you click the Link option (Figure 7.2), you can narrow your choices to just the AIFF, WAV, and AIFC sound files. These files can then be linked as cast members and shared among movies (saving disk space). AIFF files can accommodate a wide variety of sounds at different sampling rates and resolutions. They are also compatible for use as external files on both Macintosh and Windows systems (as long as you follow the DOS file-naming conventions).

## *Playing CD Audio Tracks*

If you want to play prerecorded music on the audio tracks of compact discs along with your presentation, you can use Director to control the playback of the audio tracks.

Prerecorded compact disc audio tracks and high-quality sampled sounds on CD-ROM or hard disk can be mixed in the same presentation. You may take this approach if you want to use high-quality stereo music, and medium-quality narration and sound effects. These methods are often combined to gain the advantages of both: the quality of CD audio tracks for music, and the quick turnaround time of cost-effective digital recording for narration and some sounds.

**Setting Up CD-ROM Audio Output**

To hear the CD audio tracks, the CD-ROM drive must be capable of playing audio CDs, and the audio output of the CD-ROM drive must be routed to speakers. The drawbacks are that the sounds must already be mastered onto CD audio tracks to use them. Many Macintosh models do not have built-in mixers. So, if you want to play sounds from the Mac, as well as from the CD-ROM drive's audio output, you have to use an external mixer, or combine the left-right channels of the CD-ROM drive and connect it to the left or right channel of the speaker system (with the Mac sound connected to the other channel).

You can play audio tracks on a CD or CD-ROM (hybrid-format CD-ROM discs can also have audio tracks) with Apple's SCSI-compatible CD-ROM drives and many other Macintosh models (including built-in drives in AV units). Director can control the CD-ROM drive through an XObject.

Macromedia offers the AppleCD XObjects for playing segments of music stored on either off-the-shelf compact discs or the audio tracks of CD-ROM discs.

On Windows machines, Microsoft offers the MCI interface, described in Chapter 9.

The playing of a conventional compact disc or the audio tracks of a CD-ROM disc is independent of the computer, so that you can play sound while movies are loading from disk into memory. The audio continues playing even while another movie document is loading into memory.

You can even play sampled sounds, and sound effects defined in one of the Sound channels of the score while the CD-ROM drive is playing audio tracks on the compact disc.

The AppleCD XObject provides several commands you can use in a script to play a specific audio track from the beginning. Or, you can play a segment described in the absolute time of the compact disc, in minutes, seconds, and frames. The XObject offers commands for pausing and continuing, and for returning information about the disc including the number of tracks, the current track, and the total time in minutes, seconds, and frames.

The AppleCD XObject is stored in the AppleCD XObj resource file, in the Apple CD Control folder, in the XObject folder in the Extras folder. To use the XObject, you must copy this resource file to the folder that holds your movie file, or to the movie file itself (as described in Chapter 9).

## Using the Control Panel Examples

Besides the AppleCD XObject, the Apple CD Control folder also contains movies called *AppleCD Example—Color* and *AppleCD Example—B&W*, which contain nearly all the scripts you may need to control the playing of audio tracks with a CD-ROM drive. Rather than reinventing scripts to control the AppleCD XObject, it is far easier to simply copy these scripts and cast members to your movie. Or, if you want, you can save one of these sample movies as a new movie, in order to create a movie that can play CD audio discs.

By copying the scripts and cast members of the sample movie, and putting together a simple movie that plays CD audio tracks, you can begin to understand why factories can be useful, and how to make use of them. A technique describing the use of the XObject FileIO is provided in Chapter 9, along with detailed information on using XObjects.

The two example movies *AppleCD Example—Color* and *AppleCD Example— B&W*, are set up so that you can use Save As to create a new movie containing all the scripts you need to play, stop (pause), move forward fast, move backward fast, move to the next track on the disc, and eject. Buttons are provided for these operations, and the cast member representing each button contains the script that is activated by the button. The script containing the factory definition for the AppleCD XObject is contained in a single cast script for cast member 1.

The example movies use puppet sprites to control which cast member appears in place of the buttons in the CD audio control panel that appears on the stage. The buttons are cast members with their own scripts, as in the Play button (Figure 7.3). The script for Play cast member uses factory notation to execute the "play method" (mPlay) of the factories thePanel (which controls the visual control panel) and theDevice (which controls the CD-ROM drive itself).

You can use the *AppleCD Example—Color* (or *B&W*) movie as it is—the control panel buttons work. You can play, stop, pause, eject, scan forward, scan in reverse, move to the next track, and move to the previous track. Buttons are provided to turn on or off the left and right channels. You can also click an up-arrow or down-arrow to set up the next track for the Cue button, then click the Cue button to play that track. The panel includes a message line indicating the status of the CD-ROM drive.

**Figure 7.3**
**The convenient control panel in the example file (*AppleCD Example*) for playing CD audio tracks from Director. You can copy the entire control panel and its scripts, or just the scripts (and buttons) you need.**

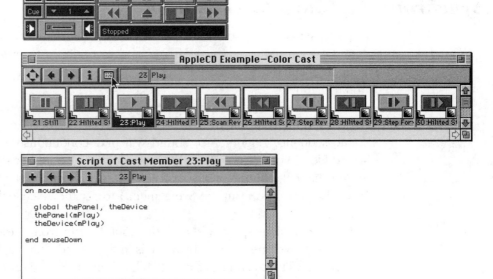

The control panel puppet, controlled by thePanel is comprised of several cast members occupying channels 1 through 16. If you use Save As to save a copy of the *AppleCD Example—Color* (or *B&W*) file, you can use it as the basis for your movie. This leaves you with channels 17 through 48 for any objects or animations you may want to add.

You can add images to the movie file using channels 17 through 48, but if you want to add a background image behind the CD sound panel buttons, you must use channel 1. However, if you move the CD sound panel cast member from channel 1 to, say, channel 17, it obscures some of the other areas of the panel that display information. What's more, you shouldn't move the cast members in channels 8 through 15 unless you modify the CD Panel factory definition in the Script window for cast member 1.

You can, however, move the cast members in channels 1 through 7 to channels 17 through 23 without changing the operation of the movie. You can also modify the cast script for cast member 1, removing the scripts and cast members that you don't need, to make room for other elements. Factory methods are described in Chapter 9.

The use of conventional compact discs is especially useful if the prerecorded music or sounds are related to the content or are the subject matter of the presentation. One can imagine a variety of music appreciation projects that can be put together with Director and conventional CDs played on the CD-ROM drive. A complete, self-paced music appreciation course could be put together.

## Synchronizing Sound to Animation

You can synchronize sound to animation by using the two Sound channels. A sound can be started from any frame, and it continues to play until it ends, or until the playback head reaches the end of the notation representing that sound in the channel.

For example, to have a particular sound play until it ends, repeat the notation for that sound over as many frames of the score as you need to play the complete sound sequence (Figure 7.4). Sound will play continuously to the end of the sound file, if you create a loop in the score. If you double-click one cell in the Sound channel, or a range of sound cells, Director displays the Set Sound dialog box (also available from the Score menu) to set the selection to a sound cast member.

To leave a silent space and start the sound again from the beginning of the sequence, leave one or more blank cells in the Sound channel, between the first sequence and the second. A single blank cell in the Sound channel, followed by

**Figure 7.4
Synchronizing
two sound cast
members to
frames in the
movie *Undo Me
prototype (IM4)*
(filename: UN-
DOIM4A.DIR).**

the notation for the sound sequence, is enough to trigger the start of the sound sequence. To be sure that the sound notation occupies enough cells in the Sound channel to play until completion, you can slow down the tempo of the movie, or add frames and extend the number of cells, or create a loop for a certain amount of time.

You can't shorten, or otherwise speed up, the sound unless you edit the sound in a sound editing program such as SoundEdit 16. However, sounds can be copied, pasted, and cleared from the Sound channel just like other score notation.

Some sound editing programs, such as SoundEdit 16, give you the ability to set loop points in the sound sequence for repeating part of the sequence over and over. You can use these loop points in sounds imported into Director movies in the SoundEdit format, so that the looping part of the sequence repeats over and over.

For example, if you define a loop to occur in the middle of a sound sequence, the sequence starts normally and then loops, until the playback head reaches the end of the score notation. Then the part of the sound sequence, after the loop, plays to its end. Thus you can synchronize the beginning, the middle (the looping part), and the end of a sound sequence to frames of animation. You must save the sound in the original SoundEdit file format for these loop features.

You can also store sounds in QuickTime movies, which are easy to synchronize. QuickTime movies are described in Chapter 8. For more tips on synchronization, see Chapter 9.

## *Chapter Summary*

In this chapter, you learned how to make use of several different types of audio. They are:

- Sampled digital audio.
- Recorded, digitized, and audio stored on disc.
- MIDI music.
- CD audio tracks and music CDs and CD-ROMs with music tracks.

You also learned about:

- Various sound file formats.
- How to control the playback of CD audio tracks.
- How to import digital sound into Director files.
- How to synchronize sound with animation.

The next chapter provides the information you need to integrate video with your Director movies, using either analog video sources, or digital video, and how to output Director animation into video formats.

# 8

## *Using Video*

**You can observe a lot just by watching.**

Yogi Berra

The essence of Director is interactive animation; however, video clips can also be part of an interactive presentation. In addition, the animation you create in Director can be exported to digital video files, or directly to analog video equipment.

This chapter explains how digital and analog video can be created and edited, how to record Director movies to videotape; how to export animation to digital video files, and how to use analog or digital video clips in Director movies.

Interactive presentations with video have the potential to be far more effective than any other type of media, especially for business and industrial training. With the combination of video and sound, you can present complex information simply and quickly. With a booming business in video training, and an enormous installed base of VCRs, people would rather watch a video than wade through pages and pages of tutorial-style documentation.

Video can be extremely entertaining and direct, capturing attention and providing much more information in a sequence of images than any other medium. The applications of *desktop video* are beginning to appear, and they include all forms of training and entertainment. Professional video production studios are using computers to assist in editing and production. Advertising firms are using Director to do rough edits of commercials to obtain approvals and make final adjustments. TV stations are using Director with professional video hardware to produce transitions between programs and other special effects. Director movies are incorporating digital video for applications as wide-ranging as games and interactive software manuals and books such as this one.

# Learning About Video

While there are many different forms of video, there are essentially two categories of video formats: *analog* and *digital*. Director can be used with both categories of formats.

*Analog* video is the form of video that most people are familiar with. Devices that record and play analog video on professional-quality tape can be found in every professional video studio, and home VCRs play analog video stored on consumer-quality VHS tape.

Professional-quality analog video is an expensive medium in which to produce content, and the costs rise dramatically for special effects. The combination of professional analog video equipment and Director provides one of the greatest benefits in this area: Animation can be created in a digital environment with Director on a desktop computer, and then saved on videotape by recording with an analog video recorder.

*Digital* video is a new form of video that is digitized and stored on hard disk or CD-ROM. Digital video can also be used with a Director movie in a number of different ways. The simplest way is to create a digital video clip with a video capture card (such as the inexpensive VideoSpigot from SuperMac for the Macintosh) and a conventional analog video camera or VCR as a source (input device). Once the clips are stored in digital video files on disk, you can import the digital video files into a Director movie and play them as part of a sequence (Figure 8.1).

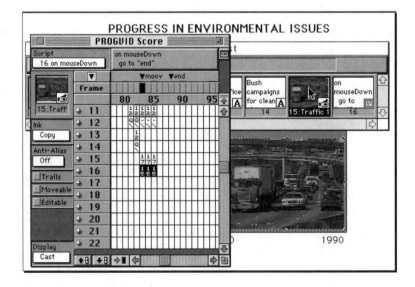

**Figure 8.1
A digital video
cast member
playing within a
Director movie
(filename:
PROGVID.DIR).**

Before digital video became available in the form of the QuickTime architecture in Macintosh systems, and the Video for Windows architecture in Windows systems, multimedia artists and producers used analog video along with Director movies. For example, prerecorded video on a laser videodisc can be synchronized with animation in a Director movie, and you can create a Director movie that plays different segments of a videodisc. The video can appear on a separate display monitor, or in a window of the display if you use a video-in-a-window display card (such as ones from Radius, RasterOps, and Truevision).

You also can record animation onto videotape for use with VCRs; or you can record the animation onto high-quality videotape for use with industrial or commercial videos. Digital video movies can also be exported directly from Director.

Sophisticated video effects can be achieved by overlaying graphics, animation, and text onto a video image in a Director movie and saving the result onto videotape or in a digital video file. One frame of video can be frozen as a still image for use in presentations and publishing projects. With professional video equipment, driven by Director, you can display video with text and graphic overlays and produce special effects of adequate quality for commercial TV broadcasts.

Before digital video hardware became widely available, the method for bringing analog video into the computer environment was called "video in a window."

The "video in a window" capability places live analog video on the same screen as the computer's display. In many cases the window is smaller than full-screen video. For full-screen video, it is usually easier to display video on a separate display monitor next to the computer's monitor and drive both monitors from the same computer. Thus, "video in a window" is an important capability for certain applications, especially kiosks that include a low-powered computer and a laserdisc player.

However, digital video has become the easiest and least expensive method of adding video to your Director movies. The tradeoff is that full-screen, full-motion digital video requires add-on hardware not found in every computer. Software-based playback with Apple's QuickTime on the Mac, and with Apple's QuickTime for Windows (both included in the Freebies section of the accompanying CD-ROM), or Microsoft's Video for Windows on Windows, offers a lower frame rate and much smaller window size than full-motion, full-screen video for today's Mac and Windows systems. More powerful computers, such as Windows systems based on a fast Pentium chip, or Power Macs based on a fast PowerPC chip, can play full-screen, full-motion digital video without extra hardware.

## How Video Works

Video production technology has its own language and standards that are not well known in the computer industry, and are not adhered to by computer display technology. In fact, the technologies have not been used together, by the same people, until very recently.

In the United States and Japan, the broadcast video signal is called *NTSC* video. It differs significantly from the video signals used in other countries (such as *PAL*, used in Great Britain, other European countries, and Australia; or *SECAM*, used in France, Russia, Germany, and the Middle East).

NTSC is the acronym for National Television System Committee; it describes a type of video signal defined in 1953 that encodes and transmits color television. NTSC video displays images, or *frames,* at the constant rate of 30 frames per second. Each frame has 525 lines of image information divided into two fields: one for the even-numbered lines and one for the odd-numbered lines in the image. In a process called *interlace scanning,* a beam sweeps across the picture tube displaying all the odd lines from top to bottom, then blanks out, and returns to the top to display all the even lines from top to bottom. This process happens continuously and faster than the eye can see (60 fields per second), providing the illusion of movement with images.

Synchronizing pulses (Vertical and Horizontal SYNC) are that part of the signal that locks the picture images in place. These pulses mark the transition points between elements of the picture. The Horizontal SYNC pulse occurs once for each line during the blanking interval, providing a measured interval for the beam to move from the end of a line, to the beginning of the next line, so that the beginnings of each line are lined up in the same column.

The Vertical SYNC occurs in the vertical blanking interval (the black bar you see when you adjust the vertical hold on your TV set), and provides a measured interval between fields of a frame. This is so that the beam can move from the bottom to the original top position and display the alternate field.

The standard computer RGB video display differs from a standard television, or video monitor, in that it uses a different scan rate and separate RGB (red, green, and blue) signals rather than one composite video signal (a composite signal includes all colors). Additional circuitry is required to combine the two different types of video information (noninterlaced computer display and interlaced television-style video) on the same display and to synchronize the signals.

A feature known as *genlocking* is required to overlay, for example, a computer image or text on top of a video signal. Genlocking is the capability to lock signals, from different video equipment, so that you can overlay them. The genlocking feature of video cards for desktop computers makes it possible to overlay graphics, including Director animation, on top of live, full-motion NTSC video.

*Keying* (also called color keying) is the capability to make a portion of a video signal transparent so that you can see another signal when genlocking. A color called the *key color* is chosen on one signal. For example, you may set the key color to be light blue, and all light blue areas of the video are replaced by another video signal. This is one method for combining, for example, a wall-sized weather map with a video image of a weather announcer standing in front of a light blue wall.

Digital video at high resolution (640 by 480 pixels, with 60 fields per line, such as the Radius VideoVision Studio card) has obviated the need for analog-oriented genlocking hardware. When you digitize video, each frame is converted into a bitmap, not unlike computer graphics. You can use an image editing program, or digital video editing program, to overlay graphics and text on the video frames. There is no need to bring an analog video stream into the computer and perform genlocking. All that is needed is a video digitizing card, and plenty (and we do mean gigabytes!) of hard disk space. We can't emphasize that too much: You need at least 100 megabytes, for example, to hold about one minute of digital video.

If this type of configuration is too much, and you want to work with analog video equipment, the genlocking hardware is still an economical choice.

## Using Camcorders

Video is recorded onto videotape using either a video camera/recorder, called a *camcorder*, to capture scenes from real life, or a videocassette recorder (VCR) for recording video off the airwaves, off cable, or off satellite.

Camcorders can be used for capturing raw video footage, which can be edited with video editing software into a video clip. Single frames of raw footage can be captured and used as images for a Director movie. The type of camcorder you choose depends on a variety of factors, such as your taste for quality, your need for portability, and your budget.

Consumer-grade camcorders fall into two major categories: 8mm and VHS (including Super VHS). Generally, the 8mm camcorders are lighter, more compact, and easier to use while traveling. The VHS and Super VHS camcorders are usually larger and record onto VHS-format videocassettes that can be played in consumer-grade VHS-format VCRs. Both types of camcorder formats offer low-priced, medium-range, and professional models.

Features to look for in consumer-grade camcorders include a power zoom lens, multiple-speed shutter, flying erase head, rechargeable battery, and the capability to connect to a TV for playback. NTSC video output is necessary for connecting a camcorder to consumer, and computer, equipment, although some equipment offers an S-Video connection.

Professional models should include SMPTE time code, which is the standard method of identifying video frames when editing video, in order to synchronize music to video. SMPTE time code is recorded directly on the tape so that the tape can be used with editing decks.

## Capturing Still Images

A still video image is similar in format to a scanned grayscale or color image. It can be edited and retouched just like a scanned photo using Director's Paint window tools, or using image editing software such as Adobe PhotoShop (Adobe Systems). However, a video image, which is 640 by 480 pixels, is usually lower in resolution than a scanned photo. For the purpose of using the image with Director movies, you can use a resolution matching the screen (72 or 75 dots per inch) and save on disk space.

A *video digitizer* can be used to capture full-screen still images from a video source. A *frame grabber* can "grab frames" of video at the speed of video (30 frames per second) and display each frame on the computer screen. However, the display may not be as fast as the speed of video.

The AV-model Macs offer built in screen-grabbing of analog video. For other Macs, cards are available from Radius (VideoVision), RasterOps (MediaTime), and other vendors that can capture video frames as 24-bit images in 1/30th of a second, fast enough for any standard video signal, without the need for pause. For PCs, there are a variety of cards that offer frame grabbing, such as IBM's Video Capture Adapter/A or Ventek's VIP 640 video capture card.

## Controlling Video Sources

One straightforward way to add prerecorded full-motion video to a Director-based presentation is to use an external display monitor for the video portion of the presentation. Connect the monitor directly to the video source device, usually a laser videodisc player, which is controlled from the computer by Director using scripts with XObjects (on the Macintosh) or Media Control Interface statements (on Windows systems).

Director for the Macintosh also supplies different XObjects for controlling specific laser videodisc players, such as the Pioneer XObject, which provides access to control features specific to Pioneer players. The *Pioneer Videodisc Color* and *Pioneer Videodisc B&W* movies, in the Pioneer Videodisc Panels folder, have player control buttons you can copy and paste into your Director movies (Figure 8.2). You can use these movies in the same way as described for using the example movies for playing CD audio tracks (see Chapter 7).

Consumer videocassette recorders (VCRs) are adequate for playing video to be captured by a frame grabber or video digitizer. However, they are not useful for interactive video projects, because the tape speed is too slow for random access.

Video can be prerecorded and mastered onto laser videodiscs and then played on videodisc players. The major benefit of producing interactive video is that the speed of a videodisc is fast enough for random access. The seek time (the time

**Figure 8.2
The *Pioneer
Videodisc Color*
movie in the Pio-
neer Videodisc
folder (in the
XObjects folder
in the Extras
folder) for the
Macintosh ver-
sion of Director
offers buttons for
controlling Pio-
neer laser
videodisc play-
ers. Shown is the
script for the
Play button.**

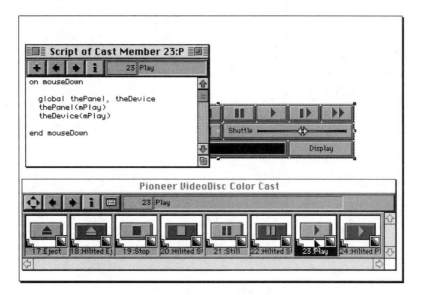

it takes to find any single frame of video on the disc) of a Pioneer LD-V 4200 is about 3 seconds. The higher-performance models, such as the LD-V 8000, can seek as fast as 0.5 second.

Laser videodiscs, encoded in the standard LaserVision format, can be played on players from Pioneer, Sony, Mitsubishi, and other manufacturers that support the LaserVision format. Commercial discs are encoded in the LaserVision format. Discs in proprietary formats can only be played on players designed to handle the particular format, and are not useful in desktop video applications.

Laser videodisc players are not equal in features. "Level 1" players, such as the Pioneer LD-V 2000, are primarily for viewing video in sequence, not for playing interactive video. "Level 2" players have built-in intelligence for playing interactive video controlled by remote keypads. However, the built-in intelligence is not useful for computer-controlled presentations, and simply adds to the price tag. "Level 3" players, such as the Pioneer LD-V 4200 and 8000 and the Sony LDP 1200, have one very important distinguishing feature: an RS-232 connector for connecting the device to a computer. Thus, only "Level 3" players are useful for interactive video.

Some players offer multispeed play capabilities, which can be useful, because the Director XObjects support it. The resolution of the display from a laser videodisc player should be close to 400 horizontal lines. Display monitors attached to the player provide the best video picture quality, but video-in-a-window cards, or digital video cards, can provide adequate quality on the computer screen.

## Displaying Video in a Window

There are several hardware products currently available for NuBus-model Macs that can display full-motion video in a window on the Mac display. The MediaTime card (RasterOps) is one example; the VideoVision (Radius) is another. The AV-model Macs already have this capability.

There are many hardware products for PCs that offer Windows drivers that can be used with Windows applications to offer video-in-a-window capabilities, such as Creative Labs' VideoBlaster. There are far to many to mention here, but the most important point to make about Windows video cards is that you must use the most recent video driver software for Windows; otherwise Director might not be compatible with it.

One popular application of full-motion video-in-a-window hardware is business television. For example, stock traders can simultaneously display the latest stock information, and a live feed from the Financial News Network, on the same screen. Media watchers can display a live newscast with closed caption text and record the captions in a transcript file. Other applications include interactive video presentations, with laser videodisc players.

## Overlaying Text and Graphics

One important application of desktop video is the capability to overlay text (such as titles) and graphics (particularly animation) onto a broadcast-quality analog video signal, effectively mixing the two media. This can be done without using full digital video, which at this time is still expensive due to hard disk requirements. This process also is called compositing, and is widely popular among video studios who use Amigas and Video Toasters for this purpose.

The output of this process can be displayed on a separate video monitor, or on the computer screen, depending on which display card you use. The output cam also be recorded onto videotape through the use of a video output feature of the display card, or a separate video input/output box. The process requires the genlocking feature to synchronize the computer and analog video signals.

For example, the NuVista+ card (Truevision/RasterOps) offers a full spate of video capture, display, and output features, with full 24-bit color images. The NuVista+ is compatible with NTSC and PAL formats and can be connected directly to RGB cameras and studio equipment. You can connect the NuVista+ to NTSC and S-video recording devices, as well as source devices such as VCRs, hand-held camcorders, and videodisc players.

For the purpose of overlaying text and graphics, the NuVista+ offers genlocking so that you can overlay graphics on full-motion video. You can then record the result onto videotape, as well as record full-motion or frame-by-frame animation prepared by Director (described next). When combining video with the computer display, you can define the key color to display the video signal through the computer signal.

# Recording to Videotape

You may want to record animation to videotape for whatever reason, or distribute a recorded version of a Director presentation on videotape. A variety of applications are best served by recording presentations to videotape, even though it means the presentation will be viewed without the benefit of interactivity.

Many of the video cards described previously (such as the Radius VideoVision), and the Mac AV models, provide the capability to output an NTSC video signal for recording onto videotape. The ones that don't provide NTSC output can be used with additional devices (such as the VideoLogic Mediator scan converter) that convert the computer signal to NTSC.

The quality of the recording is affected by a variety of factors including the quality of the output signal and the capabilities of the videotape recorder. A consumer-grade VHS VCR can record animatics for showing concepts and ideas, but it is probably not good enough for industrial-quality, and certainly not for broadcast-quality, videos. Super VHS and ED Beta consumer decks can be used for corporate and industrial training tapes. Broadcast-quality and commercial video can be recorded only with professional decks.

## Recording Frame by Frame

Although it is possible to record an animated sequence on videotape in real time, most applications call for faster animation, or more control over the presentation of each frame. This means that the recording must be done frame by frame.

The precision of professional video recording equipment is required for recording frame by frame. Macromedia provides Director XObjects for recording frames to professional videotape recorders (such as those using 8mm, ½-inch, ¾-inch, and 1-inch formats) that are driven by intelligent controllers. The *Sony VTR FramePerFrame* example in Sony VTR folder (in the XObjects folder inside the Extras folder), which comes with Director for the Macintosh, controls the Sony EVO-9650 intelligent videotape recorder.

Diaquest offers a range of video deck controllers for recording onto videotape, including the DQ-422 (for RS-422 interfacing), DQ-50P (for parallel interfacing), the Series II stand-alone controller (for serial port interfacing), and the DQ-Animaq (for the Macintosh). DQ-Animaq is available in a broadcast-quality model for serial machine control, and a desktop model for serial and parallel control with an RS-170A sync generator and SMPTE time code generator. SMPTE (The Society of Motion Picture and Television Engineers) time code is the standard method of identifying video frames in professional editing studios.

The DQ-Animaq provides frame-accurate recording of video animation, and can also be used with a frame grabber to digitize video sequences for rotoscoping effects. Captured video scenes can be composited with Director and then output frame by frame to videotape. Diaquest offers XObjects for recording frames of animation directly to videotape without having to store them on disk.

Recording frame by frame to videotape is the preferred method for showing animations of 24-bit photorealistic images, which are slow when run in real time on the Mac or PC. When recording animation frame by frame, it can take many frames to record a single transition effect between frames, but the results can be startling. You also can add transition effects directly to the videotape using professional video special effects equipment.

## Designing Graphics and Text for Video

There are a number of rules to remember when designing graphics and text for recording to videotape. One problem you may encounter is *flicker,* which occurs with very fine horizontal lines and jagged edges. You can see flicker in text and in transition areas of high contrast. Dithered patterns, fonts smaller than 18 points, and single-pixel lines are the usual suspects. Unfortunately, many clip art images are composed of dithered patterns and single-pixel lines.

The thicker the line, the less it matters, but lines that are an even number of pixels thick usually do not flicker. You also can reduce the contrast at the edges, or use a technique called *anti-aliasing,* in which you manually add or subtract pixels at high-contrast edges to soften or blur the edges.

You can avoid having sharp vertical lines appear softened, or repeated ("echoed"), by softening the edges of the lines first. Cross-hatched or repeating dark vertical lines also may cause a rainbow effect, or color fringing, and should be avoided.

NTSC video is designed to be used with televisions that *overscan* the picture tube—the total image area is larger than the tube. The Macintosh screen works the opposite way, displaying an image that is slightly smaller than the display screen. When designing animation for a 640 by 480 pixel display, which will eventually be shown in NTSC video, leave at least 15 percent of the full screen on each edge blank (or without critical imagery). This is because the video format chops off about 15 percent of the full-screen display from each edge.

Design rules for video include:

- Avoiding dithered patterns, and avoid lines that are composed with an odd number of pixels, especially single-pixel lines.

- Avoid spaces between lines that are an odd number of pixels high or wide.

- Avoid high-contrast areas, especially when white and black are adjacent to each other, such as sharp vertical lines.

- Avoid highly saturated colors, especially vivid red and orange, and use mostly pastel colors that display well in video format.

- Use the NTSC palette if you want to be sure the colors will work (other palettes may work, but the NTSC palette is guaranteed).

- Use fonts larger than 18 points.

- Plan your images to be within the "safe area" for video so that the images are not cut off.

- Preview the images on video whenever possible.

- Leave at least 15 percent of the full screen on each edge blank (or without critical imagery).

A powerful Mac or PC can be useful in virtually all of the stages of film and video production, including the preproduction and postproduction steps and for animatics. It is even possible to use a Mac or PC to control the editing of video and film in digital form and create the master tape or film.

The latest advances are in digital video editing, using QuickTime and Video for Windows tools such as Adobe Premiere and Director with compression and decompression cards such as Radius' VideoVision Studio digital video card.

## Using Digital Video

As a Director user, you have the widest possible audience available for your Director movies, both interactive and sequential. Not only can you play your movie files on any Mac and Windows-based MPC, but you can also export your animations into QuickTime digital video format and play them on a variety of platforms (including Windows-based PCs, SGI's Indigo and Indy, and various Unix workstations).

The combination of Director's interactive features, and digital video on the desktop, will have an impact not just on presentations and training, but on publishing, graphic arts, network management, telecommunications, and database access applications.

Pulling all these developments together is *QuickTime,* a media-control architecture consisting of multimedia protocols that enable applications to be developed that are completely compatible with each other in exchanging video and audio information. It provides time-based actions and a way to store various types of multimedia information—text, graphics, sound, animation, and full-motion video. Apple has implemented QuickTime so that all Mac applications can take advantage of system resources for manipulating multimedia information.

A player for QuickTime movies is also available for Windows. It is called QuickTime for Windows, is supported by Director, and can be found along with the Mac version in the Freebies section of the accompanying CD-ROM. Thus, you can use QuickTime movies with Director files on both platforms.

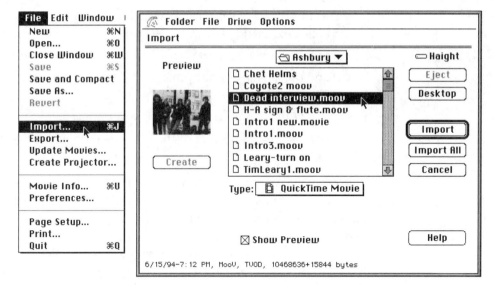

**Figure 8.3**
**Importing a**
**QuickTime movie**
**into Director.**

Another digital video architecture is available for Windows from Microsoft, called Video for Windows. There are some similarities to QuickTime, including a synchronized file format called the AVI format. Director supports AVI digital video files.

## Importing QuickTime Video into the Cast

You can import QuickTime "MOV" (aka "Moov") digital video files into Director's Cast window with the Import command in the File menu (Figure 8.3). The Import dialog box shows a poster image of the QuickTime movie.

QuickTime movies are automatically linked to the Director Cast, not stored internally in the Director movie. Since the QuickTime Moov file (which is usually very large) is separate from the Director movie, you can share the Moov file among several Director movies. If Director can't find a QuickTime Moov file when it opens the Director movie, it asks you to find it, then it updates the reference.

Since the QuickTime Moov file is linked to the Director movie file cast member, any changes you make to the cast member in the Digital Video window are made to the original file. You can cut, copy, and paste frames of video in the Digital Video window of Director. To perform more complex edits, use a digital video editing program such as Adobe Premiere.

When preparing Director movies to run on other platforms, be sure to "flatten" the QuickTime Moov files when you finish editing them. You should use either MovieShop (available on AppleLink or through APDA), or MovieConverter (on the QuickTime CD-ROM), or an editing program, such as Adobe Premiere (which offers a flattening export filter). Flattening means that all internal references to other files have been resolved, and the Moov file can run by itself on another computer, because all of its elements are contained within the single Moov file.

The final step in preparing QuickTime movies for the Windows platform is to remove the Mac header info from the resource fork of the file and merge it with the data fork, so that other operating systems can read the file. The MovieConverter program on the QuickTime CD-ROM offers this option.

## Importing Video for Windows Video into the Cast

You can import "AVI" movies that work with Microsoft's Video for Windows into the cast. "AVI" movies are the most common form of digital video on PCs.

To play back an "AVI" movie, the run-time version of Video for Windows must be installed.

In Windows systems, inks have no effect when you apply them to a digital video movie. The digital video always plays in front of the other cast members on the stage, regardless of its position in the channel hierarchy in the score.

Otherwise, you can use "AVI" movies with Director in the same way as QuickTime "MOV" movies. When you import a digital video file, a link is established to the file; the contents of the digital video file are not copied to the Director file. If you make changes to the digital video file after you've imported it, you must close and then reopen any Director file that is linked to it, in order to update the digital video cast member.

## Playing and Editing a Digital Video Cast Member

A digital video cast member can be opened and played by double-clicking the icon in the Cast window, or by choosing the Digital Video window in the Windows menu. Like other windows, the Digital Video window can be resized and manipulated, and it has controls for playing the movie backwards and forwards and adjusting the sound (Figure 8.4).

You can edit a digital video clip in this window by removing, or adding, single frames or selections of frames. To copy or cut a single frame, simply use Copy Video or Cut Video in the Edit menu to put the frame in the Clipboard. Paste Video adds a single frame from the Clipboard. To use these commands with a

**Figure 8.4**
**Playing a digital video cast member in the Digital Video window, which provides a movie controller on the bottom and the cast member icons on the top.**

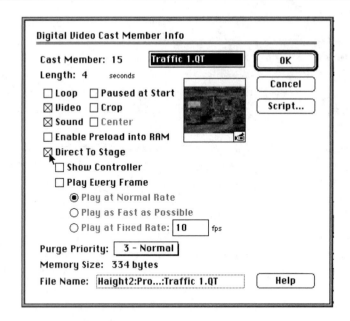

**Figure 8.5**
**Options for play-ing digital video are available in the Cast Info dia-log box.**

selection of frames, drag the slider to the first frame of the selection, and hold down the Shift key while dragging the slider bar to the end of the selection. Then use Copy Video or Cut Video. When using Paste Video after copying or cutting a sequence of frames, the command pastes the entire selection into the receiving digital video cast member.

## Digital Video Cast Member Options

The Digital Video window also offers the same icons as the Cast window for looking at the cast script and cast info. The Digital Video Cast Member Info dialog box (Figure 8.5) offers many options for controlling the playback of a digital video cast member.

Besides the options for Video and Sound (which should be turned on if you want video and sound, or if you only want video, turn off sound, etc.), the most important option to know is the Direct to Stage option, which plays the video clip in the highest animation plane, at the fastest possible speed (in Director or in a projector file). When using this option, you can't overlay any other animation, or graphics, over the digital video sprite, nor can you use different inks with the sprite. When using this option, be sure to use the highest channel and not place any graphics in front of the digital video sprite.

Turn off the Direct to Stage option, if you want to have animation occurring on top of the digital video clip, or if you want to matte, blend, or overlap digital video cast members on the stage. However, digital video may play slower with this option off. This option cannot be turned off in the Windows version.

The Loop option causes the digital video clip to loop to the beginning and continue playing.

The Paused at Start option pauses the clip before starting playback, so that the first frame of the clip is stationary.

The Crop option forces the clip to retain its original size. If you resize the bounding rectangle (reduce the size of the bounding rectangle), you will crop the edges of the digital video picture.

The Center option centers the video picture if you resize the clip's bounding box.

Another important option is Enable Preload into RAM. This option lets you load an entire digital video clip into RAM (random access memory) for fast playback. Normally, digital video clips play from files on disk or CD-ROM, which offers slower playback speed. With this option, if there is not enough RAM to hold the entire movie, Director loads only what it can fit, and plays the rest off disk or CD-ROM.

When you use Direct to Stage, you have the option to offer the user of the presentation the digital video controller (otherwise the option is not available). If the Show Controller option is checked, the controller appears below the movie when it plays (Figure 8.6). With the controller, the movie does not play until the user activates the controller's Play button.

You also have the option, with Direct to Stage, to play every frame of the digital video clip. Normally frames are skipped, as necessary, to keep up with a constant tempo (to keep sound properly synchronized, for one reason). However, if you check the option to play every frame, the soundtrack is not played, and the clip is played at a slower speed, depending on the computer's processing power. You can set the clip to play at the normal rate, to play as fast as possible (as the machine will allow), or to play at a fixed frame rate (used only if the clip is set to play at the same frame rate throughout).

Digital video cast members can also have their purge priorities set, like every other cast member. Normal, or 3, allows a cast member to be removed from memory as necessary (the default), while Never, or 0, keeps the cast member in memory at all times when the Director movie is playing.

## Arranging in the Score

To make a digital video cast member play on stage with animation, or by itself, drag the cast member from the Digital Video window directly onto the stage. You must then put the cast member in a loop of some sort, either infinite (until a click occurs), or timed.

For example, to create an infinite loop, drag the video cast member out to the stage, record for three frames, and use a go to statement (Figure 8.7) to establish the loop. Then add a push-button to move on, or make the digital video cast

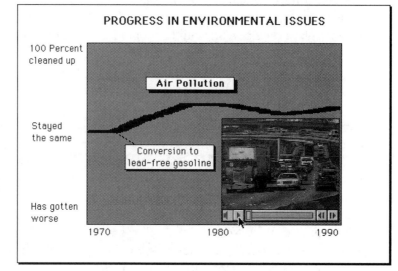

**Figure 8.6
A digital video
clip set to play
with the Direct to
Stage option and
the movie con-
troller under-
neath (filename:
PROGVID2.DIR).**

member itself "hot" by adding a cast script to it that specifies, on mouseUp, to go to another frame.

You can make the Director movie pause while a QuickTime digital video cast member plays to the end. The Wait for QuickTime Movie to Finish in Channel option is available in the Set Tempo dialog box (Figure 8.8), which is opened by double-clicking a cell in the Tempo channel, or selecting a cell in the Tempo channel and choosing Set Tempo from the Score menu.

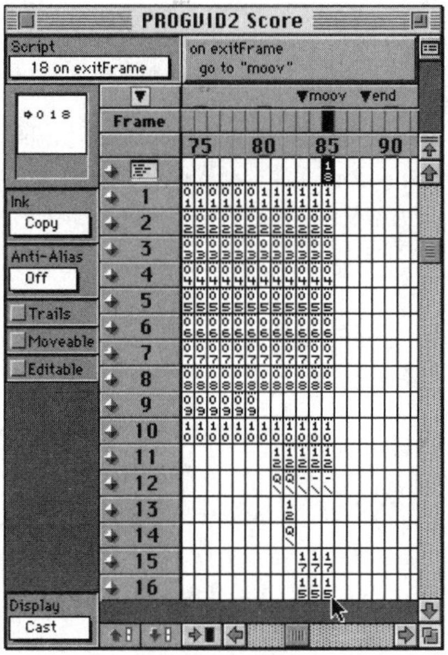

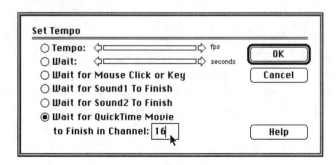

**Figure 8.7**
**Setting up a loop with the on exit-Frame go to "Moov" script in frame 85; the digital video cast member is in channel 16.**

QuickTime movies are automatically dithered to the current palette during playback in Director. You should create QuickTime movies in 16-bit or 24-bit resolution, so you can get the best possible playback on systems that offer these display resolutions.

## Exporting to Digital Video Files

While Director offers frame by frame control over animation, digital video formats such as QuickTime offer dead-on synchronization with frame playback and sound. To get the best of both worlds, you can import digital video files to use as clips in Director movies, and you can turn Director movies into digital video

**Figure 8.8**
**Using the Wait for QuickTime Movie option in the Set Tempo dialog to pause the Director movie until the QuickTime movie finishes playing.**

files. You can even combine digital video files with Director animation and export the result back to a digital video file.

Essentially, you can export animation with sound with absolutely no degradation into a digital video movie file, where synchronization is automatic. However, the digital video software will not play back every frame if the computer is not powerful enough. You can compress the digital video information using a codec (compressor/decompressor), which may degrade the image slightly, or not even noticeably, so that it will play more frames in the same duration.

You can then import those digital video files into Director and use them as part of a presentation, or play them as stand-alone movies.

## Exporting QuickTime Movies

Choose Director's File Export menu command, and then choose QuickTime Movie from the Type pop-up menu in the Export dialog box (Figure 8.9). You can select all frames, or a range of frames, to export. Export options are available by clicking on the QuickTime Export Options button.

The Frame Rate options affect the playback of the resulting QuickTime Moov file. The Tempo Settings creates a QuickTime movie with a timebase that exactly matches the Tempo channel settings used in the score. With this option, you can set the Tempo channel settings as you wish them to be when played back in QuickTime. For example, if you set the Tempo channel to 10 frames per second, the QuickTime movie will automatically synchronize playback to 10 frames per second.

> **Note:** If the machine playing the QuickTime movie is not capable of matching the frame rate, frames are dropped in order to play the sound smoothly and remain synchronized. The Tempo Settings option works best with movies that have very strict tempos that work with most machines. It does not work well with movies that are set to play at 60 frames per second, but really only play at about 5 because the frames are so complex.

The Real Time option for frame rate exports the Director movie to QuickTime with a timebase that simulates as closely as possible the last playback of the Director movie. The steps are to first lock the Director movie (as described in Chapter 3), then export the movie with the Real Time option. This option lets you limit faster machines from playing the QuickTime movie too fast. Before using this option, be sure to play the entire movie through once with Disable Lingo checked. Also, increase the chunk size of your transitions; otherwise, Director may create too many frames to duplicate each transition.

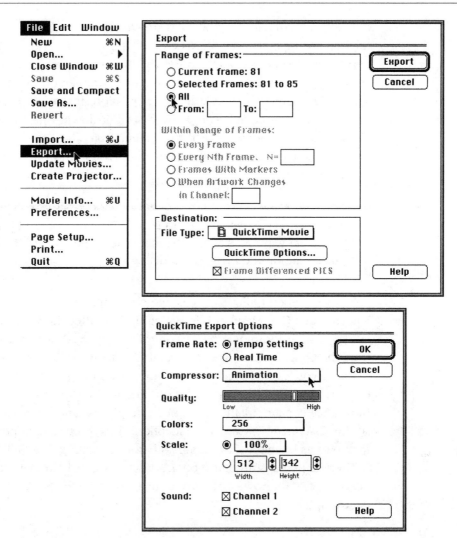

**Figure 8.9 Exporting a set of frames or an entire Director movie into a QuickTime Moov file.**

The Compressor pop-up menu lets you select how the exported Director animation should be compressed. You can choose None, standard Apple compressors, or any third-party QuickTime-compatible compressor that has been installed in the System Folder (such as Radius Studio). For most animation export operations, you can use the Animation compressor, but when exporting 8-bit animation files, the Graphics compressor often creates smaller files. Experimentation is best, but the manual suggests that Animation is good for simple animation, while Graphics is good for single frames of computer graphics, and Photo-JPEG is good for scanned images. Cinepak is good for compressing video for playback from CD-ROM.

The Quality slider lets you select the visual and temporal quality—the higher the quality, the bigger the file. The Colors pop-up menu lets you select the color depth. QuickTime is optimized for 16-bit playback, which is the Thousands of colors setting. If you plan to use the Graphics compressor, select 256 colors (8-bit). The Scale options lets you scale the animation. If you are exporting a 640-by-480-pixel animation, and you want to scale it down to, for example, a 160-by-120-resolution window, select 25 percent from the Scale percentage pop-up menu. To stretch or squash the animation, type in the values in the Scale width and height fields.

*Note:* You can create animations in the standard 160-by-120-resolution QuickTime window size by changing the Stage Size to 160 by 120 pixels (QuickTime) in the Preferences dialog box.

You can export QuickTime cast members into another QuickTime movie, but Digital Video Cast Member Info dialog options affect how the QuickTime movie is exported. If the movie has a controller displayed, it is not exported. Sound from the QuickTime movie cast member will always be exported.

When you export a QuickTime movie cast member to a QuickTime movie, they are "flattened" during the export process. This results in a single QuickTime movie that contains all the data it needs to play on another machine. Linked AIFF sound cast members are an exception. You should re-import the AIFF cast members as unlinked cast members before exporting to a QuickTime movie.

There is perhaps an entire book's worth of QuickTime and Lingo features to describe, but, for now, we'll have to make do with the tips and techniques in the next chapter.

## Exporting Video for Windows Movies

Choose Director's File Export menu command, and then choose Video for Windows from the File Type pop-up menu in the Export dialog box (Windows version only). You can select all frames, or a range of frames, to export. Export options are available by clicking on the Options button.

The Frame Rate option affects the playback of the resulting "AVI" movie file. Due to limitations in the Video for Windows format, Director can't export tempo settings or transitions, nor can it export palette transitions, to "AVI" files.

It is possible to select a compressor that is compatible with Video for Windows. As of this writing, Cinepak (described above with QuickTime), Microsoft's Video 1, and Intel Indeo compressors are available. Microsoft's RLE compressor is designed for exporting 8-bit animations and computer graphics. You can also choose Full Frames (uncompressed) to export a movie with no compression; however, this option may not work with Video for Windows version 1.1.

The Compression Quality setting determines the compression quality and size of the file. The higher the setting, the bigger the file. There are many more techniques you should learn before delving into digital video editing, but that must be a subject for another book, as this one is getting too large already.

## Chapter Summary

In this chapter you learned how Director can control laser videodisc players, how you can display video on the computer screen, and how to record animations mixed with video onto videotape. This chapter also introduced digital video, and how to use it with Director movies, including how to import and export digital video movies. Don't be deceived by the small size of this summary, a great deal of detail is contained herein!

The next, and final, chapter compiles the greatest tips and techniques we have ever encountered or thought up. You can use the next chapter as a quick tour through the capabilities of Lingo, with scripts and examples you can use in your movies.

# 9

# *Tips and Advanced Techniques*

**Once you open a can of worms, the only way to recan them is to use a larger can.**

Zymurgy's First Law of Evolving System Dynamics

**H**ow true. When working with a computer, it is common to have spent many hours trying to figure something out, or perhaps many days, and then coming across a tip or technique that solves the problem immediately. This chapter is designed to help you avoid wasting time.

The previous chapters are a prerequisite for understanding the material presented in this chapter. Now that you have learned how to create interactive Director movies, using audio and video, and you've learned basic scripting techniques, using Director's Lingo scripting language, you are ready for these tips and techniques.

The information presented here was culled from various sources, including articles in the *Macromedia User Journal* edited by the authors, and technical support answers to questions in the Macromedia Forum on Compuserve, the Macromedia section on America OnLine, and the Macromedia section on AppleLink.

## Quick Tricks

A QuickTime sprite can be "hot" so that it executes a script when the user clicks on it. You can do this by attaching a cast script to the QuickTime cast member.

The simplest script you might attach to a QuickTime cast member is to go to another frame. However, if you attach the following script to a QuickTime cast member, the user will be able to click the QuickTime sprite and bring up the standard QuickTime controller with its slider, play/pause button, and volume control. If the controller is already visible, clicking on the QuickTime sprite makes the controller disappear.

```
on mouseUp
    if the controller of cast "Intro1 moov" = 0 then
        set the controller of cast "Intro1 moov" to 1
    else set the controller of cast "Intro1 moov" to 0
    end if
    --
end mouseUp
```

This script uses the controller cast property provided for QuickTime cast members. When the mouse button is released after clicking the cast member, this script is activated. If the controller property is off (0), the script turns the controller on (1); otherwise, it turns the controller off (0).

## A Timer for QuickTime Playback

There are several ways to make QuickTime Moov files play until they are finished, then move on. The easiest is to arrange the QuickTime cast member in the score inside a simple loop that goes indefinitely, and use a timer handler to detect when to stop the Moov file and move on to another frame.

You can create a general-purpose timer handler with an argument that can receive a value, as follows:

```
on startMyTimer seconds
    set the timeoutLength to (60*seconds)
    when timeOut then go to marker(1)
    --
end startMyTimer
```

Whenever you need to use a timer for, say, 50 seconds, simply issue the command startMyTimer 50 in the score's Script channel. The value 50 is substituted for the argument seconds in the handler, and sets the timer. It is, of course, a simple problem to estimate the time needed—the QuickTime Moov is a fixed duration, and you can add extra seconds as needed.

The startMyTimer handler relies on the default settings for the timeout-KeyDown, timeoutMouse, and timeoutPlay properties: When a key is pressed, or the mouse is pressed, the timer is reset. When the time-out occurs, the movie moves on to the next marked frame by means of the go to marker(1) statement, exiting the loop.

What happens when the user presses a key or the mouse? The timeout-Lapsed property, which is the number of ticks elapsed since the last time-out, is set to zero. This has the effect of resetting the timer, which continues again to count from zero. You need this property if you are going to enable the user to click the QuickTime sprite and use the standard QuickTime controller. Why? Because the clicking that occurs while using the controller continues to reset the timer (until the user stops clicking—presumably when the user has hit the play button). The QuickTime Moov file then plays while the timer waits for the entire duration of the Moov file.

Whenever you set a time-out, there usually comes a time when you must turn it off:

```
on endMyTimer
  when timeOut then nothing
  --
end endMyTimer
```

This handler simply turns off the time-out function. You can call this handler wherever the movie branches to another movie—at the end of the movie, and in the cast scripts that activate other movies.

## Exporting PICS Files

The PICS format is invaluable for transferring animated sequences from one program to another, and is used extensively for animations converted to CD-I and 3DO formats. However, when Director exports a PICS file, it exports only the frame information. Delays, transitions, and scripts are not exported, so you lose them.

Therefore, if you want to include a 2-second delay, for example, you would need to display a still image in a range of frames. A range of 60 frames would produce a 2-second delay if the PICS sequence is played back at 30 frames per second.

## Blurring Edges with Line Art and Text

With line art and text created in other programs, or scanned with a scanner, you often want to soften the edges with a program such as Adobe Photoshop. However, when you bring the softened images into Director, you can't maintain the nice, clean edges when you make them transparent with the Transparent ink option in the score. This is because Director gets its "transparency" by making one color in the palette invisible—usually the background color. If a pixel is the background color, it's transparent; if not, it's opaque (see Figure 9.1).

When you apply smoothness to the edge of line art or text, or apply an anti-aliasing effect to line art or text, the colors are blended together. The line art or text object starts as only black-and-white pixels, but after smoothing or anti-aliasing, a ramp of gray, which can no longer be made transparent, surrounds the object.

**Figure 9.1**
**An image with an anti-aliased text object, shown at the top in Photoshop, and on the left bottom in Director on a different background with the Transparent ink set. The right bottom image shows anti-aliasing done by Director.**

If your animation uses a solid color background (set by the color palette in the Control Panel), you can make your line art or text black and set the background color to the solid color rather than white. This is so that you no longer need to make the smoothed or anti-aliased object transparent. Use the paint bucket or the Switch Colors command to color the scanned artwork or images.

If you're animating line art or text against a complex background, things get tricky. Director provides an Anti-Alias option in the score (controlled by the Movie Info dialog option), but playback speed suffers greatly.

The work-around is as follows.

1. Create an anti-aliased sequence in Director, setting the Anti-Alias option in the score window for the sequence of cells (use it only where necessary).

2. Run the sequence (it will run more slowly than usual) to be sure it looks good.

3. Export the individual frames of the anti-aliased section as a sequence of PICT files using the Export command in the File menu. The Export dialog box lets you export a range of frames as PICT files in a single operation.

4. Re-import the PICT files into Director. At that point you no longer need the Anti-Alias option for those cells, so be sure to turn it off to gain back the animation speed.

## Synchronization Tips

The technical support crew report that they often hear about the same synchronization problem.

"I ran the presentation on a Macintosh PowerBook and it was fine, but then I ran it on a Macintosh IIci and the transitions were as slow as molasses."

A variation on this theme.

"I authored on a Macintosh Quadra and it ran fine on a Pentium machine, but when I ran it on a 486-based machine, the sync was out."

Synchronicity is the albatross of animation. Depending on the content of your presentation, you may want to use a sound segment as the basis for synchronizing animation, or you may have the option to synchronize sound effects using animation as the basis. The tricks for achieving synchronization usually rely on sound as the basis. This is because sound (typically prerecorded voices and music) usually does not change in tempo. Even if you were to change tempo in the sound, you would want to play the sound back at the new rate from beginning to end, to avoid "hiccups" in the sound playback. Thus, sound becomes the basis for sync.

One solution is to export the animated sequence with sound to QuickTime, and use a QuickTime editing program such as Adobe Premiere to set the sync points for the sound and video sections of the resulting QuickTime file. You can then import the QuickTime file and play it in Director.

Newcomers to Director who are familiar with QuickTime have a particularly hard time realizing the one major difference between QuickTime movies and Director movies. QuickTime is time-based, which means that it will drop frames in order to play back in sync with the sound, whereas Director is frame-based, which means that it plays every frame and tries to play them fast enough (and if it doesn't succeed, the movie is out of sync with the sound, which always plays back at the same speed).

Exporting to QuickTime is not a good solution, if you want every frame to be played. This is because QuickTime playback might not look as smooth as Director's playback. Still images, especially, benefit from Director's playback, because frames are not duplicated to display a still image, as they would most likely be in QuickTime.

## Setting Tempo for Slowest Playback

The only way to be sure that a movie will play back at the right speed is to test the movie on the slowest possible machine it will be used on, and set the Tempo accordingly. If you are not using tempo changes (in the Tempo channel), but are instead using timers in scripts (as described next), you can set your timers in the same way—by testing playback on the slowest machine, and resetting the timers accordingly.

The Tempo channel can be used to set the upper limit of frames per second for playback, so that the movie always plays back at that rate (or slower). Play it on the slowest machine, set the Tempo to that rate, lock the movie in the score window (see Chapter 3). It should play back at the same speed every time, on that machine and on all faster machines.

## Synchronizing by Scripts

You can adjust the animated sequences to be synchronized to the beginning and end points of sounds. The simplest strategy is to pause at the last frame, or continue looping through several frames, until a sound has finished playing. You can use a delay (specified in seconds) in the Tempo channel's dialog box, or you can use the "Wait until sound is finished" or "Wait until QuickTime movie is finished" options.

However, if you use a delay or pause in the Tempo channel, Director no longer checks to see if the mouse is rolling over any objects, nor does it recognize clicks. This is because it is stuck in a single frame.

The solution is to use a timer, set to a desired duration, that matches the fixed duration of the sound segment you are synchronizing to.

Assume you have a movie consisting of several scenes, and in the first scene you have 12 frames. The first three frames are essentially the same image; the next nine form a loop that repeats and shows animation. Let's say that the first scene has a 4-second sound segment that it must be synchronized to.

In frame 1, put a script in the Score's Script channel that sets the timer's amount with the `timeoutLength` property, which is used to set the number of ticks before a time-out occurs (1 second is 60 ticks; therefore 4 seconds is 240 ticks).

```
on exitFrame
        set the timeoutLength to 240
end
```

In frame 2, put a script in the Script channel that turns on the timer and jumps to the desired frame (in this case, frame 14) when the time-out occurs.

```
on exitFrame
        when timeOut then go to frame 14
end
```

In frame 3, put a script in the Script channel that plays an external sound file.

```
on exitFrame
        sound playFile 1, "Shorty"
end
```

At frame 14, turn off the timer:

```
on exitFrame
        when timeOut then nothing
end
```

After exactly 4 seconds of looping and playing the sound file "Shorty," execution passes to frame 14 for the next scene, which turns off the timer. The loop is synchronized to the duration of "Shorty," which is 4 seconds.

By default, Director restarts the timer if the mouse is clicked or a key is pressed. These settings are controlled by the `timeoutMouse` and `timeoutKeyDown` properties. Both are set to TRUE by default. For synchronization to work even if a mouse is clicked, or a key is pressed, set both properties to FALSE before starting to use the timeout. For example, you might put these statements in a `startMovie` handler and save it as a movie script in a cast member slot.

```
on startMovie
        set the timeoutMouse to FALSE
        set the timeoutKeyDown to FALSE
        .
        .-- other statements in the handler
        .
end startMovie
```

For a universal timer that can be used in a variety of different movies, consider creating a handler as a movie script which takes care of the messy details of the timer. Such a handler could be invoked with a single statement in a frame script that also passes it a value of the number of seconds, such as `startMyTimer 6` (for 6 seconds).

Here is such a handler that could be defined as a movie script cast member.

```
on startMyTimer seconds
    set the timeoutMouse to FALSE
    set the timeoutKeyDown to FALSE
    set the timeoutLength to (60*seconds)
    when timeOut then go to marker(1)
end startMyTimer
```

For this handler to work properly, you need to use markers in the Score window. Execute the handler first, then establish the loop with a marker and the `go to marker(0)` command. The `marker(0)` function returns either the current frame, if the current frame is marked, or the most recent marked frame before the current frame, so it comes in handy when creating a loop.

The `marker(1)` function in the handler executes when the timeout occurs. This function returns the next marked frame after the current frame. At this frame, the timer should be turned off or set to another time value. You can then use the same scripts for each sequence to be synchronized.

Whenever possible, break long sounds into shorter ones. If using voice-over narration, create a separate sound sample for each sentence or paragraph. That way, if the presentation plays on a slower machine, the animation can still remain in sync with the sounds.

## Using QuickTime for Sound

Another way to synchronize loops to sound is to create the sound as a QuickTime movie (a QuickTime movie can contain only sound), and then use the QuickTime commands to control playback of the movie.

For example, you might have a QuickTime movie in sprite 20 that contains only sound. You could continually perform the following test in a loop to see if the sound has reached a certain point (greater than 10 seconds, which is 600 ticks).

```
on exitFrame
    if the movieTime of sprite 20 > 600 then ...
```

The `movieTime` property determines the current time, in ticks (one-sixtieth of a second; 60 ticks equals 1 second). It can be tested to see how long a QuickTime movie has played so far, or it can be set.

One way to test for the end of a QuickTime movie (in this case, one containing only sound) is to use the `duration` property.

```
put the duration of cast "TheSoundQTMovie" into
TotalTicks

.

.

.

if the movieTime of sprite 20 = TotalTicks then ...
```

By using a QuickTime movie for the sound, you can gain more control over synchronization, especially if you need the animation to change at different points within a sound segment.

## Button Tips

While the interactive buttons in the Tools window provide automatically the capability to invert and remain inverted, while the user clicks down on them, you can customize graphic objects to have the same property.

**Depressed Buttons**

The following tip (*courtesy of Jeff Essex*) is a standard script that can be used to swap button cast members so that the button appears to remain depressed as long as the mouse button is down.

Assuming the button cast member is in channel 1, the button in the up position is cast member 11, and the button in the down position is cast member 12, the following script swaps buttons, while the mouse is down.

> **Note:** The ¬ line continuation symbol, Option-Return, is used to extend a line to the next line, and the double hyphen (- -) indicates the start of a comment in the script.

```
on mousedown
     set the castnum of sprite 1 to the ¬
number of cast 12
     updatestage
     repeat while the stilldown
          nothing
     end repeat
     set the castnum of sprite 1 to the ¬
number of cast 11
     updatestage
```

```
        -- whatever script you want the
        -- button to execute should go here
end mousedown
```

Remember, this is a mouseDown script, not a mouseUp script. The repeat loop keeps the button swapped out (doing nothing) while the mouse remains down. When the condition `stilldown` becomes false (the mouse is up), the repeat loop ends and the swap is reversed.

To get fancy, you can also check for changes in the mouseH or mouseV (horizontal or vertical coordinate for the mouse location) while in the repeat loop to be sure that the user hasn't moved off the button while still holding the mouse down. Or, you can use the script described in the next tip.

## RollOver Depressed Buttons

The following script (*courtesy of Scott Kildall*) may be useful for managing how buttons look when you click on them.

It keeps the button depressed as long as the mouse is depressed *and* the cursor is on top of the button. Enter the script as a movie script cast member. The handler can be called from a cast script.

```
--Global rollover script
on HandleRollover destCast, theScript
    set srcCast = the castNum of sprite ¬
the clickOn
    set the castNum of sprite the clickOn ¬
to the number of cast destCast
    set isFlashed to true
    updateStage
    repeat while the mouseDown
        if isFlashed and not rollOver(the ¬
clickOn) then
            set isFlashed to false
            set the castNum of sprite the ¬
clickOn to srcCast
        end if
        if not isFlashed and rollOver(the ¬
clickOn) then
            set isFlashed to true
            set the castNum of sprite the ¬
clickOn to the number of cast destCast
        end if
```

```
        updateStage
    end repeat
    set the castNum of sprite the ¬
clickOn to srcCast
    updatestage
    if isFlashed then do(theScript)
end HandleRollover
```

The script swaps the button cast member with the one specified by an argument when invoking the handler.

For example, you might invoke the handler with the following command as a cast script.

```
HandleRollover("ButtonDown", "go to ¬
frame 20")
```

By doing so, you'd be specifying ButtonDown as the cast member to swap with the current button cast member. The second argument (go to frame 20) is the script to be executed by that particular button.

The repeat while the mouseDown loop first tests whether the is-Flashed condition is true (it starts out that way), and if the mouse is no longer rolling over the button. If so, it sets the isFlashed condition to false and swaps back the original button cast member. Otherwise, it does nothing but continue to the second test.

In the second test, if the isFlashed condition is false, but the mouse is rolling over the button, the isFlashed variable is set back to true, and button is once again swapped for the depressed button. With these two tests, the script keeps the button depressed only while the mouse is rolling over the button.

The script for the button is executed after the repeat loop finishes. If the isFlashed condition at the end of the loop is true, and the mouse is no longer down, it means the button has been properly clicked by the user, so the script performs the "do" command with the second argument theScript ("go to frame 20").

For the handler to work, the cast member for the original button must be a puppetSprite declared with the following statement (usually in a startMovie or opening handler).

```
puppetSprite 1, true
```

This assumes the button cast member is a sprite in channel 1 at the time the statement is executed. Remember that the channel you define as a puppetSprite must have a cast member in it when the definition statement is executed.

## Custom Color Cycling

Another neat trick (*courtesy of Joe Sparks*) for buttons is custom color cycling to change colors for an object while the mouse is down.

Typically, a button is a piece of black-and-white artwork in the cast. You can set the color depth of the cast member to 1 bit (or use a shape cast member). You can change the foreColor of that sprite to any color in the palette (0 to 255) without changing the palette or using the color cycling option on the stage (which cycles colors for the entire stage). You can use this method to do your own custom color cycling of one, or more, cast members, rather than the entire stage.

Make a black and white object. Set it to 1 bit. Drag it out on the stage. Select it. Type the following script into a handler inside a mouseUp or similar handler in the Score Script channel (assuming you put the object into channel 1).

```
-- script to cycle rapidly through the
-- whole palette (except white)
repeat with x = 1 to 255
     set the forecolor of sprite 1 = x
     updatestage
end repeat
-- code continues from here
```

If you need more control over the timing, you can do this:

```
repeat with x = 4 to 240
     put the timer into p
     set the forecolor of sprite 1 = x
     updatestage
     -- this part controls the timing
     -- adjust the "6" hi for slower,
     -- lo for faster cycling
     repeat while p+6 > the timer
          nothing
     end repeat
end repeat
```

Thus, you can control the timing of the color cycle.

## Using QuickTime for Button States

An interesting technique (*courtesy of Alex Zavatone*) is to use a QuickTime movie with frames representing the states (on, off, rollover) for a button. Each button is a 60 frame-per-second QuickTime cast member that contains three frames.

In Alex Zavatone's *The Equalizer Package* (in the ZAVEQ folder/directory inside the TUTORIAL folder/directory of the accompanying CD-ROM), the movie *RUNME_EQ.DIR* demonstrates this technique, with the up and down arrow buttons for volume control.

The cast script for the up (more volume) button in cast member 9 contains a mouseDown handler that checks to see if the mouse is still over the button, and then displays the proper button state by setting the movieTime property of the QuickTime sprite.

```
-- Cast Script for the Z Button "More Button"
on mouseDown
  global gVolume
  repeat while the mouseDown
    Idle
    if gVolume < 7 then
      if rollover(the clickOn) then
        set the movieTime of sprite the clickon to 1
      else
        set the movieTime of sprite the clickon to 0
      end if
    end if
    updateStage
  end repeat
end
```

The following mouseUp handler, also in the same cast script, again checks to see if the mouse is over the sprite, and sets the button's state accordingly.

```
On mouseUp
  global gVolume, gChildWindow1
  if rollover( the clickOn) then
    if gVolume < 7 then
      set the movieTime of sprite the clickon to  0
      set gVolume = gVolume + 1
      tell gChildWindow1 to adjustVolume
    end if
  end if
  HandleButtons
end
```

The movieTime property measures times in ticks (one-sixtieth of a second). The QuickTime cast member is set to 60 frames per second so that a movieTime increment of 1 tick moves the QuickTime cast member to the next frame.

The benefit of using this technique is that the button states switch very fast. Another benefit is that you use only one cast member slot for a button and all its states.

# Invisible Sprites

Let's say you need a sprite to be in a particular frame in the score, but it should not be visible. Let's also say that there is no ink treatment that will work for your purpose (or you don't want to change the ink for whatever reason).

There are several ways to make something on the stage invisible. They all involve using puppet sprites (placing the sprite under Lingo control).

## Visibility Property

Director offers the "visibility" sprite property, which you can turn on or off with scripts. It works even if the sprite is moving. For example, you might want to use these instructions (assuming your sprite is a cast member in channel 1).

```
puppetsprite 1, true
set the visibility of sprite 1 to 0
        -- the above line uses the visibility property
        -- the next line animates the sprite
        -- by moving it one pixel with the locV property
set the locV of sprite 1 to (the locV of sprite 1) + 1
updatestage
```

This works because the sprite moves (via the locV, or location-vertical, property), but when it moves, it is also invisible so that no one sees it. Be sure to set the location of the sprite back to its original position if you want to reveal it.

Other methods include placing an invisible element (with no line or fill) on the stage, then using a script to switch that element with another cast member.

A variation of this method is to use a single-pixel cast member as the "invisible" element, and switch it with another cast member (*thanks to Jeff Essex, Scott Kildall, and John Dowdell*).

## Moving a Sprite off the Stage

Another method to make a sprite invisible is to change the horizontal or vertical position to place the sprite somewhere outside the stage area. You could use a script such as the following:

```
puppetsprite 1, true
set the locH of sprite 1 to -1000
        -- or, equally effective,
        -- set the locV of sprite 1 to 1000
updatestage
```

Be careful when you place something outside the stage area—if you need it back, store the coordinates of its present location before changing the locV or locH properties.

Also, use a high number in case your user has a very large display (the sprite is visible at that location outside the stage).

## On Using Puppet Sprites

Remember that when you use puppet sprites, setting the puppet sprites to TRUE for unoccupied channels will give you unpredictable results, so be sure you actually have something in those channels when you do this.

Also, be sure to issue a `puppetsprite 1, False` command, when you no longer need to control the sprite with Lingo.

# Cross-Platform Tips

You may want to distribute movies, without the Director program, so that you can reach a large group of users who don't have Director. You can create projector files as described in Chapter 6. You can freely distribute the projector files, which can run without Director. No other software is required to run the projector file. The projector file can be made from a Director movie that refers to other movies (using `Go to movie` or `Play movie` commands), and you can distribute those movies with the projector file without requiring Director.

Unlike some authoring tools vendors, Macromedia has a simple licensing arrangement for developers who are distributing projector files created by Macromedia Director: Licensing is free with no limit on distribution.

To distribute Director 4 movies to Windows users, you need to create a projector using the Windows version of Director 4. To distribute Director 4 movies to Macintosh users, you need to create a projector using the Macintosh version of Director 4. In both cases, the projector file can then call the same Director 4 movie files. The only restriction on movie files is that they are named in accordance with PC file-naming conventions.

## Detecting Machine Type

Although most Lingo commands are supported, some Lingo commands make no sense on some platforms (such as MCI commands on a Macintosh, or `openDA` and `closeDA` on a Windows machine) and therefore do not work.

To avoid problems with unsupported Lingo commands, you can separate Macintosh sequences from PC sequences by testing the machine to see if it is a PC. The `machineType` command returns the value 256 if the current machine is a PC (DOS machine). The `machineType` command returns a 9 for a Mac IIci, a 31 for a Mac PowerBook 180, and so on (see the Lingo Dictionary manual under "machineType" ). For each processor-dependent handler, use an if-then-else statement to play a PC sequence if the `machineType` is equal to 256; otherwise play a Macintosh sequence.

## Dealing with Fonts

You'll have considerable trouble with fonts if you are using fonts on one platform that are not available on the other. This is true for interactive buttons and hot spots as well as for any textual information. Even if fonts have the same name on the different platforms, they may differ in appearance on the screen. The text rectangle stays the same size, but strange word-wrapping (due to character width and spacing differences) can occur within the rectangle. In addition, if you use an invisible rectangle, as a button over a word in a text field, the button may not be positioned over the same word when the movie is run on another platform.

These problems are best circumvented by converting all your regular text into bitmap graphics before running the movie on another platform. However, do not convert to bitmap buttons created from the Tools window, because certain button properties may be referred to by scripts—use fonts that are generally available, such as Helvetica or Geneva. Also, for editable text, you should stick with fonts that are supported on all platforms and that look the same on all platforms.

To help with font mapping from Macintosh to Windows, Director is capable of storing font information, including size and style, for each text cast member. When you start a new movie, Director looks for a file called FONTMAP.TXT in the same folder as the Director program. If there is no FONTMAP.TXT file, no font map is created. But if there is one, the file tells Director how to map Macintosh font information to Windows font information, using a font map. When the same movie is run in Windows, the font map is used to substitute Windows fonts for Macintosh fonts.

To edit the supplied FONTMAP.TXT file, open the file with a word processor. You will see the following lines, to which you can add more fonts if you wish.

```
;
; Here are sample mappings for the default Macintosh
fonts.
; You can add any fonts to this list and experiment
with different mappings.
Mac:Chicago         => Win:System
Mac:Courier         => Win:"Courier New"
Mac:Geneva          => Win:"MS Sans Serif"
Mac:Helvetica       => Win:Arial
Mac:Monaco          => Win:Terminal
Mac:"New York"      => Win:"MS Serif" Map None
Mac:Symbol          => Win:Symbol
Mac:Times           => Win:"Times New Roman" 14=>12
18=>14 24=>18 30=>24
```

```
;
; Here are sample mappings for the default Windows
fonts:
; You can add any fonts to this list and experiment
with different mappings.
Win:Arial                => Mac:Helvetica
Win:"Courier"            => Mac:Courier
Win:"Courier New"        => Mac:Courier
Win:"MS Serif"           => Mac:"New York" Map None
Win:"MS Sans Serif"      => Mac:Geneva
Win:Symbol               => Mac:Symbol
Win:System               => Mac:Chicago
Win:Terminal             => Mac:Monaco
Win:"Times New Roman" => Mac:"Times" 12=>14 14=>18
18=>24 24=>30
```

The first set are Macintosh fonts mapped to Windows fonts, which are useful for creating movies on Macintoshes and running them on Windows PCs. The second set are Windows fonts mapped to Macintosh fonts, which are useful for creating movies on Windows PCs and running them on Macintoshes.

You can change fonts in these lists, or add more fonts and their substitutions by using one of the following syntax forms.

```
Platform:FontName => Platform:FontName
Platform:FontName => Platform:FontName MAP NONE
Platform:FontName => Platform:FontName oldsize => newsize
```

The first form maps the first font to the second font. The second form, with the optional MAP NONE argument, specifies that the special characters (ASCII character values greater than 127) should not be mapped. The default is MAP ALL (unspecified but active in the first form). The third form lets you specify one or more pairs of point sizes, separated by a space, to map font sizes directly.

For example, you might use the following statement to map the Macintosh Times font to the Windows Times New Roman font, with point sizes 14, 18, 24, and 30 mapped to 12, 14, 18, and 24, respectively.

```
Mac:Times => Win:"Times New Roman" 14=>12 18=>14
24=>18 30=>24
```

You can also map special characters on one platform to special characters on another. This is useful because special characters usually have different code numbers on different platforms. The following section of the FONTMAP.TXT file deals with special characters.

```
;             Florin   Ellipsis Dagger   Upper OE left `   right `
Mac: => Win: 196=>131 201=>133 160=>134 206=>140 212=>145 213=>146
;             Left "   Right "  Bullet   short -  long -   tm       lower oe
Mac: => Win: 210=>147 211=>148 165=>149 208=>150 209=>151 170=>153 207=>156
;             Florin   Ellipsis Dagger   Upper OE left `   right `
Win: => Mac: 131=>196 133=>201 134=>160 140=>206 145=>212 146=>213
;             Left "   Right "  Bullet   short -  long -   tm       lower oe
Win: => Mac: 147=>210 148=>211 149=>165 150=>208 151=>209 153=>170 156=>207
```

As you can see, your ability to do this correctly depends on having the proper documentation to figure out the code numbers. Fortunately Director is supplied with an adequate FONTMAP.TXT file, which you can edit if you wish.

## Windows Filensames

In order to run movies on Windows systems, use a PC filename (eight characters, starting with a letter) for the name of the movie, and use PC filenames for all external files called from the movie (such as other movies and linked files).

As a user of the Windows version, this rule is a natural one to follow, as it is impossible to use any other type of filename when creating a movie or subdirectory or external file.

However, if you are using the Macintosh version and you want your movies to play under Windows, you must follow the PC filename conventions for movie files, external files, and the folders that contain them.

Also, don't use periods, blank spaces, or punctuation marks in filenames. A period has a special meaning in a PC filename: the beginning of the filename's 3-character extension. All Director movies have the same extension, so you don't have to specify it. Just specify the 8-character filename itself.

Pathnames in Windows follow the PC file-naming conventions. If you are authoring on the Macintosh, keep all movies and external files in the same folder on the Macintosh and the same subdirectory on the PC, or use PC pathname conventions (and name the Macintosh folders with PC names) to specify the file location in scripts.

## Dealing with Color

Most color displays connected to Macintoshes are set up to display at least 256 colors (8-bit color depth). However, not only do many Windows systems have color displays configured to a lower color depth, but also the colors themselves look different. PCs with a standard VGA graphics adapter can certainly display 16 colors (4 bits), and many PCs have Super VGA adapters that offer 256 colors and up.

The problem is, how you do create a movie that displays the same colors on all platforms? The technique you use depends on whether you are satisfied with restricting the movies to showing 16 colors, or whether you want to show 256 or more colors.

If you are willing to restrict the movies to showing only 16 colors, you can fix these colors in accordance with VGA display adapters by using the built-in VGA color palette. You can access this palette if your display is set to 16 colors. You can set the palette for the entire movie in the Movie Info dialog box (File menu), or set the palette as needed in the Palette channel.

For most Director movies, however, 16 colors will not be enough. When running a 256-color movie on a 16-color PC, Director makes a best guess effort to assign one of the 16 colors to each of the 256 colors. But this results in dramatic color changes and coarse gradients. If you care about the movie's colors, you will want to restrict the playback of your 256-color movies to PCs that can display at least 256 colors.

On a 256-color PC, you can get reliable color that stays the same on both platforms by using the System-Win palette when authoring on the Macintosh. Director for Windows also supports palette switching and color cycling, but the results may look a bit different from the Mac due to the difference in displays and the fact that the white and black positions on the palettes in Windows are fixed.

In fact, since the white and black colors are fixed on Windows palettes, you can't fade properly to black or white unless you first create a custom palette with black-and-white chips in palette positions other than 1 and 255. Fading to the custom palette's black or white will then work.

## Sounds in Windows

Director for Windows supports both internal sound imported into movies, and external sound files linked to movies (in the AIFF or WAV format). You can't mix two sound tracks that are different in sampling rates, because the Windows version of Director mixes the sounds in the two sound channels. To play a stereo sound, use a linked sound file that is already set up as a stereo sound file.

Sound volume controls differ on Macintosh and PC platforms. On a Macintosh, the maximum level of sound produces a loud but usually clear sound. But on a PC, the maximum level usually produces distorted sound.

It is common to set a Macintosh movie's sound very high, but if this is done, the movie will play back too loudly and somewhat distorted on the PC. If possible, do not control the sound volume from scripts (unless you also provide a volume control to the user). It is better to assume that the Windows user has already set the volume control for sound output using the sound control panel.

The sound volume setting for QuickTime movies when running under Windows is relative to the WAV driver sound volume setting. To control the sound volume of a QuickTime for Windows movie file, use the `volume of sprite` command.

**Digital Video in Windows**

Director for Windows supports QuickTime movies and Video for Windows (AVI files). QuickTime movies require the presence of QuickTime for Windows, which can be licensed for distribution. In both cases, only the Direct to Stage option is supported.

QuickTime movies must first be converted to a self-contained (or "flattened") movie using Apple's Movie Converter utility available on the QuickTime CD. This utility offers the Make movie self-contained and Playable on non-Apple computers options, both of which should be checked. Be sure to use a PC-compatible filename for the QuickTime movie.

The converted movie plays back on either Macintosh or Windows platforms, and it is a good practice to do this even for Macintosh-only titles, because the movie is self-contained and portable.

You can edit a self-contained QuickTime movie, but you must use Movie Converter again when you are finished editing.

Note that if you use Microsoft's utility for converting QuickTime movies into AVI movies, the AVI movies may be much larger than the original QuickTime movies.

## *Implementing Hypertext*

Hypertext is a form of text in which words or phrases are linked to words and phrases in other parts of the text or in other documents. Typically, one click of the mouse lets you browse from one hypertext link to another.

Director offers text chunk expressions and functions for implementing limited hypertext features. The chunk expression lets you refer to any character, word, item, or line in any container of text. For example, a word chunk is any sequence of characters delimited by spaces (any nonvisible character, such as a tab or a return, is considered a space).

Director offers the `mouseChar`, `mouseLine`, `mouseWord`, and `mouse-Item` functions for detecting when the mouse is over a certain character, line, word, or item (an item is any sequence of characters delimited by commas, such as a field in a database record).

The following scripts show how a handler can set up the variables for the chunk expressions, and how another handler can use the functions to determine where the mouse is clicking.

**Setting Up
Variables for
Chunk
Expressions**

In the first handler, global variables are set, and if the mouse is not over something applicable (such as a text cast member), then the functions return a –1 value.

```
on DoTell
    global MC,ML,MW,MI,MK
    put the mouseCast into MC
    put the mouseLine into ML
    put the mouseWord into MW
    put the mouseItem into MI
    put the mouseChar into MK
end DoTell
```

First, the DoTell handler defines the global variables, which can be referenced from other handlers. Next, the handler uses put statements to put the result of each function (mouseCast, mouseLine, mouseWord, mouseItem, and mouseChar) into its appropriate variable.

The mouseCast function returns an integer which is the cast number of the cast member under the mouse pointer (it is a complementary function to the rollOver function in that it detects where the mouse is without requiring a mouse click). If the mouse pointer is not over a cast member, the result is –1. You use mouseCast to find out the cast member under the mouse.

The mouseLine function returns an integer which is the line number of the text in the cast member under the mouse pointer. You use mouseLine to find out which line of text is under the mouse—a *line chunk* is any sequence of characters delimited by returns. If the mouse pointer is not over a field (the text in a text cast member), the result is –1.

The mouseWord function returns an integer which is the number of the word under the mouse pointer, counting from the beginning of the text field. Director recognizes a word as a sequence of characters delimited by spaces. The mouseWord function is perhaps the most useful for hypertext applications. Again, if the mouse pointer is not over a field in a text cast member, the result is –1.

The mouseItem function returns an integer which is the number of the item under the mouse pointer, counting from the beginning of the text field. Director recognizes an item as a sequence of characters delimited by commas. The mouseItem function is useful for database applications. If the mouse pointer is not over a field in a text cast member, the result is –1.

The mouseChar function returns an integer which is the number of the character under the mouse pointer, counting from the beginning of the text field. The mouseChar function is useful for single-character linking applications, such as alphabetical indexes. If the mouse pointer is not over a field in a text cast member, the result is, you guessed it, –1.

## Using the Variables

Now that the variables contain integers representing objects in the text field, these variables can be used with decision loops or other Lingo statements, such as the put statements provided in the following handler.

```
on Teller
--Puts the information gathered in handler DoTell
--into fields for the user to see
    global MC,ML,MW,MI,MK
--Make sure that all globals have pertinent info.
--Exit if any do not.
    if MC = -1 then exit
    if ML = -1 then exit
    if MW = -1 then exit
    if MI = -1 then exit
    if MK = -1 then exit

--Put the information into corresponding lines
--of fields "TellMe" and "Them"
    put "Cast" && MC into field "TellMe"
    put "Cast name:" && the name of cast MC ¬
into field "Them"

    put "Line" && ML into line 2 of field "TellMe"
    put line ML of field the name of cast MC ¬
into line 2 of field "Them"

    put "Word" && MW into line 3 of field "TellMe"
    put word MW of field the name of cast MC ¬
into line 3 of field "Them"

    put "Item" && MI into line 4 of field "TellMe"
    put word 1 of item MI of field the name of cast MC ¬
into line 4 of field "Them"

    put "Character" && MK into line 5 of field "TellMe"
    put char MK of field the name of cast MC ¬
into line 5 of field "Them"
end Teller
```

The handler starts by declaring the global variables, and checking to see if any of them have a –1 value (indicating that the mouse is not over the text cast member—set in the previous DoTell handler). If any of them do, the exit command quickly exits the handler without any further processing.

The next part of the handler is a series of put statements for placing new information in the text cast members "TellMe" and "Them". The first one puts the text string "Cast" and the variable MC into a text field in the cast member "TellMe". The field keyword refers to text within a cast member, or it refers to the cast member itself (when used with a cast member name, as in "TellMe"). The && symbol (two ampersands) performs a string concatenation of two expressions, inserting a space between them. The second put statement puts the name of the cast member into the text field of cast member "Them".

The next set of put statements puts the line number into line 2 of "TellMe" using the line...of chunk expression keyword, then puts the actual line of text into line 2 of "Them". The expression line ML of field the name of cast MC evaluates to the line on which the mouse is pointing (the ML and MC variables are set in the DoTell handler). You can use line...of to specify a line or range of lines as the source or destination.

The next set of put statements puts the number of the word pointed by the mouse into line 3 of "TellMe", then puts the actual word pointed by the mouse into "Them", using the same method as the previous set of put statements. The word...of chunk expression lets you specify a word or range of words.

In the next set of put statements, the word...of expression is used to specify only the first word of the item.

```
put word 1 of item MI of field ¬
    the name of cast MC...
```

Thus, it is possible to know which word the mouse is pointing to, and to put that word in a variable or cast member field. Basic hyperlinking can be implemented by either testing the word against an array of possible choices that execute statements, or by simply testing for a specific word and triggering a statement if the test is true (or false). The statements could display something new or lead the user to another area of a movie, or to another movie altogether.

For example, you might have this test.

```
if word MW of field ¬
    the name of cast MC = "hot" then
    go to "hot"
```

You can use handlers such as the ones above for just about any text application, and modify the Teller handler to perform such tests and execute statements. With these features you can implement a wide range of hypertext applications.

# XObjects and Factories

XObjects on the Macintosh platform are used to control external audio and video devices, and to extend the functionality to Lingo such as independent windows, pop-up menus, and other interface elements.

The equivalent extension to Lingo on the Windows platform is a combination of the Media Control Interface (MCI) and a facility to add functionality by means of dynamic link libraries (DLLs). In most cases, DLLs are designed to emulate XObjects, and the methods for using the DLLs are the same as for XObjects as described in this topic.

It is not necessary to know how to create XObjects in order to use them. You can simply copy XObjects, and the handlers that use them, from example movies to your own movies.

XObjects are organized as *factories*, which are used to create an object that is controlled by its own special set of handlers that define how the object behaves. Factories are used to create objects that are invested with certain properties and controlled by certain methods.

XObjects are exactly the same as factories, in that they define objects to which you can pass messages. The big difference is that you don't have to define XObjects—they are already defined for specific uses and ready to use, and they exist outside of your movie in a resource file in the same folder as your document. All of the movies in the same folder can share the same XObject, so you can save on disk space. Another significant benefit of XObjects is that, like factories, you can create multiple instances of an object using the same XObject code.

For example, when using an XObject that controls a laser videodisc player, you can create multiple videodisc player objects to control several players at once. Director is supplied with XObjects ready to use, including ones for controlling laser videodisc players.

XObjects exist either outside of your movie in a resource file in the same folder as your document, or as a resource within another movie. With the XObject stored in a resource file, all of the movies in the same folder can share the same XObject. If the resource is stored within a movie file, that movie file cannot run on another platform (because other platforms, such as Windows, do not recognize the resource fork of files).

Many XObjects are supplied in the XObjects folder distributed with Director. You can copy the resource file containing the XObject to the folder that holds your movie. For example, you can copy the resource file AppleCD XObj (in the Apple CD Control folder in the XObjects folder) into the folder for your movie so that your movie, and any other movie in that folder, can control one, or more, Apple CD-ROM players with audio discs.

Each movie that wants to use the AppleCD XObj resource file must execute the Lingo command openXlib "AppleCD XObj". You can copy the entire set of handlers that deal with the AppleCD XObject (including the "initialization" handler that executes the openXlib command) to your movie, without needing to know much about these handlers, except how to call them from your scripts.

When Director for Windows starts up, it looks for a file named LINGO.INI. You can edit this file to include scripts to execute at startup, such as opening a specific XObject with an openXlib command.

XObjects are similar to XCMDs and XFCNs (external commands and functions) in HyperCard's HyperTalk. Any software "driver" or segment of code can be added to the Lingo vocabulary with XObjects, which can be written in Pascal, C, or other programming languages. For more information about XObjects, you can obtain the XObject Developer's Kit from Macromedia.

## Using XObject Methods

Several standard XObjects are supplied with the Macintosh version of Director, including FileIO, Panel, SerialPort, Window, and XCMDGlue. These XObjects are opened automatically when you run Director, so you don't need to use the openXlib command.

To see the list of built-in XObjects, as well as external XObjects that are opened, type the command showXlib in the Message window (Figure 9.2). The display indicates that the built-in XObjects FileIO, SerialPort, and XCMDGlue are part of the STANDARD.XLIB XLibrary. To see a list of XObjects in a particular XLibrary, such as one that is opened as an external resource file, specify the XLibrary name after showXlib on the same command line in the Message window.

The FileIO XObject, like all XObjects, is defined as a factory. A *factory* is a script containing the instructions, which are called *methods,* that can be executed by calling them by name. A factory definition reduces the number of separate scripts that would be required to implement many instances of a particular set of instructions.

You can't see the scripts that comprise the methods, but you can see a list of the methods by typing the following Lingo instruction, substituting the actual XObject's name for *XObjectName* in the Message window.

```
XObjectName(mDescribe)
```

The word mDescribe is a built-in message that you can send to any XObject to list the methods in the XObject. Every XObject has its own set of methods, and you can find information about them in the "About..." text cast member in each sample movie that uses the XObject.

Besides mDescribe, the standard methods every XObject uses are mNew, mDispose, and mName. The mNew method creates a new object to be controlled by methods (just as with a factory). The mDispose method removes an object

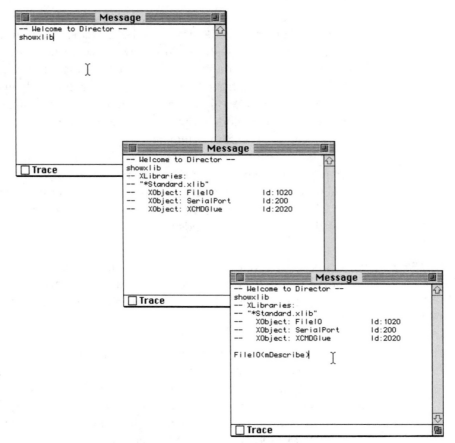

**Figure 9.2**
**Typing showXlib**
**in the Message**
**window to see**
**the supplied XOb-**
**jects, then using**
**the** mDescribe
**method with the**
**FileIO XObject.**

from memory, and mName returns the name of the XObject that created the object. The specific messages for an XObject vary from one XObject to another, but all share a common syntax.

**Using a Factory: The FileIO XObject**

In the absence of a specific database XObject that can handle input/output with a specific type of database file, your only choice is to make the FileIO XObject do the work of file input/output.

To save any information from a Director movie into an external file, use the FileIO XObject (written by John Thompson and Al McNeil), which lets you read, write, and append to text files. You can create files, read or write directly from or to a specific external file, and allow the user to select a file to open using a standard dialog box.

The FileIO XObject may seem too limited for a presentation that must save or retrieve formatted information that is designed to be stored in a database record. However, most database programs let you export a database in an entirely textual format, and also let you import text files into a database, as long as the text is formatted appropriately.

The FileIO XObject not only lets you read or write a single character or an entire string of characters, it also lets you define a *delimiter* (separator) that helps FileIO read *tokens* (fields) of data as they appear in a database record. You can also prepare a string in Lingo to mimic a textual database record (with delimiters) in order to write a formatted string to a file that could then be imported into a database record.

A typical sequence in the use of the FileIO XObject is to first establish an instance of the XObject with the mNew method, which associates a specific file with the instance for reading or writing. It returns an error code, which you can use with the mError method to display the actual error message (or consult the list below with the mError method description).

Next, use a reading method to read data, or a writing method to write data; these methods also return an error code. You may also want to use mGetLength to obtain the length (in characters) of the file; and mSetPosition to move to a character position in a file.

At the end of these operations, use mDispose to dispose of the instance of the XObject, cleaning up memory.

Some of the important arguments for the mNew method of FileIO are as follows:

```
mNew, mode, fileNameOrType
```

The mNew method creates a new instance of the FileIO XObject for use in your scripts. In effect, mNew opens or creates a file in a particular mode of operation. Most modes can open or create a file by name (which you supply in quotes for *fileName,* as in "Sample File"), but one mode ("?read") lets the user open any file using the standard dialog box, displaying only those files that match the *fileType.*

The *mode* argument in the mNew expression can be one of the following.

| | |
|---|---|
| "read" | Read file named by *fileName.* |
| "?read" | Select and read any file that has a certain *fileType.* |
| "write" | Write to a file named by *fileName.* |
| "?write" | Select a file (name suggested by *fileName*) and write to it. |
| "append" | Append to file named by *fileName.* |
| "append" | Select and append to file named by *fileName.* |

The argument *fileType* for the "?read" mode can be any one of the following:

| | |
|---|---|
| "TEXT" | Standard file type for text file. |
| "trak" | File type for an audio cd track. |
| *type* | Any four character combination used as a file type. |

### mDispose

The mDispose method disposes of the instance of the FileIO XObject (defined by mNew) to free memory.

### mWriteChar, charNum

The mWriteChar method writes a single character (supplied by the expression charNum ) to the file specified by the instance of the FileIO XObject (defined by mNew). The mWriteChar method returns an error code.

### mWriteString, string

The mWriteString method writes out a string of characters to the file and returns an error code.

### mReadChar

The mReadChar method returns a single character from a file opened for reading.

### mReadWord

The mReadWord method returns the next word from a file opened for reading.

### mReadLine

The mReadLine method returns the next line of a file opened for reading.

### mReadFile

The mReadFile method returns the remaining data, after a previous reading method, or returns all the data, in a file opened for reading.

### mReadToken, breakString, skipString

The mReadToken method reads a "token" of information—a specific data element, such as a binary character, or a database field—designated by the breakString string which acts as a delimiter to signal the XObject to stop reading. The skipString designates what characters to skip during reading.

### mGetPosition

The mGetPosition method returns the file position. You could use this method to determine the file positions before and after writing a data element. Then you can return to those exact positions, using the mSetPosition method, to rewrite (overwrite) the element in the file.

### mSetPosition, newPos

The mSetPosition method sets the file position. It returns an error code.

mGetLength

The mGetLength method returns the number of characters in the file (assumed to be text).

## FileIO: Writing to a File

You can create a general-purpose handler for saving text in a file that uses a global string variable with the FileIO methods, and use a separate handler to assign a specific set of string elements to the string variable.

For example, in a handler you might assemble the appropriate elements into the variable TextOut as shown.

```
put (Data1 & "," & Data2 & "," & Data3 & "," & Data4 &
return) into TextOut
```

This statement contains the most important information and formatting instructions. The manner in which you lay out your textual information—including the order, the use of comma delimiters, and the use of the Return character—is the sole factor determining the text file's compatibility with a particular database format.

Then, in another handler designed simply for saving whatever is in TextOut to a text file, you could use this statement.

```
Saver (mWriteString, TextOut)
```

This example assumes you have defined Saver as follows.

```
set Saver = FileIO(mnew, "append", the pathname &
"Datafile")
```

This statement uses the mNew method to open the file specified by the string the pathname & "Datafile" (which combines the pathname to the file with the name "Datafile" using the & concatenation operator). This method creates an instance of the XObject, which is called Saver in this handler. The "append" mode opens an existing file for appending new information to existing information.

The append mode was chosen so that the handler never overwrites important information. If you want to purge the file each time you write to the file, don't use this mode.

Be sure to use the following statement after finishing the file operations.

```
Saver(mdispose)
```

This statement performs the important step of file cleanup by closing the file and disposing of the instance of the XObject to free memory for other uses. Otherwise, every time you run the handler, another instance of the XObject would be created without purging the first instance.

With the data in a comma-delimited text file, what can you do with it? Most database management programs can import a comma-delimited file, and most can automatically change text fields into integer or decimal number fields. By using a comma-delimited file as a transfer file, you can confine the database operations to the database management program, and the data-gathering operation to the Director movie file.

## FileIO: Retrieving Information

To retrieve information from a database file (without the help of a special XObject designed for a particular database management program), you can use the FileIO XObject with a text file exported from the database program. You need to know the layout of text fields in the exported text file, so that you can make sense of the data you retrieve.

FileIO offers five different methods for reading text from a file.

1. mReadChar, which retrieves a single character.

2. mReadWord, which retrieves the next word.

3. mReadLine, which retrieves the next line.

4. mReadFile, which retrieves the rest of the file.

5. mReadToken, which retrieves a token.

You can retrieve text one character at a time with the mReadChar method into a string variable. One reason to do this might be to test for a particular character, such as the Return character.

```
--
--   (other statements before this)
--
--   This statement sets up the data file:
set DBfile = FileIO(mNew, "?read", "TEXT")
--   creates instance of FileIO called DBfile.
--
--   This statement reads the character:
put DBfile(mReadChar) into IncomingChar
--   Now test the character:
if IncomingChar = Return then exit
--   If the char is a Return, then leave the handler
--
--   (more statements)
--
```

The mReadWord method is useful if you are reading words from a dictionary file (words are defined as having a space on either side).

The mReadLine method reads an entire line (ending with a Return), which is useful for retrieving information stored line by line in a certain way. The mReadFile method is useful if the file is very short (just a few characters or a single line).

To retrieve data from a comma-delimited file, the best method is to use the mReadToken method. This method reads a *token* of information, such as a data field separated from the next field by a comma or similar delimiter. You tell the method what to look for as the first character of the delimiter (the *break-String*), and what characters to skip over in order to get to the next token (the *skipString*).

mReadToken, *breakString*, *skipString*

For example, comma-delimited files exported from database programs typically surround each text field in quotes as well as separate them by commas, as shown.

```
"Colligan","Bud","CEO","Macromedia","600 Townsend
Street...
```

FileIO is provided with Director as a resource and available at all times. Using FileIO's reading, positioning, and writing methods, and Lingo test and control structures, you can import and export data for use with nearly any database program, and with Lingo functions you can convert integers to strings and strings to integers.

## Using HyperCard XCMDs and XFCNs

If you are a HyperCard programmer and you want to use HyperCard XCMDs and XFCNs (external commands and functions), you can use a special XObject called XCMDGlue, supplied as a standard XObject in STANDARD.XLIB, that enables you to directly use XCMDs and XFCNs in Director movies. You can use the same HyperTalk syntax for the XCMDs and XFCNs in Lingo handlers when using XCMDGlue.

If an XCMD or XFCN resource is stored in the resource fork of the movie, it is automatically opened when you open the movie. If it is stored in an external file, you must use openXlib to open it, and closeXlib to remove it from memory (just like XObjects). Once an XCMD or XFCN is opened, you can use them in your Lingo scripts just as you would use them in HyperTalk scripts, because XCMDGlue automatically converts the instructions for you.

Most HyperCard XCMDs and XFCNs work from within Lingo scripts, but some require "callback requests" to HyperCard to do something special (some use callback requests to perform HyperCard operations such as converting information from one format to another). Lingo supports some callbacks but not all of them. You can handle the callbacks that Lingo doesn't support by defining a factory of callback routines and creating a callback object. This process is described in detail in the *Using Lingo* manual.

**Using the Media Control Interface**

The Media Control Interface (MCI) is a layer of software drivers between a Windows-based PC and external devices, such as laser videodisc players, CD-ROM drives, and other computer-controllable devices.

Director for Windows lets you send MCI commands directly from Lingo scripts to the Windows MCI command interpreter. Director ignores MCI commands when the movie plays back on the Macintosh or other platforms, but they are quite useful in the Windows world.

The Lingo command mci lets you pass MCI commands. It takes the following form.

```
mci command-string
```

The *command-string* is any valid MCI command. Here are a few examples.

```
mci open SONG.WAV type waveaudio alias song
mci play song
mci wait song
mci close song
```

This script uses MCI commands to open a WAV file and play it, then close it. The following script checks to see if a WAV file is playing.

```
mci status song mode
if the result = "stopped" then
     -- add instructions for when the sound file is
stopped
end if
```

The above script uses Lingo's the result to contain the value returned from the MCI command.

You really need to know how to use the MCI to issue MCI commands. The documentation for MCI comes with the Microsoft Multimedia Development Kit.

## *Lists and Movies in a Window*

Two of the coolest new features of Director 4 are lists, and the capability to play one Director movie, fully interactive, within another Director movie. We have an example that uses both features (*courtesy of Alex Zavatone of Macromedia*).

There are two kinds of lists. Linear lists are like arrays in that each element holds a single value. Property lists contain elements that consist of a property and a value separated by a colon (:).

## Using Lists

You can use Lingo scripts to create, sort, add to, and reorder a list, and to substitute another list's contents. To specify items in a list, enclose the items within brackets as in the following statement.

```
set mycursor to [12, 13]
```

This statement sets the cursor to a list of cast members 12 and 13 (you set it to a list so that the second cast member is used as a mask for the first one). This is a linear list.

Here is a simple example of a property list:

```
set mylist = [a:2, b:4, c:6, d:8]
```

Lists can be sorted in alphanumeric order with the sort command. Linear lists are sorted by value, and property lists are sorted by property.

Lists can serve a variety of purposes, from sorting text fields to keeping track of arrays of data. Lists are also useful when using movies in a window of a Director movie. The windowList property provides a list of all known windows in the movie.

## Playing a Movie in a Window

A fine example of movie-within-a-movie is the *Navigator* movie supplied with the Macintosh version of Director (in the Lingo Expo folder inside the Sample Movies folder). The three movies that play within *Navigator's* window (kiosk, simulation, and storybook) are separate movies playing within the *Navigator* movie.

Another is Alex Zavatone's *The Equalizer Package* (folder/directory name: ZAVEQ). The Equalizer is an example that demonstrates many of Director 4.0's new features, including movie in a window, list variables, QuickTime movies used as buttons, and cross-platform compatibility (the package runs on Windows and Macintosh). To start the movie, double-click the file RUNME_EQ.DIR and press play. Click the main display for credits.

The movies that run within the *parent* movie are set up with special handlers, such as the following ones for *initializing* (setting up) various windows, and specific instructions for initializing the volume readout window. You will find these handlers in the movie script in cast member 7.

The first handler, InitMovieInAWindow, checks to see if the movies that are used are already loaded. If they are, it starts them up from frame 1. If they are not, it calls routines that initialize them. If the windows are already open, then it tells the volume window to adjust the volume readout.

```
on InitMovieInAWindow
  global gChildWindow1, gChildWindow2, gChildWindow3
  if voidP(gChildWindow1) then
-- If the variable does not exist, then init the window
```

```
        InitVolumeReadout
    else
      tell gChildWindow1 to go to frame 1
      tell gChildWindow1 to AdjustVolume
    end if

    if voidP(gChildWindow2) then
      InitAnalogMeter
    else
      tell gChildWindow1 to go to frame 1
    end if

    if voidP(gChildWindow3) then
      InitEQModule
    else
      tell gChildWindow3 to go to frame 1
    end if

  end
```

A primary feature of running movies within a movie is the capability to send messages to the movies running in the windows. The `tell` instructions are used to send a movie-window a command, such as `go to frame 1` as used in the script `tell gChildWindow3 to go to frame 1`.

The following script initializes the volume readout window by loading the movie, setting the global variable for it, and setting all the window conditions for playing the movie in a window.

```
on InitVolumeReadout
        -- The windowList is cleared here
        -- to guarantee that we are starting
        -- with no windows. The topSide/leftside section
        -- makes the movies in a window open
        -- relative to the stage so they will
        -- open properly on all monitors.
  global gChildWindow1
  set stageRect = the rect of the stage
  set leftSide = getat(stageRect,1)-80)
  set rightSide = leftSide+64
  set topSide =  getat(stageRect,2)
  set bottomSide =  getat(stageRect,4)
  set the windowList = []
```

```
set moviePath = "Volume.dir"
open window moviePath
set gChildWindow1 = getAt(the windowList, 1)
set the titleVisible of gChildWindow1 to false
set the rect of gChildWindow1 to rect(leftSide,
topSide, rightSide, bottomSide)
end
```

This script sets the window's rectangle by using the getAt instruction to get a value from a list (the list, in this case, are the coordinates in stageRect). It then empties the windowList with the instruction set the windowList = [ ] so that there are no other movie windows.

The handler goes on to open the window moviePath (set to the movie file VOLUME.DIR), and sets the gChildWindow1 variable to the first element of the windowList, which is the newly opened movie, using the instruction set gChild-Window1 = getAt(the windowList, 1).

Finally, the handler sets the titleVisible property to false so that the movie window title does not appear in a window title bar, and the rect of the window is set to the coordinates.

Another handler changes the eq levels by grabbing the level of sound directly off the Macintosh microphone input (on Windows the eq levels are simulated). The up and down buttons adjust the volume, shown in the volume meter. The analog meter displays an average of all channels. When the average is over 80 percent of the maximum value, a red overload light will display. Stopping the movie invokes a behavior where the analog meter peaks and dies down while the channel values fade out—much like a real stereo.

You will find this example in the TUTORIAL folder/directory on the accompanying CD-ROM.

## When It Just Won't Work...

Sometimes you just don't have a clue why your complex scripts are not working. Perhaps you don't have enough memory. You can check to see how much memory you are using at a particular frame by getting values from the Lingo freeBytes and freeBlock functions.

```
put the freeBytes
put the freeBlock
```

These statements will show you how much free memory you have at the current frame.

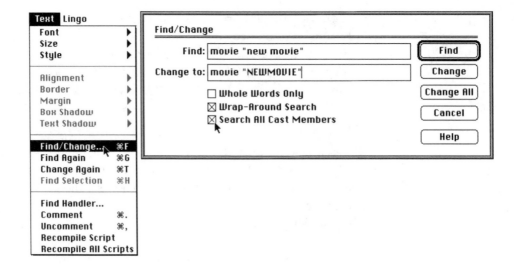

**Figure 9.3
Using Find/
Change to find
and change a
script word or
phrase.**

# Finding Script Words

With any script window open, you can use the Text menu's Find/Change, Find Again, and Change Again commands to find a particular word or phrase in other scripts and change them. These options are useful when you need to search for a particular variable or handler name, or Lingo instruction and replace it with another.

Starting with Find/Change, you can specify a script word, or phrase (Figure 9.3), and turn on the Search All Cast Members option to search all scripts. The Wrap-Around Search option starts the search again from the beginning after reaching the end.

After using Find/Change the first time and finding the first instance, use the Find Again command (or the Command-G shortcut) to display another instance of the word or phrase in another script window. If you use the Find Again enough times, every script window containing that word or phrase will eventually be displayed, so that you can find every instance. You can also use Change Again (Command-T) to automatically change each instance.

When a script window is open, you can scan through the Lingo menu for keywords and commands you don't know (and use the Help system by holding down Option and Shift while clicking). When you select a Lingo keyword, the program inserts the keyword (along with appropriate syntax elements for completing the script expression) into the script window. This feature is especially handy if you've forgotten the syntax rules for using a particular keyword.

# Disabling Features

Improper use of XObjects or XCMDs can cause problems. For example, you may have forgotten to release an XObject (with an `mDispose` or similar method) which is occupying precious memory space.

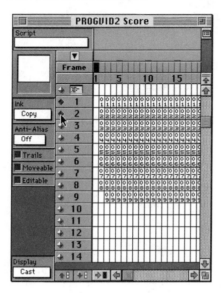

**Figure 9.4
Turning off channels 1 and 2 by clicking the buttons at the far left side of the channels, effectively removing them from the stage temporarily.**

You may also want to isolate suspicious scripts that are not working. In the score, you can turn off any channel by clicking the button at the far left side of the channel (Figure 9.4), effectively removing the entire channel from the presentation.

You can temporarily disable any set of scripts by typing dashes in front of the statements, effectively turning the statements into nonfunctional comments.

```
-- on mayItWorkOncePlease,
    -- global someday, everyday...
    -- ...
-- end mayItWorkOncePlease
```

## The Last Word

If all else fails to isolate the problem, or if Director itself is crashing, trash the Director Preferences file (located in the System folder), just in case the Preferences file is giving Director improper information.

And remember Bové & Rhodes' Theorem: *The remaining work to finish in order to reach your goal increases as the deadline approaches.* It goes along with Clarke's Third Law: *Any sufficiently advanced technology is indistinguishable from magic.*

# Index